Children and Childhoods in L.M. Montgomery

Children and Childhoods in L.M. Montgomery

Continuing Conversations

Edited by
Rita Bode, Lesley D. Clement, E. Holly Pike,
and Margaret Steffler

McGILL-QUEEN'S UNIVERSITY PRESS
Montreal & Kingston | London | Chicago

ISBN 978-0-2280-1388-4 (cloth)
ISBN 978-0-2280-1389-1 (paper)
ISBN 978-0-2280-1483-6 (ePDF)
ISBN 978-0-2280-1484-3 (ePUB)

Legal deposit fourth quarter 2022
Bibliothèque nationale du Québec

We gratefully acknowledge the generous support in aid of publication of this volume of the Symons Trust Fund at Trent University.

Funded by the Government of Canada | Financé par le gouvernement du Canada | Canada | Canada Council for the Arts | Conseil des arts du Canada

We acknowledge the support of the Canada Council for the Arts.
Nous remercions le Conseil des arts du Canada de son soutien.

Library and Archives Canada Cataloguing in Publication

Title: Children and childhoods in L.M. Montgomery : continuing conversations / edited by Rita Bode, Lesley D. Clement, E. Holly Pike, and Margaret Steffler.
Names: Bode, Rita, 1950- editor. | Clement, Lesley D. (Lesley Diana), 1951- editor. | Pike, E. Holly (Elizabeth Holly), 1958- editor. | Steffler, Margaret, 1955- editor.
Description: Includes bibliographical references and index.
Identifiers: Canadiana (print) 20220244448 | Canadiana (ebook) 20220244456 | ISBN 9780228013891 (softcover) | ISBN 9780228013884 (hardcover) | ISBN 9780228014836 (PDF) | ISBN 9780228014843 (EPUB)
Subjects: LCSH: Montgomery, L. M. (Lucy Maud), 1874-1942—Criticism and interpretation. | LCSH: Children in literature. | CSH: Canadian literature (English)—20th century—History and criticism.
Classification: LCC PS8526.O55 Z556 2022 | DDC C813/.52—dc23

This book was designed and typeset by studio oneonone in Minion 11/14

Contents

Acknowledgments

An edited volume relies on the expertise and hard work of many. We wish to thank our contributors for the care, thoughtfulness, creativity, and superb scholarly effort they brought to this project at every turn. It has been our privilege and joy to work with them in bringing this volume to fruition.

Three of the editors wish to extend a special thanks to a fourth: the concept and vision for the volume originated with Lesley Clement, whose approaches to Montgomery studies continue to inspire a wide and energetic community of Montgomery artists, readers, and scholars.

We are grateful for the work of the many scholars working on Montgomery studies worldwide and wish to extend a special thank you to Elizabeth Epperley, Mary Rubio, and Elizabeth Waterston for their ground-breaking research.

The volume first took shape under Mark Abley's valued guidance at McGill-Queen's University Press and moved forward with the help and insights of Jacqueline Mason and Jonathan Crago. We thank them and all the staff at McGill-Queen's for their encouragement, support, and exemplary professionalism.

The press's anonymous readers provided insightful, keen, and challenging critiques aimed at bringing out the best in the volume. We thank them for their time and effort.

We thank Kate Macdonald Butler, the Heirs of L.M. Montgomery Inc., and Sally Keefe-Cohen for their continuing support of Montgomery scholarship.

We are grateful to institutions whose ongoing commitment to Montgomery research actively furthers the study of her work, especially the L.M. Montgomery Institute and the Robertson Library at the University of Prince Edward Island and the L.M. Montgomery Collection at the University of Guelph Archives.

We gratefully acknowledge the generous support in aid of publication of the Symons Trust Fund for Canadian Studies at Trent University.

Rita Bode would like to thank students and colleagues at Trent University, both in Peterborough and Durham, and friends and family, with special thanks to Brian, Adam, Julia, Ella, Nolan, Mia, Casper, Laura, and David. Lesley Clement extends a special thanks to the L.M. Montgomery Institute of University of Prince Edward Island, the extended Clement family, and her co-editors for this volume of essays, Rita, Holly, and Margaret. Holly Pike is grateful for the support of colleagues and students at Grenfell Campus, Memorial University of Newfoundland, and of her partner, Marc Thackray. Margaret Steffler thanks her students and colleagues at Trent University and is grateful for the support of friends and family, especially Neil, Micah, Jeff, Gabrielle, and Stephen.

Abbreviations Used in Notes

LMM: L.M. Montgomery

FICTION

AA: *Anne of Avonlea*
AGG: *Anne of Green Gables*
AIs: *Anne of the Island*
AHD: *Anne's House of Dreams*
BAQ: *The Blythes Are Quoted*
BC: *The Blue Castle*
CA: *Chronicles of Avonlea*
EC: *Emily Climbs*
ENM: *Emily of New Moon*
EQ: *Emily's Quest*
GR: *The Golden Road*
MM: *Magic for Marigold*
RI: *Rilla of Ingleside*
RV: *Rainbow Valley*
SG: *The Story Girl*

LIFE-WRITING

AP: *The Alpine Path*

CJ 1: *The Complete Journals of L.M. Montgomery: The PEI Years, 1889–1900*

CJ 2: *The Complete Journals of L.M. Montgomery: The PEI Years, 1901–1911*

CJ 3: *L.M. Montgomery's Complete Journals: The Ontario Years, 1911–1917*

CJ 4: *L.M. Montgomery's Complete Journals: The Ontario Years, 1918–1921*

CJ 5: *L.M. Montgomery's Complete Journals: The Ontario Years, 1922–1925*

CJ 6: *L.M. Montgomery's Complete Journals: The Ontario Years, 1926–1929*

CJ 7: *L.M. Montgomery's Complete Journals: The Ontario Years, 1930–1933*

SJ 4: *The Selected Journals of L.M. Montgomery, 1929–1935* (Volume 4)

SJ 5: *The Selected Journals of L.M. Montgomery, 1935–1942* (Volume 5)

Children and Childhoods in L.M. Montgomery

Introduction

LESLEY D. CLEMENT,
WITH ASSISTANCE FROM RITA BODE,
E. HOLLY PIKE, AND MARGARET STEFFLER

Until recently, L.M. Montgomery typically has been considered a writer of children's literature, that is, a literature written for children and/or read by children, with themes and stylistic strategies children find appealing. Yet most of her central characters are what today we would consider "tweens" and "teenagers," terms that became common only in the mid- and late-twentieth century. For concepts pertaining to the adolescent years, Montgomery preferred the terms "girlhood" and "boyhood" to mark any kind of distinction between "childhood" and "adulthood," whether of age, skills, experience, attitudes, states of mind, imaginative capabilities, and/or sexual, physical, psychological, emotional, and intellectual development. Even concepts of "childhood" were fairly recent when Montgomery published her first novel, *Anne of Green Gables* (1908), at least those modern concepts based on the writings of John Locke (1632–1704) and Jean-Jacques Rousseau (1712–1778), which formed the foundation of the evolution of children's literature in what Patricia Demers identifies as the "transformative decade" of the 1740s.[1] In her discussion of "childhood" in *Keywords for Children's Literature*, Karen Sánchez-Eppler traces the historical and demographic fluidity of the concept of childhood, including the "competing theories" inspired by Locke's and Rousseau's legacies, that "seeded quite different assumptions about the most appropriate stories to tell to children," and makes the following points to challenge the essentialism of childhood: "Childhood may be widely recognized as a life stage that stretches from birth until the taking on of adult competence and responsibility, but its contours and meanings are deeply circumstantial, formed by the particulars of each historical and social situation, and the stories we tell about them. Perhaps it is because childhood simultaneously roots itself in both biological and ideological ground that it proves so potent a means of naturalizing cultural formations." Elsewhere in the same essay, Sánchez-Eppler states, "The idea of the child is repeatedly made and remade in the stories told to children."[2] These stories of "childhood," from infancy through adolescence, are featured in this volume of twelve essays and four afterwords: stories of orphans and belonging, parenting and education, father and mother figures, resilience and death, boyhood and girlhood, heteronormativity, transformative spaces, fantasy and realism, creativity and adaptation.

The twelve chapters and four afterwords in this volume also explore how the stories that are being told and retold, or "made and remade" to use Sánchez-Eppler's words, participate in continuing conversations that first Montgomery and then her readers have had with motifs, themes, and traditions reflected in books read during childhood. This introduction begins by detailing the importance of books and responsive childhood reading in shaping the beliefs, values, and attitudes of Montgomery, her characters, and ultimately her readers. It then situates this volume theoretically in terms of the conversations that responsive reading inspires and the consequent shaping and reshaping of confluent cultural products and practices. Next it outlines how Montgomery's understanding of childhood and its relationship to adulthood is a conversation that takes place at a confluent site, her acute visual memory rooted in experience and reading and often in consultation with her notebooks, which conflates multiple, interconnected past and present selves. It continues by demonstrating that scholarship on Montgomery as a children's writer – a writer for and about children – reflects cultural shifts in the twentieth century, specifically those occurring in the 1980s, when children's literature began to be valued as literature and as an area of study. It ends by arguing for the need to bring scholarship on Montgomery as a children's writer into the twenty-first century by recognizing the blurred boundaries between different stages of life out of which conversations on a variety of topics pertaining to children and childhoods arise.

Responsive Child Readers and Their Conversations with the Books They Read

Montgomery was a true bibliophile. From a young age, she read voraciously and had conversations with the books she was reading. The marginalia in her books that she read later in life, now housed in the University of Guelph archives, reflect a life-long practice, begun in childhood, of underscoring and inserting everything from exclamation points and asterisks to extended responses and musings during the reading process.[3] She placed letters and cards from friends and fans between the pages. She pasted in newspaper and magazine clippings and photographs she thought pertinent to her readings. The journals that Montgomery kept from childhood throughout adulthood contain numerous references to and reflections on what she was reading, rereading, and rereading yet again. She writes that she seems to have been "born with a capacity for reading just as for breathing or eating" and "can read books over and over again with never failing interest and zest." As a young girl, she records an eclectic range of favourites from, among many others, Edward Bulwer-Lytton's *Devereux* (1829) and *Last Days of Pompeii* (1834), whose "charm never fails," to Washington Irving's *Sketch Book* (1819–20) and Ralph Waldo Emerson's "delightful" *Essays* (1841). Of the latter, she admits that she does "not always understand him," perhaps because she is "too young" to "get right into the groove of his thought and keep steadily in it." At age twenty, she records rereading Henry Wadsworth Longfellow's poems, "which never lost their witchery for [her]," and Nathaniel Hawthorne's *The Scarlet Letter* (1850), "a marvellously powerful book, both in style and analysis." Several years later, her reading includes "all [Walter] Scott's poems over again … childhood loves that have worn well"; another favourite, Olive Schreiner's *The Story of an African Farm* (1883), which although perhaps "dangerous … for an unformed mind" is "powerful and original and fearless, and contains some exquisite ideas"; and William Thackeray's *Vanity Fair* (1848), which she acknowledges she did not like when she read it in early girlhood, "probably because it hit some of [her] pet illusions too hard," and now wonders how she "failed to see its charm before," especially "that delightful *Becky*!"[4] "Poetry pored over in childhood," she suggests, "becomes part of one's soul and nature more thoroughly than what is read in mature years can ever do." Of the poetry over which she pored, that of "Longfellow, Tennyson, Whittier, Scott, Byron, Milton, Burns," she writes, "Their music was woven into my growing soul and has echoed through it, consciously or unconsciously, ever since."[5] As well as her own conversations with books, she also records in her journals the oral and written conversations that she had with friends, pen pals, and fans about their reading and the relevance of this reading to their daily lived experiences – familial, communal, national, and, especially during the war, global.[6]

Similar conversations are reflected in the reading practices of Montgomery's characters, through recommendations, shared books, or story clubs, in which the characters recite and discuss what they are reading or – an even greater homage – recite their own derivative stories, attempting to imitate the writers they admire. These books are as much a part of their circle of friends as are Anne, Diana, Ruby, and Jane (the *Anne* series); Emily, Ilse, Teddy, and Perry (the *Emily* trilogy); or Bev, Dan, Felix, Felicity, Cecily, Peter, Sara Ray, and Sara Stanley (*The Story Girl* and *The Golden Road*), suggesting the importance that books play in the formulations of childhood. Especially valued are those books that connect them with past readers. Upon being gifted "a little, shabby, worn volume with a great many marks on the leaves" from the Awkward Man, Sara Stanley remarks, "I'd ten times rather have this than a new book. It's … one that he has read a hundred times and loved and made a friend of. A new book, just out of a shop, wouldn't be the same thing at all. It wouldn't *mean* anything."[7] As friends, books invite responsive readings that can inspire not only the comfort of accord but also the mental and emotional engagement and stimulation of dissent, as noted above in Montgomery's aversion to and then admiration for *Vanity Fair*, which generates a conversation between Montgomery as an adult reader and her younger self.

It is fitting, therefore, that Montgomery's own readers should respond as she did to their reading. In their introduction to Montgomery's *Complete Journals*, Mary Rubio and Elizabeth Waterston identify one of the stories that the journals tell as "the recording of readership" and assert that, in telling this story, "Montgomery herself becomes one of the grand purveyors of absorbing reading for many generations, in many worlds."[8] This volume of essays provides a representative sampling of the conversations, rooted in just such "absorbing reading," beginning in the first six chapters with Montgomery's own conversations with past and contemporary writers and then moving in the next three chapters to conversations that later writers have had with her books.

Throughout the twentieth and twenty-first centuries, Montgomery's readers have worked in different media – literary, dramatic, cinematic, visual, musical, digital, virtual – and continue the conversations through new forms, as explored in the three final chapters of this collection, discussed in the preface, and illustrated by the four creative responses in the afterwords.

Continuing Conversations: The Theoretical Framework of Confluence

For Montgomery, as for so many others, responsive reading – that is, having meaningful conversations with what one is reading – is at the core of cultural products and practices and the traditions that shape them, and that they then shape. Critiquing Mikhail Bakhtin's ideas on dialogical ambivalence, Julia Kristeva developed her theories of intertextuality, which challenge the potentially reductive critical practices of influence and source seeking. A gesture is made toward confluence when she famously states in *Desire in Language* (1969) that "any text is the absorption and transformation of another." Although "'two paths merg[e] within the narrative,'" one text remains the original, the other derivative: "Bakhtin considers writing as a reading of the anterior literary corpus and the text as an absorption of and a reply to another text."[9] In essence, a conversation develops between the two texts and the cultures that have shaped them, but this conversation privileges one text, one culture, over the other. In her 2017 "Introduction: Trying to Define Literature's Confluences," Catherine Bernard appeals for a concept of confluence that circumvents "the structuralist subsumption of life by discourse," which she believes characterizes both Kristeva's intertextuality and Bakhtin's dialogism, and optimistically forecasts, "From 'influence' to 'confluence,' a more organic, less agonistic poetics of creation may be in the making, on the verge of conceptualisation."[10] Confluence is "more organic, less agonistic" because, unbound from temporal and geographical restraints, it opens up sites where substantive and egalitarian conversations can occur. As Katherine Bergren outlines in her discussions of "Reading Backward" and "Reading Globally" in the introduction to *The Global Wordsworth* (2019), the (albeit impossible) conversations that transpire when a "dominant predecessor" (influencer) is no longer given hierarchical status and power can repurpose and thereby revivify ideas both within and outside their original cultural contexts.[11]

The idea of "influence" and the controversies surrounding it took on new life with Harold Bloom's *The Anxiety of Influence* (1973), as have been outlined by David Greven's discussion of "Influence Regained" in the introduction to a special issue of the *Nathaniel Hawthorne Review* on "Hawthorne and Influence" (2016) and by Marjorie Garber's *Critical Inquiry* article, provocatively titled "Over the Influence" (2016). Greven advocates for "a new theory of influence as the study of the series of exchanges, challenges, provocations, and innovations inherent in the creation of the literary" to achieve "Wai Chee Dimock's concept of literary deep time, of residues, traces, and repositories of older literary cultures."[12] Although "influence" has sometimes been used as "a kind of cultural shorthand for the diverse relationships that shape us, and the diversity of ways in which we put these relationships into words," as noted by Robert Douglas-Fairhurst in *Victorian Afterlives* (2004),[13] confluence is the preferred concept over "influence" in this volume.[14] And while the volume's twelve essays do not discuss any of the "learned plagiaries" that Garber describes, they certainly consider the allusions, the echoes, the subliminal associations, or, to use Montgomery's own phrase in a 1937 letter to pen pal Ephraim Weber, the "devilish coincidence[s],"[15] all variations on "influence" that Garber elaborates.[16] This kind of approach has formed the basis of much of the "literary borrowing" analysis that has been previously undertaken, as discussed below, even when contextualized historically. For example, in her survey in "L.M. Montgomery and Everybody Else: A Look at the Books" (2003), Virginia Careless examines similarities and differences between Montgomery's novels and earlier texts but not, as the twelve chapters in this volume do, the kind of responsive or critically engaged reading revealed through absorption in, parody and subversion of, and resistance to the ideas, motifs, and traditions met in the precursor texts.

The editorial "On Literary Debts," for a 1989 issue of *Canadian Children's Literature*, which includes two essays on Montgomery, states, "Literary borrowing, conscious or otherwise, has led to a wonderfully connected world of books" and "a deep sense of communality of books."[17] Equally, if not more important – and more important for this volume of essays – is the kind of "influence" that becomes something else – confluence – for those who participate in what Garber describes as "*reading* ... (close, distant, anxious, deconstructive, aesthetic, call it what you will) ... a critical act that depends upon a broader sense of influence ... Literature is a back formation produced by the act and the art of critical reading."[18] The essays and creative pieces in this volume address facets of literary production that engage just such reading, a kind of reading that moves backward to move forward, and forward to move backward, culturally as well as individually for each reader, as childhood merges into – and often re-emerges in – adulthood.

Child and Adult Selves: Montgomery and the Role of Memory

The kinship between child and adult selves is the main reason that the theme of children and childhoods is a productive way to focus this collection of essays. It is not just that the seeds of bibliophilia are sown in childhood, although this is an important consideration. More important for this volume is that the shifting concepts of children and childhoods inform and underpin an understanding of the confluences that shape cultural shifts in time and place. Just as there is no particular definitive event that triggers or determines a sea change culturally, so, as Marah Gubar writes in her 2013 article "Risky Business: Talking about Children in Children's Literature Criticism," "growth is a messy and unpredictable continuum. There is no one moment when we suddenly flip over from being a child to being an adult. Our younger and older selves are multiple and interlinked, akin to one another rather than wholly distinct."[19] Montgomery began to understand the "messy and unpredictable continuum" of childhood, adolescence, and adulthood at around age twenty, when leaving school and looking back through what seemed a brief passage of time to childhood perceptions of adult "occasions of state" (in this case, sitting school examinations): "there came to me a sudden chill realization that I was 'grown up' and the knowledge was not half so sweet as I had once dreamed it would be." Many of her journal entries from the mid-1890s, when she was in her early twenties, a difficult and lonely period in her life, are characterized by her lamenting – even grieving – the passing of a "carefree childhood," the fading radiance of Wordsworth's "'the glory and the dream,'" and the deepening sense that past and present selves are forever severed from one another.[20] Other entries, however, are marked by Blakean insights that childhood too has its problems and anguishes. Writing to an old school friend in 1897, she ponders, "How far away now seem those dear old days of our early teens – half childhood half girlhood. And yet, I do not really think if the choice were offered me that I would go back to them. I believe I am happier now than I was then, despite my hardships. Every age has its own troubles. My childhood and early girlhood had them and they were just as real and worrisome to me then as those of today are now."[21] In recognizing the plights that often characterize childhood, Montgomery can be aligned with earlier women writers for children (and even William Blake), who, Judith Plotz argues, "see childhood as continuous with rather than distinct from adulthood" and are "uninterested in staging 'The Child' in a decontextualized state of being," therefore "focus[ing] on multiple states of social and ethical becoming rather than on unitary states of being" that reflect "the interassimilation of adulthood and childhood."[22]

Montgomery had a formidable visual memory, often precipitated by rereading her own notebooks, which would take her back to relive childhood experiences of joy and suffering. Throughout her journals, when relaying anecdotes from her own childhood; her teaching jobs in Bideford, Belmont, and Lower Bedeque in the mid and late 1890s; her work with young people's groups in Leaskdale (1911–26) and Norval (1926–35); and her experiences as a mother of Chester (born 1912) and Stuart (born 1915), Montgomery returns to the theme of regard for a child's feelings, dreams, rights, and inquiring mind. Reliving these experiences, especially those of suffering,[23] contributed to her treating all her fictional children with respect, even when their behaviour may be misguided or humorous.

In the 1910s and 1920s, the period when most of Montgomery's books were written, Chester's and Stuart's experiences, as well as the copying out of her journals (beginning in 1919), which she had kept from 1889, triggered many of these childhood memories.[24] Throughout her life, however, it was rereading the works of favourite writers that merged present and past selves. Rereading books from her childhood and girlhood and assessing how and why they do or do not stand up through rereadings is a thread that runs throughout Montgomery's journals. "I have in mature life re-read with bitter disappointment so many books that I loved in childhood," she writes. "It is only a foolish fancy, I suppose, but to me the disillusionment is almost as painful as to meet some old loved childhood chum and find her nothing that your memory painted." Many others, however, she "love[s] … with a love that has outlived childhood." The "true test of a classic," she states, is that "it must please every age, from childhood to gray hairs."[25] For Montgomery, childhood reading seems less discriminating, less judgmental, than adult reading, especially when the ideal is pitted against the real. "Our ideals change as we grow older … We are driven to compromise with the insistent *Real*," Montgomery writes after rereading Edward Bulwer-Lytton's *Eugene Aram* (1832) and recalling conversations she had with a book-loving school friend, Nate Lockhart, about its style and "haunting impression like a cadence of dying minor music."[26] Rereading books is all the more pleasurable because she is able to reconnect with these earlier ideals and to explore the kinship of past and present selves. Later in life, it would be the books that she was reading with her sons or purchasing for their library that reinforced this sense of kinship.[27] In a 1921 journal entry that records nine-year-old Chester's asking to read *Anne of Green Gables* and her own rereading of Justin McCarthy's *History of Our Own Times* (1879–80, 1897), read "many times" since age twelve, she writes, "an old book has something for me which no new book can ever have – for at every reading the memories and atmosphere of other readings come back and I am reading old years as well as an old book."[28] In "reading old years," she is reading the flux of selves, how past and present selves are "multiple and interlinked," to use Gubar's words cited more fully earlier.

Twentieth-Century Scholarship on Montgomery as a Writer about and for Children

Because the *Anne* and *Emily* books form series, readers can track the flux of interconnected selves of both major and minor characters from preadolescence into adulthood, including late adulthood in the case of Anne and Gilbert in *The Blythes Are Quoted*. These multiple selves resist reductive categories of child, adolescent, and adult. Despite some reservations about Montgomery's ability to create strong older selves for Anne and Emily, since the 1980s readers and critics generally find the growth of both characters resonates psychologically, socially, and emotionally. Scholarship of the last thirty-five years has challenged T.D. MacLulich's 1985 assessment that Anne and Emily as adults are "disappointing" and "represent a failure on Montgomery's part of both the literary and social imagination," because Montgomery was never able to grow beyond her own personal story as an orphaned girl.[29] Montgomery scholarship has also challenged MacLulich's conclusion from another article in the same year that "Montgomery wrote most effectively when she dealt with juvenile heroines, whose difficulties appeared to be associated with a special phase of life ... she never attempted to break free from the conventions that hedged the form in which she cast the great majority of her work [the realistic girls' story]. As a result, Montgomery never made her fiction a vehicle for expressing a mature criticism of society."[30] Meanwhile, again in 1985, Rubio and Waterston were writing in the introduction to the first volume of the *Selected Journals* that, although "her books were mostly 'juveniles' in the technical sense," because of "her descriptions of the feelings of childhood, the quirkiness of human behaviour, and the landscape of her childhood haunts," her books "are unusual in that they have remained popular with children all over the world – and with many adults as well, who have retained a love for them throughout their lives."[31] The following year, in their introduction to *Lucy Maud Montgomery: A Preliminary Bibliography*, the editors, Ruth Weber Russell, D.W. Russell, and Rea Wilmshurst, observe different approaches to Montgomery's fiction that are challenging the "tide of disfavour"; however, "there is still a massive reversal that must take place before this writer receives the attention she is due – due … because her books have spoken so directly to so many millions of young adolescent girls (and boys) and continue to do so today … There are qualities in her books that touch the deepest places in the heart of childhood."[32]

MacLulich's two articles, and to a certain extent the introductions to the first volume of the selected journals and the preliminary bibliography, reflect a trend in the 1980s, coinciding with serious critical and academic exploration of children's literature as a genre or form that had both its positive and negative outcomes.[33] On the one hand, this trend contributed to bringing Montgomery back into the canon after fifty years of neglect by insistently reversing the dismissive attitudes represented by Desmond Pacey in *Creative Writing in Canada* (1952): "*Anne of Green Gables* (1908) is a children's classic, and it would be silly to apply adult critical standards to it."[34] Montgomery herself understood that she was labelled a children's writer, and although she often expressed the desire to break the mould and limitations imposed on her because of this label, it was not because she undervalued writing for young people.[35] On the other hand, by tagging Montgomery's books as "simply" juvenile literature and her fictional children as "a separate class of humanity, with special emotional and intellectual needs that adults have a duty to meet," a "privileged status" that is lost in adulthood,[36] MacLulich's articles expose attitudes characterizing two models that Gubar identifies in "Risky Business," both of which are "demeaning options": the "deficit model" and the "difference model." With the former model, "young people are viewed as lacking the abilities, skills, and powers that adults have," which is not only "condescending" but can lead to "low adult expectations" of what children can achieve. In fact, "viewing children as deficient – as unable to grasp certain concepts or skills – can help *produce* the very incapacities we claim merely to describe." The latter model results in "theories of childhood that … stress the radical alterity or otherness of children, representing them as a separate species, categorically different from adults."[37]

Bringing Scholarship on Montgomery as a Children's Writer into the Twenty-First Century

While essays in this volume cite some of the theories that Gubar critiques in terms of these two models – for example, the theories of Jacqueline Rose (1984) and Perry Nodelman (1985) – they interrogate and so contest the outcome of such theories, a "critical paradigm that holds that children do not participate in the production of children's culture," and thus "disregard[s] what young people have said, written, and done in the realm of children's culture."[38] The volume as a whole focuses *not* on the essentialism of "the child" and "childhood," as referenced earlier in the opening paragraph and as suggested by Plotz's "decontextualized state of being,"[39] but rather on children and childhoods. The volume also recognizes the validity of Gubar's "kinship model": "This model is premised on the idea that children and adults are akin to one another, which means they are neither exactly the same nor radically dissimilar. The concept of kinship indicates relatedness, connection, and similarity without implying homogeneity, uniformity, and equality."[40] Beginning the third volume of her journals on 11 February 1910, Montgomery seems to be making a distinction between the "rather shallow girl" of the first volume and the woman with a "morbid temperament, generally in the throes of nervousness and gloom" of the second volume, vowing in the third volume "to strike a better balance in it – to write out my happiness as well as my pain." The happy, carefree child and the melancholic, burdened adult – "nothing could be falser to the reality," she acknowledges, providing details in support.[41] As Elizabeth Epperly observes in a review of *A Preliminary Bibliography*,

Montgomery "goes on to insist that neither Maud is the real one, and certainly a careful reading of the entries allows most readers to see far more than two personalities at play."[42] The essays in this volume thus recognize the interassimilation of childhood and adulthood – and of the multiple, interconnected selves or personalities of the author and her fictional creations – that inspire meaningful conversations about children and childhoods.

Over the years, Montgomery's work has been discussed in relationship to other writers – whether deemed writers for children, youth, adults, or all ages – but often in only brief references rather than in the full conversations examined in this volume. For example, in Virginia Careless's 2003 article in *Windows and Words: A Look at Canadian Children's Literature in English*, mentioned above, the many comparisons made to other writers, works, and characters in critical studies up to that date are listed. The focus of the latter part of Careless's chapter is the similarities arising from historical and cultural situations, as opposed to direct borrowing between authors, and her account of the variety of comparisons made between Montgomery's work and that of other writers forms a background for the critical work in this volume, which examines in depth Montgomery's relationships with various traditions, ideas, and movements through conversations with other writers.

In addition to Careless, a number of scholars have considered Montgomery's work in light of the work of other writers. Some of these studies, such as those by Emily Woster and Clarence Karr, discuss the breadth of Montgomery's general reading, while others focus on writers from various periods.[43] Montgomery's work has also been examined in light of works by her contemporaries, both in Canada and abroad.[44] Other critics explore connections to writers through relationships with literary "heroines,"[45] conceptions of the gothic, [46] a national literature,[47] celebrity,[48] or periodical fiction.[49] These, however, are scattered analyses amongst the growing body of work on Montgomery, and while several patterns emerge (as, for example, the role of the gothic in Montgomery's works and connections with nineteenth-century writers, particularly those for children), few of these studies explicitly undertake to explore literary conversations and interactions as a topic in itself, and fewer still even touch on the depiction of childhood and children.[50] By linking Montgomery with writers representing traditions across nationalities, periods, and genres on childhood and children, this volume presents a far more comprehensive study of intersections and interactions between Montgomery and other writers and concepts than has yet been undertaken.

The first group of essays, "Conversing with the Past: Vulnerability, Resistance, and Resilience," looks at three motifs or traditions – the orphan seeking a place of belonging, death narratives, and boys' stories – upon which Montgomery drew and left her own distinctive mark in depicting children overcoming adverse and challenging situations. Integrating theories of critical literary geography, Kate Scarth, in "Emily of New Moon and Fanny of Mansfield Park: Childhood at Home in Jane Austen and L.M. Montgomery," examines two resilient orphans to show how these outsiders cope and carve out a domestic space they can call home. Lesley Clement's "L.M. Montgomery's Precocious Children: Resisting Domesticated Narratives of Death, Dying, and the Afterlife" argues that, when confronted with their own and others' mortality, Montgomery's child characters, drawing upon their inventiveness and resistance, rescript adult narratives, through humour, performance, play, and dream worlds. Rita Bode's "Vulnerable Situations: Boys and Boyhood in the *Emily* Books" demonstrates how Montgomery's "portrait of the artist as a young girl and woman"[51] opens up a study of the complicated terrain of boyhood experience, layering in and querying various boyhood traditions by looking back to the childhoods of Cousin Jimmy and Dean Priest and examining the portraiture of Perry Miller and Teddy Kent.

The second group of essays, "Conversing with the Present: Fantasy, the Ideal, and the Real," contextualizes Montgomery in her own period, as her literature enriches three traditions: female desire and dream boys, the contested spaces of the fantasy-realism dichotomy, and children's paradoxically truthful fiction in a modern world. Margaret Steffler's "The Performance of the Beautiful Dream Boy in Novels by L.M. Montgomery and Frances Hodgson Burnett" theorizes the tradition of the dream boy within two contexts – "the beautiful boy," the subject of Germaine Greer's 2003 study, and the intensification and prolongation of boyhood as investments of female desire – demonstrating ways in which the tradition is tempered by the ideal boys' experiences with less-than-ideal boys. Bonnie Tulloch's "Lost Boys and Lost Girls: The Kindred Offspring of J.M. Barrie and L.M. Montgomery" examines the liminal spaces between fantasy and realism in deconstructing what constitutes children's literature, children's roles, and childhood itself. Holly Pike's "*Magic for Marigold*,

Childhood, and Fiction" discusses the metafictive nature of one of Montgomery's later novels in its advocacy of the truthfulness of fiction and of child characters who may not be representative of a particular time and place.

The third group of essays, "Continuing Literary Conversations: Transformative Relationships and Spaces," tracks the continued and continuing presence of Montgomery in children's and YA literature that postdates her death in 1942. Åsa Warnqvist's "Loving, Larking, and Lying: Free-Spirited Children and Disciplinary Adults in the Works of L.M. Montgomery and Astrid Lindgren" traces the Swedish author's subversive reactions to her Canadian predecessor in the *Pippi Longstocking* trilogy (1945–48) and her books from the following three decades in their treatment of child behaviour, upbringing, and discipline. Heidi Lawrence's "Absent Fathers: Conversations between L.M. Montgomery and Madeleine L'Engle" explores webs of conversation generated by the idealized rescripting of the father figure and father-daughter relationships of the two authors and their fictional creations. William Thompson's "Transformative Girlhood and Twenty-First-Century Girldom in L.M. Montgomery's *Anne of Green Gables*" argues that, despite a more circumscribed environment than those experienced by twenty-first-century fictional girls such as Suzanne Collins's Katniss, J.K. Rowling's Hermione, and Disney's Elsa, Avonlea allows Anne to negotiate various imaginative, natural, domestic, and scholastic spheres, providing a transformative space for both girls and women.

The fourth and final group of essays, "Continuing Transmediated Conversations: *Anime*, Fanfiction, and Television Adaptations," focuses on twenty-first-century engagement with Montgomery's legacy. Yoshiko Akamatsu's "The Problems and Possibilities Inherent in Adaptation: *Emily of New Moon* and *Emily, Girl of the Wind*" speaks from the author's professional experiences as cultural adviser on the 2007 *anime* to argue that the choices made in the adaptations of this Canadian coming-of-age novel create a fresh view of Emily's experience that appeals to a variety of audiences. Balaka Basu's "Continuing Stories: L.M. Montgomery and Fanfiction in the Digital Era" considers four types of fanfiction – sequels set during the Second World War, the alternate-universe story, the gap-filler, and the slash fic – some of which tease out hints of both heteronormative and same-sex relationships in the source literature and reach out to contemporary readers and viewers of Montgomery narratives who desire different outcomes for Montgomery's characters and their descendants, both within and outside of heteronormative expectations. Laura Robinson's "Anne with an Edge: CBC-Netflix's Rereading of Montgomery's *Anne of Green Gables*" examines the darker, more sombre, interpretations of childhood in recent television adaptations compared to the original and earlier television versions, while exploring, too, the ways in which they nonetheless hold hope for the future.

Following these scholarly chapters are four "afterwords," with a preface introducing these creative statements from several artists on the impact that Montgomery's works have had on their respective art forms. Vappu Kannas's interview with the Finnish co-authors of *Emilia Kent*, Holly Cinnamon's "Anne's Nature," Rosalee Peppard Lockyer's "My Maud by Katie Maurice," and Kit Pearson's "Dear Maud" demonstrate that the conversations we have with stories heard and read as children continue long afterward, shaping and reshaping what childhood means personally and culturally.

In their "welcome" to the *Journal of L.M. Montgomery Studies*, launched in June 2019, editor Kate Scarth and co-editor Emily Woster provide a valuable overview of Montgomery scholarship. They quote from Elizabeth Waterston's essay on Montgomery in Mary Quayle Innis's *The Clear Spirit: Twenty Canadian Women and Their Times* (1966): "Her established audience – girls between ten and fourteen – continues to read and love the L.M. Montgomery books. But she may also lay increasing claim to our attention as adult critics. The books have an intensity because they *were* written as 'children's books.'" Scarth and Woster comment that "Waterston's essay, read with the benefit of hindsight, is a clear bellwether of coming critical respect, presaging many of the rich conversations about Montgomery and Anne – specifically about gender, childhood, and creativity" and note that, over five decades later, "The new corpus of Montgomery studies material and new outreach initiatives show us how multi-faceted Montgomery really is and how the threads of conversation about her over the last century or so have moved and changed."[52] Unravelling one of these variegated "threads of conversation" – on children and childhoods – this volume, as outlined at the beginning of this introduction, reflects on the shifts and changes that have occurred in concomitant conversations on orphans and parenting, home and belonging, recalcitrance and death, the ideal and the real, boyhood and girlhood, heteronormativity, transformative relationships and spaces, creativity and adaptation, and books and their readers. These conversations enrich and will continue to enrich projects of not only the already large community of Canadian and international readers and scholars committed to Montgomery studies but also the burgeoning interdisciplinary fields of girlhood and boyhood studies and, more generally, child and youth studies. Finally, these conversations enrich and will continue to enrich theoretical considerations and practical applications of the nuanced connections among writers themselves and among writers' ideas, whether these intersections take the form of straightforward indebtedness or serendipitous and even uncanny confluences that blur boundaries and turn in other directions through writing against or writing back in order to subvert, adjust, and resist.

NOTES

1 Demers, *From Instruction to Delight*, 132. Demers outlines and selects readings to illustrate these transformations in chapters 5 through 8.

2 Sánchez-Eppler, "Childhood," 39, 36, 35.

3 In a journal entry for 8 February 1905, Montgomery writes that, to amuse herself, she has been "jotting down in a note book all the detachable epigrams in my books. They are easily discoverable as I have them all marked. I've always had the habit of marking my books. I do it now with pencil. I was not so wise in my teens and used ink. Consequently, I cannot now erase the marks of passages and opinions I no longer agree with and they stare me in the face as reminders of my sentimental 'salad days'" (LMM, *CJ* 2:123).

4 LMM, *CJ* 1:448, 34, 226, 109, 111 (emphasis in original), 258, 448–9 (emphasis in original). In her first reading of *Vanity Fair*, she criticizes the characters as either too good – "inane, sickly-sweet things" – or attractively bad "so clear and interesting that it is vexing to see their downfall." Ibid., 228. For other extended discussions of Montgomery's rereading of childhood favourites, see LMM, *CJ* 2:67–8, 257–9.

5 LMM, *CJ* 2:216. In this journal entry, she laments not having read Elizabeth Barrett Browning's poetry at a younger age and therefore not being able to "grow into her poems." She makes the same observation about John Keats: "Perhaps if I had known him in childhood I might have so grown up with him as to love him, tinging his lines with the hues of my own life as I lived it. But I did not and he comes to me too late." Ibid., 235.

6 At age fourteen, Montgomery records conversations that she had with Nate

Lockhart on many occasions about their reading, including her surreptitious reading of the "delicious" *Undine* "under the lid of [her] desk," which leads her to exclaim, "I love books. I hope when I grow up to have lots of them" (LMM, *CJ* 1:7). See also ibid., 5, 17, 453. Several years later, she mentions "clubbing together [with a friend] to send for books," ending with "How I do love books! Not merely to read once but over and over again. I enjoy the tenth reading of a book as much as the first. Books are a delightful world in themselves. Their characters seem as real to me as my friends of actual life" (ibid., 148). As Emily Woster notes in her doctoral thesis, Montgomery's reading, as recorded in her journals "in concert with her letters to G.B. MacMillan and Ephraim Weber," is "made more complex with the many literary clippings in her personal scrapbooks, the marginalia in the books in her own library, and the pages devoted to books and reading in her published autobiography. Her reading life is a hodge-podge of different texts and thoughts, a representative sampling of life writing as a whole" (Woster, *Intertextuality and Life Writing*, 19).

7 LMM, *GR*, 21 (emphasis in original). The newly married Anne would agree. LMM, *AHD*, 102. Montgomery too says that she purchases only books that she knows "will wear well," either because she has read them before or because she has "sufficient confidence" in the author to purchase the book "'sight unseen'" (LMM, *CJ* 1:457).

8 Rubio and Waterston, Introduction, *CJ* 1:x–xi.

9 Kristeva, *Desire in Language*, 66, 68–9. Kristeva cites Bakhtin's *Problems of Dostoevsky's Poetics*, originally published in Russian in 1929.

10 Bernard, "Introduction," para. 2, 4.

11 Bergren, *Global Wordsworth*, 3–7.

12 Greven, "Hawthorne and Influence," 4.

13 Douglas-Fairhurst, *Victorian Afterlives*, 4. Although Douglas-Fairhurst consistently uses the word "influence" throughout his book, on one occasion he chooses the word "confluence." When considering the reciprocal influence of Dante on T.S. Eliot and Eliot on Dante, he says that "it is, rather, confluence as Dante and Eliot move towards one another on the page" (78).

14 It should be noted that this volume uses "confluence" in a different way from Elizabeth Epperly in her "Preface to the 2014 Edition" of *The Fragrance of Sweet-Grass*. Explaining why her book is being made "freshly available to new and seasoned scholars," she identifies four concepts: context, confluence, community, and creativity. She applies the concept of "confluence" to those "larger

forces that were converging to make Montgomery studies possible" in scholarship and "the popular world of readers and fans" during the 1970s. Epperly, Preface, ix, xvii.

15 Montgomery uses this phrase in reference to the similarity between the titles of *Jane of Lantern Hill* and Nellie McClung's *Leaves from Lantern Lane*, which was published after Montgomery had submitted her novel for publication. The title "Lantern Hill," Montgomery remarks, was in her notebook of suggestions for years. LMM, *After Green Gables*, 236.

16 Garber, "Over the Influence," 742–4.

17 "Editorial," 3. The two essays on Montgomery are Rosamund Bailey's "Little Orphan Mary: Anne's Hoydenish Double" and Constance Classen's "Is 'Anne of Green Gables' an American Import?"

18 Garber, "Over the Influence," 757–8 (emphasis in original).

19 Gubar, "Risky Business," 454.

20 LMM, *CJ* 1:221, 243, 241, 321. Montgomery quotes Wordsworth's "Ode: Intimations of Immortality from Recollections of Early Childhood," l. 57. For a later example, see LMM *CJ* 2:52. As Montgomery dramatizes and scripts her broken engagement with Edwin Simpson and unfulfilled (and unrequited) passion for Herman Leard in her journal, a noteworthy element of the narrative arc that she imposes on this period of her life (1897–98) is her transition from girlhood into womanhood. As she ends her recording of these events in her life, she mentions that even her old favourite authors, such as Bulwer-Lytton, disappoint, although by July she is reading and rereading books, "those unfailing keys to a world of enchantment" (LMM, *CJ* 1:368–78, 385–411, 413, 417–18). For Montgomery's scripting of this period of her life, see Gammel, "'I Loved Herman Leard Madly.'"

21 LMM, *CJ* 1:355–6.

22 Plotz, *Romanticism and the Vocation of Childhood*, xv.

23 Of particular relevance are the incidents described in a 2 January 1905 journal entry and discussed by Bonnie Tulloch in her chapter in this volume. LMM, *CJ* 2:117–20. Montgomery funnels the hurt her Macneill relatives inflicted on her into the Murray family's mistreatment of ten-year-old Emily after her father's death (*Emily of New Moon*, chapters 3–5).

24 In their introduction to the first volume of the *Selected Journals*, Rubio and Waterston remark: "Even before 1919 L.M. Montgomery was using her journals to re-enter the world of childhood and to create its voice and textures" (Rubio and Waterston, "Introduction," *SJ* 1:xxiv).

25 LMM, *CJ* 1:435, 452, 463.

26 LMM, *CJ* 2:136–7 (emphasis in original). See also LMM, *CJ* 1; LMM, *CJ* 2:106–7.

27 See, for examples, *CJ* 3:142, 236–7; LMM, *CJ* 4:359. Sometimes, however, the discriminating adult critic takes over, curtailing this enjoyment, as in her reading of Longfellow's *Hiawatha* with Chester. LMM, *CJ* 4:230.

28 LMM, *CJ* 4:341; cf. LMM, *CJ* 2:88–9; LMM, *CJ* 3:174–5, 236–7. Books even have the capacity to link present selves to selves from past lives, as her reading of George Rawlinson's *History of Ancient Egypt* (1881) inspires. LMM, *CJ* 4:15. In an earlier journal entry from 1908, she notes that "Scott's novels are blent with the brightest memories of those old [school] days and so have the added charm of old associations" (LMM, *CJ* 2:203).

29 MacLulich, "L.M. Montgomery's Portraits of the Artist," 91.

30 MacLulich, "L.M. Montgomery and the Literary Heroine," 16.

31 Rubio and Waterson, "Introduction," *Selected Journals* 1:xiii.

32 Russell, Russell, and Wilmshurst, "Introduction," *Lucy Maud Montgomery*, xix.

33 It also coincides with what Benjamin Lefebvre describes as "a momentum of scholarly activity," anticipated by the articles in the third issue of *Canadian Children's Literature* in 1975, an issue devoted to the works of Montgomery, which "would begin in the mid-1980s ... fueled in large part by the release of *The Selected Journals of L.M. Montgomery* (Oxford University Press) in five volumes since 1985." In this editorial for the Spring-Summer 2004 issue of *Canadian Children's Literature*, again devoted to Montgomery, Lefebvre observes that "the question of the implications of categorizing Montgomery's books as children's literature or not remains unanswered" and that "the articles and reviews published in this present issue will add to the difficulty of answering that question" (Lefebvre, "Editorial: Assessments and Reassessments," 6–7).

34 Pacey, *Creative Writing*, 106.

35 For example, as she finishes *Rilla of Ingleside* and begins what will be the seeds of the *Emily* books, she writes that she is "becoming classed as a 'writer for young people' and that only," lamenting the time and monetary considerations that prevent her from writing "a book dealing with grown-up creatures – a psychological study of one human being's life" (LMM, *CJ* 4:279).

36 MacLulich, "L.M. Montgomery and the Literary Heroine," 11. MacLulich extends his distinction between childhood and adulthood to readership: "*Anne of Green Gables* is suited for younger audiences than is *Emily of New Moon*," *Anne* for readers like his seven-year-old daughter, *Emily* "for readers who are themselves nearing or passing through the turmoil of adolescence" (ibid., 13).

Lefebvre discusses and gives further examples of "the devaluation of children's literature as a field of study or as serious literature," which notions of classifications and categories reinforce. Lefebvre, "Editorial: Assessments and Reassessments," 8.

37 Gubar, "Risky Business," 450, 451 (emphasis in original).

38 Ibid., 452.

39 See above p. 10.

40 Gubar, "Risky Business," 453.

41 LMM, *CJ* 2:286.

42 Epperly, "L.M. Montgomery and the Changing Times," 180.

43 Woster, *Intertextuality*, "Old Years," and "Readings of a Writer"; Karr, "Addicted to Reading." Epperly, *Fragrance of Sweet-Grass*, considers Montgomery's heroines within the tradition of romance novels. Earlier writers are well represented, with analyses linking Montgomery's work with: Jane Austen (Fuller, "Jane of Green Gables"); William Shakespeare (McCutcheon, "'To Skip or Not to Skip'"); Ann Radcliffe (Drew, "The Emily Connection"); Elizabeth Barrett Browning (Keen, "'So – So – *Commonplace*'"); Eliza Leslie (Dull, "Kinship and Nation in *Amelia*"); Lewis Carroll (McGrath, "Alice of New Moon"); Charlotte Yonge and Louisa May Alcott (L. Robinson, "Anne and Her Ancestors"); Charlotte Brontë (Miller, "Haunted Heroines" and "Jane Eyre's Heir"; Seelye, *Jane Eyre's American Daughters*); Thomas Carlyle (Narbonne, "Carlylean Sentiment"); Marjorie Richardson (Howey, "Reading Elaine"); Henry Wadsworth Longfellow (R. Ross, "Cultural Heroines"); and Alfred, Lord Tennyson (Howey, "Reading Elaine" and "'She Look'd Down to Camelot'"). Other critics examine Montgomery in relation to writers who followed her, including: C.S. Lewis (Dickieson, "C.S. Lewis's Theory of Sehnsucht"); Margaret Atwood (Fenwick, "The Silence of the Mermaid"; Sheckels, "Anne in Hollywood" and *Island Motif*); Ann-Marie MacDonald (L. Robinson, "Remodeling *An Old-Fashioned Girl*"); Alice Munro (Beran, "Beautiful Girlhood"; Forest, "(Re)Locating Montgomery"); Margaret Laurence (Sheckels, "Anne in Hollywood" and *Island Motif*; Beran, "Beautiful Girlhood"); W.O. Mitchell (Steffler, "Brian O'Connal and Emily Byrd Starr"); Laura Ingalls Wilder (Gates, "Image, Imagination, and Initiation"); Jane Rule (Sandilands, "Fire, Fantasy, and Futurity"); and Canadian children's writers (Meyer, "Writing after Anne").

44 For examples: Nellie McClung (Devereux, "Writing with a 'Definite Purpose'"); Stephen Leacock (Narbonne, "Lucy Maud Montgomery"); Frederick

Philip Grove (Sabatini, *Making Babies*; Gammel, "'My Secret Garden'"); Kate Douglas Wiggin (Dawson, "Literary Relations"); Susan B. Warner (Proehl, "'love of kindred spirits'"); Susan Coolidge (Jenny Robinson, "How Katy Lied"); Willa Cather (Tunc, "Teaching Anne and Antonia"); Else Ury (Gallagher, "Across Enemy Lines"); Ethel Turner (Pearce, "Constructing a 'New Girl'"); Gene Stratton-Porter (C. Thomas, "Anne Shirley's American Cousin"; Holmes, "Romantic Novelist as Naturalist"); George Bernard Shaw (Clement, "Toronto's Cultural Scene"); and J.M. Barrie (Waterston, *Rapt in Plaid*).

45 For examples: MacLulich, "L.M. Montgomery" and "L.M. Montgomery's Portraits"; C. Ross, "Calling Back the Ghost of the Old-Time Heroine."

46 For examples: Forest, "(Re)Locating Montgomery"; Miller, "Haunted Heroines"; Drew, "The Emily Connection"; Lawson, "The Alien at Home."

47 For examples: Litster, "'The Golden Road of Youth'"; Åhmansson, "'Mayflowers Grow in Sweden Too.'"

48 For examples: York, "'How a Girl from Canada'" and *Literary Celebrity*; Clement, "Toronto's Cultural Scene"; Lee, *Limelight.*

49 For examples: Gammel, *Looking for Anne*; Galletly, "L.M. Montgomery"; Roy, *Next Instalment.*

50 Litster, "'The Golden Road of Youth,'" provides the fullest analysis, comparing Montgomery's *The Story Girl* (1911) and *The Golden Road* (1913) to Kenneth Grahame's *The Golden Age* (1895) and *Dream Days* (1898) and noting how Montgomery's books deviate from a British tradition of depictions of an Arcadian childhood, particularly in her books' blurring of childhood and adulthood, both in content and readership.

51 Epperly, *Fragrance of Sweet-Grass*, 145.

52 Woster and Scarth, "Welcome." They cite Waterston, "Lucy Maud Montgomery," 218 (emphasis in original).

PART ONE

Conversing with the Past: Vulnerability, Resistance, and Resilience

1

Emily of New Moon and Fanny of Mansfield Park: Childhood at Home in Jane Austen and L.M. Montgomery

KATE SCARTH

"We might perhaps call L.M. Montgomery the Jane Austen of Canadian literature" notes a contemporary review of *Chronicles of Avonlea*.[1] Indeed, Montgomery and Austen have much in common, as Miriam Rheingold Fuller, Kathleen Ann Miller, and Jessica Seymour have shown.[2] Montgomery and Austen have similar fictional concerns: both authors depict young women negotiating maturation, family, and love. Montgomery and Austen are astute, often humorous, observers of the world around them, and that world is often the rural environs they each knew so well in Canada and England, respectively. Well-drawn, memorable characters like Montgomery's Anne Shirley and Austen's Elizabeth Bennet have been reimagined in countless adaptations, including television, film, theatre, and new media (such as vlogs). As a result, these two authors have devoted fans with nicknames – the "Maud Squad"/ "Anneites" and "Janeites." We can perhaps even label Montgomery an early Janeite; she was, after all, herself a reader of Austen.[3] Some of the homes of these two authors and the settings of their most famous novels – Cavendish, PEI, and Chawton and Bath, England – are now popular sites of literary pilgrimage. Both Montgomery and Austen have national-icon status, as recently attested to by Montgomery having her own Heritage Minute produced by Historica Canada (a well-known series highlighting significant Canadian people and events) and Austen appearing on the five-pound note in the United

Kingdom. Despite these recognitions and accolades, both wrote in environments that were not always supportive of – and sometimes actively undermined – them as women writers. For better and sometimes worse, then, Montgomery and Austen, in their writing, lives, and legacies, share much, and there is fertile ground for exploring Montgomery's conversations with this earlier acclaimed and beloved writer. This present chapter explores Montgomery's and Austen's confluences by turning attention to two protagonists who have received only brief mentions in the comparative criticism on these two writers: Montgomery's Emily Byrd Starr of New Moon and Austen's Fanny Price of Mansfield Park.[4]

I focus on Emily's and Fanny's marginal status within the novels, a liminal status that is replicated outside the text, too, in both scholarship and popular culture. While the *Emily* series is beloved by and an influence on writers, including Margaret Laurence and Alice Munro, by contrast to the more famous and seemingly ubiquitous Anne of Green Gables, Emily of New Moon's reach is considerably more truncated.[5] A recent search in the MLA International Bibliography database yields 247 hits for *Anne of Green Gables*, while *Emily of New Moon* returns just fourteen. *Anne of Green Gables: The Musical* played at the Confederation Centre of the Arts in PEI every summer since 1965, until its 2020 and 2021 cancellations as a result of the COVID-19 pandemic, but a musical adaptation of *Emily* played for just two years at the same venue.[6] In contrast to the sparkle and wit of *Pride and Prejudice*'s Elizabeth Bennet or the romantic high spirits of *Sense and Sensibility*'s Marianne Dashwood, Fanny Price's quiet morality often casts her as "Jane Austen's least popular heroine," with one critic finding her "unyieldingly charmless."[7] This present chapter, in its celebration of these two marginalized but resilient heroines, contributes to the scholarship that shows the interest and strengths of, and even explicitly defends, these "lesser" heroines and novels.[8]

My comparative reading of Montgomery and Austen, of Emily and Fanny, zeroes in on the child heroines and their relationships with home and belonging, highlighting that these two novels are stories of childhood agency and resilience. Both novels relay emotional realism in their depiction of lonely, unwanted girls finding their place in the world, and specifically in their respective homes. Austen's and Montgomery's novels share understandings of childhood; when read side by side, Emily's and Fanny's coping strategies emerge as similar, reinforcing that Montgomery and Austen have captured a particular kind of childhood experience: that of the lonely, out-of-place, but ultimately resilient, child. Both authors depict the power of (marginal) girls. Austen and Montgomery represent quiet triumphs, never losing sight of the very real (social, economic, physical) limitations placed on these two children. For both Austen and Montgomery, power is not a single, one-dimensional phenomenon, but takes on many forms – it can, for example, be social and/or physical. Power also exists at a range of scales, from the almost imperceptible, such as a quiet withdrawal from an unpleasant situation, to more obvious exertions of agency, like Emily's Murray look, which channels her formidable grandfather, even stopping his equally formidable daughter, Emily's Aunt Elizabeth, in her tracks. For both Emily and Fanny, resilience is centred on coping with and transforming initially unwelcoming domestic spaces; both girls achieve this transformation by learning to weave together self and space to create a sense of belonging. Of course, Emily and Fanny live in different times and in different places and have remarkably disparate personalities – Emily challenges authority more overtly than Fanny ever does, while Fanny's steadfast moral compass is replaced by artistic motivation in Emily. These discrepancies highlight how both heroines create a sense of belonging, a sense of self and home, suited to their individual personalities and ideal, and eventual, roles in adulthood: Emily as writer, and Fanny as minister's wife, household manager, and moral centre of the home and the community.

Spaces, specifically domestic spaces, and Emily's and Fanny's relationships with them are central to my argument, which thus builds on the well-established sub-field of critical literary geography, as developed by Andrew Thacker and others, and more specifically on spatially inflected scholarship that addresses either *Emily of New Moon* or *Mansfield Park*.[9] Domestic spaces and relations are significant in both novels, with implications for family dynamics, gender, class, literary traditions, culture, empire, and authorial development and reception, as various critics have elucidated.[10] Domestic spaces are multi-faceted, encompassing the emotional (how the girls feel in and about particular spaces), psychic (how they think in and about spaces), social (their interactions with people in spaces), and material (physical dimensions, including architecture and objects). As urban theorist Edward Soja points out, the "possibility of independent conceptualization and inquiry ... does not produce an unquestionable autonomy or rigid separation between" different facets of "spaces," because "they interrelate and overlap," creating the "construction of spatiality" that people, in fiction and beyond, encounter in lives lived in particular geographies, whether domestic, community, institutional, or national.[11] After all, a portrait hanging in one's childhood bedroom (material space) may evoke happiness (emotional space) about the portrait's subject, say an aunt (social space), leading to reflection on happy times spent with that aunt (psychic space). Fanny and Emily encounter and construct such multi-dimensional spaces, eventually creating a powerful link between self and space.

The *linkage* between a carefully delineated self and a thorough knowing of space is the mark of belonging, as advanced by Christopher Toner.[12] Various spatial critics help conceptualize this interaction – this mutually constitutive movement – between self and space. Feminist scholars like Elisabeth Grosz are concerned with how the (gendered) body "is not distinct" from the spaces it inhabits, because body and space are "mutually defining … There is a two-way linkage that could be defined as an *interface*."[13] One way that this interface plays out in everyday life is through emotions, which, according to Joyce Davidson and Christine Milligan, "might be seen as a form of connective tissue," linking an individual's "psyche and physique" with the social and material spaces people move through during their day-to-day lives. The movement between self and space is "somewhat circular in nature," Davidson and Milligan state, since particular spaces – for example, residential schools or amusement parks – elicit particular emotions, while a person's emotions can have an impact on space, say a colleague's rage undermining workplace collegiality.[14] Epperly has described this focus on self, surroundings (place, home, community), and their interface as a core feature of Montgomery's writing; for example, "each of the heroines learns to value herself in relation to the surrounding community and culture; each heroine learns to love and create a home for herself. In discovering or appreciating or creating 'home,' the heroines are creating or strengthening interconnections between themselves and the value or beauties of the spiritual or material culture around them."[15] Emily and Fanny first establish their sense of self and an understanding of domestic space, which they then weave together, gradually connecting self and space in the creation of home and belonging.

This act of connecting is an evolving process. When Emily and Fanny arrive at their new homes, they are overwhelmed with negative emotions – grief, longing, fear – that signal and intensify their distance from their surroundings. Even in this disconnection, Emily and Fanny seek out spaces where they might be themselves: they retreat into unnoticed spaces like secret corners and attic stairs to give vent to the feelings that cannot be openly displayed in the more public spaces of drawing rooms and kitchens. Then, as Emily and Fanny settle in, they carve out their own more positive spaces of retreat, spaces where they can think, feel, create: for Emily, this space is first the garret, then the lookout bedroom, and for Fanny, the East Room. In these rooms, they have agency unparalleled in other parts of the houses, and so, in these rooms, they have the physical, psychic, and emotional space to know and shape their new homes, thus creating a deeper sense of self and belonging. These rooms are emotional geographies, as in them Emily and Fanny move from homesickness to home love. They are psychic spaces too. Emily can mentally escape into her writing as a way of understanding her lived life at New Moon and hone her writing craft, a fundamental part of herself. Meanwhile, Fanny, "a strong but sensitive moral barometer if there is one in Austenworld," cultivates and develops the moral lens through which she interacts with the world.[16] These rooms crucially have social dimensions. In them, Emily and Fanny negotiate relationships with cohabiting relatives and cultivate bonds with those who are absent but are represented through letters and portraits. Portraits, as one example, point to the vital materiality of these rooms; through getting to know objects, caring for them, curating them, and adding new ones, Emily and Fanny exert power in these spaces, showcasing their own individuality and establishing a bond with the room.[17] Finally, this sense of belonging rooted in their own rooms emanates out to engender a sense of belonging across the larger scale of whole houses and the countryside around them.

Both *Emily of New Moon* and *Mansfield Park* chronicle a very specific childhood experience: the child taken in by extended family out of a sense of duty, not love. Both Emily and Fanny lack affection, power, and status within their new homes – New Moon and Mansfield Park, respectively – and society more broadly. "Remember you're not of much importance," Emily is told by her father's housekeeper, Ellen Greene, as our heroine mourns her beloved father and awaits a decision, beyond her control, of where she will be sent to live.[18]

Fanny is no stranger to such comments, as when Mrs Norris reminds her niece, "wherever you are, you must be the lowest and last."[19] At various times, family members and society dismiss or marginalize these protagonists on the basis of their female gender, youth, absent/distant parents, and their parents' status, specifically their mothers' perceived poor (marriage) choices and their fathers', and thus their own, low socio-economic standing. Given these prejudices, shared even by their extended family members who take them in, Emily and Fanny unsurprisingly feel out of place in New Moon and Mansfield Park, at least initially. After her father dies, Emily realizes "there isn't anybody in the world who loves me now," and sometimes later feels that "I didn't belong anywhere."[20] For Fanny, newly arrived at Mansfield Park, "the separation from everybody she had been used to" means that "her feelings were very acute, and too little understood to be properly attended to."[21]

When Emily arrives at New Moon and Fanny at Mansfield Park, these new domestic spaces are not emotionally accommodating to these homesick children: Emily "had terrible hours when she was overwhelmed by grief for her father and when all the splendours of New Moon could not stifle the longing for the shabby little house in the hollow where they had loved each other so," while for Fanny, "the grandeur of the house astonished, but could not console her. The rooms were too large for her to move in with ease: whatever she touched she expected to injure, and she crept about in constant terror of something or other."[22] These domestic spaces prescribe a lack of agency. Overwhelmed by emotions she cannot control, Emily longs for her father, to go back to her home with him, which is forever out of her reach: as she realizes, "there wasn't any 'back' to go to – no home – no father–."[23] Fanny's actions are curtailed in her new domestic space, as she "crept" in fear of injuring something, instead of walking properly, freely, or comfortably. For both heroines, their emotions and the space around them are not aligned: no matter how appealing the splendours of New Moon or the grandness of Mansfield Park objectively are, they are not enough to stifle Emily's homesickness for a much humbler home or to "console" Fanny's for her lack of ease in this unfamiliar territory. Both Montgomery and Austen configure the houses as living things – personified entities – that are capable of stifling negative emotions or alternatively of consoling people, pointing to the possibility of an organically evolving relationship, in the form of a person-space interface, and suggesting that this linkage should ideally be one that benefits these girls. For example, in response to these negative emotions – grief, longing, lack of consolation, and terror – Emily and Fanny attempt to exert some agency and recognize their own emotional states, staking out small-scale retreats within the house where they can give vent to their emotions, as when "Emily fled to some secret corner and cried her heart out" and Fanny "was found … sitting crying on the attic stairs."[24] They thus escape from the stoic emotional expectations of the grander, more splendid, parts of the houses. No matter how temporary, makeshift, and unhappy these small-scale retreats are, they showcase both girls' attempts to carve out space for themselves and their emotions.

Indeed, physical and emotional retreats within Mansfield Park and New Moon remain important for both children, but later develop more positive connotations. Emily finds a retreat – the garret – where she can engage with a core part of herself, her writing, and Fanny, to survive in a home that often threatens her acute emotional and moral sensibility, creates refuges within busy family spaces like the drawing room. In response to Emily's having "rolled up all the blinds" in the parlour, which is, in her childish vernacular, "dark as a toomb," Aunt Elizabeth makes her feel decidedly unwelcome in the parlour and at New Moon: as Emily writes to her father, "Aunt Elizabeth was horrified and called me a little hussy and gave me the Murray look. You would suppose I had committed a crime … Aunt Elizabeth said I was never to go into the parlour again without permission."[25] Emily reacts in a manner typical of her by retreating physically to the garret, but also, most significantly, psychically into her writing. Again and again, Emily asserts agency spatially by withdrawing to the garret to write, and through her writing, she purges negative emotions, connects with her late father, grapples with her new home, and hones the craft that will be her life's calling.

Fanny, who is not a writer but is defined by her own distinct personality of heightened sensibility and morality, also creates physical and psychic retreats. These spaces allow her to survive and even feel comfortable in her own new home in a way that suits her as an individual. Fanny is particularly sensitive to being the centre of attention and to the mistreatment of her loved ones. In both situations, she becomes adept at physically retreating in the midst of moments of social awkwardness or anxiety. So, for example, when her uncle chastises her beloved cousin Edmund for his role in the Mansfield Park amateur theatricals, "not less acutely was ['the reproof'] felt by Fanny, who had *edged back* her chair *behind* her aunt's end of the sofa, and, *screened from notice herself*, saw all that was passing before her." Fanny controls her interaction with this space, protecting herself while also being able to observe events. Then later, when too much attention is focused on her, she again creates such a personal sanctuary. During a conversation about whether Fanny, who has not yet had her coming out, should attend a party, "Fanny immediately slipped out of the room; for to hear herself the subject of any discussion with her uncle was more than her nerves could bear."[26] While such withdrawing actions might not seem like an impressive show of agency, I work against conventional dismissive readings of a Fanny characterized by "stillness and immobility," as articulated by Aileen Douglas.[27] Instead, I follow Anna Despotopoulou's persuasive argument that Fanny exerts a significant, if quiet, independence, building "a unique feminine space for herself which remains uncontaminated and uninterrupted by male involvement." Despotopoulou goes on to write,

> While not wielding any visible power in the household, she does, however, impose on the reader her gaze, which encompasses views, tastes, morality, and emotions. She powerfully withstands the male gaze of Sir Thomas, Henry Crawford, and even Edmund by consistently avoiding being looked at, a choice that renders her free of male influence. Her gaze, symbolic of her views and emotions, requires no confirmation or justification from the public world or the larger picture of politics, business, or publicity. Its self-sufficiency or domesticity is not a drawback, therefore, but a confirmation of the distinctive qualities of the female gender. In *Mansfield Park* Fanny's world is much more stable than that of the men, and with this heroine Austen seems to be presenting an alternative version to the male-defined woman of her time.[28]

Fanny's discreet movements in domestic space have empowering implications.

For both Emily and Fanny, retreating can be a show of power and self-preservation. Indeed, in both the above examples, the heroines exert physical, emotional, and psychic agency by pulling away from spaces hostile to their feelings. Aunt Elizabeth underlines Emily's marginal position at New Moon by making her feel like the ultimate outcast, a "criminal," and by requiring her to seek "permission" to enter a room in what is ostensibly her home. Fanny is often treated like an unpaid attendant, required to tend to her aunts' whims, and in her location at remote, rural Mansfield Park, she is unable to choose her own companions. She is thereby often exposed to conversations and behaviours that she finds distressing. Yet, Emily and Fanny are not only retreating *from* these unpleasant situations but retreating *into* more positive spaces in line with and supportive of their own inner lives. These are acts of resistance, even rebellion. For example, Emily fictionalizes her life, an activity to which, she later learns, her Aunt Elizabeth stridently objects, leading her to eventually stop Emily from writing fiction. Emily, moreover, writes to her father, a man of whom Aunt Elizabeth also disapproves. While Aunt Elizabeth bars her niece from parts of the house, Emily writes herself into New Moon; after all, her letters to her father are about her growing relationship with New Moon. In Fanny's case, she refuses to be party to a conversation of which she cannot approve: the chastisement of her cousin. By imagining herself dead in a dramatic drowning, Emily purges the negative emotions engendered by the mundane drawing-room scene (she writes to her father, "I felt so insulted that I came up to the garret and wrote a deskription of myself being drowned on a letter-bill and then I felt better").[29] Through her small-scale retreats, Fanny avoids becoming the target of the (negative) attention of Sir Thomas or others, rejects conversations with which she is uncomfortable, preserves her moral sensibility, and avoids the physical damage to her "nerves" that such upsets cause. The girls' creation of these retreats, which sustain mental and emotional well-being, is an act of resilience.

Emily and Fanny are figuring out a process of belonging that is reflective of themselves as individuals in and of these new domestic spaces. A significant step for them toward feeling like their respective houses are homes occurs when they acquire their own rooms. These rooms are their tiny dominions, and these spaces have distinct material and social features conducive to the girls' well-being. Emily, no longer having to share a bed with Aunt Elizabeth, "was given a room of her own," specifically what is called the lookout room at New Moon.[30] While Fanny is first given the "little white attic," marginal in location and size, as a bedroom, she eventually takes over the East Room, of which she becomes "mistress."[31] However, despite the heroines' acquisition of their own domestic spaces, Montgomery and Austen never lose sight of their heroines' marginal status in someone else's house. After all, the primary reason for Emily's getting her own room is not for her benefit but for Aunt Elizabeth's, who "could not put up any longer with a squirming bedfellow," and the new room is a static memorial to Emily's late mother before she left that room, this house, and the Murrays to elope with Douglas Starr. The room's furnishings are frozen in the moment that Juliet chose exile, a liminal status that her daughter inherits, given the Murrays' suspicions of the penurious Starrs. While it was Juliet's room, many of the furnishings are not linked to her or Emily at all but to the aesthetics of the wider space of an often-unfriendly New Moon and to Emily's aunts, who still live in their childhood home: the "room was very old-fashioned, like all the New Moon rooms" and the wall hangings, which "Emily looked at … with distaste" are from the "girlhood of her aunts."[32]

Fanny's room highlights her orphan-as-outsider status. She gets discarded furniture and portraits – "a faded footstool … too ill done for the drawing-room" and "a collection of family profiles, thought unworthy of being anywhere else" – as well as a rejected room: the East Room is the former schoolroom, no longer of use in a household of adults.[33] For much of the novel, Fanny is not permitted to have a fire in her room, but Sir Thomas does eventually correct Mrs Norris's meanness, and in her East Room, Fanny often has to host unwelcome visitors. In particular, she has to listen to her beloved – and eventual husband – Edmund, talk about his love for Mary Crawford, and has to watch them flirt while they rehearse for the illicit play. Finally, the East Room is the site of Sir Thomas's most virulent attack on Fanny when she refuses to marry Henry Crawford. Despite these disconnections and discomforts, Emily's and Fanny's rooms are more positive retreats than other domestic spaces. In these rooms, they can actively engender a firmer sense of belonging: before they are Emily of New Moon and Fanny of Mansfield Park, they are Emily of the Lookout Room and Fanny of the East Room.

Montgomery and Austen both emphasize that Emily and Fanny are individuals, whose "interfacing" with their rooms is on their own terms, in line with their emotions and movements, not with other people's, and in sharp contrast with most other spaces. For example, Emily's room can accommodate her full self (or very nearly): she could see almost all of herself – "all but [her] boots" – in the room's mirror. And the mirror takes her as she is: it does not require "craning or tipping," and "it doesn't twist [her] face or turn [her] complexion green."[34] The metaphorical implications of this literal seeing are clear: Emily is not twisted by outside forces or the opinions of others (namely Aunt Elizabeth) here, but is just Emily, no behavioural or bodily contortions required.[35] Montgomery also highlights Emily's status as a writer in this space. The smell of potpourri in the room provides Emily with literary inspiration – what she calls "the flash" – and the room has become, in her words, "consecrated" writing space, usurping the garret as *her* space. Indeed, the garret, unlike the lookout room, was never explicitly given to or sanctified by Emily. She "love[s]" the new room, which is "almost like a living thing to her – a sharer in gladness – a comforter in sorrow"; this "sharing" of emotions results in an interfacing between Emily and her "living" room, which is capable of comforting her, while she, in turn, loves it. This mutual exchange, this growing rapprochement, between Emily and her lived space is bound up with love of home and belonging. Indeed, from the first moments in the room when "she flit[s] about examining everything," Emily makes a decision: this is "her room – she loved it already – she felt perfectly at home. 'I belong here,' she breathed happily."[36]

For Fanny, the East Room is a space of physical, emotional, and psychic retreat: "the comfort of it in [Fanny's] hours of leisure was extreme. She could go there after anything unpleasant below, and find immediate consolation in some pursuit, or some train of thought at hand." After her cousin Tom accuses her of ingratitude for her refusal to act in their amateur theatrical production, Fanny, "agitated by the shock of such an attack from her cousin Tom, so public and so persevered in," is unsure how to proceed and, finding the little attic room "incompetent to suggest any reply, she ha[s] recourse … to another apartment [the East Room] more spacious and more meet for walking about in and thinking."[37] The East Room is accommodating, allowing Fanny to walk and think freely. While in her room, Emily writes, the central activity of her life; Fanny can most adequately reflect on moral matters – a central part of her personality – by entering into a kind of cognitive and kinesthetic conversation with her East Room. The East Room, moreover, unlike the now inadequate attic room, "suggest[s] a reply" to her problems. Like Emily, Fanny is simultaneously cultivating self, space, and the links between the two.

Emily and Fanny love these rooms, their own small queendoms, because they explore and come to know them intimately. On Emily's first night in her new room, "left alone in her lookout, lighted dimly by the one small candle," she investigates "every bit" of the room "with keen and thrilling interest." Emily's exploration leads to an intimate inventory of the room's features: its wallpaper, pictures, carpet, rugs, bedstead, bed, quilt, table, window, windowpanes, chairs, washstand, ottoman, mantel, vases, cupboards, and a small fireplace. Not only does Emily explore the room, but she enthusiastically becomes its caretaker: "I dusted *everything* – and when I went out I knelt down and kissed the doorstep," justifying this action to Aunt Elizabeth by saying that she kissed it "because I love my room so much."[38] Emily emphasizes the thoroughness of her dusting – the thoroughness of her jurisdiction over and knowledge of this room – with italics, and links this physical caretaking with emotional caring for the room. The kiss is a physical interfacing between Emily and the room, and her love for it is so strong that she is willing to not only demonstratively exhibit it but to defend this act to her stern Aunt Elizabeth.

Fanny's love of her room is also achieved through detailed knowing of the space. Like Montgomery, Austen provides an inventory of the East Room's furniture; Fanny's room includes "*her* plants, *her* books – of which she had been a collector from the first hour of her commanding a shilling – *her* writing-desk, and *her* works of charity and ingenuity, [which are] all within *her* reach." This room becomes beloved by Fanny, as Emily's is by her; Austen writes that "the room was most dear to [Fanny], and she would not have changed its furniture for the handsomest in the house." Fanny learns to negotiate and even care for the objects that were discarded by others. For both girls, the rooms' materiality – the things in them and how those objects are laid out – is closely connected to a psychic and emotional sense of belonging as characterized by terms like "dear," "value," "love," and "keen and thrilling interest." So, while both Emily and Fanny intimately know, curate, and have agency in these rooms, in contrast to other domestic spaces, Fanny has considerably more scope than Emily to add new objects to her room: "gradually, as her value for the comforts of [the East Room] increased, [Fanny] had added to her possessions, and spent more of her time there; and having nothing to oppose her, had so naturally and so artlessly worked herself into it, that it was now generally admitted to be hers."[39] There are practical reasons for this divergence between the two heroines – Fanny is older than Emily and lives with a much wealthier family – but this difference also speaks to their particular personal development. For Emily, whose physical spaces and belongings are so decidedly determined by others, namely her Aunt Elizabeth, Montgomery's most biographical heroine has, appropriately for a budding writer, a relationship to space that relies heavily on her imaginative and psychological interpretations of space, as we will see in more detail below. Fanny's spatial experience relies less on imagination, but she has more scope for rudimentary household management – of shillings and household goods – and she claims the East Room for herself, anticipating her eventual household management as Edmund's wife.

Reflecting the influence of Romantic ideals of nature, the heroines' loving attachments are cemented by these two rooms' access to nature and related emotional and psychic benefits. Emily's looks "to the garden," and having "no curtains" means she can easily, and happily, see the sky and listen "to the sonorous sweep of the night wind among the great trees in Lofty John's bush."[40] Fanny decorates her room with "her plants," and hopes that "by giving air to her geraniums she might inhale a breeze of mental strength herself."[41] Both Emily and Fanny, like their creators, may love the natural world, but Emily's is outdoor, noisy, and wild, while Fanny's is decidedly indoor, domestic, and contained. For Emily the wind is a source of artistic inspiration – the Wind Woman, the friend of her imagination, is a clear example of this – while Fanny sustains the life of an organic being. Their disparate settings are brought into relief – a windswept island in eastern Canada and a landscaped country estate in the English Midlands – but so are their ultimate ambitions: writer, on the one hand, and minister's wife/community (spiritual) leader, on the other.

For Emily and Fanny, space and people are intimately entwined, with social and emotional aspects of domestic spaces engendering belonging. Emily is given her late mother's room, where "she felt deliciously *near* to her mother – as if Juliet Starr had suddenly become real to her." Physical proximity, emphasized not only by a shared room but by the sensual language of taste, even if accompanied by temporal distance, cultivates emotional nearness. Not only do Emily and her mother in a sense share a room, but "there was a picture of her mother hanging over the mantel," and "this picture … was all her own. She could look at it – talk to it at will." Emily's exertion of "will" in accessing Juliet's likeness in the bedroom is contrasted with her mother's picture in New Moon's drawing room: "Emily seldom saw it."[42] Emily can, for the first time, actively craft a relationship with the mother she never knew and deepen her bond with this shared room too.

In the East Room, Fanny fosters a space of emotional and social resonances that is also conducive to her well-being: "she could scarcely see an object in that room which had not an interesting remembrance connected with it. Every thing was a friend, or bore her thoughts to a friend." These objects are key to the room's status as a refuge within Mansfield Park. For example, when uncertain how to respond to her cousin Tom's desire to force her into the Mansfield theatricals, "to [her] nest of comforts Fanny now walked down to try its influence on an agitated, doubting spirit – to see if by looking at Edmund's profile she could catch any of his counsel."[43] And, of course, Fanny and Edmund also have many intimate tête-à-têtes in her East Room, as outlined above.

Emily's and Fanny's rooms are also bases from which they continue relationships with those who are not present via letter writing to beloved relatives. Through letters, Emily and Fanny can bring – at least emotionally and psychically, if not physically – the most beloved people from their earlier lives, namely, Emily's late father and Fanny's seafaring brother, into these new domestic spaces. Letter writing becomes an emotional and social act, independent of Emily's and Fanny's physically present but often overbearing guardians. Emily writes herself into New Moon's domestic spaces through these letters, telling her father about details of the house – its rooms, routines, traditions – and she also negotiates more negative aspects of life there: sometimes she "poured out her bitterness and perplexity."[44] She thus exerts power by explaining and understanding her relationship to this home from her perspective, with herself, not Aunt Elizabeth, as the central player. Once installed in the lookout room and feeling more connected with its previous inhabitant, her mother, Emily starts writing to her as well, thereby psychically creating a connection with her mother through this space and through these letters. Meanwhile, Fanny uses letters to maintain and foster a relationship with her brother – and through him her immediate family back in Portsmouth: "Fanny had never known so much felicity in her life, as in this unchecked, equal, fearless intercourse with the brother and friend who was opening all his heart to her," while also being interested in her Mansfield home.[45] The psychic space that Emily and Fanny create in their letters is markedly dissimilar to their early encounters with New Moon and Mansfield Park. For example, by contrast to the unhappiness, restrictions, and discomfort characterizing her early life at Mansfield, in these letters Fanny achieves a happy freedom, feeling "unchecked" and "fearless" and experiencing unparalleled "felicity." Like Emily with New Moon, Fanny writes herself into Mansfield Park by sharing all "the comforts and all the little hardships" of her life there. However, a significant contrast again emerges between the two heroines. Emily, with dead parents and no siblings, writes to people (her late parents) who cannot write back, and her letter writing is thus both an act of imagination and of faith, serving the emotional need to write and providing an informal apprenticeship for her to hone her craft. Fanny, in contrast, not only shares her own feelings and experiences but is also confidante and counsellor to another person – in this case, her brother – a role that she also fulfills for her future husband, Edmund.

Emily and Fanny extend the weaving together of self and space – including emotional, psychic, social, and material spaces – that engage their respective rooms in the wider homes. Emily's comprehensive knowledge of her lookout room is eventually replicated on the wider scale of New Moon as a whole: "Emily had lived long enough at New Moon for it to get pretty thoroughly into her blood," and "she fitted into its atmosphere as a hand into a glove. She … loved *every* stick and stone and tree and blade of grass about it … *every* 'tradition' of its history."[46] Emily and New Moon are intertwined then at the bodily level; this place is Emily's birthright, and Montgomery even invokes that (now) clichéd image of "a hand into a glove," the ultimate idiom for describing a good fit. Emily's relationship with New Moon is no passive interfacing but reflects Emily's active power in getting to know her new home intimately and with relish. Similarly, Fanny's in-depth knowledge of space, evident in the East Room, is also translated across Mansfield. When Fanny leaves Mansfield for the first time since moving there, her emotional attachment is comprehensive: "her heart was completely sad at parting. She had tears for *every* room in the house, much more for *every* beloved inhabitant." As with Emily, the physicality of self and of space are connected. From Fanny's earlier uncertain movements through Mansfield, she now realizes the positive influences, the "animation, both of body and mind" that home, and its signs of spring, have on her.[47]

Austen and Montgomery layer detail upon detail of New Moon and Mansfield Park, inviting readers, like the heroines, to come to know, and care about, these spaces. Emily and Fanny arrive in houses already resonant with strong personalities and traditions, where they are expected to fall in line. It could therefore be possible for their young, newly formed personalities to disappear beneath Aunt Elizabeth's rules or Mrs Norris's demands. Yet Emily and Fanny both establish, showcase, and cultivate their own developing temperaments, tastes, and dreams. For example, when Aunt Ruth catalogues Emily's faults so that she may change them, Emily insists on her self-worth, standing up to her elder by stating, "But I don't *want* to be a different girl." Emily's antagonist is usually Aunt Elizabeth, and "once in a while she came up against that curious streak of granite in Emily's composition which was unyielding and unbendable and unbreakable." Emily's "curious streak of granite" is significant. Emily remains "unyielding and unbendable and unbreakable" no matter how marginalized she is as a young girl, financially insecure and dependent, without parents, while the adults around her often undermine her passion, writing, and expect continuous demonstrations of gratitude. Emily is assisted in this resistance by having the "Murray look," the facial expression that reminds authoritarian Aunt Elizabeth of her own stern father and results in Emily getting her own way in skirmishes with her aunt. While Emily cannot control the appearance of this expression, when it does appear, it asserts her Murrayness, her belonging at New Moon, and her own iron will. Emily is resilient, explicitly acknowledging her own selfhood: "'I am important to myself,' cried Emily proudly."[48]

Emily channels strength from her Starr and Murray familial lineages and from her writing ability. Meawhile, Fanny, too, although she is often found tending to her aunts' needs, has an unbreakable spirit firmly tied to her strong moral compass, which she carefully safeguards. Emily develops her writing voice, while Fanny finds her speaking voice. While her cousins seemingly ignore the roots of their wealth in Antiguan plantation slavery, Fanny questions her plantation-owner uncle, explicitly reflecting to Edmund on her increasing courage when it comes to Sir Thomas: "But I do talk to him more than I used. I am sure I do. Did not you hear me ask him about the slave-trade last night?" Later, in the East Room, she defies Sir Thomas, the "master at Mansfield Park," and his entreaties for her to marry the wealthy, but dissipated, Henry Crawford, by deploying a series of simple declarative sentences of "Yes, sir" and "No, sir." Unlike her cousins, she is not completely enamoured of the alluring personalities of the fashionable Crawfords, Henry and Mary, and voices the unpopular opinion that they act "so dishonourably and unfeelingly!" And so the timid Fanny resists her uncle even when he, deploying language not unlike Aunt Elizabeth's words to Emily, accuses Fanny of being "wilful and perverse," selfish and inconsiderate: "you can and will decide for yourself, without any consideration or deference for those who have surely some right to guide you – without even asking their advice."[49] When Henry Crawford's affair with her cousin, Maria, is made public, Sir Thomas and all must acknowledge Fanny's good sense. It is no accident that Austen houses Fanny in the East Room, formerly the schoolroom, as she is the character who most embodies the importance of adequate moral education.

Eventually, Emily can declare, "I am Emily Byrd Starr of New Moon," feeling "as if she belonged to this old cradle of her family" and wondering, "How could she live away from dear New Moon?" since "there is no place just like dear New Moon."[50] For Fanny, too, the bond with her new home is clear: "Portsmouth was Portsmouth; Mansfield was home."[51] Emily and Fanny both move from outsider to insider status, becoming integral to New Moon and Mansfield Park, and thus becoming Emily of New Moon and Fanny of Mansfield Park. These houses have become homes through a three-part process in which the girls develop their sense of self in these domestic spaces while learning about and shaping their new homes. Finally, self and space become inextricably connected through psychic, emotional, and physical interfacing, as these domestic spaces become the sites of and inspirations for writing, reflecting, and speaking about experiences, declaring love and expressing sadness, and cleaning, decorating, and collecting objects and memories, all of which create the heroines' sense of belonging, of home.

This belonging is underlined by Emily's and Fanny's growing realizations of their own importance and value in their respective homes. Even with Aunt Elizabeth's stern standards, Emily suspects that she now belongs to New Moon's emotional fabric: "'I don't believe I'm a duty to Aunt Elizabeth any more,' she thought exultantly."[52] When Fanny is away in Portsmouth, she worries that "*there* [at Mansfield] she might be missed to a degree that she did not like to think of"; after all, at "Mansfield Park, she was useful, she was beloved."[53] As these two heroines leave childhood behind and grow into young women on the precipices of careers as writer and minister's companion, they are Emily of New Moon and Fanny of Mansfield Park. While confronting how home and domestic life are sometimes limited or distressing, L.M. Montgomery and Jane Austen, through Emily Byrd Starr and Fanny Price, both celebrate children's and young women's strength and agency in the spaces of everyday life.

NOTES

1 "Concealment of Art," 133.

2 See Miller, "Haunted Heroines," 125; and Fuller, "Jane of Green Gables," para. 1 and 2.

3 See Fuller, "Jane of Green Gables," para. 2.

4 Despite the convergences between Montgomery and Austen, only three articles compare them. Fuller's 2009 article is the first, investigating the "connections between Anne Shirley, Austen's heroines, and Montgomery herself." Fuller is particularly interested in how "Montgomery uses Austen's romance scenarios": Montgomery "does not … replicate these heroines and their experiences but alters them to reshape her fictional self and to comment on Austen's treatment of her heroines." In a 2010 article, Miller grants Montgomery an active role in a tradition of women's writing, specifically in the subversive Gothic genre, stating that "Montgomery's manipulation of Austen's Gothic does not exist as mere mimicry, but rather it participates in an intertextual tradition of women's Gothic that advocates novelistic responses to scenes of writing and reading in Gothic texts." The juxtaposition of Austen and Montgomery in Miller's article is centred on the *Anne* books, and she examines the *Emily* series, as do other scholars, in relation not to Austen, but to Charlotte Brontë. Miller's intertextual argument also pays attention to Montgomery's cultural legacy, specifically Kevin Sullivan's television adaptations of the *Anne* books. Jessica Seymour (2015) extends this engagement with meta-fiction, analyzing five web series adaptations of classic novels, including *Anne of Green Gables*, reimagined as *Green Gables Fables*, and Austen's *Pride and Prejudice*, translated into *The Lizzie Bennet Diaries*. Fuller, Miller, and Seymour then make successful strides in establishing the many connections between Austen's fiction and Montgomery's, the *Anne* series in particular.

5 For discussion of *Emily*'s influence on Laurence and Munro, see Beran, "Beautiful Girlhood," 148–60.

6 For information on this production, see Kenneth Jones, "Canada's *Emily*, of New Moon, Sings Again in Revised Musical Revival," *Playbill* (14 December 2006). https://www.playbill.com/article/canadas-emily-of-new-moon-sings-again-in-revised-musical-revival-com-137063.

7 Burton, "In Defense of Fanny Price," para. 2; and Auerbach, "Jane Austen's Dangerous Charm," para. 1.

8 See Clement, "Visual Culture"; Epperly, "Reading Time"; Burton, "In Defense of Fanny Price"; and Despotopoulou, "Fanny's Gaze."

9 The sub-field of critical literary geography was formally established by Thacker's 2005–06 field-formative essay, "The Idea of a Critical Literary Geography," in which he outlines the potential for better understanding materiality, history, and power through the interdisciplinary analysis of literature and geography.

10 For *Emily of New Moon*, see, for example: Lawson, "The Alien at Home" and "Adolescence and the Trauma of Maternal Inheritance"; L. McMaster, "The 'Murray Look'"; and Posey, "Ethereal Etchings." On *Mansfield Park*, for instance, see: Despotopoulou, "Fanny's Gaze"; Aileen Douglas, "Austen's Enclaves"; Himes, "Fanny Price"; Kasmer, "'That Was Now the Home'"; Mucignat, "Theatrical Revolutions"; and Parrish, "Shadows and Houses."

11 Soja, *Postmodern Geographies*, 120.

12 Toner, "'With What Intense Desire,'" addresses the importance and multifacetedness of domestic spaces in Austen's fiction, addressing human relationships, physical comfort, financial security, and social well-being.

13 Grosz, *Space, Time, and Perversion*, 108 (emphasis in original).

14 Davidson and Milligan, "Embodying Emotion," 524.

15 Epperly, *Fragrance of Sweet-Grass*, 8, 7.

16 Graham, "Jane Austen and the Labor of Leisure," 176.

17 For discussion of portraiture and *Emily of New Moon*, see Clement, "Visual Culture."

18 LMM, *ENM*, 25.

19 Austen, *Mansfield Park*, 218.

20 LMM, *ENM*, 28, 62.

21 Austen, *Mansfield Park*, 14.

22 LMM, *ENM*, 108; Austen, *Mansfield Park*, 14–15.

23 LMM, *ENM*, 69.

24 Ibid., 108; Austen, *Mansfield Park*, 15.

25 LMM, *ENM*, 118.

26 Austen, *Mansfield Park*, 182 (emphasis mine), 215.

27 Aileen Douglas, "Austen's Enclave," 152.

28 Despotopoulou, "Fanny's Gaze," 570–1.

29 LMM, *ENM*, 118.

30 Ibid., 342.

31 Austen, *Mansfield Park*, 148.

32 LMM, *ENM*, 342, 343.

33 Austen, *Mansfield Park*, 150.

34 LMM, *ENM*, 344.

35 The importance of Emily's "body agency," particularly in terms of eroticism, has been highlighted by Irene Gammel in "The Eros of Childhood," 106.

36 LMM, *ENM*, 345 (emphasis in original), 382, 345.

37 Austen, *Mansfield Park*, 149, 148. For discussion of Fanny's attic as a liminal space, see Schneider, "The Little White Attic," 227–8; and Parrish "Shadows and Houses," 41.

38 LMM, *ENM*, 343, 344, 346 (emphasis in original).

39 Austen, *Mansfield Park*, 149–50 (emphasis in original).

40 LMM, *ENM*, 343, 344, 346.

41 Austen, *Mansfield Park*, 149, 150.

42 LMM, *ENM*, 345 (emphasis in original).

43 Austen, *Mansfield Park*, 149–50.

44 LMM, *ENM*, 373.

45 Austen, *Mansfield Park*, 230.

46 LMM, *ENM*, 226 (emphasis mine). For similar inventories of New Moon, see also LMM, *ENM*, 91, 108–9, 118–19.

47 Austen, *Mansfield Park*, 370 (emphasis mine), 428.

48 LMM, *ENM*, 360 (emphasis in original), 368, 178, 25.

49 Austen, *Mansfield Park*, 195, 366, 222, 311–13, 341.

50 LMM, *ENM*, 323, 108, 377, 342.

51 Austen, *Mansfield Park*, 427.

52 LMM, *ENM*, 382.

53 Austen, *Mansfield Park*, 366 (emphasis in original), 457.

2

L.M. Montgomery's Precocious Children: Resisting Adult Narratives of Death, Dying, and the Afterlife

LESLEY D. CLEMENT

In an 1897 journal entry, L.M. Montgomery records that in rejecting, at the age of eight or nine, what she refers to as the "literal," "primitive" view of the afterlife as celestial city or fire-and-brimstone hell, other related beliefs "seemed to drop away like an outgrown husk."[1] Ann Douglas's chapter "The Domestication of Death," in the contentious but still important *Feminization of American Culture* (1977), discusses nineteenth-century representations of heaven "scaled to domestic and pastoral proportions" as a reaction to these "primitive" views of death, dying, and an afterlife. Douglas's main examples are Elizabeth Stuart Phelps's *The Gates Ajar* (1868) and her two sequent books, *Beyond the Gates* (1883) and *The Gates Between* (1887).[2] In the 1897 journal entry, Montgomery concedes that she has not yet formulated any idea of an afterlife to replace those she had "outgrown" and then, several paragraphs later, mentions reading *The Gates Ajar.* Despite desiring to believe in Phelps's "pleasing conception" that a heavenly life will be much like an earthly one until we slowly "expand into perfect holiness," Montgomery cannot will herself to accept it.[3] This chapter uncovers Montgomery's conversations, throughout her writing career, with various narratives of death, dying, and the afterlife through her child characters' inventiveness and resistance when confronted with their own and others' mortality.

Montgomery's child characters retain their youthful joy, vitality, and creativity, fuelled by their curiosity, in an environment saturated with death.

Orphaned at three months old, Anne Shirley later experiences the deaths of two foster fathers, Mr Thomas and Mr Hammond, before she arrives in Avonlea at age eleven. Throughout *Anne of Green Gables* (1908) and *Anne of Avonlea* (1909), death, dying, and the afterlife are frequent topics of conversation and sources of literary inspiration and dramatic play for Anne and her Avonlea friends. Orphaned at age six, Davy Keith understands that his mother has welcomed death as an end to her suffering. His inquisitive nature prompts him to quiz Anne on the nature of heaven and hell, resulting in many humorous exchanges between them throughout *Anne of Avonlea* and *Anne of the Island* (1915). Orphaned by both her biological and adoptive parents, twelve-year-old Mary Vance joins the motherless Meredith children, who have transformed the old Methodist graveyard into their own playground, an environment that inspires them to reflect on their Presbyterian upbringing in conversations threaded throughout *Rainbow Valley* (1919). At age six, fatherless Marigold Lesley, from *Magic for Marigold* (1929), witnesses the gradual decline and death of Old Grandmother, who holds court in the spare bedroom with tales of dead brides and Death as a lover; meanwhile, Marigold has created a celestial Hidden World to counter the flux of her adult-dominated environment.

These widely different child characters demonstrate the "precocity" – the verbal acumen, lively imaginations and curiosity, resourcefulness, and resilience – that Marah Gubar, in *Artful Dodgers: Reconceiving the Golden Age of Children's Literature*, observes in late-Victorian and Edwardian literature and that, after the mid-nineteenth century, was increasingly represented and critiqued as disturbing. Gubar's research demonstrates the widespread phenomenon whereby precocious children were treated as docile prodigies to be flaunted by parents or, worse, "artful children whose precocious abilities" and perceived malleability were exploited by impresarios in circuses, theatres, and music and dance halls, or were put on display for voyeurs in art and advertising. Nevertheless, as Gubar argues, "whereas the Child of Nature paradigm [generally in adult literature by male writers] insists that such precocious knowledge is enfeebling and even deadly, children's stories frequently suggest that young people have enough resourcefulness or recalcitrance to deal with (and even profit from) worldly influences." Gubar's examples of "artful dodgers," then, contest theories, such as those of Jacqueline Rose and James Kincaid, fixated on the Victorian "cult of the child" premise, "that there ought to be a strict dividing line separating child from adult."[4] As in the children's literature that

Gubar examines, primarily texts by women writers, Montgomery's child characters exhibit precocity and, indeed, join others that Gubar argues are "capable of reshaping stories, conceiving of them as artful collaborators in the hope that – while a complete escape from adult influence is impossible – young people might dodge the fate of functioning as passive parrots." They also dodge the deadly fate of precocious characters such as Charles Dickens's Little Nell and Paul Dombey and Thomas Hardy's Father Time, precocity being a "one-way ticket to the grave" in many nineteenth-century texts.[5] Despite being surrounded by the deaths – real and imagined – of others from accident, heartbreak, disease, and old age, Montgomery's child characters are not killed off. Through rescripting the narratives of death, dying, and the afterlife that they have inherited, her precocious child characters are better able to confront – and sometimes even defy – the reality of death.

Statements interspersed throughout Montgomery's writings might suggest that her fiction reflects not the continuum and kinship of childhood and adulthood, such as Gubar outlines in "Risky Business,"[6] but rather polarized states of childhood innocence – with its associated qualities of naïveté and vulnerability – and adult experience, with the realization of death marking the transition from child to adult. The night before Matthew Cuthbert dies, the narrator says of sixteen-year-old Anne Shirley, "no life is ever quite the same again when once that cold, sanctifying touch has been laid upon it."[7] Two years later, when Anne's Avonlea friend Ruby Gillis is dying of consumption, death again enters and changes "something for her. Life held a different meaning, a deeper purpose."[8] When, in *Emily of New Moon* (1923), thirteen-year-old Emily Byrd Starr recuperates from a near-death fever, during which her eyes "looked into death and read the riddle of a buried thing" (that is, that Ilse Burnley's mother, Beatrice, had not run off with a lover but had fallen down and drowned in a well), Dean Priest concludes that she has "left the childhood of her soul behind, though she is still a child in body." The narrator comments, "One cannot go down to the depths of hidden things and escape the penalty" of the knowledge of sexuality and death.[9] Statements such as these suggest that these transitions are both empowering and disempowering in the way that Roberta Trites describes in *Disturbing the Universe*: "Accepting one's mortality is indeed a powerful rite of passage predicated on understanding oneself as finite. The knowledge of death may thus prove both more repressive and more empowering to adolescents than are discursive interactions with socially constructed institutions, authority figures, or sexuality." Trites's comments on the repressive yet empowering knowledge that *adolescent* characters in *adolescent* literature attain are pertinent to characters such as Anne and Emily once they have entered their teen years. Because sexuality and death are both "biological imperatives," Trites argues, they are "linked inviolably" as not only biological but also cultural concepts.[10]

Trites's thesis that "for many adolescents, trying to understand death is as much of a rite of passage as experiencing sexuality" is exemplified by Anne's delayed recognition of her love for Gilbert until the third book in the series, *Anne of the Island*, a recognition prompted by his near deadly bout of typhoid fever and the revelation of her own mortality when she realizes he is vital to her very existence: "She knew that she could no more cast him out of her life without agony than she could have cut off her right hand and cast it from her … If Gilbert went away from her, without one word or sign or message, she could not live."[11] It is also exemplified by the lasting effects of the Byronic Dean Priest's rescue of Emily, already haunted by the mystery of Beatrice's death a year before her transformative vision, from a fall down a cliff, when she entertains dramatic visions of her own death and mourners.[12] However, in Trites's dismissing the representation of death in children's literature as not outward-looking (as in adolescent literature) but inward-looking – children's literature is all about achieving *personal* power and *self*-control, disengaged from any social context, according to Trites – she fails to do justice to the ability of child characters and child readers to negotiate complicated social and cultural networks. Trites thus concurs with Jacqueline Rose's contention that children's literature "sets up the child as an outsider to its own process, and then aims, unashamedly, to take the child *in*."[13] This chapter argues that, by rescripting adult death narratives, Montgomery's precocious child characters – those with verbal dexterity, active imaginations and curiosity, resourcefulness, and resilience – are instrumental in exposing coercive social and cultural practices and systems that threaten to insulate children from developing the skills necessary to survive in an often dangerous world.

First among these precocious children is Anne Shirley. Newly arrived at Green Gables, eleven-year-old Anne defies Marilla's command to provide just the "bald facts" without any of her "imaginings" by immediately deviating from a faithful history of her death-saturated life. Building on a vague description from her foster mother, Mrs Thomas, Anne envisages in detail the "weeny-teeny little yellow house in Bolingbroke" where she was born and her parents died. Anne challenges Mrs Thomas's assessment of her homeliness as a baby, preferring a narrative in which she was not a disappointment to her mother during the three months mother and daughter had to bond. In recounting her history until age eight, when Mr Thomas was killed falling under a train, and then until age eleven, when Mr Hammond died, Anne continues to digress from the "bald facts," although alluding to the abuse and overwork she has endured and the abandonment she has experienced after each death. Based on her history, Anne concludes that her fate is to be rejected, but Marilla "read[s] between the lines" of Anne's narrative. Given Anne's consumptive constitution, rejection in the form of being returned to the orphanage or slaving under Mrs Blewett would certainly have sealed her "death warrant by consumption."[14] The narrative arc of Anne's life changes from death to survival in these early chapters due to her ability to win over her adoptive parents and then her adoptive community through her precocious imagination.

The stories of death and near-death interwoven throughout *Anne of Green Gables* are all about love, especially between friends, and belonging. From imaginatively nursing the smallpox-stricken Diana back to life, a story Anne retells during the raspberry cordial scene, and then envisioning Mrs Barry's remorse when Anne dies of grief from being separated from her bosom friend after getting Diana drunk, to relishing the romance of actually saving Minnie May from the croup (an excellent example of Anne's precocious resourcefulness), to confronting the terrors of the Haunted Wood, inhabited by the ghosts of a grieving woman, a murdered child, and a headless man, to walking the ridgepole "in an affair of honour," to the "unfortunate lily maid" dramatic reenactment of "Lancelot and Elaine," Anne exploits deathbed scenes as opportunities not only to savour their romantic and gothic potential but also to assert control over her environment.[15] Her literary inspirations are varied – Gothic novels and romances, ghost stories, boys' adventure stories, in which certain values are worth dying for, and Tennyson's *The Idylls of the King* (1859), among others – but they are always tailored to current circumstances and players. As Ann Howey concludes about Montgomery's treatment of the Elaine story, these scenes "provide models of ways to read against cultural texts; they also suggest the power of readers – even child readers – to construct meaningful self-narratives." The "Unfortunate Lily Maid" chapter accomplishes this because it "privileges not peril but physical comedy."[16]

The early *Anne* books are consistently filtered through Montgomery's trademark humour, delivered with understanding of and sympathy for children's sensitivity. Therefore, while the narrator frequently conveys that the adults who are privy to the children's playacting and storytelling find the melodrama, pathos, and sentimentality absurd, most respond with respect and even encouragement. For example, the two deaths in Anne's "sad, sweet story," "The Jealous Rival; or, in Death Not Divided," are so melodramatic as to be ridiculous. Predictably, Marilla, who is "as fond of morals as [Lewis Carroll's] Duchess of Wonderland," responds that this, like all Anne's stories, is "stuff and nonsense," a waste of time, but Matthew, the "kind of critic" Anne likes, thinks her story is "fine." Similar stories flow from the pens of the Avonlea girls when they form the Story Club. Although the minister and his wife, Mr and Mrs Allan, and Aunt Josephine laugh at all the wrong places, these adults do not dismiss the girls' stories as trivial or misguided.[17] *Anne of Green Gables* and the novels that follow do not satirize children's detachment from reality in their renderings of death but rather parody the literature written by adults in which undying love, sacrifice, loyalty, and honour are categorically presented as values worth taking risks and dying for. These values are all debated by the children in the games they play, stories they tell, deaths they witness, and occasionally in their own near-death experiences.

If *Anne of Green Gables* is saturated with stories of death, *Anne of Avonlea* explores concepts of heaven. The Avonlea girls – now aged sixteen to seventeen – discuss everything, from the smells, seasonal cycles, and geography of heaven to the appropriate fashion and demeanour of celestial souls. In these scenes, Montgomery is parodying the kind of nineteenth-century domestic and pastoral narratives that prompted Emily Dickinson to question, in a poem from the early 1860s, "Is Heaven a Place?" and respond, "Unto the Dead / There's no Geography –."[18] When Dickinson wrote these lines, a wave of consolation literature surging out of the New England states featured the deserving dead taking up residence in mappable towns with street signs directing newcomers to their final resting places: neat little houses with flower boxes in bloom, where their dearly departed kinfolk waited patiently to greet them.[19] Drawing upon Philippe Ariès's chapter "The Age of the Beautiful Death" in *The Hour of Our Death*, Elisabeth Bronfen writes of this period, "Death became a private event, assuring continuity in the form of a family unity and an androcentric domestication of heaven that saw it as a continuation or repetition of earthly existence, not as a completely other sphere."[20] Ann Douglas observes of the consolation literature rooted in concepts of a "beautiful death" – "obituary poems and memoirs, mourners' manuals, prayer guidebooks, hymns, and books about heaven" – "Death must become, not exactly life, but a controlled extension of the feelings, and property rights, of the living."[21] What Bronfen and Douglas refer to as the "domestication of death" is a reaction against the heaven that Dickinson's persona had been taught about as a child – an unmappable, nebulous celestial city with pearly gates, golden roads, and bejewelled palaces – and that she and others were now interrogating, each in her own way.

Best known of these domesticated and pastoral heavens that material bodies of the recently deceased seem to reach and navigate by foot is Phelps's vastly popular *The Gates Ajar*, published several years after Dickinson wrote her poem. Winifred Forceythe, the novel's authority on all things celestial, finds great amusement in others' "notions … of the heavenly body." She describes these notions to Mary Cabot, the narrator and Winifred's niece, who is recording her aunt's observations seemingly verbatim into her journal: "Vague visions of floating about in the clouds, of balancing – with white robes on, perhaps – in stiff rows about a throne, like the angels in the old pictures, converging to an apex, or ranged in semi-circles like so many marbles." She concludes, "The truth is, that the ordinary idea, if sifted accurately, reduces our eternal personality to – *gas*."[22] Although Winifred seems intended to be taken as modest and respectful of more orthodox views than her own, dismissive passages such as this have prompted Desirée Henderson, in *Grief and Genre in American Literature, 1790–1870*, to conclude that *The Gates Ajar* is better described as a "conduct book" than as "consolation literature," because, whereas Dickinson's fractured "manuscripts return authority to the reader," Phelps's novel silences viewpoints other than the one Mary adopts – Aunt Winifred's – and "establish[es] authority over loss by directing the feelings and actions of the mourner along clearly defined paths of approved behavior."[23]

In Montgomery's 1897 journal entry with which this chapter begins, she describes the "primitive" views of heaven and hell that she held as a child – heaven a celestial city "spread all over the other side of the blue sky above us" and hell a fiery lake "situated away off to the southeast" – and the "great many bitter spiritual struggles" that she underwent without adult supervision or intervention but which nevertheless challenged her "'to be a Christian.'" It was "the fine old hell of literal fire and brimstone [that] went first," other beliefs gradually and inconspicuously fading away. At age twenty-three, when she is writing this entry, she has "not yet formulated any working belief to replace that which [she has] outgrown."[24] Whereas Phelps satirizes what she sees to be the alienating metaphors of disembodied souls and a celestial city and replaces them with more comforting literal domestic and pastoral commonplaces, Montgomery's *Anne* novels parody these reductive readings and find in the old metaphors, so often taken literally by children, if not comfort, an imaginative catalyst to engage her young protagonists in their inquiries and rescripting narratives about their final home.

A recurring satire in *The Gates Ajar* is directed at those who have taken biblical metaphors of heaven so literally that they would prefer any alternative resting place as their final celestial abode. Phelps's main target of satire is the potato farmer, Deacon Quirk, whose son Abinadab is a lapsed church member because he fears that he is not fit for his father's heaven and would not find eternal rest endlessly and tunelessly singing in a celestial choir. Phelps's satire becomes pathos when the eminent parish minister, Dr Bland, loses his wife (ironically) in a fire, and his vision of heaven fails him. Rather than the "blank heaven of his belief," he seeks solace from Winifred's "pleasant" heaven and even burns an "old blue manuscript" of a sermon. This is the sermon that Mary, grieving the loss of her brother Royal in the Civil War, has critiqued as leaving her "hungry, hopeless, blinded … empty, uncomforted, groping. I wanted something actual, something pleasant, about this place into which Roy has gone. He gave me glittering generalities, cold commonplaces, vagueness, unreality, a God and a future at which I sat and shivered."[25] Winifred's domesticated and pastoral heaven provides a welcoming home, where Dr Bland and Mary can be reunited with deceased family members and resume their old habits and customs of life.

Literal perceptions of a domesticated and pastoral afterlife as filtered through the perspectives of children and adolescents provide a source of gentle humour in *Anne of Avonlea*. Anne and her friends disagree about the nature of heaven and who or what will reside there. Early in the novel, Anne rhapsodizes that a perfect heaven would provide "a whiff of dead fir as you went through its woods. Perhaps we'll have the odor there without the death," prompting the pragmatic Diana to contest Anne's suggestion that trees have souls, although Diana does allow that dead fir needles make an aromatic stuffing for cushions. Later in the novel, Anne describes heaven with seasonal quadrants, imagined as geographical places within a celestial space. Jane Andrews, "a good girl, a member of the church, who … believed everything she had been taught," finds Anne's image of heaven uncomfortable. The absurdity of Anne's image is less absurd when she describes passing from one district to the other by choice, more reflective of the traveller's state of mind, and hence to be taken figuratively, rather than crossing or navigating actual terrain, borders, or time zones. But Anne has not completely abandoned time travel in her conception of heaven, as she hopes to wear pink "a few centuries at first," since her red hair has barred her from doing so in this world.[26]

The girls' amusingly fanciful perceptions – especially Anne's – are balanced by young Davy Keith's attempts to explain logically the location and nature of heaven, resulting in many humorous conversations. Phelps's recently widowed Aunt Winifred explains to her young daughter, Faith, that her favourite food, gingersnaps, will be available for consumption in heaven, giving her child "*pictures* of truth that she can understand" to ease her fear of death and cultivate her desire to join her father when the time comes.[27] Similarly, Davy thinks there will be celestial jam, in his case, however, not because of any adult's placating metaphor but rather from his own misconstruing (and mispunctuating) of the catechism passage he has been learning that we should love God "because He makes preserves, and redeems us." While young Anne's precocity is characterized by verbal acuity, Davy's is characterized by curiosity and determination to find rational explanations for situations that just do not make sense. Although Davy understands that his mother has willingly succumbed to death as an end to her suffering, his inquiring mind leads to his questioning authority figures about heaven. For example, he provides what he believes is a perfectly reasonable explanation of why he does not want to go to heaven. After he has offended his Sunday-school teacher, who had answered with a brusque "heaven was where God was" in response to Davy's query about heaven's location, his friend Milty Boulter has told him a tale in which the minister and mourners cast their eyes upward to Uncle Simon's garret when speaking of the old man's final resting place. Davy decides that, if heaven is in Uncle Simon's garret, he will go anywhere else – including hell – to avoid this man he dislikes.[28] In a 1911 journal entry, Montgomery draws a parallel between Davy's belief and her own: "When I was a child heaven was only seven miles away. But now! Is it not beyond the furthest star?"[29]

Anne is always cognizant that the staid Presbyterian Marilla, who is bringing up Davy "in the good old ways of theology," would be shocked by Anne's "fanciful speculations" and would be as concerned for Anne's soul as for Davy's because of his "lively curiosity." All these discussions between Anne and her friends and between Anne and Davy are grounded by the anxiety of Mrs Allan, the minister's wife, over the possible loss of a second child (the first died in infancy) and the persistent cough of the shiftless Timothy Cotton, slowly dying of consumption, and the effect this has on his children. Ten-year-old Mirabel Cotton, for example, believes her family has nothing to bestow prestige in the community except "an uncle who persisted in walking about houses after he had been decently interred." The Cotton family's ghost prompts spectral stories from the children and a range of responses, from bravado to trepidation.[30] The framing of death scenes with humour comes to the foreground in the chapters of *Anne of the Island* that narrate the death of Anne's Avonlea friend, Ruby Gillis, who has been gradually dying of consumption. Literal-minded Davy may think that heaven is directly above him in the garret, but he does not fear, as obedient Dora does, the consequences of fishing or swearing on the Sabbath – God knows "a fellow must have some way of 'spressing his feelings" – because the "other place" is "very far off." As I argue elsewhere, the rounding off of chapter 14, "The Summons," in which Ruby dies, with Anne and Davy's conversation as to whether Ruby will laugh in heaven and Davy's decision to smoke to ward off germs and untimely death "undercuts onerous gravity and excessive sentimentality in the contextualization" of Ruby's death.[31]

Throughout the late 1800s and the 1910s, when Montgomery was writing most of the books in the *Anne* series, her "spiritual struggle" over ideas on death, dying, and an afterlife continued as she experienced personal loss in the deaths of the grandmother who raised her (1911), her stillborn son Hugh (1914), and her cousin and dear friend, Frederica (Frede) Campbell (1919), as well as public loss in the mass deaths of the First World War. Montgomery's sense of an afterlife became much less literal, much more abstract – heaven is less a physical, domestic, and populated place and more a metaphysical, remote, and ethereal space. When copying out her journals in 1920, Montgomery elaborates on the 1897 entry that opens this chapter and on how her continuing interrogation of the binaries inherent in "Orthodox Christianity" as a belief "seemed to take shape within [her] mind slowly and relentlessly [through] experience and comparison and reflection": "The hope of heaven is too dearly balanced by the fear of hell and the one thing implies the other. I believe in neither; but I believe that *life* goes on and on endlessly in incarnation after incarnation, co-existent with God, and Anti-god, rejoicing, suffering, as good or evil wins the upper hand. To me, such an anticipation is infinitely more attractive than the dull effortless, savorless existence pictured to us as the heaven of rest and reward. Rest! It is a good thing; but one does not want an eternity of it. All we ask rest for is to gain fresh strength for renewed effort ... Our best reward is the joy of the struggle."[32] While these ideas are explored in two deaths affecting Anne in *Anne's House of Dreams* (1917) – that of Anne and Gilbert's baby, Joy, who dies on the same day she is born, and that of Captain Jim, who rejoins his Margaret after crossing over the bar – this novel does not contextualize death, dying, and the afterlife within a child-focused fictive world, a world to which Montgomery returns in the novel that takes place thirteen years later, *Rainbow Valley*.

With the shadow of mass deaths hanging over *Rainbow Valley*, published in 1919 but set in the years immediately preceding the First World War, the characters' experiences of death move beyond Green Gables and Avonlea, Ingleside, Four Winds, and Glen St Mary, but are again contextualized within child-centric communities, even when the conversations are between adults rather than children. Montgomery's desire for eternal rest becomes increasingly urgent by the early-to-mid 1920s; however, in *Rainbow Valley*, Anne can still have a light-hearted conversation with Miss Cornelia about "this everlasting rest doctrine" and, to quote Anne, death as "open[ing] a gate and [going] through – on – on – to new, shining adventures." For Miss Cornelia, heaven will be one big kitchen after a brief respite: "I want to bustle round in heaven the same as here. And I hope there'll be a celestial substitute for pies and doughnuts ... the very tiredest could get rested in something short of eternity."[33] Just as the younger Anne would have enjoyed Winifred's heaven as depicted in Phelps's *The Gates Ajar*, a place where bodily blemishes (such as red hair) are airbrushed and joyful laughter abounds, so too Miss Cornelia would fit right in with its promise of potato fields to cultivate, pianos to play, and gingersnaps to bake for children to consume. But neither Anne nor Miss Cornelia claims, as does Phelps's Winifred, to have the final word on heavenly matters. And, indeed, Susan spoofs theories of perfect celestial beauty when, in the opening conversation of the novel, she asks, "I have no doubt we will all be beautiful when we are angels, but what good will it do us then?"[34] The open-ended conversations on death, dying, and an afterlife continue throughout *Rainbow Valley*, with allusions to the next novel, *Rilla of Ingleside* (1921), when Anne suffers the greatest loss of all, that of her soldier son, Walter.

Rainbow Valley, an ensemble piece, one that does not profile any central character, features the interactions among ten children: the six Blythe children – Jem, age thirteen; Walter, twelve; Nan and Di, ten; Shirley, eight; and Rilla six – and the four motherless Meredith children – Jerry, age twelve; Faith, eleven; Una, ten; and Carl, eight – whose father is the local Presbyterian minister. As well, there is the no-nonsense twelve-year-old Mary Vance – perhaps most akin to the Dickensian "artful dodger" of which Marah Gubar speaks – who has been orphaned by both her biological and adoptive parents. Mary is a self-described "hustler," always on the move, especially when it comes to spreading gossip and attempting to control situations and conversations through her "superior" knowledge of the world, attained through experience – or later, when adopted by Miss Cornelia, eavesdropping. Although Anne compares Mary's orphaned state to her own before coming to Green Gables, Miss Cornelia states emphatically that she does not "think this Mary-creature is or ever will be much like [Anne] … She's a cat of another colour. But she's also a human being with an immortal soul to save." "Mary of little faith" is a scrapper, and while she can weave stories as far-fetched as those of Anne, there is a slyness, wiliness, and mean streak about her that make her a very different kind of "artful dodger" – one who survives by her wits – than any character Montgomery has created in previous novels.[35]

The Meredith children have annexed the old Methodist graveyard adjacent to the Presbyterian manse as their own personal playground. Here, much to the horror of some parishioners, both Methodist and Presbyterian, the children pursue their own games and lines of inquiry. After they tire of a "scandal[ous]" praying competition, a "sacred concert" that features a resounding "Polly Wolly Doodle" as finale, and leapfrogging over and dancing a hornpipe around the tombstones, they engage in theological discussions, such as whether they will be haunted by the dead if they speak ill of them; whether it is better to be dead or half-dead (and what it is like to be either); the different sizes and shapes of souls; where is hell, who goes there, and why; and the difference between an earthly and celestial heaven. Given the Reverend Meredith's absent-minded proclivity to answer questions with "True? What is truth?" the children are free to develop their own answers. Mary thinks that hell is a specific place – New Brunswick – because Mr Wiley, who was from New Brunswick, "was always telling folks to go there," and she infers that the devil "just roamed round" from place to place. The Presbyterian-raised Meredith children know differently, however: the devil resides in hell, an "awful place" says Faith, "with the dramatic enjoyment that is born of telling dreadful things." The children have developed these ideas about hell from the bible and Sunday school, obviously not from their father, whom Norman Douglas, impressed by Faith's feistiness, bribes to deliver "a good rip-roaring sermon on hell once every six months – and the more brimstone the better. I like 'em smoking." Anne encourages her children to read the bible figuratively and to perceive the divinity and heaven subjectively. In an extended conversation about heaven, which the children have in Rainbow Valley, their favourite evening playground, their perceptions of heaven range from literal to metaphorical, from pragmatic to fanciful, from orthodox to subversive. Nan seems to grasp what her mother has meant when she says that each person's metaphors of heaven's geography reflect that person's temperament and values as shaped by circumstances, past and current. Faith and Una round off the conversation with the understanding that although, as minister's daughters, they "know" as much as Walter about heaven, he has the benefit of imagining.[36]

Walter, the incipient poet, under the "shadowy Piper's thrall," is unique among Montgomery's precocious child characters, because he already seems destined for the grave: "All the joy and sorrow and laughter and loyalty and aspiration of many generations lying under the sod looked out of [his eyes'] dark-gray depths."[37] Walter's childhood precocity evolves into the empathy that, in young adulthood, as narrated in *Rilla of Ingleside*, provides him access into the minds of the victims of war – compelling him to enlist – and later into the minds of the dead, which he captures in his poetry. Throughout *Rainbow Valley*, Walter's "piper" assumes more and more sinister connotations until the final chapter – "'Let the Piper Come'" – when the piper's associations with death, and specifically the mass deaths of war, become "too real," as it advances nearer and nearer, entering the valley and piping the young men away.[38]

Considering *Rainbow Valley* as an ensemble piece in her chapter in *L.M. Montgomery's Rainbow Valleys: The Ontario Years*, Elizabeth Waterston comments, "The intriguing new title with its double references to physical elements of sky and earth promises a new emphasis on place rather than person." She begins her chapter by noting the biblical connotations of the title: "the rainbow of hope that God sent to the world after the flood, as well as the valley of the shadow of death that psalmist David had to walk through."[39] The two settings that the children primarily frequent – Rainbow Valley and the graveyard – both profile not only the inevitability of death and the knowledge of death entering the children's lives but also the tools – exuberance, creativity, curiosity, tenacity, courage – that enable them to remain resilient in the face of death.

As with other graveyards in the *Anne* novels – most notably, the rural churchyard of Avonlea in the first three novels and the urban burying ground of Kingsport in *Anne of the Island* – the Methodist graveyard of *Rainbow Valley* is a liminal landscape that provides visitors the opportunity to commune and connect with the absent dead. Conversely, in the new town cemeteries being built throughout North America, as best exemplified by Summerside's "Old" Cemetery in chapter 5 of *Anne of Windy Poplars* (1936), "death and the dead were placed out of sight and out of mind," ensconced behind "an established perimeter (a high wall or hedge) along with a formally marked entrance," thus "sequester[ing] the dead from the living."[40] But, in the Avonlea graveyard, Anne can give presence to a newly manifested Matthew, whose body sleeps in the country churchyard and whose soul has been greeted on the other side by the souls of his beloved white roses, which connect him to his ancestral past.[41] Anne is first attracted to Old St John's in Kingsport because of her need for trees like those in Avonlea, but she is soon wandering "the long grassy aisles … reading the quaint, voluminous epitaphs," which eventually enable her to discover a deep-rooted heritage, a sense of belonging in her home province of Nova Scotia.[42] Because the living and dead reside peaceably together, Avonlea's old church graveyard and Kingsport's urban burying ground are sites for Anne's imaginative resurrection of and engagement with the dead lingering in the recesses of personal or communal memory. Similarly, *Rainbow Valley*'s manse and adjacent graveyard is a space where "inner and outer worlds join hands," a space where Reverend Meredith looks down from his study while "reflecting deeply on the immortality of the soul," and his children weave their own stories and engage in games and other creative enterprises in the face of the inevitability of death.[43]

Nevertheless, the scene near the end of the novel in which Carl brings a near-fatal pneumonia upon himself after a penitential evening spent on Hezekiah Pollock's tombstone, a punishment the children administer in their attempts to meet their community's criteria for "good conduct," is a reminder that, as Gubar remarks, while resistance is admirable, "complete escape from adult influence is impossible."[44] This reminder is compounded and nuanced by the detail that Carl's act of penance is a consequence of his fear of what is thought to be the ghost of an abused child, Henry Warren. Although the children's fear is treated comically – the ghost proves to be nothing but an old woman in search of her knitting needle – their compliance to what is deemed "good conduct" almost kills Carl, as it has similarly caused the "dead faint" of Una in an earlier scene after a day of fasting in penance for the "sacred concert" held in the graveyard.[45] Compliance is, therefore, no guarantee of survival.

Nan, Di, and Jem have questioned the truth of Mary's Henry Warren ghost story, but for Faith, Una, and Carl, "Death! What was death compared to the unearthly possibility of falling into the clutches of Henry Warren's grovelling ghost?"[46] Montgomery's precocious child characters do not fear death or what lies beyond, although they often grapple with images of the suffering and pain associated with dying and spectral manifestations of restless souls. A source of this fearlessness can be found in Montgomery's reflections on her own life experiences. In a journal entry from 1934, Montgomery explains retrospectively how the idea of death became "*comforting*" for her after her grandfather's death in 1898 when she "was beginning to find life sad and hopeless" and saw "nothing before [her] but dreary unloved years of toil and frustration." The "old stars of a summer night," the "faint surf-thunder on the faraway dunes," and the ghost-like kiss of a "little night-wind" have inspired the thought that this bleak life "cannot go on *forever*. Some day there will be an end – some day death will save [her]." These are all images from her childhood intimacy with the natural world and are what give continuity to her life, leading her to conclude that she has never "in all [her] life had any fear of death *as* death." She begins this recollection with her response to Francis Bacon's "To die is as natural as to live": "Of course. Death would never have become the thing of horror it is considered if it had not been for the sadistic imaginations of fanatics and mad theologians." She ends with thoughts of joyful days at Park Corner, particularly of Frede's laughter, and then cites Ernest Renan – "'If, even as we are, we could once a year at odd moments see the loved ones we have lost long enough to exchange a few words of greeting, death would be no longer death'" – adding, "True, oh, true!"[47] These are the conversations that inform *Magic for Marigold*, but with a new emphasis on the stultifying effects of fear, which confrontation with death and renewed commitment to life can allay, themes also explored in Montgomery's "adult" novel *The Blue Castle* (1926), published three years prior to *Magic for Marigold*.

Fatherless Marigold must negotiate Lesley clan rituals – such as the family's hesitation in consulting a doctor from outside the clan, especially a woman (Dr Marigold Richards) – even to survive infancy, a struggle with which the novel begins. Marigold is named after not only her mother's dead girlhood friend but also this very alive and life-giving woman, who becomes her aunt after marrying into the family. The novel suggestively conflates past, present, and future, as Holly Pike develops in her chapter in this volume, arguing that "childhood is presented not as simply a period of life in this novel, but as either a state of mind or a memory."[48] Thus childhood and adulthood are not distinct but overlapping, forever in flux, as the child actively engages with and responds to the world of family, community, and beyond. From age six to twelve, Marigold shapes her beliefs about life and death, heaven and hell, as she overcomes fears and navigates through clan rituals and legends surrounding death, the outside world of child zealots and child unbelievers, and her fantasy world of the Hidden Land.

Marigold's early beliefs are challenged when witnessing the aging of Old Grandmother, whom Death defeats in her goal to reach the age of one hundred. For six-year-old Marigold, Old Grandmother represents "The Things That Always Have Been"; therefore, when Old Grandmother dies at age ninety-nine, Marigold must adjust to a knowledge of the mutability of life and inevitability of death. Even before Marigold spends the final evening of Old Grandmother's life alone with her, her "daring little imagination … falter[s]" in trying to conceive of her dead grandmother as "a radiant being with long white wings and halo of golden curls, soaring easily through sunset skies." Marigold remembers Old Grandmother frozen in time in her room, surrounded by photographs of dead Lesley brides, including that of Clementine, Marigold's father's first wife, who died with her daughter six years before Marigold was born. She remembers her grandmother's pride in the "famous Skinner doll," a waxen image of Old Grandmother's aunt's dead baby, about which Marigold, like the Lesley children before her, has heard tales with "fear and awe." She remembers her last evening with her grandmother, when the old woman talks of Death as no longer a foe but a lover, someone who calls her "Edith," not "Old Grandmother." She remembers that final gift she gives her grandmother: "a moment of youth," when Marigold calls Old Grandmother "Edith," as she has requested. What Marigold ultimately gains from Old Grandmother, however, is a sense of the fluidity of "Things That Always Have Been" and things as they are and will become; of childhood and adulthood, with their many shifting phases; of life and death, in all their permutations. This final evening with Old Grandmother bequeaths Marigold confidence that, because this world is constantly in flux, her beliefs are as valid and valuable as those of others:

> "The blinds were drawn. The doors were purple-bowed. The Lesleys came and went decorously. A terrible, abysmal loneliness engulfed Marigold.
>
> And then she suddenly ceased to believe Old Grandmother was dead. That was not Old Grandmother – that little ivory-white creature in the big flower-banked casket. *That* was not the Edith of the old orchard. *She* was living and laughing still – if not in the orchard then somewhere else. Even in heaven – which must and would become an entirely different place the moment Old Grandmother arrived there."[49]

After Old Grandmother's death, Marigold more consciously addresses fears that she has allowed a fence to be erected around Cloud of Spruce, and so comes to understand more fully what her grandmother meant by her comment that the "more things you can believe the more interesting life is." Forays outside the gates of Cloud of Spruce, from T.B. Phin's certainty that death is an end and preferable to a "dull" heaven, to Paula Pengelly's "games" to achieve the elect station of sainthood to enter heaven and her "harangue[s], mainly compounded of scraps of her father's theology," to Bernice Willis's dismissal of heaven and hell as "fairy-tale," all shape Marigold's maturing perception of life and death.[50]

Even before witnessing the death of Old Grandmother and before broadening her world beyond the Lesley clan, Marigold has sensed the Hidden Land, with its celestial overtones. At age six, Marigold begins to expand her consciousness beyond the familiar "past and present, all tangled up together." Listening to the murmurings of "mysterious" trees and winds and wondering what she cannot see beyond the "long red road of mystery" and the "mysterious ships that came and went" out of the harbour, cradled by hills, she ponders what lies beyond "those long dark hills that laughed to you and beckoned – but always kept some secret they would never tell." In particular, the spruce hill has an "irresistible charm for her," a "lure" that would not only let her "touch the sky" but suggested that with "a little spring she *might* land right in heaven." Beyond the hills is the Hidden Land. Marigold overcomes any "dread" of climbing far and high and travelling in the dark, as well as disappointment in discovering that the Hidden Land is even farther and higher than she first thought, when she experiences a sunset whose beauty over the "far-off purple seas" inspires a vision of "that dream city of towers and spires whose gates were of pearl."[51]

Although she cannot gain entry to the Hidden Land during this lifetime, Marigold finds enhanced joy in her own material world through another imagined place, among the hills, reached through the Magic Door and Green Gate, where she plays with the imaginary Sylvia. Unlike the Little White Girl of the spring, who is an abstract reflection of herself, Sylvia has, for Marigold, a physical presence; therefore, when young grandmother prevents Marigold from playing with her imaginary friend, Marigold "pine[s] and pale[s] more visibly every day" and speaks of dying. Grandmother remembers a prediction from Great-Aunt Elizabeth that Marigold "is too glad to live. Such gladness is not of earth." Great-Aunt Elizabeth is proven wrong. Because hers is a "mind prowling in all sorts of corners," Marigold is thankful that her thoughts are her own and she can explore all these corners. Her exuberance, curiosity, and imagination underpin the mantra that she uses to overcome fear: "it *would* be int'resting" even if "she would die of it."[52] Marigold does not allow fear to hold her back from confronting mentally and emotionally all of life's mysteries, including its final mystery – death.

Whether through misunderstanding adult narratives of death or through their own sheer inventiveness, Montgomery's precocious children understand death – including their own mortality – and experience grieving in their own way and on their own terms. Like the "artful dodgers" that Gubar discusses, Montgomery's children are "immersed from birth in a sea of discourse [but] can nevertheless navigate through this arena of competing currents in diverse and unexpected ways."[53] They converse among themselves about adult conversations that they have overheard. They converse with literature written by adults for children's edification on topics of life and death. They converse with social and cultural practices that threaten to curtail their experiencing life to its fullest through fear, compliance, and inertia. Most importantly, however, they are not simply "dodgers" but "artful dodgers," as they construct from and through these conversations their own narratives – sometimes humorous, sometimes melodramatic, sometimes gruesome, sometimes fantastical – to interrogate and resist adult narratives imposed on them.

NOTES

1 LMM, *CJ* 1:380, 382.
2 Ann Douglas, *Feminization of American Culture*, 223–6.
3 LMM, *CJ* 1:382.
4 Gubar, *Artful Dodgers*, 151, 6, 3–4. In particular, chapter 5, "The Cult of the Child and the Controversy over Child Actors," provides examples of the links between the perception of children as "innocent" and the potential for exploitation.
5 Ibid., 6, 181. Gubar also discusses the tendency of "British novelists, scientists, and journalists … to pound home the message that 'precocious children usually die early'" with reference to Frances Hodgson Burnett's Sara Crewe from *A Little Princess* (1905) (ibid., 35–6). Dickens's *The Old Curiosity Shop* (Little Nell) was serialized 1840–41, and *Dombey and Son* (Paul Dombey) 1846–47; Hardy's *Jude the Obscure* (Father Time) was serialized in 1894–95.
6 See introduction to this volume, 9.
7 LMM, *AGG*, 346.
8 LMM, *AIs*, 129.
9 LMM, *ENM*, 399, 397.
10 Trites, *Disturbing the Universe*, 140, 117, 122.
11 Ibid., 117; LMM, *AIs*, 290. For a discussion of Anne's delays, her "pleasures of postponement," see Gubar, "'Where Is the Boy?'"
12 LMM, *ENM*, 316–20. For discussion of Dean Priest's Byronic and generally gothic qualities, see Epperly, *Fragrance of Sweet-Grass*, 155–9; Gammel, "Eros of Childhood," 108; and Bode, "Vulnerable Situations," in this volume, 76–8.
13 Trites, *Disturbing the Universe*, 2–3, 83; Rose, *Case of Peter Pan*, 2 (emphasis in original). For a discussion of other theoretical perspectives on children (fictional and real) and their responses to narratives about death, dying, and the

afterlife (perspectives such as those found in Juliet Dusinberre's *Alice to the Lighthouse: Children's Books and Radical Experiments in Art* [1987, rev. 1999]; M.O. Grenby's *The Child Reader, 1700–1840* [2011]; Judith Plotz's *Romanticism and the Vocation of Childhood* [2001]; and Gillian Avery's "Intimations of Mortality: The Puritan and Evangelical Message to Children" and Kimberley Reynolds's "Fatal Fantasies: The Death of Children in Victorian and Edwardian Fantasy Writing," both in *Representations of Childhood Death* [2000]), see Lesley D. Clement, "Introduction: Flying Kites and Other Life-Death Matters," *Global Perspectives on Death in Children's Literature*, edited by Clement and Leyli Jamali (New York: Routledge 2016), especially 4–10.

14 LMM, *AGG*, 45–9, 99, 295.

15 These incidents are narrated in chapters 16–18, 20, 23, and 28 of *Anne of Green Gables*.

16 Howey, "Reading Elaine," 87, 98. See Clement, "From 'Uncanny Beauty' to 'Uncanny Disease,'" 44–53, which considers Anne's resistance to the consumptive-maiden narrative.

17 LMM, *AGG*, 69, 245–9.

18 Dickinson, "We pray – to Heaven –," stanza 2.

19 For example, Phelps, *Gates Ajar*, 138–41.

20 Bronfen, *Over Her Dead Body*, 87.

21 Ann Douglas, *Feminization of American Culture*, 201, 207.

22 Phelps, *Gates Ajar*, 117 (emphasis in original).

23 Henderson, *Grief and Genre*, 146, 127.

24 LMM, *CJ* 1:380, 382. For a discussion of a similar struggle articulated in a later journal entry (21 October 1921) and the tensions created between various personae from childhood through adulthood adopted in Montgomery's journal writing, see Steffler, "'Being a Christian' and a Presbyterian in Leaskdale," especially 54–9.

25 Phelps, *Gates Ajar*, 180, 217–20, 73.

26 LMM, *AA*, 45, 122.

27 Phelps, *Gates Ajar*, 185–6 (emphasis in original).

28 LMM, *AA*, 132, 66, 154–5.

29 LMM, *CJ* 2:356–7.

30 LMM, *AA*, 133, 148–9, 129, 209–10.

31 LMM, *AIs*, 114–15, 132; Clement, "From 'Uncanny Beauty' to 'Uncanny Disease,'" 51.

32 LMM, *CJ* 4:244–5 (emphasis in original).

33 LMM, *RV*, 139. Anne's reference to death as an adventure is perhaps an allusion to J.M. Barrie's *Peter Pan*. See Clement, "From 'Uncanny Beauty' to 'Uncanny Disease,'" 55–6, for a discussion of death as an adventure in *Peter Pan* and *Rilla of Ingleside*.

34 LMM, *RV*, 4. Winifred says to Mary, "Beautiful, too, I suppose we shall be, every one. Have you never had that come over you, with a thrill of compassionate thankfulness, when you have seen a poor girl shrinking, as only girls can shrink, under the life-long affliction of a marred face or form? The loss or presence of beauty is not as slight a deprivation or blessing as the moralists would make it out" (Phelps, *Gates Ajar*, 123).

35 LMM, *RV*, 42, 82–3, 75.

36 Ibid., 209, 246–9, 29, 37, 30–1, 44–5, 213, 157, 101–3.

37 Ibid., 74, 22.

38 Ibid., 299. For a discussion of Walter's piper, see Clement, "From 'Uncanny Beauty' to 'Uncanny Disease,'" 55–8.

39 Waterston, "Leaskdale," 31, 21.

40 Young and Light, "Interrogating Spaces," 64.

41 LMM, *AGG*, 352.

42 LMM, *AIs*, 30–1, 41.

43 LMM, *RV*, 26–7.

44 Ibid., chapter 31; Gubar, *Artful Dodgers*, 6, quoted more fully above.

45 LMM, *RV*, 253, 246 (chapter title).

46 Ibid., 262.

47 LMM, *SJ* 4:255–6 (emphasis in original). Bacon's observation comes from the first paragraph of his essay "Of Death," during his discussion of how the "weak" natural fear of death in children is "increased with tales"; the passage Montgomery cites actually reads, "It is as natural to die as to be born." The quotation from Renan is from *The Apostles*, 62.

48 Pike, "*Magic for Marigold*, Childhood, and Fiction," 146–7.

49 LMM, *MM*, 57–8, 3–4, 66, 75–7 (emphasis in original).

50 Ibid., 72, 154–5, 206–7, 247.

51 Ibid., 29–34 (emphasis in original).

52 Ibid., 34–5, 94–5, 27, 29 (emphasis in original).

53 Gubar, *Artful Dodgers*, 32–3.

3

Vulnerable Situations: Boys and Boyhood in the *Emily* Books

RITA BODE

In a 2016 episode of the popular Canadian television detective drama *Murdoch Mysteries*, aspiring novelist Maud Montgomery makes an appearance. The episode, entitled "Unlucky in Love," has *Murdoch*'s clever but somewhat bumbling Constable George Crabtree, from his position of authority as the published author of *The Curse of the Pharaohs*, advising Maud on her talent and prospects for a successful writing career. After reading the first few chapters of Maud's manuscript, George assures her that "there is no question in my mind, Maud, you have a real gift." But he follows this initial encouragement with increasingly stringent and dismissive criticisms, citing Anne's adoptive family as singularly "dull," finding too much "nature stuff" in Maud's material, and building up to a final observation, delivered with pompous self-confidence, that Maud should "consider making Anne a boy, and that way she would have *real* adventures." To the credit of the *Murdoch* series creators, their fictional Maud, much as Montgomery herself might have done, emphatically rejects George's suggestion for a "Dan of Green Gables" – an Anne with a D![1] – but the real Maud Montgomery, while keeping her focus firmly set on her girl characters and their subsequent incarnations as women, also pays attention to boys and boyhood, a subject that has generally received short critical shrift in Montgomery scholarship. In *The Meaning of the Men and Boys in the Anne Books* (1997), one of the few studies to focus on the male presence in Montgomery's work, Sylvia DuVernet comments that "although the Anne novels were indisputably feminine in orientation … the men and boys who were included were essential to the stories," and their participation was "inevitable." Her observation that Montgomery "pushes and shoves men into her stories"[2] resonates with the way in which Montgomery's boy stories sometimes seem to emerge from the interstices of her heroines' experiences.

The stories of boys and men in the Montgomery books are less evident than her tales of girls and women, but her engagement with girls – girl-children, adolescent girls, and their womanhoods – makes room for the inclusion of their male counterparts. In the three books to which Emily lends her name, Montgomery seems particularly intent on providing a gender-balanced context for her protagonist's central position. Not only does she find a lively bosom friend for Emily in the independent Ilse, who demands her own attention, but she also introduces a cohort of male characters that includes boy-peers, as well as older friends whose boyhoods inform their adult situations. Montgomery's "portrait of the artist as a young girl"[3] opens up to a study of the complicated terrain of boyhood experience. In the *Emily* books, Montgomery reveals her stories of boys, boyhood, and young men's lives subtly but surely, drawing, as she does with her stories of girls and girlhood, on both personal and literary experiences. In the years leading up to the publication of the *Emily* books, Montgomery's vast reading and literary interests continued amidst the birth of two sons, in a time, moreover, when educators and social scientists were bringing their boyhood studies to the public's attention. The *Emily* books reveal a heightened awareness of boyhood in their recognition that the vulnerable state of childhood is part of both male and female experience. Her imaginative responses in revealing the boyhoods of Cousin Jimmy and Dean and in tracing the boyhoods of Perry and Teddy speak, in multiple ways, to the vulnerable situations of boy children.

By the time that Montgomery came to write the *Emily* books, successful and popular novels with a female protagonist as the central interest had long been abundant on both sides of the English-speaking Atlantic. In addition to her own *Anne of Green Gables*, an obvious, earlier example is *Jane Eyre*, which has a palpable presence in Montgomery's work. As our introduction notes, Montgomery criticism shows her drawing her Victorian predecessor into conversation with her own texts in various ways, especially in the *Emily* books.[4] While there are numerous allusions to Brontë and *Jane Eyre*, both direct and indirect, Emily significantly never refers to Brontë's character Jane. And yet her wide-ranging reading includes coming-of-age stories from the same era. In her diary in *Emily Climbs*, Emily records reading and crying over Charles Dickens's *David Copperfield*, the story of a boy-orphan, who, like Emily, is especially close to the parent of the opposite sex, ends up living with an aunt, and finds companionship and a quasi–father figure in the supposedly simple-minded member of the aunt's household. Emily's own first novel, moreover, develops from a story that incites in Aunt Elizabeth, not the most receptive audience for fiction, what Emily identifies as an "Oliver Twist complex." "And that little chap, *Jerry Stowe*," remarks Aunt Elizabeth in response to Emily's second story of the *Applegaths* in *Emily's Quest*, "What happens to him when he grows up, poor child?"[5] Emily's reading, as well as her writing, affirms the fictional George Crabtree's claims for greater interest in male protagonists, but more significantly, her literary activities suggest that Montgomery herself was not willing to leave the boy's story behind.

In her journal entry of 24 August 1920, Montgomery declares, "I am done with *Anne* forever." Having just completed *Rilla of Ingleside*, she writes about wanting "to create a new heroine now," one with "black hair and purplish gray eyes," a heroine, still young and female, but in appearance at least, in clear contrast to Anne. "She is already in embryo in my mind," Montgomery continues, "she has been christened for years. Her name is Emily." But in the very next paragraph of this brief two-paragraph entry, Montgomery expresses other literary ambitions that appear distinct from the *Emily* project, declaring her desire "to write – something entirely different from anything I have written yet." She laments the public's perception of her as "a 'writer for young people' and that only … I want to write a book dealing with grown-up creatures," she continues, "a psychological study of one human being's life." As with her conception of her new kind of heroine, this new kind of novel is in imaginative process. "I have the plot of it already matured in my mind," she states and then goes on to reveal its surprising title: "The name of the book is to be 'Priest Pond.'" Not only does Montgomery's choice of a title veer away from her usual association of a female protagonist with place, but it also directs its focus on a name invoking patriarchal traditions and implications. The entry becomes even more complicated as Montgomery designates this latter work, "Priest Pond," as her "real novel," and aligns the obstacles to writing it with her sons' futures: "I can't give up my profitable 'series,'" she notes, "until I have enough money salted down to give the boys a fair start in life – for the 'real novel' will not likely be a 'best seller.'"[6] The presence of Dean Priest in the *Emily* "series" suggests that Montgomery collapsed at least some of her plans for her "real novel" into the *Emily* books, which proved profitable and also highly gratifying for their creator, who came to love "dear little 'Emily' ... far better than I ever loved 'Anne.'"[7] The inclusion of Dean in Emily's story exposes in multiple ways some of the conflicts and tensions that were confronting Montgomery as she undertook the creation of the *Emily* books.

The *Emily* years saw Montgomery immersed in boys and boyhood. Her sons, Chester and Stuart, born in 1912 and 1915 respectively, grew from eight and almost five to fourteen and eleven in the approximately six years encompassing the writing and publication of the *Emily* series.[8] As children do, they made demands on her time and attention. Referring to her inability to get to work on her "real novel," "Priest Pond," she notes in the 24 August 1920 journal entry that "the boys are too young."[9] Six years later, in a journal entry of 20 November 1926, recording her relief at having sent the final revisions of *Emily's Quest* to the typist, she laments that the book "is no good. How could it be?" and longs for "a few unbroken spare moments!"[10] Montgomery's domestic responsibilities in the *Emily* years were multiple, and while she does not specifically mention Chester and Stuart in this entry, growing, developing boys were part of her immediate and ever-intensifying experience, restricting her time for writing and preoccupying her thinking. As her sons interfered with the writing of her "real" novel, so they at the very least intervened in the creation of her "best seller." Their presence was a constant reminder of the challenges that boyhood entails.

Montgomery's personal focus on boyhood during the writing and publication of the *Emily* books was sharpened, moreover, by public interest in the study of boys and male adolescence in the early decades of the twentieth century. Chester's and Stuart's childhoods coincided with the boy-study movement, which tended to position the human boy as essentially a wild creature in need of taming and training. The first of the significant handbooks on boyhood published during this time, *The Boy Problem* (1901), by American Quaker William Byron Forbush, implies in the choice of words for its title that boyhood presents difficulties requiring attention. William Henry Gibson, a leader in the YMCA movement, provided a name for the study of boyhood when in

1916 he published *Boyology, or Boy Analysis*. Although it is not known if Montgomery read *Boyology* specifically, the ideas and attitudes that Gibson articulates about boy traits and tendencies and how these should best be handled for optimum character-building were prevalent in North America during Chester's and Stuart's boyhood and adolescence. As Kenneth Kidd points out in his book on boys in American literature and culture, Gibson's study is representative, "a standard example of the American primers of boy education and management published during the first two decades of the twentieth century." Montgomery was familiar with the work of psychologist Granville Stanley Hall, who founded the child-study movement and on whose work on adolescence Gibson and the other boyologists drew.[11] She records reading Hall's autobiography, *Life and Confessions of a Psychologist*, in 1924, finding it "very interesting in some parts – very dull in others."[12]

"Analysis," as Gibson's alternate title to *Boyology* suggests, is a significant component in the boy-study movement and is reflected in Montgomery's own propensity to observe and analyze her boys. On Stuart's sixth birthday, 7 October 1921, for instance, she muses that "every year seems to make him smarter and more lovable," but when she turns to contemplate Chester, worries emerge: "I see qualities in him that may interfere seriously not only with his success in life but with his happiness and the happiness of those he lives with." While Montgomery's concerns about Stuart focus mostly on his temporary physical ailments, her journal entries regularly reveal a persistent anxiety in her scrutiny of Chester's character and behaviour and her attempts to manage him. She continues her 7 October entry on Chester by observing that he is "an exceedingly difficult child to train, especially in the more superficial aspects of existence – table manners, social observances, etc."[13] Her comments reflect the boyologists' aims to civilize and socialize the young male's primitive tendencies. Montgomery also expresses worries over the possibility that the troubling traits of her husband, Ewan, may surface in Chester. One of Hall's interests was genetic inheritance; Hall saw the inheritance of behaviours as open to modification over time, and hence his views further supported the emphasis on the proper training and handling of boys. Linking her husband's early physical maturity, which he seems to have passed on to Chester, to Ewan's "constitutional tendency to melancholia," Montgomery fears the presence of a "lurking mental unsoundness" in Chester. Ewan further troubles her attempts "to teach and train Chester as wisely as possible" through what Montgomery sees as his inadequacy in being a strong masculine role model. In sending Chester off to St Andrew's boarding school in the fall of 1925, Montgomery echoes the prevalence of the boyology mandate that privileged the presence of male authority in boys' lives. Expressing her sense of loss at Chester's coming absence, she also states her satisfaction that "he will be under masculine influence henceforth – and, as I hope and believe, good masculine influence."[14]

The boyology movement as reflected in Montgomery's worries over Chester and her concerns about the experience of childhood also point to another aspect of boyhood that the work of Forbush, Gibson, and others introduced: they recognized the vulnerability inherent in boyhood and male adolescence. Although the boyologists set out prescriptive goals for character-building that emphasized conformity through teamwork over individuality, they saw that boys needed adult guidance and help in negotiating their development into adulthood. Their approach reflected a fear that, without support, boys would not reach their adult potential to function as upright citizens and leaders. Gibson's foreword to *Boyology* speaks of the boy as "ever … a new subject for discussion and analysis" and "in need of friendly interpreters … who will secure for him the unalienable rights of boyhood and genuine sympathy during the struggles of youth."[15] Montgomery's perspective when writing of Stuart in January of 1922 shows similar sentiments and a concern over his character, but in a different way than her worries about Chester: "What is before him, the little, loving starry-eyed fellow?" she wonders: "Somehow I have always felt vaguely anxious about his future. He is so sensitive. Will the world use him gently? Will it love him too much – or not enough?" She describes an incident with Chester, whom she consistently sees as hardy and robust, when he tripped and hit his head on the hard ground outside, but "sprang up with a gay laugh … and then bolted through the front door." Finding "the spunky little chap" crying, she sees that he "had braved it off before others." Montgomery recounts that, in taking "his poor little head close to my heart, he said piteously, 'O, mother, it hurts!'" Her response is to cuddle and kiss him: "I … felt that this was what mothers were made for – to comfort behind the scenes."[16] Like the boyologists, Montgomery takes the side of the boy in seeing his need for support, but her thoughts and responses suggest a different emphasis. Although she often refers to her own failed attempts to "train" Chester, and lauds the opportunity that he will have at school for exposure to positive masculine role models, she also values her maternal influence and guidance and foregrounds her sympathy. Kidd points out that "boyology was not an exclusively male domain, but its authoritative figures were men," with mothers positioned at the sidelines, their contributions viewed as secondary rather than central.[17] Boyology's aim to civilize and build the character of boys through organized group activities, developed for and aimed exclusively at boys and initiated and facilitated by masculine authority figures, may well have seemed too facile an approach to Montgomery, with her deep awareness of childhood's pain and difficulty, regardless of gender. In her fiction, especially, Montgomery turns from the direction in early-twentieth-century boy studies that embraces group conformity and gender exclusivity, but she aligns with its tendencies toward behavioural analysis and its recognition that boys, like girls, are vulnerable, in their dependent, childhood states, to the vagaries of their worldly circumstances.

Returning to her journalling after a three-month silence following Chester's birth, Montgomery expresses the deep, emotional fulfillment that has come to her in motherhood, but she notes, too, that maternal love has intensified her anguish over childhood's difficulties: "Always when I read of a child being neglected or ill-used," she writes, "I would thrill with indignation and horror. But now I can scarcely endure to read such a thing because of the anguish it causes me – for in every child I see my own child – and I picture him undergoing that. I have cried aloud at the pain that came with such a picture."[18] Montgomery knew that neglect and ill-use can take many forms. She never forgot the deep hurts of her own childhood.[19] The *Emily* trilogy shows in Emily's striving for fulfillment the restrictions placed on young female lives, but at the same time, Montgomery does not lose sight of the boyhood challenges and obstacles experienced by her male characters. In her journal, in August 1923, when *Emily of New Moon* was published, Montgomery writes, "I very seldom draw a character 'from life,'" and asserts that while "'Emily's' inner life was my own," the "events and incidents were fictitious."[20] In representing boyhood, Montgomery did not draw her fictional boys directly "from life" either. She observed, studied, and gauged with sensitivity and understanding the male experiences around her, and she fitted her responses to what she read and imagined, bringing to her depictions of boyhood the literary experiences of her broad reading and the exercise of her vibrant imagination on both lived and fictional experience. In the *Emily* books,

Montgomery gives us glimpses of the "inner life" of several boyhoods, including those of some of the adult male characters. Montgomery's creation of the boyhoods of Jimmy, Dean, Perry, and Teddy reveal a range of physical, emotional, psychological, and social challenges that come in insightful and usually complicated combinations.

Childhood suffering hovers over both Cousin Jimmy and Dean Priest. Cousin Jimmy's adult self, as already noted with reference to Emily's reading, is a literary cousin of Dickens's Mr Dick from *David Copperfield*. Both characters provide a source of humour as well as irony. Like Mr Dick, Cousin Jimmy is considered "simple," even foolish, but, in the tradition of Shakespeare's wise fools, both characters show insight into the weaknesses of society and human character and display what current psychology deems emotional intelligence, with its ability to include feelings in informed decision-making. Emily's assessment of Cousin Jimmy, that "whatever part of him was missing, it wasn't his heart," is entirely accurate and equally applicable to Mr Dick. Both characters display childlike tendencies, but both also give consistently sage advice and intervene successfully on behalf of others. They also both have literary talents: Mr Dick is preoccupied with writing his memoir, while Jimmy is adept at oral poetry. But a crucial difference between them signals Montgomery's intent in her depiction of Cousin Jimmy, for while Mr Dick cannot confront his past traumas directly, as indicated in the persistent intrusions of Charles I's head into his memoir, Cousin Jimmy himself and everyone else in the *Emily* books constantly refer to his life-altering childhood accident.

Before Emily and the reader even meet Cousin Jimmy, Ellen Greene establishes that "he ain't quite all there … He's a bit simple – some accident or other when he was a youngster, I've heard. It addled his head, kind of. Elizabeth was mixed up in it some way." Shortly after Emily's arrival at New Moon, Cousin Jimmy, in one of his first interactions with Emily, details at some length the "way" in which Elizabeth was involved. "Elizabeth bosses the farm," Cousin Jimmy confides, "but she lets me run the garden – to make up for pushing me into the well." Jimmy recounts how a childhood game of tag went terribly wrong when, to avoid a targeted blow from Elizabeth, he fell headfirst into the open well. "I was took up for dead," he continues, and while he recovered "pretty near as good as new[,] folks say I've never been quite right since – but they only say that because I'm a poet, and because nothing ever worries me." Jimmy admits that he had made "Elizabeth mad ... 'twasn't *hard* to make her mad, you understand," and also acknowledges that "Elizabeth didn't mean to ... We were just children,"[21] but Montgomery nevertheless includes the accident in all three *Emily* books, coming back again and again in different ways to the childhood mishap and its irrevocable results.[22]

Although Aunt Elizabeth, as instigator, was also affected, and she does make efforts at reparation, the persistent reminders of the incident are also reminders of her harsh character and augment the indictment of her severity toward Emily. In what she did to Cousin Jimmy, inadvertently or not, lurks a warning of what her inflexible attitudes might do to Emily. Aunt Elizabeth's development into adulthood, bringing with it her childhood traits, whether good or bad, moves forward, but the accident checks Cousin Jimmy's transition into maturity. Despite the instances that show Cousin Jimmy's strong moral perspective and just thinking, the numerous references to his past are reminders of his lost potential. One of the most poignant moments that speaks to Jimmy's awareness of a life lost to him with the childhood accident occurs in the final *Emily* book, when Emily has found the Lost Diamond: "The Lost Diamond will bring you luck, Emily ... I'm glad they've left it with you," he says with his usual generosity, and then adds: "But will you let me hold it sometimes, Emily – just hold it and look into it. When I look into anything like that I – I – find myself. I'm not simple Jimmy Murray then – I'm what I would have been if I hadn't been pushed into a well. Don't say anything about it to Elizabeth, Emily, but just let me hold it and look at it once in awhile."[23]

The Priest surname of the other adult character who forms a particularly close friendship with Emily roots Dean in Montgomery's desire "to write a book dealing with grown-up creatures," as already noted in her 1920 journal entry, but her explanation that this entails the "psychological study of one human being's life" directs Montgomery toward the boyhood of this troubling and troubled figure, who, like Cousin Jimmy, endured a childhood of loss.[24] A less sympathetic figure than Cousin Jimmy to readers, especially in contemporary times, Dean has also received little critical approbation in large part because his need to possess and control Emily is alienating. As Mary Rubio suggests, and as Kit Pearson points out in the afterword to this volume, there is a "creepy" aspect to his adult personality.[25] Elizabeth Epperly's commentary on Dean is particularly apt, for she recognizes that the perception of Dean as a Byronic outlier figure, represented by Charlotte Brontë's Edward

Rochester, stems from his own self-imaging, revealed when he places the flower that Emily had crushed and abandoned "between the leaves of an old volume of *Jane Eyre*."[26] Dean's position as the novel's ambivalent gothic hero/villain, equally capable of deep love and self-involved, threatening cruelty, is confirmed by Emily's early response to him: instinctively liking him, she is nonetheless repulsed when he jestingly lays claim to her for having saved her life. It is with reason that she feels "as if a cobweb fetter had been flung around her."[27] Dean's self-positioning as the romantic gothic figure, wronged yet deserving, sinning but also sinned against, speaks to a sense of entitlement that is often accompanied by a self-justification for insidious behaviours – he does, after all, openly subvert Emily's writing ambitions – and twenty-first-century readers and critics, who have learned to challenge the predatory practices of powerful men, can see his "sinister" quality, with "its disturbing sexual aura."[28]

And yet, the contexts in which Montgomery places Dean's outcast status, with the shifting significance that he shares with the Byronic hero, imply that she has an even more ambivalent trajectory for him. Other self-identifying markers intensify Dean's alien position, for Montgomery shows him internalizing the way in which others see him, that is, through a lens of disability; like Cousin Jimmy's intellect, Dean's body, with "wan av his shoulders … a l'il bit higher than the other,"[29] reflects the social construction of disability that theorist Susan Wendell, among others, articulates in identifying the "subtle cultural factors that determine standards of normality and exclude those who do not meet them from full participation in their societies."[30] Both his family and his community read Dean's non-conforming body as a disadvantage and use it to cast him as an outsider. By routinely and repeatedly referring to him as Jarback, a designation that signals his bodily difference, instead of by his given name, they turn his physical differentiation into his identity. Montgomery presents Dean as acutely self-conscious of his physical appearance; he tells Emily after their engagement that "of course the Priests find it hard to believe that you are marrying me because you care anything for me. How could you? I find it hard to believe myself," and he includes his expressed self-image of "old – lame as I am" in his vow to make her happy.[31] At the same time, however, he remains aware of an innate superiority that his intellect, imagination, and the world of books, art, and culture have given him. To his family and community, Dean cultivates the gothic-hero stance of the alienated and arrogant outcast-wanderer, the "cynic," as Aunt Nancy calls him,[32] suggesting that his behaviours and activities are an adult strategy of social self-preservation, an active resistance to the communal and societal attempts to cast him as inferior because of his physical non-conformity. His adult self-positioning, however, part-subconscious, part-deliberate, tells only half his story. The other half lies in his boyhood.

Montgomery's most telling complication in Dean's presentation is her placing of his Byronic persona in conversation with his boyhood past. Dean's adult self looks back to a suffering boyhood that still held out some promise of escape from oppression. Montgomery provides a context of childhood sorrows arising from the abuses visited on him because of his bodily non-conformity. Dean refers to his school days casually and matter-of-factly, but his words reveal a dark underside of emotional and psychological hurt. From the first, Montgomery associates his attraction to Emily with his keen awareness that she is Douglas Starr's daughter. "I knew your father," he tells Emily on their first meeting, "he was the only friend I had at school – the only boy who would bother himself about Jarback Priest, who was lame and hunchbacked and couldn't play football or hockey." Dean is thirty-six years old when he meets Emily, but Montgomery makes his boyhood experience, its pain as well as its hope, still present to him. As he parts from Emily on their first meeting, his thoughts are not so much on Emily as on the lone friend of his boyhood as he thinks, "She is Douglas Starr's child – *he* never called me Jarback."[33] His past derails his cynical Byronic-hero stance by foregrounding the pain of his schoolboy experience, but also recalling a time before his bitterness hardened his adulthood. Emily, in the present, brings that double-edged past forcefully back to him, echoing her father's attitude as she tells Dean, "I *never* think of you as Jarback," and assuring him that his self-description of being "lame – and crooked … doesn't make a bit of difference – and never will."[34] Emily recalls for him a sense of boyhood possibilities outside of societal prejudices. In her "company," the narrator states, Dean "was not a cynic; he had shed his years and became a boy again with a boy's untainted visions."[35] Dean's threat to Emily's selfhood intensifies as she matures, but Montgomery carries his complicated inner world beyond the potentially deviant attraction of an older man for a girl-child as she traces a sense of lost hopes in the hurt and pain of his boyhood experiences.

The boyhoods of Jimmy and Dean that Montgomery depicts in the *Emily* books speak not of male privilege but of boy vulnerability. Boyhood studies and her own motherhood, as I have suggested, increased her sensitivity to the precarious nature of boyhood. Her imagination worked in both joyful and dark ways. For Jimmy and Dean, she creates boyhoods that would not have easily fit in with the boyologists' approach to cultivating manhood. The boyhoods of both these fictional characters fall outside their community's parameters of social acceptance. In the years leading up to the *Emily* books, moreover, Montgomery experienced the profound sorrow of losing her second-born son. Stillborn Hugh's death in 1914 coincided with the beginning of the First World War, during the course of which the destruction of young male lives was personal, global, and massive.[36] The sense of loss that the events of the second decade of the twentieth century ushered in aligns with Montgomery's perspectives on boyhood. In Jimmy and Dean, Montgomery depicts boyhood as susceptible to injury and adversity. Beyond the accepted trials of boyhood, theirs are troubled lives with no easy means of repair or restitution.

In addition to the companionship and guidance offered Emily by these older male figures, Montgomery places her protagonist in a circle of young friends – two girls, Emily and Ilse, and two boys, Perry Miller and Teddy Kent – that provides a gender-balanced context for the playing out in the three *Emily* books of multiple *Bildungsromans*. As literary descendants of the Victorian period, all four are full or partial orphans, and three of them are potential artists. But Montgomery also resists a monolithic view of children and their experience. In his history of American childhood, *Huck's Raft* (2004), Steven Mintz disputes the idea "that childhood is the same for all children, a status transcending class, ethnicity, and gender."[37] Marah Gubar's "kinship-model" for critical approaches in children's literature and childhood studies privileges connection and relatedness, but nonetheless also acknowledges "that children – like adults ... are such a diverse population that we can rarely (if ever) indulge in confident generalizations about them."[38] As with Jimmy and Dean, Montgomery's presentation of Perry and Teddy offers little promise that her two young males could ever become successful recruits among the boyologists. Both boys are achievers, but they choose their own paths forward. Perry's striving for success does not come at the expense of his iconoclastic perspectives on the very society in which he seeks distinction, and Teddy's artistic activities require focused individual attention of both mind and heart, rather than physical group activity and team-building games. In depicting the boyhoods of Perry and Teddy, Montgomery not only gives them different personalities and different backgrounds and situations but also employs different methods in their presentation, while at the same time exploring the experience of each in a context of hardship and resilience and its implications for social commentary.

Despite his being the most disadvantaged among the four young people, facing the greatest material and social hardships because of his poverty and class status, Perry has the most straightforwardly happy childhood in negotiating most successfully the vulnerable situations in which he finds himself. Like Emily, Perry is a full orphan who also lives with his aunt – "my old beast of an Aunt Tom down at Stovepipe Town," as he puts it, a description that Emily would likely not mind applying to her own Aunt Elizabeth. Although the most illiterate, he is also the most obviously literary child character in the *Emily* books. He not only resembles Montgomery's own Anne in his self-reliant resilience, which consistently helps him to forge ahead, but he also bears a strong likeness in both his background and demeanour to several acclaimed literary boy heroes. Perry's father was "a sea captain and I uster sail with him when he was alive – sailed everywhere," he confides to Emily by way of further introduction, displaying hints of Robert Louis Stevenson's Jim Hawkins and a knowledge of a better world beyond his present circumstances. He captivates Emily with "fassinating stories after his lessons are done" based on his own adventures,[39] like those perhaps of Frederick Marryat's Mr Midshipman Easy, in whom Montgomery shows interest early on.[40] In his first meeting with Emily, Perry's heroic status as the "gallant rescuer" who saves her from the pending charge of a bull is quickly undermined by his Huck Finn–like slang and vernacular talk. His wearing, moreover, "as few clothes as decency permitted" again recalls Huck's sartorial discomforts, and, like Huck, he displays a sense of impromptu accommodation to welcoming circumstances, deciding, at the sight of Emily, that he will hire out as the chore boy at New Moon.[41] Perry, like Huck, is a good "bad boy," a literary type with which Montgomery was familiar.

Emily Woster points out that, in a 12 May 1902 journal entry, Montgomery attributes the origins of her own journal writing to her reading of "A Bad Boy's Diry," published in 1880, which the young Maud read when she was around nine and decided to emulate in her own diary version.[42] As types of the literary bad boy, both the "diry's" author, "little Gorgie,"[43] and Huck create mischief rather than committing crime, and Perry falls in line with such activities, in the process initiating much of the first *Emily* book's humour; Perry, nonetheless, emerges as a different version of the bad boy than Huck. Rather than embracing life on a raft, as Huck does, and deciding "to light out for the Territory" to head off being "sivilize[d],"[44] Perry is, from the first, determined to succeed and attain a position of authority and influence in the mainstream affairs that exclude a poor boy from Stovepipe Town. In being the bad-boy type who makes good, he is closer to the literary models of the self-made boys of the dime novels, especially the rags-to-riches boy heroes that Horatio Alger created, starting with Ragged Dick in 1868. Alger's books remained very popular through the second decade of the twentieth century, the years leading up to the *Emily* series.[45] Like Dick and other Alger boys, Perry is brave, a trait that he consistently demonstrates in his interactions with his peers and adults alike. Montgomery elaborates and extends Ragged Dick's attributes to show her true valuing of Perry's qualities. Emily's admiration for Perry's fearlessness in *Emily Climbs* – "Perry always brags that he is never afraid of anything – doesn't know what fear is … I wish I could be so fearless" – adds to the increasing importance of this quality as a meaningful human attribute in the Montgomery canon. Mr Carpenter's condemning of fear as "a vile thing … at the bottom of almost every wrong and hatred of the world" anticipates John Foster's guide to living in *The Blue Castle* (1926), when he writes that "*Fear is the original sin … almost all the evil in the world has its origin in the fact that someone is afraid of something*," and looks ahead to "the stultifying effects of fear" in *Magic for Marigold*, as Lesley Clement articulates in this volume.[46] In Perry, Montgomery suggests the strength that resisting fear imparts to the individual. Like Alger's boy heroes, Perry is "plucky."[47] He laughs off, or laughs "loud and long," as Emily notes,[48] at the pronouncements directed at him by figures of authority or challenges those pronouncements, especially when they involve standing up for the unjust treatment of others, while, at the same time, willingly accepting responsibility for his actions. Like Dick, he is industrious, an example of the Protestant work ethic, and he is also practical, focusing astutely on how to achieve his goals. As the four young people make their education plans at the beginning of *Emily Climbs*, Emily notes that Perry is penniless, which drives his decision to attend "Shrewsbury in place of Queen's Academy … [because] it will be easier to get work to do in Shrewsbury, and board is cheaper there."[49]

The Ragged Dick–type stories are openly didactic fiction, popular for their moral perspective – work hard, especially with the intention of glorifying some higher power, and success will come, both in terms of material well-being and societal respectability and acceptance. They are formulaic stories of uplift. But the popularity of their subject matter, ragged, disadvantaged orphan boys whose purpose is to engage the tender feelings of readers,[50] carries beyond the immediate moralistic one to other significant effects, which Montgomery takes up in her own fiction. In her representation of Perry, Montgomery recognizes that the Ragged Dick–type character contains a powerful resistance to sentimental victimhood. Montgomery's critical reputation for much of the twentieth century suffered from the dismissive view of her as a sentimental writer, with all the implications of emotional excesses, superficiality, and manipulation, not to mention purple prose, which such a categorization carries. The re-evaluations of sentimentalism in critical thinking, starting in the last decades of the twentieth century, have led not only to new understandings of sentimentalism's intents but also to acknowledgments of its absence where it is expected.[51] While the emphasis on industry to explain the Ragged Dick figure's personal success, with a corresponding lack of industry to explain failure, helped lessen the guilt feelings of the wealthier classes at socio-economic disparities and injustices, it also, as seen in Perry, has the potential to transcend its sentimental appeal in imparting to the disadvantaged and disenfranchised the possibility of agency and autonomy.

Alger's boys are motivated, and hard-working, but their advancement is inevitably facilitated by luck. Some form of extra help – an unexpected, fortuitous inheritance; a rich gentleman who singles out one poor orphan boy among many to patronize – supplements their hard work. In contrast, Montgomery provides no arbitrary external aids for Perry. No lucky opportunity or rich patronage serendipitously comes along to help Perry realize his goals. Even his old Aunt Tom, with her "bit o' money," refuses to help with the cost of his "eddication" unless he manages somehow to get Emily's promise to marry him when they grow up.[52] The commendatory attention and support that Perry receives from Emily and others – like Mr Carpenter, their teacher; Dr Hardy, the principal of Shrewsbury High School; or Mr Abel, the lawyer – are not random, but rather a response to his talents and industry. His successes are solely the result of his determination and hard work. Without any training from the boyologists, Perry takes the lead in his own advancement, rejecting conformity as he reaches for any opportunity that he sees, regularly and often casually challenging the barriers and boundaries that would limit him, and, significantly, avoiding the pursuit of his goals at the expense of others. Perry consistently shows himself to be both self-reliant and self-confident. As he says to Emily, "I've got to hoe my own row," and he does.[53]

Montgomery does not make light of the obstacles that Perry faces in his drive to get ahead. With her representation of strict social hierarchies continually pointing to formidable boundaries for social mobility, she makes his vulnerable situation amply evident. To Aunt Elizabeth's consciousness of Murray family stature, Perry as the "hired boy" seems not just of a different class but of a different species. Even as his "status at New Moon … change[s] subtly and steadily," and Aunt Elizabeth realizes that to "have some small share" in the making of "a future premier" is entirely desirable, ingrained prejudices against Perry's Stovepipe Town origins endure.[54] Somewhat shocked at Emily's engagement to Dean Priest, whom she considers unsuitable, Aunt Elizabeth nonetheless has to admit that an announcement of marriage to Perry of Stovepipe Town would be worse. Emily's Aunt Ruth sees Perry as among the "off-scourings of the gutter," and it is only when she realizes that "the help-boy at New Moon" has transitioned into "Dr Hardy's guest" that her derision lessens.[55] Perry functions as a kind of barometer of the intolerance and prejudice operating in the community, revealing the snobbery and self-aggrandizing qualities in which its discriminations are rooted. Montgomery looks to the attitudes toward Perry's social progress as much as to his Stovepipe Town roots to suggest the debilitating social prejudices at work, since, rather than seeing his achievements as proof that Stovepipe Town inhabitants have worth, social attitudes position him as the exception. They reject his accomplishments as representative and thus keep ignorant, discriminatory practices toward Stovepipe Town origins firmly in place.

Emily's female counterpart, Ilse, who is secretly in love with Perry throughout the three books, camouflages her desire in scorn and, in the process, forcefully articulates the cruel, deep-seated intolerance toward the socially disadvantaged in the community's thinking. When Perry brags to her that someday he will be a "finer gentleman than anyone" she knows, she retorts mercilessly – "'Gentlemen,' said Ilse in a nasty voice, 'have to be born. They can't be made, you know'"[56] – and in protesting too much to Emily, she questions rhetorically that even if Perry were to become premier some day, "won't you always smell the herring-barrels of Stovepipe Town?" on him.[57] Perry's self-confidence and determination act as buffers to the discrimination that his circumstances engender. He remains focused on his goals, and although marrying Emily is one of them, he turns even this setback of a final romantic break into an affirmation of their continuing friendship. Rather than the moral of hard work bringing good luck and success as in Alger's stories, Montgomery suggests in Perry's resilience a defiance against the hostile prejudgments directed at him. Her bad boy never turns pious. He offers little material with which the boyologists could work, for he steadfastly rejects conformity. Montgomery does not make Perry overly complex – he remains a source of humour and fun throughout the *Emily* books – but neither does she see him as superficial.

Montgomery does not dwell on dark corners in her presentation of Perry's character. In contrast, the story of his counterpart in the *Emily* series, Teddy Kent, has the potential to reveal several. Teddy's literary past is most evident in the range of suggestive resemblances to Louisa May Alcott's Laurie, to which Dawn Sardella-Ayers draws attention in her study of the love triangle in *Little Women* and the *Emily* books. But Montgomery situates her young male artist differently than Alcott positions Laurie. While Laurie, like Teddy, is lonely and longing for emotional interactions beyond his home, he is also privileged, living with his wealthy grandfather and with access to resources and opportunities that such a position provides. Montgomery's introduction of Teddy in *Emily of New Moon* suggests no corresponding advantages. Montgomery situates him, like Jimmy and Dean, as vulnerable. When she first draws attention to him, he has been out of school all June, and Dr Burnley has "been absorbed all through July trying to save [his] life." Once he is out of danger, the doctor's instruction to Ilse and Emily to go up to the Tansy Patch to cheer him up, because he is "lonesome and moping" and not recovering fast enough, suggests that he also has psychological susceptibilities.[58] His boyhood is the most enigmatic depiction of childhood and young adulthood in the *Emily* series, for, as Emily discovers, he lives in a troubling atmosphere with a mother whose all-consuming love for her son is itself diseased. Emily is Teddy's interpreter. Montgomery embeds the portrait of the artist as young boy and man into her portrait of the young female artist. Emily is able to recognize instinctively Mrs Kent's unhappiness, but her insight into Teddy's home circumstances and her ability to understand his inner life are more limited – partly, perhaps, because of their romantic involvement. Montgomery, however, provides signposts to Teddy's untold story.

Mrs Kent's demanding, exclusionary attitude toward her son is a constant that Teddy must negotiate and accommodate from an early age. He keeps his "pictures in the barn loft because his mother doesn't like to see them," Emily confides in one of her letters to her father, but even this does not prevent Mrs Kent's maternal destructions: "She's burned some of [the pictures]," Teddy tells Emily. "They're missing from the barn wall and I can't find them anywhere." Teddy lives with his mother's immediate hatred of "*anything*" or anyone for whom he shows affection. His home life reflects displaced abuse, as he bears witness to drowned kittens and lives with the threat of poisoned dogs. And yet he affirms unequivocally to Emily, "I love Mother,"[59] and his repeated assertion that "she's always lovely when we're alone" rings true.[60] In her depiction of Teddy and his mother, Montgomery offers an affirming rewriting of sorrowful boyhoods and fraught mother-son relationships. While they share similarities, Mrs Kent stands in contrast to figures like Thomas Hardy's Mrs Yeobright, whose maternal love is closely tied to her ambitions for her son, Clem, in *The Return of the Native* (1878), or D.H. Lawrence's Mrs Morel, whose passionate involvement with her son, Paul, becomes an obstacle in his emotional ties to others, especially women. Well read in Victorian fiction, Montgomery likely knew Hardy, and if she did not read Lawrence's *Sons and Lovers*, which was published in 1913, just before the outbreak of the First World War, she most likely would have heard of and/or read about the book. However, she would not even have had to do that for her to write her own aesthetic response to this most intimate relationship, the intricacies of which are recorded in her journal responses to her boys.

Teddy's devotion to his mother is not entirely misguided, and it effectively negates Ilse's view of him as selfish, which she attributes to lifelong maternal adoration and his great appeal to the opposite sex. "Teddy likes to be adored," Ilse tells Emily as she critiques the way in which he handles expressions of female devotion by "graciously bestowing a smile – a look – a touch as a reward" and saying what he knows his admirers want to hear.[61] These responses that Ilse condemns offer another interpretation. Teddy's interactions are consistently characterized by sympathy, by meeting what he senses are the needs of others. His imagination brings not only recognition but also understanding to human frailty. His fury at mad Mr Morrison for having frightened Emily in *Emily Climbs* dissipates before "the old man's piteous entreaty … the ageless quest in his hollow, sunken eyes" for his lost Annie. "No – no – I don't know where she is," Teddy replies "gently," "but I think you will find her sometime."[62] "Poor little mother," he says to Emily in the final *Emily* book. "She hasn't changed. She isn't proud of my success – she hates it. She thinks it has taken me from her. The years have not made it any easier for her … I've never known her any other way, but I think she must have been different once." Teddy's sympathetic imagination is powerful in its understanding and forgiveness. Although for the wrong reasons, Ilse's prediction that Teddy will have success as "a wonderful portrait painter" is not inaccurate.[63] He understands and tolerates the wide expanse of human motivations. Confronted by the weaknesses of others, Teddy reacts with compassion, making him a worthier person for Emily to spend her life with than some have thought.[64]

In *Emily Climbs*, Emily records her reaction to a story that "ended unhappily. I was wretched until I had invented a happy ending for it," she comments, and then vows "to always end my stories happily."[65] Emily's creator has a similar resolve. Montgomery provides the conventional happy ending to the *Emily* books in uniting Emily and Teddy and further intensifies romantic satisfaction by bringing together Perry and Ilse, thus providing a happy resolution for all four of her young characters. But Montgomery's narrative reveals other kinds of happy endings lurking behind the conventional one as the challenging boyhoods that she depicts transform into satisfactory adulthoods. Her maternal responses are affirmed and worries about her sons are assuaged through the outcomes that she allows to her fictional boys, whose boyhoods lie outside the insistent advice of the boyologists. Teddy turns out well. His mother's potentially suffocating possessiveness does not damage him. He carries on forging his own way, yet remaining compassionate to her troubling love. In depicting this relationship, Montgomery presents a reassuring vision of enduring family ties that carry the promise of overcoming both maternal and child inadequacy, concepts that extend, too, to the care-giving adults who assume responsibility for young and vulnerable lives. Teddy's compassion, moreover, aligns with Perry's openness to others, which his ambitions never compromise. For the two older characters whose boyhoods Montgomery examines, adulthood is more shadowed by their pasts, but still marked by a resilience that keeps a sympathetic imagination for others in play. Despite his limitations and childhood setback, Cousin Jimmy is a just and generous adult with a creative spirit that brings him fulfillment. Even Dean overcomes his selfish motivations in a magnanimous gesture of continuing a friendship that has brought him at least as much joy as sorrow. To various degrees, Montgomery writes a happy ending for all four of the boyhoods that she presents in the *Emily* books. Perhaps the happiest resolution of her trilogy lies in its quiet acknowledgment that the pain and sorrows of childhood need not determine the rest of life, nor need they stand for the whole of life.

NOTES

1 "Unlucky in Love." *Murdoch Mysteries*, written by Lori Spring, based on the creations of Maureen Jennings, and directed by Cal Coons, season 9, episode 12, Shaftesbury Films, 1 February 2016. A transcript of the episode is currently available at https://transcripts.foreverdreaming.org/viewtopic.php?f=13&t =25019 (emphasis in original).

2 DuVernet, *Meaning of the Men and Boys*, 1, 8.

3 Epperly, *Fragrance of Sweet-Grass*, 145.

4 See, especially, Epperly, *Fragrance of Sweet-Grass*, 154–67; Miller, "Haunted Heroines"; L. McMaster, "The 'Murray Look.'" See also Gerson, "L.M. Montgomery and the Conflictedness," 68–9, 72; and Lefebvre, *L.M. Montgomery: A Name for Herself*, on Montgomery and the Brontës, 314–15.

5 LMM, *EQ*, 171, 169.

6 LMM, *CJ* 4:279.

7 LMM, *CJ* 5:41.

8 See also in this volume, Steffler, "The Performance of the Beautiful Dream Boy," 97, 107–10, on Montgomery and her sons.

9 LMM, *CJ* 4:279.

10 LMM, *CJ* 6:92.

11 Kidd, *Making American Boys*, 67; Kidd includes Hall's two-volume *Adolescence: Its Psychology and Its Relations to Physiology, Anthropology, Sociology, Sex, Crime, Religion, and Education* (1904) among the influential works on boys circulating in the United States.

12 LMM, *CJ* 5:237.

13 LMM, *CJ* 4:339–40.

14 LMM, *CJ* 5:219, 402.

15 Gibson, *Boyology*, ix.

16 LMM, *CJ* 5:4, 41–2.

17 Kidd, *Making American Boys*, 68. Generally, the boyology movement was unfriendly to women only in so far as favouring male leadership for boys. In current times, the idea of boys as vulnerable and the importance of meeting their particular needs are concepts that are sometimes exploited by anti-feminist advocates in some branches of the male-rights movement who see feminism's demand for gender equality as disadvantaging boys and men.

18 LMM, *CJ* 3:73.

19 Tulloch, "Lost Boys and Lost Girls," 114–35, in this volume, touches on Montgomery's painful experiences in childhood; see also, for example, Montgomery's journal entry for 2 January 1905 (LMM, *CJ* 2:117–20).

20 LMM, *CJ* 5:178.

21 LMM, *ENM*, 26, 41, 26–7, 80–1 (emphasis in original).

22 In *Emily of New Moon*, there are further reference to Jimmy's childhood accident in chapters 8, 15, 18, 20; in *Emily Climbs*, in chapters 1, 5, 6, 10, 15, 18; and in *Emily's Quest*, in chapters 18, 22.

23 LMM, *EQ*, 167.

24 LMM, *CJ* 4:279.

25 Rubio, *Lucy Maud Montgomery*, 292; Pearson, "Dear Maud," this volume, 300.

26 LMM, *ENM*, 329; Epperly, *Fragrance of Sweet-Grass*, 155.

27 LMM, *ENM*, 328.

28 Rubio, *Lucy Maud Montgomery*, 292.

29 LMM, *ENM*, 285.

30 Wendell, *The Rejected Body*, 36.

31 LMM, *EQ*, 74.

32 LMM, *ENM*, 321.

33 LMM, *ENM*, 323–4, 329 (emphasis in original).

34 LMM, *EC*, 30 (emphasis in original).

35 LMM, *ENM*, 331.

36 See, for instance, Cavert, "'To the Memory of,'" and Clement, "From 'Uncanny Beauty' to 'Uncanny Disease.'"

37 Mintz, *Huck's Raft*, 2. Plotz's studies in Romantic literature, as referenced in the Introduction, also resist essentialist readings of children and childhood.

38 Gubar, "Hermeneutics of Recuperation," 300.

39 LMM, *ENM*, 183, 188.

40 LMM, *CJ* 1:148. Stevenson's *Treasure Island* was published in volume form in 1883; Marryat's *Mr. Midshipman Easy* in 1836.

41 LMM, *ENM*, 181, 182, 183.

42 Woster, "Readings of a Writer," 210; LMM, *CJ* 2:54. The book was published initially as *A Bad Boy's Diary*; "by little Georgie" was added only in later editions. The spellings of "diry" for the title and "Gorgie" are Montgomery's.

43 LMM, *CJ* 2:54.

44 Twain, *Huckleberry Finn*, 229.

45 See Scharnhorst, "Demythologizing Alger," 182.

46 LMM, *EC*, 12–13; *BC*, 30–1 (italics in original); Clement, "L.M. Montgomery's Precocious Children," 62–4, in this volume.

47 Alger, *Ragged Dick*, 111.

48 LMM, *ENM*, 185.

49 LMM, *EC*, 7.

50 In his Preface to the 1868 volume edition of *Ragged Dick*, Alger writes: "The author hopes that, while the volumes in this series may prove interesting as stories, they may also have the effect of enlisting the sympathies of his readers in behalf of the unfortunate children whose life is described, and of leading them to co-operate with the praiseworthy efforts now making [sic] by the Children's Aid Society and other organizations to ameliorate their condition" (1).

51 For a re-evaluation of literary sentimentalism, see Dobson, "Reclaiming Sentimental Literature."

52 LMM, *ENM*, 275.

53 LMM, *EC*, 371.

54 LMM, *ENM*, 185, 363.

55 LMM, *EC*, 255, 282.

56 Ibid., 8.

57 LMM, *EQ*, 52.

58 LMM, *ENM*, 147.

59 Ibid., 152, 339 (emphasis in original).

60 Ibid., 358; *EC*, 89.

61 LMM, *EQ*, 133.

62 LMM, *EC*, 58.

63 LMM, *EQ*, 137–8, 77.

64 See, for example, Epperly, *Fragrance of Sweet-Grass*, 170–1, and Clement, "Visual Culture," especially the section entitled "From 'Smiling Girl,'" for appreciative readings of Teddy, and Waterston, *Magic Island*, 149–50, for a negative one.

65 LMM, *EC*, 259.

PART TWO

Conversing with the Present: Fantasy, the Ideal, and the Real

4

The Performance of the Beautiful Dream Boy in Novels by L.M. Montgomery and Frances Hodgson Burnett

MARGARET STEFFLER

In a curious journal entry in 1910, thirty-five-year-old L.M. Montgomery, not yet a mother, records an unusual meeting with her cousin's son, four-year-old Kenneth Ritchie, whom she sees for the first time on her visit to Boston in November. Montgomery is immediately overwhelmed by Kenneth's beautiful appearance and "disposition," professes her love for him in her journal, and claims to cry and long for him after they part.[1] In a later entry in July 1913, almost three years after the initial meeting, she records her "queer little disappointment" upon meeting seven-year-old Kenneth, who appears as a "total stranger," retaining only the "beautiful brown eyes" of the "little dream boy" she once loved and has now lost. "The present Kenneth Ritchie," Montgomery mourns, "seems as nothing to me."[2] In this chapter, I argue that the unknown, passive, and silent four-year-old Kenneth functions as a receptacle to receive Montgomery's "desire" for boyish beauty and artistic genius, resulting in the fleshing out of the "dream boy," which she extends into her fiction of this period, most notably in the character of Anne's student, Paul Irving, in *Anne of Avonlea* (1909). What drives Montgomery's creation of a fictional dream boy in *Anne of Avonlea* and her strange formulation of Kenneth Ritchie? Although Montgomery continues to create the beautiful, artistic, and sensitive boy in later characters, such as Walter Blythe in *Rainbow Valley* (1919) and *Rilla of Ingleside* (1921) and Teddy Kent in the *Emily* trilogy (1923–27),[3] these characters are less dreamy than the earlier Paul Irving and Kenneth Ritchie, who seem to be idealized primarily to elicit and receive love and admiration from their creator.

This idealized figure, extreme in his beauty and goodness, was popularized by Frances Hodgson Burnett in her 1886 novel, *Little Lord Fauntleroy*. In his article, "Reluctant Lords and Lame Princes: Engendering the Male Child in Nineteenth-Century Juvenile Fiction," Alan Richardson describes Little Lord Fauntleroy as a "veritable icon of boyish effeminacy, the definitive mama's boy," and discusses how the excessive attention accorded to him and the novel constituted a craze or cult. Richardson draws attention to similar characters in John Ruskin's *The King of the Golden River* (1851), George MacDonald's *Back of the North Wind* (1871), Jean Ingelow's *Mopsa the Fairy* (1869), Mark Lemon's *Tinykin's Transformations* (1869), and Dinah Maria Craik's *Little Lame Prince and His Travelling-Cloak* (1875).[4] Burnett's character was not the first of his kind, but he was certainly the most popular. Through its titular character of Cedric Errol, Burnett's novel offers the epitome of the dream boy whose qualities reflect those who came before and set the standard for those who follow. The reviewer of *Anne of Avonlea* in *The Scotsman*, for example, declares that "one small chap [Paul Irving] is just another Little Lord Fauntleroy."[5] It comes as no surprise to learn that, in January 1902, Montgomery had reread Burnett's *Little Lord Fauntleroy*, a story she originally read in serial instalments in the *Montreal Witness* when she was about ten. She is enthusiastic about what she terms the "charm of the story,"[6] and there is no doubt that the endearing qualities of Burnett's character are reflected in Montgomery's Paul.

Montgomery's construction of Kenneth Ritchie speaks to the role played by authorial desire in the creation of fictional characters. Such desire, as established in Jacqueline Rose's well-known 1984 study, *The Case of Peter Pan or The Impossibility of Children's Fiction*, can result in the construction of a character in whom the writer is deeply invested and who blatantly reflects and serves the adult's needs. Susan Honeyman in *Elusive Childhood: Impossible Representations in Modern Fiction* (2005) agrees that at times "the concept of childhood serves as a *tabula rasa* for adult constructions."[7] Rose understands "desire to refer to a form of investment by the adult in the child, and to the demand made by the adult on the child as the effect of that investment, a demand which fixes the child and then holds it in place."[8] James R. Kincaid's work on "child-loving" is also based on this concept of authorial investment and reflection in its view of childhood as a "wonderfully hollow category, able to be filled up with anyone's overflowing emotions, not least overflowing passion." According to Kincaid, the child, whose "presence testifies only to our need," fulfills "functions necessary to our psychic and cultural life." He sees the child as "that which we are not but almost are, that which we yearn for so fiercely we almost resent it, that which we thought we saw in the mirror and almost wanted to possess yet feared we might."[9] This particular school of thought speaks to the inexplicable relationship between Montgomery and the unknown, silent four-year-old who serves as a tabula rasa to be created according to her desires and needs. Kenneth's blank inaccessibility makes possible Montgomery's construction of him as a beautiful and innocent boy, who exists primarily to draw out and receive her love. According to Kincaid, the Romantic child, "as an inversion of Enlightenment virtues," was "strangely hollow right from the start: *un*corrupted, *un*sophisticated, *un*enlightened," and the child of purity merely "another empty figure that allows the admirer to read just about anything into its vacancy."[10]

A case of filling innocence and purity with emotion, need, passion, and desire can certainly be made for Burnett and her fictional Little Lord Fauntleroy, as well as for Montgomery and Paul Irving. The fictional characters not only receive and satisfy the desires of the writers, but also serve as receptacles and reinforcements for the desires of the novels' characters. This phenomenon does not, however, render the child characters passive figures, limited to serving and fulfilling the needs of adults. Neither does the process depend on what Marah Gubar identifies as a dangerous emphasis on "the radical alterity or otherness of children, representing them as a separate species, categorically different from adults."[11] In persuasive arguments, Gubar and David Rudd, among others, take issue with views of the child as a passive character produced and controlled by adults.[12] Montgomery's and Burnett's characters are neither passive nor controlled. The creator's development of the child character animates him into possibility and substance as opposed to the hollow emptiness that results from assumptions, such as Rose's, that the child is inaccessible as a character and thus impossible to create. Taking my lead from Burnett and Montgomery, who believe in the possible rather than the impossible, I do not see the child – reader or character – as empty or Other. In my argument, adult desire does not limit or control the child character but energizes him into independence accompanied by agency. And, in terms of the adult writer's distance from the child reader, it is important to remember that Burnett and Montgomery retain and cultivate close ties to childhood that emphasize the continuum of childhood into adulthood, demonstrating the artificiality of divisions and separations based on age and stage. As the introduction to this collection of essays stresses, Montgomery's keen visual memory and use of her journal contribute to the ease with which she is able to recreate and re-enter childhood in a fluid manner.[13]

The suffering, vulnerability, and loss experienced by the dream boy or beautiful boy recall the qualities of various boyhoods explored by Rita Bode in this collection's previous chapter. The dream boy and beautiful boy function as recognizable poses and performances in the manner theorized by Judith Butler in *Gender Trouble: Feminism and the Subversion of Identity*.[14] The performance in this case is that of vulnerability and sensitivity in boy characters treated as outsiders by society. Bode, in her discussion of boyology, draws attention to the movement's goals to train, tame, and civilize boys and their temperaments. The dream boy, although not subjected to the correction aimed at the bad boy, is similarly pressured to join the mainstream. Sharing qualities with the artistic and sensitive boy – with Teddy rather than Perry – the dream boy must move himself from the quiet margins of thought, contemplation, and beauty to the robust activity of society.

In this chapter, I examine the conversation that emerges when dream boys in Montgomery's *Anne of Avonlea* and Burnett's *Little Lord Fauntleroy* are read together within the context of the Kenneth Ritchie episode and the western tradition of what Germaine Greer identifies as that of "the beautiful boy." I then introduce *The Secret Garden* (1911) into the conversation, focusing on the pairing of the dream boy with a foil who accentuates and makes more specific his idealized qualities. The partnerships of Paul Irving and Davy Keith in *Anne of Avonlea* and Dickon Sowerby and Colin Craven in *The Secret Garden* work in ways that both promote and temper the idealized boy of beauty and charm. I argue that this pairing of opposites accentuates the artificiality of the contrast between two extremes. The breaking of the rigid opposition mitigates the space between the two "types," freeing both characters from their impossible designations as purely good or unrelentingly bad. Paul and Dickon are released from the tension holding them firmly in place within their circumscribed ideal positions. Moreover, the writer is released from her investment in fixing the character in idealized beauty and goodness once he begins to demonstrate agency beyond the scripted behaviour of the beautiful boy. When Paul and Dickon break out of their passive positions, they become fuller characters, complicating and surprising readers' assumptions and expectations through this release into independence, action, and agency following the fulfillment of their roles as ideals. Importantly, the beauty and goodness of the dream boy are powerful and influential, bringing about changes in the adult world, rather than being controlled and manipulated by that world. I conclude this chapter by briefly considering the role played by "real" children – Montgomery's sons, Chester and Stuart Macdonald, and Burnett's sons, Lionel and Vivian Burnett – in the creation and nuanced complications applied to the dream boy.

In *Everyday Magic: Child Languages in Canadian Literature*, Laurie Ricou articulates the challenges of writing from and through the point of view of the very young child, arguing that "the writer, it seems, must use enough child's language to give a consistent feel of what the child would say, yet exploit fully his mature technical resources to suggest the complexity of the child's mind."[15] Honeyman, more extreme in her assessment, argues that "there is a language gap, an inherent inaccessibility, between the concept of 'child' and the adult minds that create it."[16] Montgomery falls prey to that perceived gap when the *Spectator*'s reviewer of *Anne of Green Gables* finds fault in Anne's "precocity," based on an objection to an eleven-year-old's appreciation of the lines, "Quick as the slaughtered squadrons fell / In Midian's evil day." Not surprisingly, Montgomery, who was only nine when "those lines thrilled [her] very soul," dismisses the reviewer's condescending assumptions and assessment of Anne as precocious.[17] Rose, like the reviewer, focuses on the impossibility of accessibility, pointing out that "children's fiction sets up a world in which the adult comes first (author, maker, giver) and the child comes after (reader, product, receiver), but where neither of them enter the space in between."[18]

Such views have been challenged by Gubar in her proposal of a kinship model, in which "our younger and older selves are multiple and interlinked, akin to one another rather than wholly distinct."[19] And, most importantly, in my view, an emphasis on impossibility and inaccessibility based on a supposed void separating child and adult sells the child short through a misuse of the term and concept of "the precocious child," which essentializes and limits the child's abilities as unnaturally strange and not really her own in their adult-like qualities. As Lesley Clement points out in her chapter in this volume, precocious child characters, "those with verbal dexterity, active imaginations and curiosity, resourcefulness, and resilience," are well placed to develop the skills needed to negotiate dangerous challenges and thus survive.[20] Verbal dexterity includes the child's appreciation and use of what is considered adult-like language. Perry Nodelman persuasively points out that children's literature is "rich in irony, in ambiguity, in linguistic subtlety."[21] Ricou's assessment of the creation of child language as challenging stresses its possibility, albeit difficult, rather than its impossibility. He delights in the complexity of successful creations of such language in Canadian literature. Montgomery's and Burnett's child languages are the basis of the irony, ambiguity, and, most importantly, subtlety at play in their novels. Such language is neither precious nor precocious, although it may be viewed as such by undiscerning adults.

The enforcement of the child into blankness and innocence "comes at the child as a denial of a whole host of capacities, an emptying out," to use Kincaid's words.[22] Such a fixing and holding obviously takes place during Montgomery's initial meeting with Kenneth Ritchie and is disrupted by the later meeting, during which the more active and articulate seven-year-old fails to live up to the earlier ideal. The fictional Paul Irving, on the other hand, created by Montgomery one year before she met Kenneth, is initially fixed and held in place much more easily than the real boy, because he does not unexpectedly or prematurely break the mould or disrupt the ideal. Unlike the strangely silent and static Kenneth, however, Paul speaks eloquently and performs romantic acts of boyish love, his ideal qualities clearly lodged in his beauty, poetic imagination, and altruistic gestures. There is depth and complexity to his character that Montgomery allows to develop in ways that imbue the developing boy with individuality and agency, particularly as he grows into love and family.

The prototype for Paul Irving is clearly Burnett's Cedric Errol. The numerous and lavish descriptions of Cedric emphasize his "curly yellow hair," his "handsome and strong and rosy" qualities, his "cheerful, fearless, quaint little way of making friends with people," his "confiding nature," "kind little heart," quickness "to understand the feelings of those about him," and "a childish soul [that] was full of kindness and innocent warm feeling."[23] When Anne first sees Paul Irving, she thinks "he had the most beautiful little face she had ever seen in a child," with "features of exquisite delicacy and refinement, framed in a halo of chestnut curls." She notes his "crimson lips" and a smile that signals "the outflashing of a hidden personality, rare and fine and sweet."[24] The outer beauty of Paul, like that of Cedric, reflects precious inner gifts.

Physically, Cedric and Paul fit into the tradition of the beautiful boy as established and recognized in western culture. In her study of this figure, Greer emphasizes the "short-lived charm of boys," itemizing the climax of the boy's beauty perceived over the centuries as occurring when "his cheeks are still smooth, his body hairless, his head full-maned, his eyes clear, his manner shy and his belly flat." The description highlights conventionally feminine qualities and a lack of development or maturation. Greer's study exposes the historical tradition of boyhood as an intensely brief and transient stage, its fragility apparent through the belief that "the more beautiful the boy, the less likely he is to survive." The resistance to the end of boyhood is seen in the observation that "for centuries European mothers wept when their sons were breeched and their hair shorn." Greer details how the "charms of extended boyhood" were valued and even worshipped, as established by the prevalent position of Apollo as boy-god. Most significant perhaps in Greer's discussion of the boy's physical attributes is her observation that sixteenth-century portraits show "male children as elfin creatures with floating curls and muslin skirts or as tough mini-men in breeches."[25] The boy is either feminized or toughened into static positions and postures. Cedric and Paul, although feminized, are not static – they are beautiful in action and temperament as well as appearance. Cedric's generous philanthropy and Paul's artistic temperament provide them with a sensitivity that invigorates their actions with dynamic energy, producing a beauty of wholeness that renders the external appearance less startling or out of place precisely because it is viewed in conjunction with extraordinary actions that confirm internal as well as external beauty. Rather than persisting as a flat type or thin concept, the beautiful boy character in Burnett's and Montgomery's novels is deepened, filled, and animated.

Kenneth, unlike the fictional characters, unexpectedly outgrows the beauty of young boyhood, in what Montgomery judges to be awkward and disturbing ways. The sources of disappointment that meet her in the seven-year-old Kenneth consist of his hair being "clipped to the bone" and his shapeless clothing giving him the appearance of being a "grown-up dwarf." She makes a half-hearted attempt to reclaim the ideal boy through his "beautiful brown eyes," the only familiar feature untouched by maturation, but seems to resent the effort such a reclamation would entail. She maintains that had she tried to "get acquainted with him all over again," she thinks she would have found him "loving and charming *enough* in his new incarnation," suggesting the requirement of a strange minimum standard of charm dependent on her own effort and investment.[26] Montgomery realizes that the changes in hair and clothing have transformed the ideal boy – small and feminine – into a boy who shows signs of disorder and masculinity, and that her attempt to fix Kenneth through a kind of Peter Pan syndrome into a boy arrested before his development has been undone by the passage of time. He eludes such fixing by growing older, larger, and awkward. The fictional Cedric and Paul make much more pleasing transitions from an American boy to a British lord and from a sensitive child to an artistic and loving son, respectively, never forfeiting or outgrowing their beauty and goodness but growing gracefully into it.

Paul becomes the object of desire for both his teacher, Anne Shirley, and his potential mother, Miss Lavendar. The ways in which the fictional characters of Anne and Miss Lavendar fulfill their desires through interactions with the dream boy in the form of Paul Irving reflect how Montgomery satisfies her own desires for beauty and genius through her construction of this idealized character. Desire for the writer Montgomery, the teacher Anne Shirley, and the unfulfilled Miss Lavendar is based on a need to prolong and return to that moment of boyhood that immediately precedes the acquisition and demonstration of any language, thought, or behaviour conveying male power and authority. Honeyman, referring to the process of "reversing development," examines the common movement or impulse to return to childhood as a state and stage that is "intuitive, natural and untainted by socialization."[27] Similarly, Rose refers to the backward momentum as a move to "a primitive or lost state to which the child has special access."[28] This is the role and space that Montgomery gives to four-year-old Kenneth. His malleability and receptivity invite her to fill and shape him according to her desire for the pure, the natural, and the primitive.

The eloquent Paul, in contrast to Kenneth, is anything but blank. Significantly, however, Anne forms her initial bond with him in silence, through the gaze and a "quick interchange of smiles … before a word had passed between them." Unlike Kenneth, Paul, through what Anne describes as an "outflashing," projects a personality "rare and fine and sweet." Moreover, he reflects and duplicates Anne, who realizes that "there was a soul subtly akin to her own gazing at her out of the very dark blue eyes that were watching her so intently."[29] Disturbingly narcissistic, the uncanny mutual gaze seems to exist to reinforce for Anne her own temperament. As a created fictional character, Paul, unlike Kenneth, can behave in ways that confirm, feed, and duplicate not only Anne's but also Montgomery's desire for beauty, goodness, and creativity.

Miss Lavendar never allows her "dream boy," who eventually becomes a form of Paul, to "get any older than eleven or twelve," thus serving her maternal desire for the prepubescent boy, as well as arresting the passage of time to prolong the possibility of recovering opportunities of lost love. Paul is diminutive and feminine, stepping into Miss Lavendar's desire for a Peter Pan–like child who resists growing up. Anne's comments that Paul at ten "looked no more than eight" and that "he had a sober, grave, meditative expression, as if his spirit was much older than his body" accentuate the retention of a feminine boyish beauty, along with a remarkable genius, in one who appears much younger than he is. Contributing then to the unusual attraction of Paul is the impression that "his spirit was much older than his body."[30]

Similarly, the charm of Cedric lies in a disparity between appearance and age – in "a mixture of maturity and childishness." Those he meets are delighted by his "sage little air," the combination of "his occasionally elderly remarks and the extreme innocence and seriousness of his round, childish face," which is "irresistible." His powerful impact on Mr Havisham, the lawyer, is based in this startling mixture: "His beauty was something unusual. He had a strong, lithe, graceful little body and a manly little face; he held his childish head up, and carried himself with a brave air" and had "innocently fearless eyes." Although it is his beauty that initially attracts attention and his mixture of boyishness and maturity that captivates those around him, it is his kindness that wins people over and brings about change. The response of the rector, Mr Mordaunt, to Cedric's smile, for example, focuses on "his kind little heart": "He liked the little fellow from that instant – as in fact people always did like him. And it was not the boy's beauty and grace which most appealed to him; it was the simple, natural kindliness in the little lad which made any words he uttered, however quaint and unexpected, sound pleasant and sincere."[31]

Cedric has a positive impact on many, but it is his influence on his grandfather, the Earl, that brings about the most astounding change. In a reversal of adults filling the emptiness of the child figure with their needs and desires,

Cedric fills his grandfather with his own admirable and precocious boyish qualities, resulting in Cedric's goodness being reflected back to him. For the Earl, "to see each of his ugly, selfish motives changed into a good and generous one by the simplicity of a child was a singular experience."[32] Cedric's confidence in the good and generous qualities of his grandfather is more than simply a desire to see the positive. His automatic assumption of the presence of his own positive traits in his grandfather constitutes a faith in all of humanity, which lifts the Earl into the optimistic world in which Cedric walks. Cedric does not so much influence his grandfather as fill him with a goodness that displaces the selfishness Cedric is incapable of seeing. Although such faith is somewhat naive, it is also empowering in its affirmation of the impact of the child's needs and desires on those around him and on the world in which he lives and loves.

Anne sees in Paul her own imagination and love of beauty reflected back to her. He reinforces the qualities and temperament she holds dear in both child and adult – and confirms that these qualities, subdued in so many by the passage into maturity, will be retained by Paul as she herself has retained them. The more complex interaction is between Paul and Miss Lavendar. When he asks her if she has any boys of her own, she replies that she has a little dream boy; in response to Paul's question about how old he is, she replies: "About your age I think. He ought to be older because I dreamed him long before you were born. But I'll never let him get any older than eleven or twelve; because if I did some day he might grow up altogether and then I'd lose him."[33] The dream boy is a receptacle for Miss Lavendar's maternal love, disappointment, and regret, and performs a major role in her attempt to arrest time. The entry of Paul and all that he brings into her life breaks the spell she has cast, breathing life into her frozen figure and allowing time to progress. Paul allays the disappointment and loneliness of Miss Lavendar; Cedric softens and humanizes the Earl. Cedric allows for the creation of a grandfather, while Paul brings motherhood to Miss Lavendar. The dream boys are unaware of their roles in reversing the static positions of the older generation. Through their genuinely sincere performances of beauty and goodness, they fill the emptiness of loss with love. Rather than being fixed by others, they initiate the movement that releases the adults they love from the static positions those adults have imposed upon themselves. Cedric and Paul refuse to remain fixed in place by those who gaze in wonder at them, responding to those gazes with actions that release their much-needed beauty and goodness into the adult world.

The gaze attempts to fix in place the figure gazed upon. Greer, who describes the female gaze on the young boy as "desirous," points out that, regardless of the gender of the artist and subject, "the viewer is masterful and empowered; the viewee mastered." The same can be said of the writer. Greer devotes a chapter of *The Beautiful Boy* to "The Passive Love Object," whose "function is not to do love but to allow love." She uses the example of the sleeping boy as the embodiment of passivity that, similar to emptiness or blankness, invites external desires to fill and awaken the figure. Greer's thesis that "art is fundamentally narcissistic and elegiac" can be applied to Montgomery's and Burnett's fixing of Paul and Cedric, respectively, in a dream boyhood, a state initially imposed by the gaze of the writers and reinforced by the gazes of characters.[34] The desire to retain the boyish qualities of the dream boy are seen in characters such as Miss Lavendar, who resists the presence of masculinity and the passage of time. Significantly, however, the dream boy in *Little Lord Fauntleroy* and *Anne of Avonlea* does not remain static in that role but enacts his goodness and beauty, thus breaking the fixed position and serving as the source of movement that allows time to progress and the future to arrive.

It is through the contrasts between the good and bad boy that more specific qualities of beauty and goodness come to light in Burnett's and Montgomery's versions of the dream boy. For example, the naughty Davy Keith in *Anne of Avonlea* and the sour Colin Craven in *The Secret Garden* highlight by contrast the affiliation of the beautiful boy with the natural world. Written only two years apart, these novels endorse the importance of nature and the outdoor world in the development of the child and locate the source of the unusual beauty and goodness of the dream boy in his relationship with nature.

In *Magic Island: The Fictions of L.M. Montgomery*, Elizabeth Waterston notes the literary convention of twins, including the predecessors of *Anne of Avonlea*'s Davy and Dora Keith. She also points out the "bad boy books" that influenced Montgomery's creation of Davy and the impact of "stories of the double," in which "the strongly contrasted pair imply a deeper duality of disruption and conformity, both in society and in the individual psyche."[35] The working out of psychological and societal polarities through Davy's and Dora's gendered behaviour is central to *Anne of Avonlea*, but the focus on duality extends to include the good- and bad-boy dichotomy of Davy and Paul as well. The difference is lodged in the ways the boys "play" with nature. Caroline Jones, in her article "Idylls of Play: L.M. Montgomery's Child-Worlds," stresses the importance of nature and demonstrates that "Montgomery's child protagonists use play not simply to have fun but to find and make a place for themselves, particularly as they face families or communities that fail to understand or value them,"[36] which is certainly the case for both Davy and Paul. Davy brings nature indoors when he thrusts a "furry squirming caterpillar" down Lauretta White's neck in church and puts a toad in Marilla's bed.[37] Davy, in his conversations with Anne after such boyishly mischievous acts, brings in the perfection of the slightly older Paul, whom he assumes Anne views as a desirable role model for good behaviour. One of the main differences between the two boys, as noted by Anne, is Davy's practicality and complete lack of imagination as opposed to Paul's imaginative creativity. Paul may be seen by many in Avonlea as having too much imagination, approaching that category of "queerness" that makes Avonlea's inhabitants so uncomfortable, but for those who know Paul well, his imagination provides the strength that allows him to cope and is the foundation of his beauty and goodness.[38] The source of the imagination itself lies in Paul's intimate relationship with the natural world. This relationship is clearly displayed for Anne and the reader when Paul is "stretched out on the grassy bank beside the thick fir grove that sheltered the house on the north, absorbed in a book of fairy tales."[39] Uniting the imaginary and the natural through the act of reading fairy tales in the grove, Paul, by taking the book from the indoor setting into the outdoor world, reverses Davy's perverse placement of the outdoors in the indoor spaces of church and bedroom. Paul's reading of the fairy realm and natural world expands his vision, whereas Davy's use of nature to trick and upset others diminishes him, placing him in the role of the bad boy.

Significantly, it is through Anne's gaze that the reader sees Paul at home in nature, "sitting on the fence in the shadows of the spruces … a boy with big, dreamy eyes and a beautiful, sensitive face."[40] Responding to Paul with deep understanding, Anne sees her own sensitive and imaginative temperament reflected back to her in Paul's face and her own devotion to nature in his comfortable position among the trees. Although Anne sincerely delights in Paul's sensitive nature, her response is partially a reinforcement of the childhood values she holds dear, even while others, such as Diana, are growing away from them. Davy is the bad boy who does not even touch the edges of the rich world of nature and fancy inhabited by Paul and Anne, and yet Anne loves him despite his somewhat shallow temperament. He is lovable but does not reflect Anne's own desires back to her, so is a project rather than a mirror.

Paul's letter about the rock people who live at the shore affords a glimpse into his elaborate mixture of the fanciful and the natural. Firmly based in named caves and rocks on the actual shore, these imaginary friends travel through moonglades into the moon and sail into the sunset, "a land all flowers, like a great garden."[41] The natural setting of the shore, where the voyages begin, and the transformation of the imaginary destinations into gardens, meadows, and flowers involve both real and fanciful nature; the real rock shore nurtures Paul in his daily life, providing "scope for imagination,"[42] while the garden growing out of the journeys of the shore people is the product of his imaginary impulses. Physical and imaginary journeys begin and end in the natural world for Paul, often in flowers and gardens, in a novel in which Hester Gray's garden is both a real and an idealized space of romance and story. Jones points out that Paul's imaginative play in the natural world involves an "opening of [Annis] Pratt's feminine 'green world' to masculine characters of a certain sensibility."[43]

The dichotomy between the interior domestic world and the natural world is much more pronounced in the good- and bad-boy pairing in *The Secret Garden*, with the badness of Colin Craven, confined to his bedroom, contrasting with the goodness of the earthy Dickon, who essentially lives on the moors. Rather than one boy bringing the outdoors in and the other bringing the indoors out, or one using nature to trick and shock and the other transcending nature to access an imaginary fairyland garden, *The Secret Garden* works with the more literal extremes of interior and exterior spaces. One boy is shut indoors, where he cannot benefit from the natural world at all, and the other is immersed in the natural world that sustains him and his family physically, emotionally, and psychologically. Dickon, "a common moor boy" conversant with squirrels, pheasants, and rabbits, dwells with the "heather and grass and leaves" that lend him their scent. Dickon possesses the unusual qualities of the "beautiful boy"; his cheeks are "as red as poppies," his eyes "round" and "blue," his mouth "wide, red, curving," and his hair "curly, rust-colored." He is gifted, as he works his magic on those who need it most, and, like Paul, he brings together those who have been estranged. Deriving his unusual empathy and understanding from the earthiness of nature and its creatures, Dickon possesses a healthy body and mind that works directly and indirectly on the unhealthy Colin. Like Paul, Dickon is an astutely perceptive reader of others. As "an animal charmer he could see more things than most people could and many of them were things he never talked about. He saw some of them now in this boy [Colin]."[44] Montgomery believes in the imagination; Burnett believes in what she terms magic. The infusion of the conclusion of *The Secret Garden* with the suggestion of uncanny magic places Dickon's powers within the larger forces at work in the scientific world of the time and within Burnett's own beliefs that science and nature hold elements of magic that call for wonder and positive thinking.[45]

Whereas Paul moves from the rocky shore to imaginary worlds, Dickon digs into the dirt to connect with what is actually there – with the life that grows out of the ground. Paul does not have much of an impact on Davy beyond serving as a role model to improve his manners and behaviour. His real impact is on Miss Lavendar. Dickon, on the other hand, works magic on his doppelgänger, Colin – magic that originates in him but involves forces beyond himself. Both Paul and Dickon work through other characters to reach the one who needs their influence the most – Paul working through Anne, and Dickon through Mary Lennox – characters who join with the dream boy they admire to bring about much-desired changes from loneliness to love.

The power of Paul resides in his presence, which encourages the recovery of lost love by bringing together his father and Miss Lavendar. Paul's romantic imagination initiates the forward movement of time in the slowed-down world of Echo Lodge. Dickon's healing power, which unites Colin with his father, Archibald Craven, is derived from his affinity with the natural world and works its magic on the sterility of Misselthwaite Manor. The impact of the beautiful boy resides in his gifted ability to break the spell of arrested development lodged in disappointed characters and relationships. Instilling desire in others to connect with those who can still love them after a passage of time, Paul and Dickon bring together, through the imagination, faith, and power of the natural world, forces and people who have been apart. The result is a more holistic family and community. The position and qualities of the beautiful and good dream boy, poised on the edge of adulthood but not yet there, provide the influences and power that can bring about these connections and changes.

Both Montgomery and Burnett incorporated elements of their own sons in their fictional boys. Montgomery's sons were born after the publication of *Anne of Avonlea* in 1909, so did not influence the early creation of the dream boy in the form of Paul Irving, but they resonate with later versions of the idealized figure, such as Walter Blythe and Teddy Kent. The darkness and worry associated by Montgomery with Chester, as documented by Bode in chapter 3 of this volume,[46] placed Stuart in an ever-increasing light, resulting in the two sons becoming studies in contrast as Chester sank ever lower into troubled and disturbing behaviour. The dichotomy was not simply between good and bad but between decent and deviant, as Montgomery herself recognized. Burnett's sons, Lionel (1874–1890) and Vivian (1876–1937), were also paired as opposites. Lionel died at the age of sixteen, twenty-one years before the publication of *The Secret Garden*. Elizabeth Lennox Keyser proposes that "the idealized Colin seems to represent [Burnett's] elder son, Lionel, and his recovery a wish-fulfilling revision of what actually happened."[47] Lionel's illness and early death confirmed him as the lost son, leaving Vivian, who had been the model for Little Lord Fauntleroy, to be loved and indulged as the remaining son. This pairing of opposites is based on the dichotomies of the ill and healthy, the dying and thriving, the absent and lasting. Both Montgomery and Burnett were deeply devoted to their sons, pouring passionate maternal love and hope into them. Each felt the keen disappointment of losing sons, whether through disillusionment or death, resulting in an even deeper investment in the ones who remained.

Montgomery's resistance to her sons' transitions from infancy to boyhood to adolescence reflects a desire for the safety of what she sees as the innocence of earlier states, along with a sense that transitions themselves are dangerous. Mary Douglas, in *Purity and Danger*, discusses early-twentieth-century beliefs that "to have been in the margins [of transition] is to have been in contact with danger, to have been at the source of power." The French ethnographer and folklorist Arnold van Gennep, who is best known for his pioneering work on "rites of passage" and liminality, also saw danger in transitional states; in the words of Douglas, van Gennep believed that "because transition is neither one state nor the next, it is undefinable" and the person making the transition is "in danger and emanates danger to others."[48] As Chester leaves infancy, Montgomery mourns the increasing distance between son and mother, which seems strangely and ominously threatening. When Chester is finally weaned in May 1913, she refers to him as "a big sturdy man-child" in his creepers and, one month later in June, as "my little man-child." The hyphenated label of man-child and the contradictory applications of the adjectives "big" and "little" convey a disturbing intersection of innocence and maturity in the transitioning child. The most extreme mourning for the passage away from infancy takes place in October 1912, when Montgomery and her cousin, Frede Campbell, "shorten" Chester, after which she says she "could have wept" and "felt as if he were dead." According to Montgomery, the short clothes lacked the "sacredness" of the infant's garments, and with the disappearance of "my little baby" came "just a big fat chubby-legged 'bouncing boy'" in his place.[49]

Most significantly, the acquisition of language changes the maternal relationship with Chester. With his first words he becomes a "wee man," "a big boyish boy."[50] Attempts to make the man small and the boy, although large, still boyish, result in almost "oaf"-like qualities that recall the "dwarf"-like appearance of seven-year-old Kenneth. The transitional state and its results proclaim an unsettling mixture of life stages and appearances that fail to coalesce. This is not an example of a wiser and older spirit residing in a younger body, but is instead an unsettling combination of disparate physical characteristics and inner qualities. The difficult transition extends to behaviour as well as appearance. Honeyman emphasizes that "the receding linguistic barrier" separates the child from the infant, the word "infant" "com[ing] from the Latin and French for 'not yet speaking.'" With the acquisition of language comes the ability not only to reason and communicate but also to lie. Honeyman astutely points out that "the lying child is a literary representation of the romantic philosophy that language itself is unavoidably deceitful."[51] The lying child is, of course, a major motif in Montgomery's work, as seen, for example, in the character of Davy, who lies about shutting Dora in Mr Harrison's toolhouse,[52] and in Anne Shirley's story about the amethyst brooch, as discussed by Åsa Warnqvist in her chapter in this volume.[53] For readers of Montgomery's journals, who learn about the lies and deceit of Chester's adolescent and adult behaviour, this original acquisition of language becomes all the more significant and poignant.

In her journaling, Montgomery, through Chester and Stuart, explores precocious boyish activity, turning from ideal forms to amusing and charming anecdotes when, to quote Ricou, "the child finds his experience constantly running ahead of his language." The child figure, both real and fictional, is at times and to degrees constructed and used by Montgomery in a manner identified by Ricou as "a presence, a vehicle representing a way of seeing, rather than an individual who has been part of the writer's own personal experience."[54] Throughout her life and career, Montgomery's own desires played a role in her construction of the fictional child, but never at the expense of the character's independence and agency. Her accurate observations, engaged interest in psychology, and belief in the child's unusual value and abilities assured the creation of fictional children who display the agency and power in which she so fervently believed.

In his biography of his mother,[55] Vivian Burnett claims that her "sweetest and most complete romance was her children." The son-biographer goes on to say that "to be a gay, helpful, understanding companion to her little boys, was the ideal for which she strove, and not to have been considerate, not to have understood, to have added one ounce to the weight of their smallest childish woes, would be crimes long to accuse herself of committing." In the chapter entitled "Dearest and Her Children," Vivian recounts the brushing and curling of hair as "a sort of sacrament of mother worship in which no doubt the fragrance of the laddies' hair was a sort of incense."[56] The use of Vivian as a model for Little Lord Fauntleroy did not go unnoticed by the public. In a newspaper article, Burnett wrote back against criticism of the way she dressed and posed her sons:

> That the little boys have been beautiful has not been my fault nor their misfortune. Their tendency to pose I have sometimes had reason to regret. I have seen them repose in attitudes replete with grace, suspended by their feet from apple trees with their hyacinthe locks sweeping the dust and having somewhat the appearance of an entirely new species of yellow mop. I have seen them pose upon one foot upon the top of an iron-spiked fence; I have seen them pose on adjacent roofs, their purely Greek countenances aglow with rapt contemplation at the thought that at least they had attained an altitude which a mis-step could cause to result in their being dashed into minute fragments; and a maternal feebleness has led me at such times to deplore the rooted tendency to the ideal, the sublime and the beautiful in posturing.[57]

Lionel and Vivian were, for Burnett, the most beautiful of boys. Like Montgomery, she mourned their growth away from boyhood and revelled in the precocious and posed performances she encouraged, particularly in the boyish clothing and posturing that delighted her. A sheet of manuscript paper with a paragraph outlining the qualities of Vivian marks the genesis of the character of Lord Fauntleroy: "He was such a handsome, blooming, curly-headed little fellow that when he sat down and nursed his knee with his chubby hands and conversed with such guileless wisdom, his hearers were always tempted to lead him on asking him questions to see what he would say." Lionel's death devastated Burnett, and, as she sat by his deathbed, she saw and described a boy much younger than his sixteen years: "I have suffered so much I cannot forget it. I cannot get over it. My poor boy was so beautiful and so sweet. He grew lovelier every hour, and every hour we were dearer and nearer to each other – Oh! *how* we loved each other! No one can know."[58]

The beautiful boy of genius, purity, and imagination, as seen in Kenneth Ritchie, as created in Cedric Errol and Paul Irving, and as developed in Dickon Sowerby, Walter Blythe, and Teddy Kent, existed in the real Chester and Stuart Macdonald and in the real Lionel and Vivian Burnett before they outgrew a boyhood of smooth skin, precocious language, and naive goodness. The heartache caused by Chester, beloved in his early years and the cause of anguish as he matured, exemplifies the grief, suffering, and disappointment brought about by the replacement of the idealized beautiful boy with an emerging and difficult man-child.[59] The idealized boy is arrested and held by Burnett in the dying figure of Lionel and in the dress and performance of Vivian as Little Lord Fauntleroy. The two extremes of the beautiful boy and the lost boy seen in the actual sons of Montgomery and Burnett introduce nuanced layers to their fictional creations of boyhood. In the fictional character, they can prevent or at least manage to some extent the Wordsworthian "Shades of the prison-house" as they "begin to close / Upon the growing Boy"[60] in a way that they cannot do for real children, especially their own. Montgomery's and Burnett's fictional boys, however, like real boys, do take on lives of their own, growing into themselves as they are animated into substance and agency by writers who, like Wordsworth, both "create and perceive," initially creating through desire and subsequently perceiving their characters at work in the text and the world.[61]

NOTES

1 LMM, *CJ* 2:322.

2 LMM, *CJ* 3:110.

3 "Uncle" Paul, as a famous poet, is named as Walter Blythe's "model" in *Rainbow Valley*. LMM, *RV*, 22.

4 Richardson, "Reluctant Lords," 6.

5 "Studies in Canadian Village Life," 77.

6 LMM, *CJ* 2:42.

7 Honeyman, *Elusive Childhood*, 2.

8 Rose, *Case of Peter Pan*, 3–4.

9 Kincaid, *Child-Loving*, 12, 5, 7.

10 Kincaid, *Erotic Innocence*, 53 (emphasis in original), 16.

11 Gubar, "Risky Business," 451.

12 See Gubar, *Artful Dodgers*, 29–33, and Rudd, *Reading the Child*, 17–38.

13 "Introduction," 10–11, in this volume.

14 Butler, *Gender Trouble*, 171–90.

15 Ricou, *Everyday Magic*, 2.

16 Honeyman, *Elusive Childhood*, 4.

17 LMM, *CJ* 2:352.

18 Rose, *Case of Peter Pan*, 1–2.

19 Gubar, "Risky Business," 454.

20 Clement, "L.M. Montgomery's Precocious Children," 50, in this volume.

21 Nodelman, "The Case of Children's Fiction," 99, 100.

22 Kincaid, *Child-Loving*, 73.

23 F.H. Burnett, *Little Lord Fauntleroy*, 9.

24 LMM, *AA*, 38–9.

25 Greer, *Beautiful Boy*, 7, 196, 14, 49, 37, 14.

26 LMM, *CJ* 3:110 (emphasis added).

27 Honeyman, *Elusive Childhood*, 80.

28 Rose, *Case of Peter Pan*, 9.

29 LMM, *AA*, 39, 38, 39, 38.

30 Ibid., 288, 38, 39.

31 F.H. Burnett, *Little Lord Fauntleroy*, 38, 34, 18, 59.

32 Ibid., 63.

33 LMM, *AA*, 288.

34 Greer, *Beautiful Boy*, 236, 228,105.

35 Waterston, *Magic Island*, 23.

36 Jones, "Idylls of Play," 105.

37 LMM, *AA*, 70, 73–4.

38 Walter Blythe shares Paul's love of reading in nature. In chapter 3 of *Rainbow Valley*, for example, he is introduced in a position that defines him – reading a volume of poems underneath the White Lady. LMM, *RV*, 22.

39 LMM, *AA*, 186.

40 Ibid., 144.

41 Ibid., 107.

42 LMM, *AGG*, 12.

43 Jones, "Idylls of Play," 113.

44 F.H. Burnett, *Secret Garden*, 117, 114, 116, 117, 325–6.

45 See Adams, "Secrets and Healing Magic," 52, for one discussion of how magic works in the conclusion of *The Secret Garden*.

46 Bode, "Vulnerable Situations," 72–4, in this volume.

47 Keyser, "'Quite Contrary,'" 10–11.

48 M. Douglas, *Purity and Danger*, 120, 119.

49 LMM, *CJ* 3:99, 101, 84.

50 Ibid., 157.

51 Honeyman, *Elusive Childhood*, 116, 129.

52 LMM, *AA*, 87–90.

53 See Warnqvist, "Loving, Larking, and Lying," 167, in this volume.

54 Ricou, *Everyday Magic*, 50, 93.

55 One month after his mother's death, Vivian Burnett began to devote his time and energy to researching and writing the biography of his mother, *The Romantick Lady: The Life Story of an Imagination* (see Gerzina, *Frances Hodgson Burnett*, 304). In the late 1970s, Stuart Macdonald contacted Mary Rubio to publish his mother's journals and to write her biography (see Rubio, *Lucy Maud Montgomery*, 5–7). Both sons wanted input into how their mothers' lives were depicted and remembered.

56 V. Burnett, *Romantick Lady*, 129, 135.

57 Quoted in ibid., 137.

58 V. Burnett, *Romantick Lady*, 144, 213 (emphasis in original).

59 See Bode, "Vulnerable Situations," 72–3, in this volume, for references to Montgomery's fear that Chester's early maturation could have been inherited from

Ewan and could bring other undesirable qualities with it. This early and intense maturation exacerbates the already uneasy feelings associated with Chester's transition from boy to man.

60 Wordsworth, "Ode: Intimations of Immortality," ll. 67–8.

61 For the concept of both creating and perceiving, see Wordsworth, "Lines Composed a Few Miles above Tintern Abbey," ll. 106–7, and *The Prelude*, Book 2, l. 274 (1805), l. 258 (1850).

5

Lost Boys and Lost Girls: The Kindred Offspring of J.M. Barrie and L.M. Montgomery

BONNIE J. TULLOCH

Classic children's books like J.M. Barrie's *Peter Pan* (1911) and L.M. Montgomery's *Anne of Green Gables* (1908) reflect one of the powerful ways adults invent ideas about childhood.[1] In their narrative depictions of children's lives, adults explore their perceptions of how children and, by extension, they themselves should be and behave. The problem with these narrative inventions, however, is that they are often premised on a binary logic that subverts the reality they attempt to represent, for, as Jacqueline Rose points out, if childhood and adulthood are separate stages of existence, how is it possible for adults to create *children's* literature?[2] Viewed from this perspective, children's literature functions as a nonsensical space, one that the adult writer and the child reader cohabit. And yet, as a seemingly impossible creation, it is entirely possible that some children's literature purposely subverts the *sense* underlying cultural narratives of childhood. Such is the case, this chapter argues, with *Peter Pan* and *Anne of Green Gables*. Barrie's and Montgomery's casts of lost characters invite readers to recognize that, regardless of their age, people never stop being children.

This argument concerning the possibility of lifelong childhood extends to the authors themselves. Read in relation to their personal memoirs, one can see how writing *Peter Pan* and *Anne of Green Gables* allowed Barrie (1860–1937) and Montgomery (1874–1942) to question the logic of the cultural roles that defined their lives as adults. In the creation of these novels, both authors were able to access experiences that their society suggested were lost to them as mature human beings. According to Jackie Wullschläger, the Victorian era privileged two views of childhood, the first being that it is "a special state," with the child functioning "as a symbol, in a prosperous, progressive society, of hope and optimism," the second being that children are "good, innocent and in some way connected with spirituality and imagination." Between the Victorian and the Edwardian eras, she observes, a shift occurred "from an emphasis on the child as moral icon, emblem of purity, to a craze for the child as fun-loving playboy hero."[3] Barrie seems to promote this latter view when he describes children as "gay and innocent and heartless."[4] Situated within the changing cultural context of these eras and their different views of childhood, the fictional worlds of Neverland and Avonlea provide him and Montgomery, respectively, with the space to deconstruct some of the problematic assumptions that separate adults and children. These assumptions include the association of children with imagination, play, and nonsense, and the association of adults with reality, work, and sense. In their novels and autobiographical writing, Barrie and Montgomery question the logic of these associations and the age limitations they place on human experience.

But what is the age limit associated with childhood? While the exact number of years varies across time periods and contexts (not to mention personal experiences), Barrie's and Montgomery's writing indicates that the age of twelve marked a significant year in both of their lives.[5] In his memoir of his mother, *Margaret Ogilvy* (1896), Barrie states that "nothing that happens after we are twelve matters very much."[6] The fact that Montgomery spends much of her own memoir, *The Alpine Path* (1917), discussing her pre-teen years implies her agreement with this statement.[7] Of course, Barrie's and Montgomery's continued fascination with the events of their younger years suggests that the age of twelve did not mark the end of their childhood per se, as much as it did their awareness that this was the time society started viewing them differently. Wullschläger writes that "the 1833 Factory Act, limiting children under thirteen to eight hours work a day, was the first legal definition of childhood in terms of age in English history."[8] For Barrie and Montgomery, the age of thirteen also seemed to signify a new period of maturation.[9] In *Anne of Green Gables*, Anne acknowledges the significance of her thirteenth birthday, telling Diana, "I can scarcely realize that I'm in my teens. When I woke this morning it seemed to me that everything must be different … In two more years I'll be really grown up."[10] While Barrie does not state the ages of Peter or the Darling children in *Peter Pan*, his older brother David was thirteen years old when he died in an accident. David's death likely contributed to Barrie's view that the most important life events occur by the age of twelve.

These personal observations and others related to Barrie's and Montgomery's youth demonstrate their awareness of the cultural expectations that shaped their growth as individuals. Montgomery recalls that, at age seven, she fully embraced the distinction between childhood and adulthood, noting that "either you were grown-up or you were not, that was all there was about it."[11] Barrie also felt this distinction, which, he admits, led him to fear growing up. Describing how stories of his mother's maturation inspired fear of his own, he writes, "The horror of my boyhood was that I knew a time would come when I also must give up the games … I felt that I must continue playing in secret, and I took this shadow to her, when she told me her own experience, which convinced us both that we were very like each other inside. She had discovered that work is the best fun after all, and I learned it in time, but have my lapses, and so had she."[12] Barrie's fear of adulthood stemmed from his realization that growing older meant that he must "give up" the fun and games he enjoyed. Significantly, this "shadow" of loss is a point of connection between him and his mother, who also had "lapses." Barrie's choice of the word "lapse" to describe his playful adult moments reveals how cultural assumptions underlying childhood and adulthood affected his perception of himself. Defined as "a slight error typically due to forgetfulness or inattention" or "a temporary deviation or fall especially from a higher to a lower state,"[13] the word *lapse* carries inherently negative connotations. Barrie's use of it here, while somewhat facetious, suggests his recognition that his society did not approve of adults engaging in childlike behaviour.

Montgomery, on the other hand, does not describe her adult forays into imagination as lapses, but rather as "glimpses."[14] These glimpses, while fleeting in some respects, serve as a constant source of pleasure throughout her life. Although Montgomery often romanticized her youth,[15] it contained its share of struggles. Raised by her strict maternal grandparents, the Macneills, the "shadow" of Montgomery's younger years was that she often felt misunderstood by the adults around her.[16] In a journal entry dated 2 January 1905, she observes, "The older I grow the more I realize what a starved childhood mine was *emotionally*. I was brought up by two old people, neither of whom at their best were ever very sympathetic and who had already grown into set, intolerant ways."[17] Unlike Barrie, Montgomery was not brought up by adults who condoned "lapses" in their behaviour or her own. Later in the same entry, she writes, "It was never as happy as childhood should be and as it easily might have been; and there *were* times when it was fiercely unhappy." Even so, consoling Montgomery through these unhappy times is the realization that she has "always" felt "very near to a kingdom of ideal beauty." She acknowledges that "a thin veil" separated her from this ideal world and that "sometimes a wind fluttered it and [she] seemed to catch a glimpse of the enchanting realm beyond." Looking back, the author asserts that "those glimpses have always made life worthwhile."[18] Similar to Barrie's lapses, then, Montgomery's "glimpses" provide a connection to her younger self. For her, however, they are not sources of shame (as facetious as Barrie's shame may be), but genuine sources of hope.

These personal reflections offer insight into the sense-making processes that shaped the fictional worlds of Neverland and Avonlea. Barrie's and Montgomery's lives had more in common than their Scottish heritage and love of islands.[19] While both authors cherished their younger years, they also associated them with personal loss – either of experiences had or experiences not had. What is most interesting from the viewpoint of this chapter, however, is that their literary professions allowed them to recover part of that loss. Writing was a childhood pastime that Barrie and Montgomery did not have to "give up" as they matured.[20] Describing his earliest stories, Barrie writes, "They were all tales of adventure (happiest is he who writes of adventure), no characters were allowed within if I knew their like in the flesh, the scene lay in unknown parts, desert islands, enchanted gardens, with knights (none of your nights) on black chargers, and round the first corner a lady selling watercress."[21] Montgomery offers a similar catalogue of her own early writing in a 1911 newspaper article for the Toronto *Globe*, "How I Began to Write": "Sometimes I wrote prose; and then all the little incidents of my not very exciting existence were described. I wrote descriptions of my favourite haunts, 'biographies' of my pets, accounts of visits and school affairs – and even 'critical' reviews of books I had read. Sometimes I broke out in verse, and wrote 'poetry' about flowers and months, or addressed 'lines' to my friends, and enthused over sunsets."[22] Both authors credited the trajectory of their careers to their early fascination with the "work" of writing, which, in their experience, doubled as a form of play.

Barrie and Montgomery were, therefore, children's writers at an age when their society considered them as actual children. The narrative ingredients for Neverland (such as adventure, desert islands, enchanted gardens) and Avonlea (such as little incidents of existence, favourite haunts, poetic speech) are found in their descriptions of their early writing. These narrative connections to their past experiences suggest that the "work" of writing *Peter Pan* and *Anne of Green Gables* allowed both authors to play with and question the cultural norms that had shaped their existence since birth. This psychological play aligns with the constructivist belief that people's understanding of the world evolves in response to their experiences, which either affirm or negate the ideas that guide their actions in it. In his theory of personality, psychologist George Kelly refers to these ideas as personal hypotheses – the psychological constructs that shape people's understanding of reality. Stories, Kelly observes, allow people to rework their personal hypotheses with limited risk to themselves. "In the use of stories," he points out, "the self is only gradually involved and the new constructs which are developed are allowed to replace only gradually those undesirable role constructs which have continued to exercise control in the client's life after having outlived their validity."[23] Viewed from this perspective, the story worlds of Neverland and Avonlea provide Barrie and Montgomery with the opportunity to question the undesirable role constructs that exercised control in their lives.

The islands in *Peter Pan* and *Anne of Green Gables* are ideal locations for these psychological experiments, because they function not only as metaphors for the individual but also as microcosms of society. According to Susan Naramore Maher, the island, "from Defoe on, serves as an archetypal laboratory for a society's ideology."[24] To the extent that the island serves as an ideological testing ground, it is useful for developing personal constructs. Kelly theorizes that "a laboratory is a situation in which there is present, for the person to re-sort, a sufficient amount of the stuff out of which new constructs can be formed."[25] As archetypal laboratories, the island locales of Neverland and Avonlea provide Barrie and Montgomery with effective spaces for sorting out the ideological "stuff" underlying cultural constructions of childhood and adulthood. All inhabited islands, after all, were once deserted islands, and it is the process of their domestication that presents a powerful analogy to human experience. Understood as a figurative territory, the human mind is its own wilderness, one that every individual must explore in an attempt to reach a sense of self.[26] Cultural role constructs, by extension, serve as the psychological maps that help or hinder people on their journeys to self-discovery.

Barrie establishes this figurative connection between the island and the psyche in his description of Neverland, the geography of which resembles a child's mind.[27] "I don't know," the narrator explains, "whether you have ever seen a map of a person's mind. Doctors sometimes draw maps of other parts of you, and your own map can become intensely interesting, but catch them trying to draw a map of a child's mind, which is not only confused, but keeps going round all the time." While constantly changing, the narrator suggests that "Neverland is always more or less an island." Describing the difficulty of charting this landscape of "coral reefs," "savages and lonely lairs," "gnomes," "caves," and "princes," etc., he claims, "It would be an easy map if that were all; but there is also first day at school, religion, fathers, the round pond, needlework, murders, hangings, verbs that take the dative, chocolate-pudding day, getting into braces, say ninety-nine, threepence for pulling out your tooth yourself, and so on; and either these are part of the island or they are another map showing through."[28] The island metaphor thus serves to illustrate the complex relationship of the self to society. Barrie's description of Neverland identifies the various cultural influences that attempt to shape children's sense of reality and themselves, including institutions (schools, religion, health care, the criminal-justice system), authority figures (fathers), and domestic life (needlework, chocolate-pudding day). He presents the child's consciousness as a psychological wilderness – an exotic island – that is made more complex by the processes of socialization that seek to develop it.

While Montgomery does not explicitly connect Anne's mind to Prince Edward Island, she nevertheless promotes this association through the orphan's distinctively red hair and the island's red roads,[29] as well as through the narrator's romantic descriptions of its landscape, which, as Elizabeth Epperly observes, align with the little girl's perspective. The result, Epperly explains, is that "we identify Anne herself with Prince Edward Island and with all the enchantment of its moods and features."[30] Like Barrie's description of the child's mind, Montgomery presents Anne's mind as a constantly changing, confusing place. The orphan states, "There's such a lot of different Annes in me. I sometimes think that is why I'm such a troublesome person. If I was just the one Anne it would be ever so much more comfortable, but then it wouldn't be half so interesting." The revolving nature of Anne's mind reveals itself in her constant chatter, which quickly moves from topic to topic. Listening to her on their ride to Green Gables, Matthew finds "it rather difficult for his slower intelligence to keep up with her brisk mental processes." Marilla also struggles to map out Anne's mind, telling Matthew, "I don't like children who have so much to say. I don't want an orphan girl and if I did she isn't the style I'd pick out. There's something I don't understand about her." Thus, while Anne's mind, like the child's mind Barrie describes, is "a real interesting little thing,"[31] it is precisely the interesting aspects of her personality that prove the most elusive and frustrating to those who are trying to socialize her into a certain "style" of child.

Peter Pan and *Anne of Green Gables*, in this respect, present the child's mind as a nonsensical space. Hypothetically speaking, adults cannot fully access this space, because they cannot chart all of the different "stuff" it contains.[32] Susan Stewart contends that, "in everyday discourse, nonsense is used as a category that is both negative and residual. Like its companion categories of Fate, Chance, Accident, Miscellaneous, and even *etc.*, it gives us a place to store any mysterious gaps in our systems of order."[33] Barrie's description of the disorderly conglomeration of thoughts that fill the child's mind creates the impression that childhood is just such a residual space. He presents Neverland and Peter Pan, two symbols of enduring childhood, as mysterious phenomena. The narrator remarks that "occasionally in her travels through her children's minds Mrs Darling found things she could not understand, and of these quite the most perplexing was the word Peter."[34] Alternatively, Anne's arrival at Green Gables and her subsequent experiences there are characterized by "Fate, Chance, [and] Accident," as demonstrated by Mrs Spencer's mix-up and Anne's various "mistakes," which often result in "catastrophe." Like Peter, Anne is also depicted as mysterious and "queer"; she is described by Matthew as a "freckled witch," who, Marilla observes, possesses the power to "cas[t] a spell over" others.[35] Anne's arrival at the Cuthbert home, then, just like Peter's arrival at the Darling home, upsets the systems of order that govern the household.

On the surface, this association between childhood and nonsense appears to support the binary thinking that separates children from adults. However, it is actually by introducing this association early in *Peter Pan* and *Anne of*

Green Gables that Barrie and Montgomery are able to deconstruct its logic throughout their narratives. "Nonsense," Stewart argues, "always refers back to a sense that itself cannot be assumed. The locus of the investigation must be in the nature of the *not* that stands between the domain of common sense and the domain that takes its identity as 'not common sense.'"[36] Focusing on the incomprehensible aspects of childhood allows Barrie and Montgomery to question the common sense by which children are rendered incomprehensible to adults. Mysterious characters like Peter and Anne serve as the *not* that stands between childhood and adulthood. Readers are inevitably tasked with asking why Peter and Anne do not make sense and whether the problem lies with the characters themselves or with the logic through which they are understood. From the beginning of their novels, Barrie and Montgomery set up a dialectic between the "nonsense" of the child and the "sense" of the adult.[37] This dialectic provides them with the means to forefront and question the differences that separate children from adults. In doing so, the authors attempt to bridge the gap that keeps older people out of Neverland and younger people in it.

One of the ways Barrie and Montgomery bridge this gap is by changing the systems of order/sense that govern their fictional landscapes. The fantasy worlds associated with their child characters (Peter, Wendy, John, Michael, and Anne) are presented as counter to the real worlds of England and PEI that are associated with their adult characters (Mr and Mrs Darling, Matthew and Marilla). And yet, both Barrie and Montgomery gradually rework this distinction, until the boundaries between fantasy and reality are completely blurred. Mrs Darling, for instance, dreams of Neverland, only to wake to find Peter in the nursery. "The dream by itself," the narrator observes, "would have been a trifle, but while she was dreaming the window of the nursery blew open, and a boy did drop on the floor."[38] Anne's arrival on PEI, in turn, marks the transition of her dreams into reality. She exclaims to Matthew, "I used to imagine I was living here, but I never really expected I would. It's delightful when your imaginations come true, isn't it?" Anne expresses this delight multiple times on her first ride to Green Gables, including the moment when she discovers that the farm is located near a brook. In fact, by the end of the ride, she comments that her "arm must be black and blue from the elbow up," because she has "pinched [herself] so many times" in fear that it was all a dream. Describing her wish for a bosom friend, she tells Marilla, "I never really supposed I would, but so many of my loveliest dreams have come true all at once that perhaps this one will, too. Do you think it's possible?"[39] That Anne does find a bosom friend answers her question. Through the fulfillment of the orphan's "loveliest dreams," Montgomery's story, like Barrie's, suggests that fantasies can and do become realities.[40]

Through this deconstruction of the boundaries separating fantasy and reality, *Peter Pan* and *Anne of Green Gables* challenge their readers to re-sort their understanding of the world by making the impossible possible. Barrie's and Montgomery's descriptions of the child's mind as a hybrid, liminal space, containing fantasy-based and reality-based thoughts, highlight the inherent relationship between imagination and experience. Both of their stories illustrate the significance of dreaming as a real event that is not always accounted for by common-sense representations of reality. "Common-sense thinking," Stewart argues, "must see the lifeworld as a stable and ordered phenomenon in order to get on with the business at hand. An investigation that accepts this as the nature of the everyday world will then be in a quandary with regard to explaining changes in our perception of the world."[41] Adults like Mr Darling and Marilla embody this common-sense approach to getting "on with the business at hand." When Mrs Darling confronts her husband about the existence of Peter, he replies, "Mark my words … it is some nonsense Nana has been putting into their heads; just the sort of idea a dog would have."[42] Likewise, when Anne tells Marilla about her imaginary friends, Katie Maurice and Violetta, Marilla responds, "You seem to half believe your own imaginations. It will be well for you to have a real live friend to put such nonsense out of your head."[43] Throughout both novels, however, Mr Darling and Marilla find themselves in a "quandary" when their views of the world fail to account for their children's experiences and their own. At one point or another, their mental maps prove to be inadequate guides.

The map of the adult mind, therefore, is just as central to Barrie's and Montgomery's stories as the map of the child's. In *Peter Pan* and *Anne of Green Gables*, adults are the ones whose psychological hypotheses are ultimately put to the test. Marilla even describes the adoption of Anne as an "experiment." For Marilla, this experiment results in the realization that she understands Anne more than she originally thought, and this understanding emerges in those moments when the orphan challenges the systems of order that structure the older woman's life. For example, when Marilla rebukes Anne for acting inappropriately toward Mrs Rachel Lynde, Anne cries, "Just imagine how you would feel if somebody told you to your face that you were skinny and ugly." Marilla, it turns out, does not have to imagine, because she experienced a similar situation as "a very small child." Remembering this moment from her past, she is able to see the world through Anne's perspective and feel the injustice of Mrs Lynde's remarks. Similarly, when listening to the orphan's critique of church, Marilla is confronted with "the undeniable fact that some of the things Anne had said, especially about the minister's sermons and Mr. Bell's prayers, were what she herself had really thought deep down in her heart for years, but had never given expression to." Thus, while Marilla (and Victorian society) may not approve of a child who has "so much to say,"[44] it is Anne's ability to speak her mind that makes it possible for Marilla to see the resemblance between them. In Anne's mind, Marilla sees her own Neverland begin to surface – the parts of herself that she has repressed in an attempt to comply with the cultural role constructs that control her life.[45]

Mrs Darling undergoes similar realizations when interacting with her own children. At first, the mother claims to know nothing about Peter. However, upon reflection, she recalls that she has heard of him before. Describing this remembrance, the narrator states, "after thinking back into her childhood she just remembered a Peter Pan who was said to live with the fairies … She had believed in him at the time, but now that she was married and full of sense she quite doubted whether there was any such person." Here again, the dialectic between nonsense and sense divides children and adults. And yet, this divide decreases as Mrs Darling's belief in Peter gradually returns, culminating in her meeting him in the nursery: "But in her dream he had rent the film that obscures the Neverland, and she saw Wendy and John and Michael peeping through the gap." The only evidence Mrs Darling has of her encounter with Peter is the "shadow" he leaves behind, a shadow that symbolizes Mrs Darling's own childhood, remembered only when her children mention Peter's name.[46] Similar to Barrie's experience of bringing the "shadow" of growing up to his mother, the Darling children bring the shadow of growing up to theirs. Mrs Darling's handling of this shadow signifies her own "lapse" in "sense," which allows her to see and experience the Neverland that adults supposedly cannot access.

Through these "lapses" and "glimpses," Barrie and Montgomery present a counter hypothesis to cultural narratives of childhood and adulthood. Specifically, they suggest the possibility that childhood is not something that can be lost as much as it can be forgotten. The Neverland of one's imagination is ever present for those who choose to access it. Reflecting on her grandparents' lack of imagination, Montgomery writes, "their children left them early in life and they remained alone together with no influence to prevent them from growing narrow and set and warped. Emotionally they grew old before their time, getting into a rut of feeling and living which suited them but was utterly unfitted to anyone who was yet growing in soul or body." While critical of her grandparents' lack of imagination, Montgomery still leaves space for the possibility that there are people who do not grow "narrow and set and warped" as they mature. In the same journal entry, she suggests that "the gap between youth and age is too wide to be bridged, save by those exceptional natures that do not grow old in heart."[47] In Montgomery's view, growing older in body does not necessarily mean growing "old in heart" as well. The real reason adults cannot access the Neverlands of their imagination is that they have stopped growing – they have closed their minds to all of the "interesting" things there are to find out about the world.[48] And yet, as Montgomery points out, there are "exceptional natures" that do not fall prey to this "rut of feeling and living."[49] The mysterious gap between youth and age is not impossible to bridge.

Barrie and Montgomery highlight these "exceptional natures" in the adult characters that fill the pages of *Peter Pan* and *Anne of Green Gables*. Mr and Mrs Darling are not bystanders in their children's play, but active participants. They engage with Wendy, John, and Michael in "lovely dances" and "romps." During the family's playful dances, the "gayest of all was Mrs Darling."[50] While Anne admits that it "wouldn't be dignified" for Mrs Allan to "dance and sing," she nevertheless finds a "kindred spirit" and sympathetic adult in the new minister's wife. Describing her fondness for the Sunday-school teacher, Anne tells Marilla, "She said right away she didn't think it was fair for the teacher to ask all the questions, and you know, Marilla, that is exactly what I've always thought. She said we could ask her any question we liked, and I asked ever so many." The narrator offers a similar account when describing the new Avonlea teacher, Miss Stacy, in whom Anne finds "another true and helpful friend."

Miss Stacy, readers learn, is "a bright, sympathetic young woman with the happy gift of winning and holding the affections of her pupils and bringing out the best that [is] in them mentally and morally."[51] In these exceptional adults, Anne is able to see reflections of her own self, particularly her ever-present interest in, and appreciation for, learning more about the world. Although technically grown up in body, Mrs Allan and Miss Stacy are still "growing in soul."[52]

Montgomery's conceptualization of a "kindred spirit," of course, also allows for the possibility that one's nature can become more exceptional later in life. Growing up does not mean that one's mind has to become "narrow and set and warped," but, even if it does, imagination can give it the "scope" it needs to change. Kindred spirits like Miss Josephine Barry and Marilla, for example, are more difficult to recognize than Matthew, Mrs Allan, and Miss Stacy; it is not until Anne reminds these older women of their imaginations that they are able to relate to her. Anne's apology to Miss Barry leads the latter to confess, "I'm afraid my imagination is a little rusty – it's so long since I used it … I dare say your claim to sympathy is just as strong as mine." Miss Barry's change of heart reinforces the idea that a person's soul can transcend the physical limitations that come with age. Reflecting on it, Anne says to Marilla, "Miss Barry was a kindred spirit, after all … You wouldn't think so to look at her, but she is." Montgomery underscores this distinction between body and soul once again when Marilla describes her past romance with John Blythe. The older woman tells Anne, "You wouldn't think so to look at me, would you? But you never can tell about people from their outsides." Throughout the novel, Anne and Marilla learn that their insides have more in common than their outside appearances suggest. Just as Mrs Allan and Miss Stacy teach Anne, so does Anne teach Marilla the importance of appreciating the "interesting world" around her, thereby bringing more "scope" into the older woman's life.[53]

Through these character transformations, Montgomery demonstrates the difference between being old and acting old. The problem with adulthood does not lie with age as much as it lies with the fixed mentality that supposedly accompanies it. Although brought up by the older Cuthberts, Anne does not suffer the same misfortune Montgomery did. Matthew and Marilla, unlike the Macneills, change through their interactions with their adopted daughter.

According to Holly Blackford, this is the "central thesis" of Montgomery's novel: "the romantic child, a Pan figure reminiscent of J.M. Barrie's 1904 creation of Peter Pan, could with play and imagination cross the threshold of an 'infertile' Victorian town and forever transform it." Like Peter, Blackford argues, Anne is "a character serving the traditional function of a liminal spirit who beckons others to cross into lands of enchantment." Through Anne's interactions with Marilla and other adults, Blackford notes, "Montgomery teaches us how to read and receive her child as an inner one. Anne *awakens*."[54] In fact, the transformation of seemingly ordinary, common-sense people like the Cuthberts suggests that staying connected to one's inner child is not as exceptional as society considers it to be. On the contrary, staying disconnected from this part of oneself actually appears unnatural and illogical, because it prevents people from embracing all the aspects of their personalities.

Barrie's depiction of adults like Mr Darling, in turn, suggests that attempts to ignore this inner child are often nothing more than a pretence, as are Barrie's own when he feigns contempt for his "lapses."[55] Despite Mr Darling's efforts to present himself as a mature adult, he is ultimately shown to be as immature as his children. In fact, the narrator observes that the father "might have passed for a boy again if he had been able to take his baldness off."[56] To be sure, Mr Darling's mood swings, his dependence on his wife, his pride, and his forgetfulness all bear a strong resemblance to Peter Pan and Captain Hook.[57] This resemblance is further emphasized by Peter's impersonation of the father and the pirate in various instances, as well as through Mr Darling's response to his children's absence. Living in Nana's kennel, he becomes somewhat of a celebrity, with crowds of people, particularly "little boys," cheering him on. Indeed, when the lost boys return home with Wendy, John, and Michael, Mr Darling assumes Peter's role as their chief: "'Then follow the leader,' he cried gaily. 'Mind you, I am not sure that we have a drawing-room, but we pretend we have, and it's all the same. Hoop la!'" Through the construction of these parallels, Barrie presents Mr Darling as another lost boy. True, the father knows, or at least pretends to know, about "stocks and shares," but that does not stop him from having temper tantrums when he cannot tie his dress tie, nor does it change the fact that he does not like taking his medicine, pouts when his pride his hurt, and still enjoys a good "romp."[58] Mr Darling might be grown up by his society's age standards, but he certainly has not grown out of the behaviour patterns his society considers childlike.

These adult-child parallels in Barrie's and Montgomery's novels problematize the constructs that prevent people from being themselves. The more one examines the "nature of the *not* that stands between" the domains of childhood/nonsense and adulthood/sense, the more one realizes the flawed nature of the logic that keeps them apart.[59] While *Peter Pan* and *Anne of Green Gables* appear to support this logic, their child characters reject it in various ways. Anne and Wendy, for example, actively look forward to growing up. Anne tells Marilla, "It must be lovely to be grown up,"[60] and Barrie's narrator informs us that Wendy "was one of the kind that likes to grow up."[61] While Marilla does not share Anne's enthusiasm for adulthood,[62] the older woman's dissatisfaction no doubt stems from her acceptance of the narrow cultural narrative associated with it. Anne, however, is determined to find "scope for imagination" in everything and, as her renaming of people and places demonstrates, is not opposed to changing cultural narratives to suit her own preferences. Early on, she tells Marilla, "It's been my experience that you can nearly always enjoy things if you make up your mind firmly that you will. Of course, you must make it up *firmly*."[63] Like Anne's mind, the Darling children's minds are not "*firmly*" against growing up. On the contrary, acting grown up is one of their favourite games of make-believe, one that they play in the nursery and in Neverland with Peter and the lost boys. Speaking of Wendy's maturation, the narrator notes, "in the end she grew up of her own free will a day quicker than other girls."[64] The character of Wendy, like the character of Anne, presents readers with a contradiction. She, too, is able to accomplish the seemingly impossible task of changing while staying "just the same."[65] Of all the children in Neverland, she is the one who is most eager to grow up and assume the adult roles of wife and mother, and yet she is also the only one of the children who is able to return to Neverland more than once.

Barrie and Montgomery, in this respect, do not actually present growing up as an unhappy event. Their characters remind readers that life is an adventure that everyone plays at. Living is a balance of work and play, as Barrie's own mother's childhood attests. Describing Margaret Ogilvy's youth, he writes, "She was eight when her mother's death made her mistress of the house and mother to her little brother, and from that time she scrubbed and mended and baked and sewed, and argued with the flesher about the quarter pound of beef … all these things she did as a matter of course … then rushing out in a fit of childishness to play dumps or palaulays with others of her age."[66] Barrie's description of his mother's youth highlights the significant disparity between cultural constructs of childhood and people's actual experiences. Accounts of his own life do the same. Inspired by his make-believe games with the Llewelyn Davies boys, *Peter Pan*, while fantastical, carries the authenticity of a real imaginative experience. In Barrie's dedicatory essay, "To the Five," which appeared in the 1928 republication of the 1904 drama, he writes, "What a game we had of Peter before we clipped him small to make him fit the boards. He was the longest story on earth."[67] To the extent that *Peter Pan* tells the story of human maturation, it is the "longest story on earth." Barrie conveys its timeless significance at the end of the narrative, when he describes the maturation of Wendy's daughter, Jane, and speculates on the subsequent maturation of Jane's daughter, Margaret.[68] Peter's story, he points out, is never-ending because it is told and retold, and lived and relived, generation after generation.

Understood in this way, the game of storytelling emerges as a central sense-making practice in *Peter Pan*, one that allows characters of all ages to rework their experiences into narrative form. In Barrie's novel, storytelling violates the logic that keeps adults out of Neverland. Wendy never stops playing "mother" or telling stories[69] and, therefore, does not truly lose her connection to the land of make-believe. Every time she recounts her adventures to her daughter, grown-up Wendy relives the game she played when she was young. Montgomery offers a similar view of storytelling in *The Story Girl* (1911), when she writes that "singers and poets and artists and story-tellers" are "just people who have never forgotten the way to fairyland."[70] Like Barrie's Wendy, Montgomery's Anne is also a storyteller who knows the way to the land of make-believe.[71] Mary Rubio notes that "Anne seems partly magical because she uses her imagination as a passport to fairyland; and the fairyland provides either a haven from or a visionary vantage point from which to view the real world."[72] Montgomery's heroine, in other words, reveals the power of storytelling not only as a game but also as a game changer. Anne's imagination is a passport to fairyland, but it is also a passport to changing her reality. According to Rubio, "Anne's imaginative flights of fancy" are not what resonate most with readers; rather, what resonates most is "the recognition that our perception of reality often becomes the blueprint for our lives."[73] Consequently, it is through the storytelling characters of Anne and Wendy that Montgomery and Barrie convey the transcendent power of imagination, which allows people to connect their pasts and futures in the present moment, giving them a sense of their own lives.

This focus on storytelling in *Peter Pan* and *Anne of Green Gables* allows one to see how the island metaphor transcends the narratives to encompass the reading situation. These stories, which create a sense of both connection to the world and isolation from it, offer readers a place for their imaginations to cultivate a sense of self. Reflecting on the intergenerational popularity of *Anne of Green Gables*, Montgomery writes, "I never dreamed that it would appeal to young and old. I thought girls in their teens might like to read it, that was the only audience I hoped to reach. But men and women who are grandparents have written to tell me how they loved *Anne*, and boys at college have done the same."[74] Like *Peter Pan*, *Anne of Green Gables* appeals to people of all ages, because it is written for children of all ages. Barrie and Montgomery remind their readers that childhood is a lifelong experience. Hence the importance of mothers in both of their novels. While Anne's dreams are fuelled by her desire to be someone's child – to "belong" to someone,[75] Peter, despite his dismissal of mothers, keeps returning to bring one back to Neverland. In both narratives, parents are the people who make children's existence possible. Their role as parents, however, does not change the genealogical fact that they, too, are children. Grown-up Wendy is still the daughter of Mr and Mrs Darling, just as Matthew and Marilla Cuthbert are still the children of their father and mother, who built Green Gables.[76]

The same pertains to Barrie and Montgomery, who, like Wendy and Anne, retained their child identities through imaginative storytelling and a strong sense of loyalty to their parents, whom they never forgot. Unlike the lost boys, for instance, Barrie did not have trouble remembering his mother's eyes.[77] According to him, they revealed that she was created "to open the minds of all who looked to beautiful thoughts," which, he observed, "is the beginning and end of literature."[78] Given Barrie's appreciation for his mother, it is not surprising that she figured prominently in the stories he wrote.[79] While presented as friendly adversaries, mothers and Peter Pan perform the same function – they keep the "window" to the nursery (and by extension, childhood) open.[80] Although Montgomery never had the opportunity to know her mother,[81] what she did learn about Clara Woolner Macneill became, like Barrie's own understanding of Margaret Ogilvy, "a talisman to make life beautiful."[82] Montgomery inscribes her lasting devotion to both her parents in *Anne of Green Gables*, which is dedicated to their memory. Like the birth name that served as her pen name, her novel acts as a public reminder that she never forgot her child identity or her sense of connection to the people who made it possible.

Reading Barrie's and Montgomery's novels alongside their personal memoirs, therefore, reminds readers that children's literature is only impossible for adults who forget that grown-up writers are also children. The only person who can truly shut the window to one's childhood is oneself. *Anne of Green Gables* and *Peter Pan* open people's minds to the possibility that childhood does not have a beginning and end, but rather a middle; it is the story of human existence. A confusing and often nonsensical space, it "is important for members making a transition between realizable domains. It is a place to stand in the middle of change."[83] Children's books like *Peter Pan* and *Anne of Green Gables* highlight the "messy continuum"[84] that separates the "realizable domains" of birth and death and, in doing so, give people "a place to stand in the middle of change."[85] By providing readers with narrative laboratories through which to re-sort the undesirable role constructs that shape their lives, Barrie and Montgomery give them the space to redefine the systems of order that determine what is or is not possible in life. Growing up, they reveal, is a continual process of exploring and discovering oneself. Society has rules for how it expects people to play the game, but for those who possess the imagination to live outside those rules, adventure is never very far away.

NOTES

1 Historian Hugh Cunningham notes that, throughout the centuries, "what we hear are adults imagining childhood, inventing it, in order to make sense of their world" (Cunningham, *Invention of Childhood*, 12).

2 Rose notes that "children's fiction sets up a world in which the adult comes first (author, maker, giver) and the child comes after (reader, product, receiver), but where neither of them enter the space in between" (Rose, *Case of Peter Pan*, 1–2).

3 Wullschläger, *Inventing Wonderland*, 12, 109. Wullschläger dates the start of this transition to approximately 1880. She credits the Edwardian view of childhood in part to "the role of Edward, the Prince of Wales, as the irresponsible, pleasure-seeking playboy of Europe" (ibid., 109). While "playboy" is a loaded term,

one can see how it might have been used in this context to connote an avoidance of the cultural responsibilities associated with adulthood.

4 Barrie, *Peter Pan*, 201.

5 For fuller discussion on this distinction between childhood and adulthood, particularly as it applies to Montgomery's work, see the introduction of this volume, 9–11.

6 Barrie, *Margaret Ogilvy*, 32.

7 Justifying her focus on the early years of her life, Montgomery writes: "I have written at length about the incidents and environment of my childhood because they had a marked influence on the development of my literary gift" (LMM, *AP*, 52).

8 Wullschläger, *Inventing Wonderland*, 14.

9 Montgomery makes a distinction between her childhood and girlhood. See LMM, *AP*, 19.

10 LMM, *AGG*, 244.

11 LMM, *AP*, 28. Montgomery notes the following about her younger self: "I had no conception of age at that time" (ibid.) This statement suggests the ways she began to think differently about age as she matured.

12 Barrie, *Margaret Ogilvy*, 23.

13 "lapse," *Merriam-Webster.*

14 LMM, *CJ* 2:119.

15 See LMM, "The Gay Days of Old," and *The Alpine Path.*

16 Montgomery also uses the metaphor of a "shadow" in her description of the unhappy aspects of her life. In a journal entry dated 15 October 1908, she responds to a positive review of *Anne of Green Gables* with the observation: "Thank God, I can keep the shadows of my life out of my work" (LMM, *CJ* 2:199).

17 Ibid., 118 (emphasis in original).

18 Ibid., 119 (emphasis in original). In their introduction to this volume, the editors explain Montgomery's ability to remain connected to the imaginative worlds and experiences of her younger years through memory and the effect these had on her reading and writing practices. See the introduction of this volume, 9–11.

19 A fan of Barrie's work, Montgomery visited the places in Scotland he wrote about during her honeymoon trip to the British Isles. Describing Kirriemuir, otherwise known as "the 'Thrums' of Barrie's stories," she observes that the

red of its paths, which were like those of PEI's "island roads," made her "feel at home" (LMM, *AP*, 87). Jennifer Litster notes that "the infant Chester Macdonald was nicknamed 'Peter Pan' by his mother," as revealed in a unpublished letter to MacMillan dated 16 March 1913. Litster, "'The Golden Road of Youth,'" 69. Montgomery was also compared to Barrie as a writer. See LMM, *CJ* 7:21.

20 Barrie, *Margaret Ogilvy*, 23. Barrie explicitly compares the profession of writing to a game. Speaking of his decision to be an author, he writes: "From the day on which I first tasted blood in the garret my mind was made up; there could be no hum-dreadful-drum profession for me; literature was my game" (ibid., 40).

21 Ibid., 39.

22 LMM, "How I Began to Write," 67–8. Montgomery notes that, "Other children found their recreation in games and romps. I found mine in creeping away into some lonely corner with a pencil and a 'letter bill,' and writing verses or sketches in a cramped, schoolgirl hand" (ibid., 68).

23 Kelly, *Theory of Personality*, 162. Kelly observes: "In the clinical experience of the writer it has been relatively easy to develop new constructs for children in connection with story elements and thus give them form, definition, and usefulness before they come into conflict with the constructs which they are eventually to replace" (ibid., 162).

24 Maher, "Recasting Crusoe," 169.

25 Kelly, *Theory of Personality*, 169.

26 In her study of the island setting in children's literature, Virginia L. Wolf notes the way that the island can function as "a symbol for the self" ("Paradise Lost?" 53).

27 See Blake, "The Sea–Dream," 170. She notes: "The island is the land of dreams (it is the landscape of a child's mind) and its presiding spirit, Peter, is good form, a kind of embodiment of the play spirit, playing at islands" (ibid.)

28 Barrie, *Peter Pan*, 7.

29 Juliet McMaster notes that Anne's "red hair connects her deeply with the island of her adoption ... We are meant to recognize a propitious kinship between Anne's red braids and Prince Edward Island's red roads" (J. McMaster, "Taking Control," 63).

30 Epperly, *Fragrance of Sweet-Grass*, 31.

31 LMM, *AGG*, 191–2, 18, 35.

32 Kelly, *Theory of Personality*, 169.

33 Stewart, *Nonsense*, 5.

34 Barrie, *Peter Pan*, 8.

35 LMM, *AGG*, 209, 63, 103, 18, 42.

36 Stewart, *Nonsense*, 4–5 (emphasis in original).

37 Citing the work of Erhard Reckwitz, Maher notes that the island in the robinsonade supports a dialectical structure ("Recasting Crusoe," 169). The dialectical structure is also found in nonsense literature. See Sewell, *The Field of Nonsense*. Both the island settings and the play between nonsense and sense we find in *Peter Pan* and *Anne of Green Gables* can thus be seen to support the dialogues that Barrie and Montgomery create between childhood and adulthood.

38 Barrie, *Peter Pan*, 12.

39 LMM, *AGG*, 17, 26, 68. On her first ride to Green Gables, Anne tells Matthew: "Fancy! It's always been one of my dreams to live near a brook. I never expected I would, though. Dreams don't often come true, do they? Wouldn't it be nice if they did?" (LMM, *AGG*, 19).

40 The publication of *Anne of Green Gables* was the fulfillment of Montgomery's own childhood dream. Reflecting on this, she writes in her journal, "Well, I've written my book. The dream dreamed years ago in that old brown desk in school has come true at last after years of toil and struggle. And the realization is sweet – almost as sweet as the dream!" (LMM, *CJ* 2:173).

41 Stewart, *Nonsense*, 12.

42 Barrie, *Peter Pan*, 9.

43 LMM, *AGG*, 70. It's interesting to note that Montgomery modelled Anne's imaginary friends after her own fictional playmates. Describing their significance to her, she writes, "All this sounds like the veriest nonsense, but I cannot describe how real it was to me" (LMM, *AP*, 74).

44 LMM, *AGG*, 57, 79, 80, 97, 35. Cunningham notes that among the contrasting images of childhood Victorian society presented was that of "little children who should be seen and not heard" (*Invention of Childhood*, 140). Anne repeats this idea to Matthew when she tells him, "It's such a relief to talk when one wants to and not be told that children should be seen and not heard. I've had that said to me a million times if I have once" (LMM, *AGG*, 18).

45 For a discussion of some of the psychoanalytical implications of Anne and Marilla's relationship, see Blackford, "Introduction," xiv.

46 Barrie, *Peter Pan*, 9, 12, 13. There is a notable similarity between Barrie's word choice of "film that obscures the Neverland" and Montgomery's own description of the "thin veil" that separates her from the "kingdom of ideal beauty." Barrie, *Peter Pan*, 12; *CJ* 2:119.

47 LMM, *CJ* 2:120.

48 LMM, *AGG*, 18.

49 LMM, *CJ* 2:120.

50 Barrie, *Peter Pan*, 5–6.

51 LMM, *AGG*, 202–3, 224–5.

52 LMM, *CJ* 2:120.

53 LMM, *AGG*, 18, 188, 189, 354, 18.

54 Blackford, "Introduction," xii, xxiii, xv (emphasis in original).

55 Barrie, *Margaret Ogilvy*, 23. Describing his fear of growing up, Barrie states: "this agony still returns to me in dreams, when I catch myself playing marbles, and look on with cold displeasure" (ibid., 23).

56 Barrie, *Peter Pan*, 183–4.

57 This resemblance is underscored by Mr Darling and Captain Hook being viewed as "twin roles," played by the same actor. See Birkin, *J.M. Barrie and the Lost Boys*, 109.

58 Barrie, *Peter Pan*, 186, 193, 2, 18. For examples of Mr Darling's childish behaviour, see also, 17–18, 21–3.

59 Stewart, *Nonsense*, 5 (emphasis in original).

60 LMM, *AGG*, 174.

61 Barrie, *Peter Pan*, 199.

62 Marilla responds to Anne's exclamation "with a brief sigh" and says, "I don't know about that" (LMM, *AGG*, 174).

63 Ibid., 18, 44 (emphasis in original).

64 Barrie, *Peter Pan*, 199. For descriptions of the Darling children's make-believe "grown-up" games, see 16, 91.

65 LMM, *AGG*, 326.

66 Barrie, *Margaret Ogilvy*, 22.

67 Barrie, quoted in Birkin, *J.M. Barrie and the Lost Boys*, xi.

68 Barrie, *Peter Pan*, 206–7.

69 Peter first encounters Wendy and the Darling children when he comes to listen to Mrs Darling's stories in the nursery. The primary reason Peter asks Wendy

to come to Neverland is to tell him and the lost boys stories and be their mother. Ibid., 37–8, 75.

70 LMM, *SG*, 145.

71 See Frever, "Anne Shirley, Storyteller: Orality and *Anne of Green Gables*," for further discussion of Anne's role as a storyteller.

72 Rubio, "*Anne of Green Gables*: The Architect of Adolescence," 70.

73 Rubio, "Satire, Realism, and Imagination in *Anne of Green Gables*," 34.

74 LMM, *AP*, 76.

75 LMM, *AGG*, 15.

76 Matthew and Marilla live on the farm their father built. Ibid., 4. Also, it is noteworthy that Marilla insists on going by her first name, the name by which she has always been addressed since childhood. Ibid., 65.

77 See Barrie, *Peter Pan*, 90. Wendy develops testing methods to help the lost boys and her brothers remember their parents.

78 Barrie, *Margaret Ogilvy*, 4.

79 Barrie devotes a whole chapter to this topic in his memoir of his mother. See Barrie, *Margaret Ogilvy*, 130.

80 Barrie, *Peter Pan*, 129.

81 Clara Woolner Macneill died when Montgomery was only twenty-one months old.

82 LMM, *CJ* 2:117.

83 Stewart, *Nonsense*, 203.

84 Gubar, "Hermeneutics of Recuperation," 294.

85 Stewart, *Nonsense*, 203.

6

Magic for Marigold, Childhood, and Fiction

E. HOLLY PIKE

Shortly after the publication of *Magic for Marigold* (1929), a series of letters written by both local residents of and visitors to Prince Edward Island appeared in the Charlottetown *Guardian*, beginning with an American visitor writing to ask whether L.M. Montgomery's depiction of Prince Edward Island in that novel is "true" or "fictitious and untrue,"[1] and ending with a letter from Montgomery responding to all five writers at once. These letters, and Montgomery's response to them, constitute a conversation about the nature of fiction and its connection to the real world. In her own letter to the paper, which closed the exchange, Montgomery asserted that her depiction of her home province, the village of Harmony, and the Lesley family is both fictional and true; more importantly, she claimed that her central child character, Marigold, was an "ageless daughter of imagination," rather than "Miss 1930," as the first letter writer asserted, or "Miss Any-age."[2] In this public discussion, as I will demonstrate later in this chapter, Montgomery defended not only her own fictional locale and child creation but also fictionalized versions of real places and fictional children more generally. That is, she defended both realism as it is broadly understood – "works concerned with representing the world as it is rather than as it ought to be, with description rather than invention"[3] – and works that depict "ageless" child characters "found occasionally in every age of a nation's history."[4]

In making this defence, Montgomery explicitly addressed questions of genre, audience, and creative practice that she raised indirectly through the metafictive aspects of *Magic for Marigold*. Montgomery's choice to set the novel in the present, while referring to that present as long past; questions of false representation and make-believe in Marigold's episodic interactions with Varvara and Gwennie; child substitutes, such as the Skinner doll and Mrs Delagarde's Delight; and Marigold's desire for a "real chum, of the kind you read about in books,"[5] all raise questions about the relationship between truth, fiction, and the imagination in the depiction of children. By asserting in her letter that children of Marigold's type do exist in all times and places, including the contemporary world, Montgomery directly and publicly addresses how the valuation of what Colin Hill describes as her mode, "realistic local-colour works," is changing during the 1920s. Hill claims with reference to *Anne of Green Gables* and other Canadian novels of the early-twentieth century that they belong to a past tradition: "whatever the significance of these early examples of realistic writing, they have much more in common with European and American nineteenth-century realism than with Canadian modern realism."[6] In a simultaneous process, as Cathryn M. Mercier notes, assumptions about realism came to be a problematic for children's literature: "As [late-nineteenth-century] apologists for the novel based their argument on realism, they also cast children's literature away from adult literary concerns and positioned it as [a] separate entity."[7] Furthermore, as Carole Gerson argues, "from approximately 1918 to the 1940s, the canon of English-language Canadian literature was particularly arbitrary and malleable, governed less by cultural consensus than by the whims and agendas of certain individuals in positions of power."[8] The assessment of Montgomery's work in the 1920s, therefore, was affected by shifts in the understanding of what constituted "literature," leading to her works being categorized as stories for girls, rather than for a general audience. I have argued elsewhere that Montgomery was aware of this process and engaged with it in the *Emily* series,[9] also published during the 1920s, and will argue here that, through the depiction of both a contemporary Canadian scene and a timeless imaginative world in *Magic for Marigold*, Montgomery implicitly participates in contemporary conversations on what constitutes "serious" fiction, and that, through her participation in the *Guardian* discussion of fiction, she explicitly enters a conversation on the popular understanding of fiction and child characters.

That Montgomery sees herself at odds with modernist realism as frequently understood in the 1920s is clear in her journal, when, in 1928, she famously describes Morley Callaghan's view of "Literature" as "photograph[ing] a latrine or pigsty meticulously and hav[ing] nothing else in the picture."[10] However, her comments also indicate an active engagement with and response to contemporary literature in the period during which she wrote the Marigold stories and then developed them into a novel. For example, as Mary Henley Rubio documents, Montgomery admired Frederick Philip Grove's early work, and wrote letters encouraging him after the publication of *Over Prairie Trails*, although she deplored his later focus on tragic endings.[11] Her letters to Ephraim Weber also give a sense of her familiarity with contemporary Canadian literature – including assessments of Wilson MacDonald, Norah Holland, Morley Callaghan, and Mazo de la Roche – and demonstrate her awareness of contemporary criticism through references to articles in *Saturday Night* magazine and comments on William Arthur Deacon's "malice" toward her and her works.[12] Montgomery, that is, is fully aware of how her work is being judged in the public sphere and shares her knowledge with Weber, even telling him about the *Delineator* rejecting her commissioned Marigold stories.[13] While Montgomery seems to share what Hill describes as the view of "conservative segments of the literary world who used 'realism' as a euphemism for 'sexually explicit,'" Hill's definition of Canadian modern realism as "a realism that could simultaneously document a surface world of appearances and the hidden processes of human consciousness" could reasonably be applied to *Magic for Marigold*, which depicts Marigold's surface world and explores her psychology and perceptions.[14] Montgomery's active engagement with Canadian literature and criticism during the late 1920s makes it difficult to avoid seeing *Magic for Marigold* as a site on which questions of literary value were contested.

Magic for Marigold is relentlessly up to date in its cultural references, including allusions to Coué, chromosomes, and girls who look like sticks and have bobbed hair.[15] As well, both Marigold's perception that the "hobbles and huge hats of the tens" belong to "that legendary time before she was born" and Old Grandmother's reference to dandelion wine from sixty years ago as "the vintage of the sixties" firmly place the events of the novel in the 1920s, the decade in which it was published. Yet the narrator's comments on Marigold and what she learns from her childhood experiences place these apparently contemporary events in a past that Marigold has long outgrown; we are told that "in after life [Old Grandmother's speeches] were to come back to her" and that some of what Old Grandmother tells her she only understands "twenty years later."[16] Similarly, the narrator places the events of the novel in a completed past being described from the perspective of the present by using the present tense to express Grandmother's perplexity at a change in Marigold's and Gwennie's behaviour – "Grandmother can't understand it to this day." In fact, Marigold's entire life is placed in the past when the narrator notes that Marigold "*always* believed that she also ate two crickets" at a picnic and that "to the day of her death" she believed that she saw the chairs dancing when she was locked in the parlour for punishment.

To further complicate the chronology of the novel, while Montgomery explicitly grounds it in the contemporary world of its original readers, she also places it in the realm of fairy tales, beginning with the opening lines, "Once upon a time – which, when you come to think of it, is really the only proper way to begin a story – the only way that really smacks of romance and fairyland."[17] The phrase "once upon a time" suggests that the story takes place in a distant or mythic past, and the reference to "romance and fairyland" suggests that the story that follows will not be a work of contemporary realism. The novel's epigraph, "To Nora, in memory of a world that has passed away," also directs readers to think of the book as connected to a past – and presumably valued – state of existence.[18] Thus the account of Marigold's childhood experiences and development is associated with a particular state of mind – romance – that is associated with a remembered past. Through these strategies, Montgomery encourages the reader from the start to assume that the novel depicts events of the past rather than of the present, and not to expect it to depict the real-world experience of a realistic child, despite the carefully realist contemporary setting, thus both referencing the popular conception of her novels as depictions of rural child life and asserting the timelessness of her apparently realist presentation.

While the opening reference to fairyland may suggest that this is a book for children, that has not necessarily been the understanding of its readers. In her discussion of *Magic for Marigold* in *Harvesting Thistles* (1994), Elizabeth Waterston asserts that the novel was "written for children," but in *Magic Island* (2008), she expands her analysis of the child development theories at play in the novel without specifying the novel's audience, noting, however, that it is "a new kind of 'L.M. Montgomery book.'"[19] Elizabeth Epperly, in *The Fragrance of Sweet-Grass*, claims that Marigold "belongs to the worlds of poetry, fairy tale, and enchantment," thus drawing attention to a common assumption about what is appropriate for children's literature. However, she then suggests that the novel works against this assumption when she states that Marigold's world "is full of hidden ugliness" and that Old Grandmother's stories, "while in questionable taste in a supposed children's story ... are certainly the stuff of real life,"[20] addressing the assumed disjunction between realism and children's literature to which Mercier refers.

Some contemporary reviews of *Magic for Marigold* similarly address the question of readership and genre. The *New York Telegram* states that "it certainly is not a novel" but is "one of the stories about children ... which older people like to read, too," and the *Nottingham Journal* identifies the book as "light reading," which implies that it is intended for adults. The *Auckland Star*, referring to Marigold's "biography" as "an excellent study in character," also notes that "Marigold is a dreamer, and finds real life an adventure not to her liking. Modern girls may think this strange,"[21] suggesting that the realist elements of the novel are at odds with the "dreamer" who experiences them. The description of the book as "an excellent study in character" seems directed at an adult readership, but the description of Marigold as a dreamer and out of step with modern taste and the real world seems directed at younger readers and identifies Marigold with fictional practices of the past. The *Montreal Daily Star* regards the book as suitable for both adult and child readers, as adults "will recall the days when we were young and reveled in the land of make-believe," and children will receive "an enrichment of the imagination."[22] The reviewer in the *Pioneer* of Allahabad states that "the author has a remarkable insight into the youthful mind" and argues that, while it "can be read with real pleasure as a novel," it also works as "an object lesson to parents – almost a study in child psychology,"[23] clearly suggesting that its audience will be adult.

Montgomery does not offer a clear indication herself as to whether she thinks a story *about* children is necessarily *for* children. Her first Marigold stories were written for the *Delineator*, an American magazine originally established to sell sewing patterns that for some time produced a Canadian edition.[24] Under the editorship of Marie Mattingley Meloney (1921–26),[25] the *Delineator* had published stories from the *Emily* novels in 1925 and had accepted stories about Marigold in 1925, publishing them in 1926.[26] Further stories were requested early in 1927 under editor Loren Palmer, but his replacement, Oscar Graeve, did not publish these stories, judging them, according to Montgomery, "not 'sophisticated' enough" for his audience.[27] The demand for sophistication, which in 1927 would suggest consonance with modernist literature, certainly suggests that the *Delineator* did not expect the stories it published to be read by a young audience. The American edition of the magazine in fact had a separate children's section, "The Little Delineator," in the 1920s, with craft ideas, stories, and activities,[28] making it all the more likely that the *Delineator*'s fiction was intended for adult readers. It is probable that Montgomery, having already produced stories for the magazine, understood that to be the case, though, in writing to G.B. MacMillan in 1929, she says of *Magic for Marigold*, "It is about a little girl but some of the chapters may interest an adult."[29] However, immediately after referring to the advertisement of *Magic for Marigold* in her journal, Montgomery writes that "I am working now on an adult story,"[30] with the qualifier "adult" implying by contrast that Montgomery did not consider *Magic for Marigold* an adult story.

Nevertheless, the narrator of *Magic for Marigold* seems sometimes to directly address an adult audience through comments that assume a shared understanding of how children experience the world and differ from adults – and that are more explicit than the "shadow text" and "double readership" that Perry Nodelman posits.[31] For instance, in describing the infant Marigold, the narrator refers to "the arrogant, superior smile of babies before they have forgotten all the marvelous things they know at first," suggesting that children are innately connected to a world of wonders that is lost with maturity. Similarly, after describing Marigold's interaction with the natural world on a walk with her mother, the narrator comments, "Marigold knew naught of Grecian myth or Anglo-Saxon folklore but the heart of childhood has its own lovely interpretation of nature in every age and clime, and Marigold was born knowing those things that are hidden forever from the wise and prudent and sceptical." The references to myth and folklore clearly appeal to an adult reader rather than a child reader; furthermore, the child is separated from adults not merely by the passage of time but by a difference in attitude that causes some things to be "hidden forever" from those who attain the supposedly adult characteristics of being "wise and prudent and sceptical."[32]

The narrator's reliance on the shared knowledge of adults is shown most clearly in the chapter titled "It," in which, during a visit to cousins, a single louse is found on Marigold's head. Marigold is completely unaware of why "an expression of profound horror" comes into Aunt Stasia's eyes as she looks at Marigold's head, why Cousin Teresa speaks in "a low shamed voice" when she asks if there is "a *comb*" in the house, and why Aunt Stasia claims "there has never been any need of one here, thank heaven" when Marigold is aware that there is a comb in every bedroom. She does not know what the "it" found on her head is, and, as the narrator never identifies "it" either, an understanding of the incident relies on the reader's knowledge of what "a comb" might refer to, and what might be spotted on the head that would cause such consternation. Marigold's fears about what "it" might be and the possible consequences clearly are presented for the reader's amusement. The use of free indirect discourse particularly calls attention to Marigold's thought processes and the disparity between her reaction and the actual circumstances. Marigold fears "she must have some terrible disease. Yes, that must be it. Leprosy was an awful thing. Suppose she had leprosy – or smallpox. Or that dreadful thing Uncle Klon flippantly called T.B.?"[33] However, the adult reader, informed by the preceding conversation about combs, recognizes how overblown her reaction is and realizes that her fear is caused by the overreaction of the adults she is visiting, who have not shared their knowledge with her. The comedy is emphasized through the printing of IT in small capital letters throughout the episode, a visual clue that dramatizes the child's reliance on adult knowledge and authority and the undue importance the adults attach to the incident. Once she knows what IT is, Marigold dismisses the incident as a matter of no importance, and is supported in this judgment by Aunt Marigold's professional opinion,[34] thereby justifying the narrator's mockery of the adult reaction and reinforcing the idea that there is a gap between child and adult understandings and knowledge. Marigold's young cousins, Nancy and Beulah, having seen the removal of the louse from Marigold's head, understand what the problem is (as may some young readers), so Marigold's failure to understand also reinforces the difference between Marigold and other children that the narrator draws attention to later in the novel, when it is noted that Marigold has no particular friends among the girls at school and that "the sense of cleavage deepened as she grew older, instead of disappearing."[35]

While it is a common trope for the central character of a novel to be differentiated from her peers in some significant respect, in *Magic for Marigold*, the differences between Marigold and the other child characters are specifically linked with issues of fictionalization and representation. Marigold feels that "it would be nice to have a real chum, of the kind you read about in books," a statement that explicitly draws attention to the fictional depiction of children in this book. Marigold's inability to "compromise with second best"[36] in the choice of a friend, and her attachment to her imaginary friend, Sylvia, suggest that the kind of chum to be found in books is an idealized one. During the composition of *Emily of New Moon*, Montgomery writes in her journal that "the public and the publisher won't allow me to write of a young girl as she really is," noting that "when you come to write of the 'miss' you have to depict a sweet, insipid young thing" rather than depicting the "very vivid love affairs" that she knows young teenage girls often have. However, she states, "one can write of children as they are; so my books of children are always good."[37] That is, she claims that her child heroines are realistic, even if she must gloss over some aspects of older characters. However, the tension she creates between a clearly contemporary world and a magic fairy-tale world in *Magic for Marigold* undercuts her claim to be writing in the realist mode, especially since, within this explicitly fictional world, child characters are further fictionalized, particularly through Sylvia, whose activities are narrated exclusively by Marigold, her creator. Sylvia develops from Marigold's seeing a plum bough in blossom and briefly mistaking it for a girl's figure, and Marigold can access her only by leaving the house through what she calls the Magic Door, leaving the garden through the Green Gate, and saying a rhyme she has composed. Thus, Sylvia is tied to a particular physical location and accessed through a ritual that is appropriate to her explicit association with fairyland, where, Marigold believes, "there was no such thing as time."[38] This further separates her experiences with Sylvia from real-world experience or a realist fictional depiction of experience.

As a character, Sylvia is clearly an extension of Marigold, her knowledge and interests limited by Marigold's knowledge and interests. Marigold celebrates Sylvia's birthday, assigns her characteristics, such as bravery, and gives her likes and dislikes, such as a preference for plum jam over gooseberry. When their activities include finding an echo "'way, 'way back in the hilly land," Marigold's admission that she might be "a little scared to go so far back" shows that, in believing Sylvia is brave, Marigold is giving her a quality that she feels she lacks herself, just as Sylvia's preference for plum jam complements her own preference for gooseberry. Similarly, when Marigold reports that Sylvia told her "God was a very nice-looking old gentleman" and that they saw elephants drinking at a fountain, she is creating stories that reflect her own behaviour – asking Mr Lord if he is God and imagining grey monkeys and four moons in her play with Varvara.[39] An imaginary friend is by definition an imagined friend, just as a fictional character is imagined by an author, so the nature of a child character's imaginary friend reflects the author's sense of what that character can imagine. Therefore, the child character's imaginary friend reveals what the author thinks children in general can imagine and what factors influence their imaginations, or what needs their imaginary friends address. In creating an imaginary friend, the child character stands in for the author, and the child character's version of "child" reifies the values, interests, and fears ascribed to children by the author.

In Marigold's interactions with Varvara and Gwennie, considerations of fiction, false representation, and make-believe underscore the problematics of depicting "real" children. Marigold's encounter with Princess Varvara links her imaginative life to her real life. When Marigold "almost" wishes for a "real little girl to play with," her wish seems to be answered when the narrator begins the next section of the chapter with "Perhaps this *was* a Magic Day," possibly "brewed up" by the cat, the Witch of Endor. Since Varvara "looked different in every way from the Harmony little girls," and appears "suddenly" and "uncannily," it seems that she is somehow outside of Marigold's world and is conjured specifically to meet Marigold's need, as is Sylvia. The uncanniness of her sudden appearance is reinforced by her initial refusal to name herself ("I'm me") and her description of herself as "just the right age." Even when Varvara does give an accurate account of herself, Marigold interprets it as fiction, saying "There are no princesses in Prince Edward Island. And you wouldn't be dressed like that if you were a princess."[40] At the end of their day together, Marigold is forced to accept as fact what she initially thinks is fiction and learns that, although "she had been used to pretend 'Suppose a Princess dropped in to tea,'" when it actually happens it is nothing like her make-believe version. While she is "very well satisfied" to go back to Sylvia, despite having "felt a vague discontent with [her]" and, at the start of the chapter, "*almost* wish[ing] [she] had a real little girl to play with," the narrator states that Marigold is "the poorer for a lost illusion,"[41] thus reinforcing the idea that the value of childhood resides in its separation from the real world and its concerns.

In her encounter with Gwennie, Marigold mistakes fiction for reality. She and Gwennie have been given idealized versions of each other by Aunt Josephine, leading to mutual suspicion and jealousy, so, when they are together, each modifies her behaviour to meet this fictional standard. If Gwennie is a chum of the kind found in books, the version of her that is presented by Aunt Josephine might be from a "Pansy" book, as she is described as impossibly good, pious, well-behaved, and scholarly. The "Pansy" books were written by Isabella Macdonald Alden and were described in her own time as "Sunday-school books" and "good, pure books for young and old alike."[42] The stories typically feature a religious conversion and a central character who struggles to live a Christian life in the face of personal difficulties or opposition; characters frequently hold discussions of evangelical biblical interpretation, Christian behaviour, and good works. As another contemporary put it, "[Pansy] has dedicated her work to the advancement of the Christian religion in the home life and in the business life."[43] While Montgomery refers to these books in her journals as part of her childhood reading, even as a girl she notes their disjunction from her own experience. Her description of having to take over a Sunday-school class in Prince Albert as "like a chapter out of a 'Pansy' book – but I did not feel at all like a 'Pansy' heroine," separates her experience from Alden's fictional depiction of such an incident.[44] As an adult, Montgomery purchased and read a "Pansy" book that she had wanted as a girl and finds it "ghastly," writing that "It *must* have been worse than the others. Surely even at twelve years I couldn't have read such mush with pleasure."[45] Her adult assessment underlines the disjunction between this "mush" and what she tries to depict in her fiction about girls' lives. The Gwennie who emerges once she and Marigold become aware they have been given false accounts of each other evokes another type of fictional child, the impossibly ill-behaved one – perhaps, as Rita Bode suggests in chapter 3 with respect to Perry Miller of the Emily series,[46] a version of the hero of *A Bad Boy's Diary* by Metta Victoria Fuller Victor, which Montgomery admired, or of Peck's Bad Boy, which she records her son Stuart reading.[47] When Montgomery rereads *A Bad Boy's Diary* as an adult, she finds it "even funnier" than when she first read it and "made a hero and model out of 'little Gorgie,'" who was "always in mischief."[48] Gwennie and Marigold do not enjoy each other's company until the fictions are recognized as such and each starts to behave in her usual way. Marigold misses Gwennie for a few days when she leaves, but feels "it was very nice to be alone with Sylvia again," still finding the "different world" and "beautiful hours" with her imaginary friend more satisfying than the real world and real friends.[49] By depicting Gwennie through two well-known child-character tropes, Montgomery differentiates Marigold from popular literary depictions of children and draws attention to the artificiality of those depictions, encouraging readers to evaluate her child characters from a different point of view.

The references to child substitutes in the novel further develop the distinction between real and imagined children. The Skinner doll, for instance, is "a waxen image" of a dead child, an image which the mother kept "beside her always and talked to it as if it had been alive." While it functioned in the past as a child substitute to the grieving mother, for subsequent generations it is merely an art object that "conferred a certain distinction" on the Lesleys, or an object which, by being "so lifelike," causes aversion: "Lorraine always shuddered when she passed it." The substitute, the fictional child, because of its approximation to a real child, is perceived as unnatural and unacceptable. When Marigold removes the doll from its glass case to play with it, she declares she does so because the doll "wanted to be loved so much," and she and her friend pretend to feed it, crown it with flowers, and treat it as royalty. Marigold's play with the doll is much like her imaginary play, such as supposing a princess came to visit or giving to Sylvia the complements to her own feelings; Marigold is loved, so she ascribes to the doll the desire to be loved. Similarly, Marigold encounters Mrs Delagarde, another mother who has lost a child and is trying to maintain the fiction that the dead child, named Delight, is living. At one point, she thinks Marigold is her lost child. When she puts Marigold in Delight's room, where the toys and clothing are left as they were at the time of her death, Marigold feels "a prickling in the roots of her hair" and perceives the dresses hanging in the closet as "awfully like Bluebeard's wives,"[50] responses that emphasize how unnatural and unreal is the fictional construct around the dead child. Mrs Delagarde's encounter with Marigold leads to her return to emotional health, as Marigold, in the perceived character of Delight, expresses the forgiveness the mother had been seeking from the lost child. The mother's belief that the child will return – that is, her belief in an imagined child – is an unhealthy state, which she must abandon for healthy participation in the real world.

Because it is associated with fairyland and make-believe, childhood is presented not as simply a period of life in this novel, but as either a state of mind or a memory. Marigold's childhood ends not when she reaches a certain age, but when she ceases to believe in fairyland, when she can no longer conjure up Sylvia after telling Budge, a neighbour boy, about her. The narrator does not specify the cause of that loss, instead asking questions about it: "Was it because she had told Budge about her? Or was it because she had suddenly grown too old and wise for fairyland? Were the 'ivory gates and golden' of which Mother sometimes sang, closed behind her forever?" While the reason for Marigold's loss of fairyland is not spelled out, the novel presents that loss as a natural and healthy progression. At the start of the final chapter, Marigold's mother thinks "it would not be a good thing if the wild secret charm of fairy-playmates spoiled Marigold for the necessary and valuable companionship of her kind."[51] Young Grandmother's attitude toward Marigold's imaginary world is also based on the belief that fairyland must be abandoned for a healthy life. However, when she prevents Marigold from going through the Magic Door to the fairyland Sylvia inhabits, Marigold becomes not just unhappy but unhealthy. During this illness, Marigold believes she is dying, which she does not regret, because she believes that "when I die I can go through The Magic Door without any key." As Lesley Clement argues in chapter 2, "Marigold does not allow fear to hold her back from confronting mentally and emotionally all of life's mysteries, including its final mystery – death."[52] This association of fairyland and access to her imaginary friend with an afterlife – a life outside the earthly and time-bound – further undermines the insistent contemporality of the novel's setting and separates Marigold's experience from the contemporary world of the novel. Childhood and access to fairyland and imagination are taken outside the life cycle to support the notion that childhood is not just a temporal phase but is equally a state of mind. That the mind has power to create a seemingly real state is asserted by Grandmother's friend Dr Clow, whose up-to-date assessment of Marigold's state – "neurosis caused by a suppressed desire for her playmate" – leads to the same recommendation as his statement that her "pretenses" are "truths to her" and that "she sees things invisible to us." He recommends that she be allowed to use her imagination now, as "she will lose it as she grows older."[53]

As noted above, Montgomery claims in her journal that young girl characters must be depicted like children, unaware of "the basic realities of life and reactions to them."[54] That is, she believed childhood to be separated from adolescence and adulthood by perception, and that the key difference was the child's lack of understanding of the "basic realities of life." Marigold's loss of Sylvia is prepared for through experiences that teach her some of the realities: that Bernice's father is in jail, that Paula suffers deprivation, that she cannot have Budge all to herself, that loss can be survived in different ways, all of which suggest that the novel "represent[s] the world as it is rather than as it ought to be."[55] While Marigold and her friends all engage in imaginative play, the other child characters are not given imaginary friends. Lorraine's sympathy with Marigold's attachment to Sylvia – possibly due to her own childhood imaginings and those of Marigold's father – and Dr Clow's understanding of her power of imagination both suggest that some adults, even if they cannot access fairyland themselves, remember it. When Dr Clow says that Marigold "will have to forego its wonder and live, like us, in the light of common day,"[56] he acknowledges that this change is a loss and should be delayed as long as possible. Marigold will not tell other children about Sylvia, as she "was so much her own," but Sylvia is changing all the same: she is "not so vivid – so living – so *real*." Marigold's acknowledgment of the fiction weakens her sense of Sylvia's reality, and once the story of Sylvia is communicated to Budge, she no longer exists, even to her creator. That is, the attempt to reify the imaginary child through description ironically establishes its fictionality, rather than creating the impression of reality. Although Marigold weeps because "her lovely dream was gone," the loss of the imaginary friend does not mean the loss of imaginative play, as Marigold and Budge go grail-hunting two days later. However, imaginative play now has a real-world outcome, for, instead of the grail, they find one of Grandmother's best cups, lost at a picnic two years earlier, and are rewarded with a plate of cookies. Aunt Marigold, in trying to help Marigold deal with both the loss of Sylvia and Budge's behaviour, refers to "our earthly house of love," reinforcing the difference between fairyland and the real world. The disjunction between child and adult perception is also reinforced in the narrator's statement that "if [Aunt Marigold] smiled over it Marigold did not see it." Marigold accepts that "the old magic was gone forever – gone with Sylvia and the Hidden Land and all the dear, sweet fading dreams of childhood."[57] Thus the state of childhood is always already in the past. Childhood as an identifiable state exists only in memory.

As noted at the beginning of this chapter, *Magic for Marigold* specifically – and fiction more generally – were discussed in a series of letters published in the Charlottetown *Guardian*, the writers focusing on the meanings of "real," "true," and "fictitious" as they critique and defend Montgomery's literary practice. The first writer, Mrs Edith Frank Fisher, an American visitor, notes that, if *Magic for Marigold* is "true," then strangers like herself have no right "to criticize the thoughts and life of [Prince Edward Island's] people," however "peculiar" and "antiquated" they might seem. However, in the continuation of that sentence, Mrs Fisher declares that Montgomery "has no right" to use real place names if the work is "fictitious" and "untrue." She further equates "fictitious" and "untrue" with "unreal": "I would certainly resent her exposing such bigotry if it were unreal."[58] In responding to this letter, "Islander" asserts that "this book must be purely fiction," but also that "good fiction should depict life in its real sense."[59] The third writer, "Outsider," interprets the issue raised in Mrs Fisher's letter as whether the book is "derogatory to the people of Prince Edward Island or, as an alternative, insincere." The association in these letters of "real," "true" and "sincere" in opposition to "fictitious" draws attention particularly to assumptions about the nature of fiction. To these readers, it seems that fiction must represent a believable time and place, but not an actual time and place; they expect realism, but not reality. Part of Outsider's defence of *Magic for Marigold* is based on the assumption that its setting is thirty years before, and that Marigold "differs from 'Miss 1930,' whose time is the present, and whose view is bounded by the car, the pictures and whatever amusement can be got out of life," because she is "a dreamer of dreams, an idealist."[60] Outsider's assertion indicates the potential confusion caused by Montgomery's narrative strategy: is the story set in the present decade so frequently alluded to, in the completed past suggested by references to Marigold's later life, or outside the realm of time, as suggested by the references to fairy tales and imagination? Even the writer who most explicitly defends the novel, who refers to "visitors [who] question the truth" of the work while seeming to suggest that Montgomery's depictions should be verifiable by residents of Prince Edward Island, asks "do not all authors draw somewhat on their imagination?"[61] suggesting that Montgomery must be expected to have deviated from a strictly documentary presentation of the real world.

In her clearly exasperated response, published 1 September 1930, Montgomery, in order to assert the literary value of her work, employs multiple strategies. These show some of her thinking about fiction in general and about *Magic for Marigold* and child characters in particular. To make the claim that her work, like other works with broad appeal, should not be read as dependent on verifiable local information, Montgomery gives details of her international fame, namedropping "the Hon. Stanley Baldwin, then Premier of Great Britain" and referring to her fan mail "from all over the world." She also establishes her authority on the topic of Prince Edward Island as a descendent of early settlers, before addressing the nature of fiction. Her first claim about fiction is that "human nature does not change" and that her "characters are 'types' that are found wherever human beings congregate." When she states that, regardless of the period depicted, "the fictitious incidents of [her] books" will never match the tragedy or comedy actually experienced by Islanders, she claims both that fictitious incidents cannot replicate actual human experience and that all human societies, no matter how small or remote, undergo the full range of human experience. Montgomery ridicules the notion that real places are not to be used in fiction by reference to Sinclair Lewis, Theodore Dreiser, and Mazo de la Roche, and states that it is "back-country" to believe that the opinions of characters are those of the author,[62] thus establishing both her own knowledge of contemporary realism and her cosmopolitan attitude. By asserting the universality of human behaviour, the difference between actual experience and fictional depiction, and the separation between author and characters, Montgomery outlines her theory of fiction, effectively claiming to write realism, but not merely to describe the contemporary world.

When Montgomery then describes Marigold in her letter as "one of those ageless daughters of imagination and vision that are to be found occasionally in every age of a nation's history,"[63] she claims that the questions of time and place raised by the letter writers are irrelevant to Marigold's characterization. This statement strongly suggests that the tension between past and present and between overtly fictionalized and supposedly realistic child characters in this novel is a deliberate strategy on Montgomery's part to remove *Magic for Marigold* from the realms of children's literature and regionalism with which she is generally associated, a response to what Waterston identifies as "Montgomery's recognition of a major shift in literary topics and styles."[64] While Montgomery may insist that Marigold "is not intended to be 'Miss 1930' or Miss Any-age,"[65] she has in fact explicitly presented her as a contemporary child, even if her assertion that human nature does not change allows a contemporary child to be also "ageless." By claiming a theoretical ground that she implies is also inhabited by writers such as Dreiser (who, incidentally, had earlier in the century edited the American edition of the *Delineator*) and Lewis,[66] Montgomery also claims literary sophistication, despite the novel's focus on a child character, a choice which, as discussed above, seems to have caused some confusion among reviewers and readers in light of Montgomery's earlier works. While Montgomery contests a concept of realism dominant in the 1920s that she associates with "photograph[ing] a latrine or pigsty meticulously,"[67] both implicitly through the metafictive elements of *Magic for Marigold* and explicitly in her public defence of her composition, she claims realism as an aspect of her writing.

Early in 1930 Montgomery seems to have been engaged in an internal conversation about her career. In her long journal entry of 1 March 1930, she records having reread her books over the previous few weeks and enjoyed them, noting of *Rilla of Ingleside* "how clearly it reflected the atmosphere and background of those war years."[68] She then records excerpts from reviews of all her books, drawing attention to the conflicting assessments, responding to some criticisms, and asserting that "I have written to please myself. It has not mattered much what anyone else thought."[69] With her previous remarks on latrines and pigsties clearly in mind, she also defends the romanticism which was one of the factors in the devaluation of her work at that time: "I always tried to catch and express a little of the immortal beauty and enchantment of the world into which I have sometimes been privileged to see for a moment – the moment of Emily's 'flash.' Those who never have that glimpse cannot believe there is such a world. I can but pity them."[70] Montgomery undertakes this review and assessment while writing *A Tangled Web*, which she describes in her journal as "an adult story"[71] and which also has an explicitly contemporary setting. The *Guardian* discussion of *Magic for Marigold* just a few months after this reflection on her career may have revived her anger over the *Delineator*'s rejection of the second batch of Marigold stories in 1927. Montgomery was particularly wounded by that rejection, as she said she wrote the Marigold stories not for the money "but for the kudos their appearance in *The Delineator* would give me."[72] That is, she recognized that publication in the *Delineator* was of particular significance for her reputation as a serious writer, not just for children, but for adults as well. She defends *Magic for Marigold* on the grounds that, while it is fiction, it is based on reality, and that, while it is apparently set in the present, it depicts timeless situations and a timeless child character, who is herself a creator of fictions. Her defence, that is, resists the categorization of her work.

Montgomery's focus in *Magic for Marigold* on issues of fictionality in the depiction of children and its undercutting of its own claim to contemporary reality can be read as her demonstration of narrative sophistication. Her public engagement with readers on the question of her fictional strategies and her criticism of reductive and simplistic readings of her work constitute an assertion of the value of her career at a time when the tide of taste in fiction was moving away from what is perceived as her usual style. The day after the publication of her letter in the *Guardian*, Montgomery finished writing *A Tangled Web*,[73] which Benjamin Lefebvre has analyzed as Montgomery's attempt to explore some aspects of modernist experimental form.[74] The relative neglect of *A Tangled Web* and *Magic for Marigold* in Montgomery scholarship is perhaps a result of their differences from her earlier work and the tendency of readers to seek unifying concepts of a writer's career. Contending with that tendency, Montgomery's active engagement through *Magic for Marigold* and the *Guardian* letter with questions of how realistically children can or should be portrayed in fiction shows a writer consciously interrogating her culture and her place in it, a reminder that critical conversations are never closed.

NOTES

1 Fisher, "Letter 1 – 12 August 1930," 263.

2 LMM, "Letter 6 – 1 September 1930," 270.

3 "Realism," *The Cambridge Guide to Literature in English.*

4 LMM, "Letter 6 – 1 September 1930," 270.

5 LMM, *MM*, 179.

6 Hill, *Modern Realism*, 21, 22. Hill specifically refers to Duncan Campbell Scott, Sara Jeannette Duncan, Nellie McClung, and Ralph Connor, as well as Montgomery.

7 Mercier, "Realism," 198.

8 Gerson, "The Canon between the Wars," 47.

9 Pike. "(Re)Producing Canadian Literature."

10 LMM, *CJ* 6:243.

11 Rubio, *Lucy Maud Montgomery*, 479–80.

12 Montgomery, *After Green Gables*, 163, 164, 177–8, 169–70, 148 and 163, 180–2.
13 Ibid., 154.
14 Hill, *Modern Realism*, 9, 76.
15 LMM, *MM*, 8, 96, 72, 83.
16 Ibid., 62, 76, 41–2, 46.
17 Ibid., 142, 260 (emphasis added), 44, 1.
18 For a fascinating discussion of time in *Magic for Marigold*, see Epperly, "*Magic for Marigold*: Engendering Questions about What Lasts."
19 Waterston, "Marigold and the Magic of Memory," 161; Waterston, *Magic Island*, 153.
20 Epperly, *Fragrance of Sweet-Grass*, 239, 241.
21 "Another Little Girl," 299; "In a Small World," 300; "Strange to Modern Girls," 305.
22 "Suffused with Whimsicality," 303.
23 "Simple Story, but Fine Character Drawing," 305.
24 Mott, *History of American Magazines*, 481–2.
25 Ibid., 489.
26 LMM, *CJ* 5:259, 421; C. Collins, *Annotated Bibliography*, 37–8.
27 LMM, *CJ* 6:105–6, 185. For an account of the shift in literary taste that may have led to this rejection, see Sutherland, "Advocating for Authors."
28 For examples, see "Prosperity and Thrift: The Coolidge Era and the Consumer Economy, 1921–1929," on the Library of Congress's *American Memory* website. https://memory.loc.gov/cgi-bin/query/r?ammem/cool:@field(NUMBER+@band(dl1))::bibLink=D?coolbib%3A1%3A./temp/~ammem_hDFX%3A%3A; https://memory.loc.gov/cgi-bin/ampage?collId=amrlgs&fileName=dl1page.db&recNum=18&itemLink=D? coolbib:1:./temp/~ammem_hDFX.
29 Montgomery, *My Dear Mr. M.*, 140.
30 LMM, *CJ* 6:260. The novel referenced is *A Tangled Web.*
31 Nodelman, *Hidden Adult*, 8, 303 *passim.*
32 LMM, *MM*, 6, 35.
33 Ibid., 102–4 (emphasis in original).
34 Ibid., 107–8.
35 Ibid., 179.
36 Ibid., 179.
37 LMM, *CJ* 5:197.
38 LMM, *MM*, 34–5, 92, 79, 90.

39 Ibid., 89, 91, 90–1, 81, 43, 122.

40 Ibid., 118–120 (emphasis in original).

41 LMM, *MM*, 130, 118 (emphasis in original), 131.

42 Marquis, *Who's Who in America*, 19; Willard and Livermore, *A Woman of the Century*, 14.

43 Rutherford, *American Authors*, 653. I base this description partly on my personal knowledge of *One Commonplace Day*, *The Man of the House*, *Four Girls at Chautauqua*, *The Chautauqua Girls at Home*, and *Ruth Erskine's Crosses.*

44 LMM, *CJ* 1:56. In *Chautauqua Girls at Home*, Flossy Shipley takes over a Sunday-school class of teenage boys, with immediate success.

45 LMM, *CJ* 6:224.

46 Bode, "Vulnerable Situations," 80–1, in this volume.

47 LMM, *CJ* 2:54; LMM *CJ* 5:223.

48 LMM, *CJ* 2:54; other bad-boy books are identified at the George W. Peck website: http://www.georgewpeck.com/index.html.

49 LMM, *MM*, 178.

50 Ibid., 4, 45, 196–7.

51 Ibid., 269, 264.

52 Clement, "L.M. Montgomery's Precocious Children," 64, in this volume.

53 LMM, *MM*, 90, 94, 97.

54 LMM, *CJ* 5:197.

55 "Realism," *The Cambridge Guide to Literature in English.*

56 LMM, *MM*, 79–80, 97.

57 Ibid., 266 (emphasis in original), 269–70, 272, 273.

58 Fisher, "Letter 1 – 12 August 1930," 263.

59 Islander, "Letter 2 – 19 August 1930," 265.

60 An Outsider, "Letter 3 – 22 August 1930," 265, 266.

61 A.M.C., "Letter 5 – 27 August 1930," 268.

62 LMM, "Letter 6 – 1 September 1930," 269–70.

63 Ibid., 270.

64 Waterston, *Magic Island*, 151.

65 LMM, "Letter 6 – 1 September 1930," 270.

66 Hutchisson and Pastore, "Sinclair Lewis and Theodore Dreiser," 71. Both Dreiser and Lewis were nominated for the Nobel Prize in 1930, Lewis receiving the award. The contest was a subject of public discussion in the weeks before

the announcement in November; see also Lunden, "Theodore Dreiser and the Nobel Prize."

67 LMM, *CJ* 6:243.

68 LMM, *CJ* 7:12.

69 Ibid., 26.

70 Ibid., 26.

71 LMM, *CJ* 6:260.

72 LMM, *CJ* 6:185. In September 1926, the title on the magazine cover changed from *The Delineator* to *Delineator*, but Montgomery uses the earlier form here.

73 LMM, *CJ* 7:57.

74 Lefebvre, "Pigsties and Sunsets."

PART THREE

Continuing Literary Conversations: Transformative Relationships and Spaces

7

Loving, Larking, and Lying: Free-Spirited Children and Disciplinary Adults in the Works of L.M. Montgomery and Astrid Lindgren

ÅSA WARNQVIST

In an essay on her childhood reading, world-renowned Swedish author Astrid Lindgren (1907–2002) describes her experience of reading L.M. Montgomery's *Anne of Green Gables* (1908) as an eleven-year-old: "And then there's Anne of Green Gables, of course. My unforgettable Anne, forever riding the buggy next to Matthew Cuthbert underneath the apple blossoms of Avonlea! The times we had together! My sisters and I spent a whole summer playing Anne of Green Gables in the big pile of sawdust up by the saw, I was Diana Barry and the mud puddle behind the barn was the Lake of Shining Waters."[1] In this essay, Lindgren references a number of classic boys' and girls' stories, and of all the works mentioned, *Anne of Green Gables* is the one she lingers on the longest and the one she describes in the most enthusiastic terms. Like Montgomery, as this volume's introduction outlines,[2] Lindgren was an avid reader, alluding at length in her books and articles to literary works she had read.[3] And, like Montgomery, when Lindgren spoke of her own reading, she often returned to that of her childhood.[4] Among these works, Montgomery's *Anne of Green Gables* was of particular importance to Lindgren, not only to her as a reading child but also to her as the adult author. As I will argue in this chapter, one important reason for this is that Montgomery describes and discusses the issues that develop when imaginative children are brought in contact with disciplinary adults, a topic also dear to Lindgren. In Montgomery, Lindgren found a conversation partner in matters concerning child rearing and child autonomy. As the perspectives of her literary characters indicate, Montgomery was progressive in these matters in her time, and when Lindgren wrote her works some decades later, Montgomery's stories offered a platform from which she could develop her own even more progressive ideas, in line with new pedagogical concepts. As I will show in the following analysis, Montgomery's presence in Lindgren's work helps Lindgren question the process of socialization dictated by adults and the limits of freedom to which children are subjected.

Much research with a comparative perspective has been undertaken to identify the traces of Montgomery in Lindgren's textual universe by scholars such as Sarah Death, Vivi Edström, Cornelia Rémi, Eva Söderberg, Gabriella Åhmansson, and me.[5] In this chapter, I will look at these traces as Lindgren's *responses* to Montgomery by analyzing Montgomery's presence in Lindgren's work as the result of a responsive reading of her novels and short stories.[6] The theoretical inducement for this perspective comes from Swedish literary scholar Kjell Espmark's theorizing of dialogues between texts. Drawing on Mikhail Bakhtin's dialogism, Espmark discusses allusions and references to another author's works as "responses." Following Espmark's lead, I will argue that Montgomery is a clearly identifiable voice in several of Lindgren's texts, and that Lindgren, by engaging in a response, articulates her progressive attitudes and beliefs concerning child rearing and child autonomy.[7] Several of Lindgren's works – particularly the *Pippi Longstocking* trilogy (1945–48), some of the short stories in *Kajsa Kavat och andra barn* (1950) [*Brenda Brave and Other Children*, not translated into English], the *Emil* trilogy (1963–70), and the two books about Madicken (1960, 1976), or Mardie as she is called in the English translations – can be seen as responses to Montgomery's *Anne* and, in some cases, to the *Emily* books.

My analysis is also inspired by Sarah Death's notion of the *Pippi Longstocking* trilogy as a tribute to, and a subversion of, *Anne of Green Gables*. Death makes a comparison between the two, and although she never poses the question of *why* Lindgren so carefully reinterprets and transforms Montgomery's depictions and the social structures of the late-nineteenth century, the subtitle of her article, "tribute and subversion," offers an important clue. While she only indirectly returns to these ideas in her analysis, she clearly considers the *Pippi* trilogy to be both similar to Montgomery's novel (and therefore a tribute) and dissimilar (and therefore a subversion).[8] The notion of "tribute and subversion" in the *Pippi* trilogy is a fruitful approach to not only this trilogy but also other works by Lindgren in which Montgomery's presence is strong. The notion informs my analysis of how Lindgren's responsive and critically engaged reading of Montgomery results in writing that celebrates but also subverts some ideas and traditions concerning children and childhood(s) met in Montgomery's texts.

The traces of Montgomery in Lindgren's work are strongest in depictions of playful, imaginative children in the presence or absence of disciplinary adults. The celebration of free-spirited children is a recurring theme with both authors, but while Montgomery conveys the idea that playfulness and imagination characterize childhood and need to be subdued as children mature to assume adult responsibilities, Lindgren emphasizes free, autonomous children, who do not want to – and do not have to – assimilate. Both authors are affected by the pedagogical ideas of their time. Montgomery was an educated schoolteacher, reputedly a good and popular one, who, according to Mary Rubio, "used her quick verbal skills and her sense of humour to keep order."[9] As Elizabeth Waterston notes, Montgomery would have known the predominant pedagogical orientation of the nineteenth century, for instance that of German educator Friedrich Froebel and philosopher and educational reformer John Dewey. The former advocated individual development and believed in nurturing children as flowers in a gentle setting, while the latter had a more practical outlook and claimed that children must interact with their environment to learn and become productive members of a democratic society.[10] Ideas from both thinkers can be discerned in the practices of likeable schoolteachers in Montgomery's novels, such as the kind and gentle Miss Stacy, who encourages her students to make field exhibitions and partake in concerts, or Mr Carpenter, who lets his pupils present their exercises orally, recite poems, and make speeches. Lindgren, for her part, was influenced by philosophers and educators like Bertrand Russell and A.S. Neill, whose books advocating a pedagogy of freedom were published in Swedish in the 1930s.[11] Their new ideas manifest themselves in Lindgren's work, for example through her critique of prevailing disciplining methods and her highlighting of autonomous, imaginative children who enjoy free playing. The latter is a central aspect of Lindgren's views on children. In almost all her stories, children are either playing or wishing they could.[12] Influenced by the changing views on child rearing that attracted attention from the late-nineteenth century through the mid-twentieth century, Lindgren responded to the ideas expressed in Montgomery's novels through emphasizing her own views on children and disciplining methods. In her response to Montgomery, Lindgren pays tribute to her predecessor's depictions of imaginative children and authoritative adults, but also rewrites these by embracing the subversive power of free children.

Lindgren publicly expressed her ideas on child rearing early on. In a newspaper debate in 1939, five years before she made her debut as a children's book author, she expressed critical ideas of the sovereignty of adults in contemporary society and what children must endure as adults dictate every aspect of their lives, from what they should eat and when they should go to sleep to their future and outlooks. According to Ulla Lundqvist, Lindgren's insights into how children's lives and wishes are circumscribed by adults led her to believe that children long for freedom and sovereignty, and that they deserve and have the right to demand respect from adults. Lindgren found confirmation of these notions in the new pedagogical ideas, which resulted in her writing, in Lundqvist's words, "an emancipation proclamation of the children,"[13] that is, the ground-breaking children's book *Pippi Långstrump* (1945) [*Pippi Longstocking*, 1950].

Pippi Longstocking is Lindgren's best-known free-spirited child. Pippi's traits – power and strength, love and generosity – can be directly connected to the ideas of Russell and Neill.[14] In the letter accompanying the first *Pippi* manuscript sent to the first prospective publisher (who rejected it), Lindgren mentions Russell's *Education and the Good Life* (published in English in 1926 and in Swedish in 1933) and highlights Russell's ideas on children's fantasies about having power: "Bertrand Russell … informs me that the noblest instinctive trait of childhood is the desire to become an adult, or perhaps rather the desire for power, and that in her imagination the typical child will amuse herself with fancies that involve the desire for power. I don't know if Bertrand Russell is correct, but I am inclined to believe he is, judging by the downright shocking popularity that Pippi Longstocking for several years has enjoyed among my own children and their friends."[15] By drawing on Russell as an authority, but at the same time claiming that she does not know whether Russell is right, Lindgren expresses an awareness of how controversial these ideas were at the time and that they might be provocative to the publisher. She is also aware of how progressive the Pippi character is at this point: she does her best not to alienate the publisher by emphasizing that "Pippi's behaviour has not had a harmful influence" on her own children and their friends, who understand that "Pippi is an eccentric, in no way fit to serve as a role model for ordinary children."[16]

In *Pippi Longstocking*, Lindgren portrays a motherless nine-year-old girl, living without adults or guardians, who moves into Villekulla Cottage accompanied only by a horse and a monkey, and visited only occasionally by her father, the king of a South Pacific island. Pippi is said to be the strongest girl on earth, and a bag full of money leaves her financially independent. In the absence of adult authority, she takes care of herself and develops unconventional approaches to social norms. She does what she pleases, whether it means sleeping with her feet on the pillow or having cake for breakfast. She jokes, lies, and tells plenty of tall tales. In confrontations with Pippi, adults are often shocked by her behaviour. Nevertheless, because she defines her own moral outlook and standards, she is a fair-minded, good-hearted, and generous child.

Pippi is thus shaped by the modern pedagogical ideas about child autonomy, but she is also shaped by Lindgren's close connection to *Anne of Green Gables*. Anne, too, is a young girl living without her biological parents and who, different as they may seem, has much in common with Pippi. In Lindgren's own initial drawing of Pippi, on the front page of the original manuscript of *Pippi Longstocking* given to her daughter on her tenth birthday, Lindgren portrays a girl with bright red hair in braids that stick out from her head.[17] The image echoes the novel's description of Pippi's hair as "the same colour as a carrot" and "braided in two stiff pigtails that stood straight out from her head," but is also reminiscent of her Canadian predecessor, with her "two braids of very thick, decidedly red hair."[18] Born in 1907, Lindgren would have read the first Swedish edition of *Anne of Green Gables* (1909), the novel's first translation, which was reprinted with the same cover until 1920. On the 1909 cover, the unknown illustrator depicts a girl with strong and confident posture, who looks straight at the reader. She wears a knee-length dress and carries a suitcase, similar in shape and size to Pippi's suitcase full of money in Ingrid Vang Nyman's original illustrations. The Swedish 1909 Anne is portrayed with bright orange-red hair far more conspicuous than the hair of the Gibson Girl image on the cover of the original US publication from L.C. Page Co. (Boston). It is so bright, in fact, that Montgomery herself reacted to it.

When receiving her copy of the translated book, Montgomery noted in her journal that Anne had "hair of a literally *scarlet* hue."[19] In her autobiographical essay *The Alpine Path*, she added that the cover always gave her "the inestimable boon of a laugh."[20] When Lindgren bestowed on her heroine the same kind of bright red hair she was very likely influenced by this cover. These early visual interpretations of Pippi and Anne underline the parallels between the two girls, and the red braids have over time become synonymous with both of them. The hair colour signals power and subversion, but the intense colour of Pippi's hair, combined with the braids sticking straight out from her head, suggests an even stronger subversive force in the Pippi character.[21]

The visual parallels signalling subversion extend beyond the girls' hair. When Åhmansson compares the capacities and appearances of the two girls as they are described in each text respectively, she concludes that both heroines are subversive: "The red hair symbolizes visibility when girls are supposed to be invisible; the mouth speaks of a voice capable of speaking in a loud voice when well-bred girls are supposed to be silent; the unorthodox dress contradicts the perfect image of a clean and neat little girl."[22] While Åhmansson is concerned with how the details of the girls' appearance are subversive from a gender perspective, these details also link both Anne and Pippi to the notion of child autonomy. What Åhmansson does not discuss is how the depictions of the two girls differ in terms of subversion, differences that begin to outline Lindgren's response to Montgomery's text concerning key elements of free children.

In contrast to Åhmansson, Death emphasizes the girls' appearances as a concrete example of how they differ.[23] She notes details such as Anne's acute self-consciousness about her red hair and freckles, in contrast to Pippi's pride when she states, "No, I do *not* suffer from freckles … I like them!"[24] When Anne's hair turns green after a failed attempt to dye it black, she is devastated and forced to have her hair cut. Pippi, on the other hand, considers deliberately dying her hair green in preparation for a journey to the South Pacific. These examples, I argue, effectively show Lindgren's work responding to Montgomery's through subverting the ideals of feminine beauty expressed in *Anne of Green Gables*. Juliet McMaster, who analyzes the mythopoetic depiction of hair in Montgomery's work, has concluded that "adjusting our hair is a female declaration of independence."[25] That Pippi is proud of her freckles and does *not* dye her hair are strong examples of the freedom manifested in this character. Unlike Anne, Pippi does not need to declare her independence; she is already independent. This is also underlined by her financial independence and physical strength, which can be seen as a response to Anne's initially less privileged situation and references to her consumptive constitution. While Anne carries all her possessions in her broken suitcase when arriving at Green Gables, Pippi has a house of her own; moreover, her suitcase is full of money, a difference in socio-economic terms that Lindgren creates to manifest the freedom of the Pippi character.

Death also elaborates on how differences in appearance reflect more substantive differences between their characters, an observation that I wish to extend further.[26] As opposed to Anne, Pippi refuses to adapt to the society in which she lives, as exemplified by their contrasting attitudes toward school and education. While Anne loves reading and learning and aspires to a career in teaching, Pippi has little interest in such conventional activities. Both girls rebel against school rules, but in different ways and with different consequences. For instance, after the teacher, Mr Phillips, punishes Anne for losing her temper when Gilbert Blythe calls her "Carrots!" she refuses to return to school. Anne is angry, humiliated, and insulted – doubly so because Mr Phillips has spelled her name without an "e." But Anne eventually returns to school and decides to become a "model pupil," not because she has forgiven the teacher but because she misses her friend Diana and, perhaps more importantly, understands that, as the narrator observes, although Mr Phillips is not a "very good teacher," she is the kind of "pupil so inflexibly determined on learning" that she "could hardly escape making progress under any kind of a teacher."[27]

Pippi, on the other hand, does not attend school, but one day two friends convince her to go. Pippi's objective is to experience a Christmas break, indicating that learning and scholarly progress are of no importance to her. Pippi thus has a very different approach to school than Anne: playful and rebellious. She deliberately arrives two hours late on her first and only day, and makes a loud, grand entrance. Among other rebellious acts, Pippi refuses to read and calculate when asked to and questions why she should answer the teacher's questions when the teacher already knows the answers herself. Pippi also tells tall tales, and, when asked to draw, makes a life-size drawing of her horse on the floor, a scene that can be seen as the inverse of Anne and Mr Phillips's interactions. The friendly, patient teacher forgives Pippi's behaviour, since Pippi assures her that she does not know any better, but they mutually agree that Pippi should leave school for now and return when she is older. Lindgren here reverses Anne's situation, flipping and exploring what happens when the pupil does what she pleases, and the teacher responds patiently. While Anne acknowledges the rules and eventually returns to school to become a "model pupil," Pippi refuses to accept any rules at all and stays away from school. These examples suggest that Anne, despite her occasional rebelliousness, mainly represents adjustment, while Pippi represents norm-breaking and becomes an extreme manifestation of Russell's and Neill's free children.

Also exemplifying and emphasizing Pippi's norm-breaking as Lindgren's inverse response to Montgomery is the depiction of the two girls' homes. Edström stresses the subversive properties of Pippi's home when she points out that "Villekulla Cottage – the name itself suggests chaos – is a deconstruction of a famous home from the traditional children's classics, the calm and orderly Green Gables."[28] While Green Gables is neat and tidy in the hands of the fastidious Marilla, Pippi's home, Villekulla Cottage, has become the archetype of a fun, disorganized home. With no adults to impose restrictions, Pippi can keep a horse indoors, prepare cookies on the floor, decorate any way she likes, and not worry about keeping the place tidy – an order that works perfectly fine for Pippi. In Swedish, the two names Grönkulla and Villa Villekulla have a kinship through their ending "kulla," a suffix alluding to, respectively, the Swedish word for hill and the playground game of tag. Villekulla also resembles the Swedish word "villervalla," meaning turmoil. Whereas the name of Anne's home links it to nature, Pippi's home is thus linked to play and upheaval, a difference that emphasizes how the two homes are constructed. Mavis Reimer points out that "a child inside a family home is a naturalized image" and "the depictions of stable and safe housing in narratives for children can be read as the adult promise, or hope, that the world is a place in which children can not only survive, but also thrive."[29] The promise of Green Gables is Reimer's naturalized image of the safe and nurturing home, while the promise of Villekulla Cottage is freedom and the overthrowing of societal norms. As a response to Montgomery, Lindgren has constructed Pippi's home as a place for a free-spirited child to thrive – not in a stable family home, but in a parent-free existence where she has the power to make all decisions by herself. Lindgren's response to Montgomery's ideal home deconstructs not simply

Green Gables but any ideal home in children's literature, in favour of an alternative whereby children's freedom comes first.

As the analysis above shows, in *Pippi Longstocking* Lindgren attacks authorities and the social norms of her time by portraying a physically and mentally strong girl who rejects the rules of the adult world. Similar tendencies are noticeable in other Lindgren texts where Montgomery's presence is strong. The short story "Under körsbärsträdet" ["Under the Cherry Tree"] in *Kajsa Kavat och andra barn* (1950) provides another example of Lindgren's responsive reading of *Anne of Green Gables*, here in terms of the portrayal of a fanciful child. The story begins with a romantic description of the protagonist Ann, sitting under a cherry tree on a summer night, watching the swallows fly. Sitting under her "wishing tree," Ann indulges in not only the experience of nature but also fantasies of death and of being an orphan.[30] When a woman sits down next to her, Ann tells her that she is an orphan, just like her mother before her. However, her embroidered tall tale is exposed when she claims her mother died as a young girl after having fallen from the very tree under which they are sitting. In many respects, Lindgren's Ann appears to be a projection of Montgomery's Anne. They share the same name, are preoccupied with the idea of being orphans, and are easily carried away with their own stories. From the outset, both are chatty, romantic, and placed in a spring setting, where a blossoming cherry tree sends their imaginations reeling, as Montgomery's Anne's imagination does when she first arrives in Prince Edward Island and imagines that she will sleep in a cherry tree when there is no one there to meet her.

Despite the strong kinship with Anne, however, Ann also takes after Pippi, especially when it comes to lying, which is not one of Anne's traits. Anne might be fanciful, but she is not known for telling lies. As Marilla points out, after having accused Anne of stealing her amethyst brooch and been proved wrong, "I shouldn't have doubted your word when I'd never known you to tell a story."[31] Both Anne and Pippi express their creativity through their imagination, but whereas Anne expresses hers as fantasies, Pippi often presents hers as facts. As a consequence, Pippi's fantasies are often received as lies. The same can be said about Ann, who takes her lying even further. She is scolded by the woman she lies to, but, despite the impossibility of her tale, Ann maintains she is right: "'My mother *did* die when she was little,' Ann angrily yells after her." When the woman has left, Ann quickly forgets about the whole conversation, turns her gaze back to the wishing tree, and, with the arrival of her mother on the scene, is exposed to the reader as not an orphan but a liar who even lies about her lying. The short story concludes with Ann "obediently" telling her mother that she is coming in, but remaining under the cherry tree. Ann's "Yes, Mum, I'm coming" is the only occasion in the short story when Ann recognizes an adult authority; however, she quietly rebels by lingering "under the cherry tree, watching the swallows fly," a small, but significant, act of independence.[32]

The peaceful, romanticized ending of the short story shows a narrator who sides with the child and does not condemn, but instead accepts the child's delight in letting her imagination run wild. In fact, the narrator does not judge this little liar at all, which is characteristic of Lindgren's writings, with the celebration of imaginative and playful children being a recurring theme. While Montgomery reveals a similar celebration of imaginative children, her novel does not overlook and thereby condone lying. On the contrary, lying is considered a serious misdemeanour, so much so that when Anne is accused of stealing the brooch, it is not the lost brooch that is Marilla's concern but the idea that Anne has lied: "It's a dreadful thing to think she tells falsehoods … It's a fearful responsibility to have a child in your house you can't trust."[33] In this sense, Lindgren enters into a conversation with Montgomery about the limits of freedom to which children are subjected: both stress the importance of imagination and play, but Lindgren's texts incorporate them unconditionally. Lindgren condones lying as the right of free, imaginative children; in contrast, honesty is at the very core of a moral conduct instilled in children in Montgomery's work.

Because the norm-breaking actions of Lindgren's Ann and Pippi are portrayed in a positive light, these stories reflect a critique of the process of socialization dictated by adults. By choosing settings, scenes, and characters so similar to *Anne of Green Gables* in both the *Pippi* trilogy and "Under körsbärsträdet," Lindgren highlights her subversion of key elements of Montgomery's novel and, by extension, her critique of late-nineteenth- and early-twentieth-century views on children and methods of discipline. This strategy is particularly evident in the trilogy about Emil of Lönneberga.

Emil was first introduced to readers in the 1960s through three books in which he pesters the residents of a rural, late-nineteenth-century Swedish community: *Emil i Lönneberga* (1963) [*Emil in the Soup Tureen*, 1970]; *Nya hyss av Emil i Lönneberga* (1966) [*Emil's Pranks*, 1971]; and *Än lever Emil i Lönneberga* (1970) [*Emil and Piggy Beast*, 1973]. By regularly getting into new mischief, Emil tests his family's – in particular his father's – patience. As a disciplining method – but not a very effective one – Emil's father locks him up in the tool shed to make him ponder his actions. Disciplining unruly children is yet another topic with which Lindgren engages in response to her predecessor. Three of Montgomery's child characters bear a particularly strong kinship to Emil: Anne Shirley; the mischievous Davy Keith, who has his most important appearances in *Anne of Avonlea* (1909); and Lionel Hezekiah from the short story "The Miracle at Carmody" in *Chronicles of Avonlea* (1912). In all these works, adults deem these children unruly and in need of disciplining.[34]

As the examples previously discussed show, one of Lindgren's strategies in her response to Montgomery is first to connect the characters that she wishes to contrast by making them resemble each other physically or mentally or by placing them in the same kind of setting. This strategy is also apparent in the *Emil* trilogy, where similarities in descriptions between Emil and one or more of the Montgomery characters alluded to are common. Many phrases uttered by Emil and other characters echo lines from the Swedish translations of Montgomery's texts. For example, both Emil and Lionel rarely intend to do mischief and never pull the same stunt twice. Anne, too, claims that she "never [makes] the same mistake twice."[35] Both Davy and Lionel are six-year-old orphans, roughly the same age as Emil, and all three are described similarly as blond cherubs.[36] Moreover, while there are also similarities between their antics, many of them are classic boyish pranks, not unique to these particular boys (such as frightening people with snakes, rats, or frogs, or painting their own or a sibling's face with watercolour or ink).[37] The parallels are most evident between Emil and Lionel, especially the boys' environments. They both have one strict guardian, who wants to lock the boy in a tool shed (Anton) or tether him in the yard (Judith), and one lenient guardian, who is indulgent and makes excuses for him (Alma/Salome).[38] Montgomery often sets up this kind of strict-lenient pairing with parental figures – for example, Marilla and Matthew, and, in the *Emily* trilogy, Aunt Elizabeth and Aunt Laura – although they are not so sharply contrasted. In Lindgren's *Emil* trilogy, this pairing is seen with Anton and Alma, and also with the kind farmhand, Alfred, and the strict maid, Lina, strengthening the connection to Montgomery's stories.

Moreover, there are several parallels between *Anne of Green Gables* and *Emil and Piggy Beast* in scenes where the stories centre on the main characters' rule-breaking with positive outcomes. In both cases, Anne and Emil accidentally get themselves and/or another character drunk.[39] A few chapters later, both children are given the opportunity to redeem themselves by venturing out into a winter landscape to save the life of another character. While readers likely consider their drinking mishaps inadvertent "mischief," their rescue missions involve deliberate rule-breaking and going against the commands of their parents or guardians.[40] The latter are absent during the ordeals, reappearing only when an authority, in both cases a doctor, praises the children's actions. In this manner, the deliberate violation of rules becomes a way of making amends for their previous unintentional "mischief" and results in a moral victory for the children.[41]

The many similarities in terms of scenes, lines, and descriptions between Montgomery's and Lindgren's unruly children suggest that Lindgren's aim is twofold: to affirm Montgomery's portrayal of the unruly children, but at the same time subvert it. The core point in Montgomery's depictions is that, although the children may be unruly, they are lovable too – a notion that recurs in Lindgren's stories. In *Anne of Avonlea*, Anne points out that Davy is "really a dear little chap," and that she likes Davy better than his twin sister, the obedient Dora.[42] Both the attitude and the phrasing can also be found in Lindgren's work. Emil, too, is described as a dear little boy by his mother.[43] The authors differ, however, when it comes to their attitudes to disciplining methods. In Montgomery's stories about Anne, Davy, and Lionel, attempts to discipline the children are made regularly. For instance, most of Davy's appearances are accompanied by a comment on how he should or should not behave. These attempts at discipline often lead the guardians to punish the children, by such methods as forcing the children to go to bed without supper or requiring them to apologize. The best-known example of the latter is the scene when Anne, confronting Rachel Lynde for calling her ugly, is then forced to apologize. The scene stresses that Anne needs to apologize when she does something social norms consider wrong; however, it also clearly reflects a triumph for Anne, who finds a way to apologize without compromising her integrity. She turns the apology into a form of play and enjoys the performance. Nevertheless, despite the emphasis on justice and the clever child's victory, the adults remain in charge, inflicting punishments and deciding when apologies are in order. As Söderberg points out, this notion is characteristic of early-twentieth-century girls' fiction in which female characters always, by extension, move toward being domesticated.[44] In Montgomery's texts discussed here, the same occurs for little boys.

Lindgren's treatment of an unruly child in the *Emil* trilogy is similar to Montgomery's in many respects, but it also reveals important differences. In the *Emil* books, the adults are in charge in theory, but not in practice. Although Emil may not repeat the same mistake twice, he still does essentially as he pleases. He is rarely scolded, but instead is sent straight to the tool shed. He is never asked to apologize, and as he does not seem to mind the hours spent in the tool shed, he is, in fact, never actually punished. On the two occasions when he does object to being sent to the tool shed – when there is a party at the family farm, Katthult, and when he wants to go swimming with Alfred – he easily escapes, which indicates that he usually stays in the tool shed of his own free will. In neither case is a punishment administered. Instead, his breakouts pay off; in one case, Emil fills up on delicious sausages, and in the other, he enjoys swimming in the nearby lake with Alfred.

Katthult is not the only place where unruly children go unpunished in Lindgren's works. Lundqvist considers this a key attitude: "although there are lots of mischievous children … there is hardly any punishment at all. When somebody has earned a penalty, like Emil, the whole thing is turned into triumph. Emil is happy to be locked up in the tool-shed carving his little figures, very well aware that he is much smarter than his father, who thinks the boy is ruefully contemplating his sins."[45] Punishment works quite differently in Montgomery's novels. Even if her child characters occasionally escape punishment for actions disapproved of by their guardians, the moral outlook is not the same as in Lindgren's work. One example from *Emily of New Moon* (1923), translated into Swedish by Lindgren's sister, Stina Hergin, in 1955, reveals an interesting difference in morals compared to the two Emil breakouts described above, despite the similarities of the narratives. Aunt Elizabeth locks Emily in a room as punishment for going barefoot to the shop, but Emily escapes through the window, and when she returns home, only Aunt Laura is there. Emily believes she has "got off better than she deserve[s]," since she knows that Aunt Laura will not give her away. Unlike Emil, Emily expresses awareness of her naughtiness and disciplines herself. Despite Aunt Laura's encouragement to continue going barefoot but avoid being caught – "What

Elizabeth doesn't know will never hurt her" – Emily does not agree. "You oughtn't to be so good to me because I *was* bad today," she responds, claiming that she has disgraced her family by her behaviour. She also decides that from now on she "must obey Aunt Elizabeth because she's the head of the family."[46]

This kind of respect and voluntary adjustment shows a very different outlook on adult authority than is expressed in Lindgren's *Emil* books. Since the *Emil* trilogy is narrated by an external, omniscient narrator, who does not always tell us what Emil's objectives are, it is sometimes impossible to tell whether Emil's antics are deliberate. However, his reactions – mainly that he never blames himself – suggest that he does not consider his behaviour to be mischievous. Consequently, Emil is not ashamed, and throughout the three novels, he expresses regret only once.[47] Apologizing never even seems to cross his mind, nor, as mentioned above, is he ever told to apologize. On several occasions, however, he is angry over what he considers to be unfair treatment. In this sense, Emil's attitude toward his actions differs greatly from both Emily's and Anne's. Being an orphan without a proper upbringing, Anne actually *wants* to be disciplined. Anne is described as feeling sincere regret in many situations when she has done something wrong, and the reader follows her development into a young woman who leaves mischief behind.

Lindgren's responsive reading of the disciplining of unruly children in Montgomery's works results in depictions of children who refuse to adapt to the adult world and its expectations of children. While the prime example of an autonomous child in Lindgren's novels is Pippi, who has no adult authorities to whom she must answer, Emil, too, is in many ways an independent child. Like Pippi, he is very much in charge in practice, and, like Pippi, he represents rebellion during the period of his life that the stories cover. Although all his actions serve a logical purpose in his games, the adults fail to see this. The reason for this and for the strong reactions to his actions is, I argue, that he refuses to be restrained. Emil is a child who, unlike Anne but similar to Pippi, rebels against the rules established by adults. Like Pippi, he refuses to adjust, and therefore his attitude and actions become a form of rebellion against adult power and wrongful discipline. Because the omniscient narrator can foretell the future, there is no need for readers to worry about what will become of Emil. The narrator assures readers, not once but five times throughout the trilogy, that Emil will grow up to become chairman of the village council, which suggests that the author sympathizes with Emil rather than the father and his methods; the free, playful child grows up to be a respectable adult. To do so, at one point or another in his life, Emil would undoubtedly need to conform and make certain concessions, but since Lindgren never follows her protagonists into adulthood, she can, unlike Montgomery, focus solely on her conviction that children's longing for freedom and sovereignty needs to be acknowledged.

The publishing of the *Emil* trilogy overlapped with the publishing of Lindgren's two books about Mardie, *Madicken* (1960) [*Mardie*, 1979] and *Madicken och Junibackens Pims* (1976) [*Mardie to the Rescue*, 1981]. Notably, the *Mardie* books also illustrate Lindgren's questioning of prevailing methods of discipline in favour of imagination and play. Focusing on the everyday life and adventures of Mardie and her younger sister, Lisabet, both books are set during the First World War. With their main theme being social and economic differences, they are two of Lindgren's most political books. Mardie leads a good life in a middle-class environment, with kind and supportive adults around her. She plays and regularly gets into mischief, but she is also exposed to social inequality and reflects on the injustices around her.

As Rémi has shown, there is an emphasis on play and imagination in the *Mardie* books, with strong ties to *Anne of Green Gables*. Rémi analyzes the two books, starting with Lindgren's statement that the *Mardie* books are primarily inspired by the author's own childhood games. These metapoetic games create a bond, Rémi argues, since Lindgren attests to having played Anne of Green Gables as a child. Rémi finds traces of Montgomery's novel in several scenes, motifs, and descriptions. For instance, she notes that Mardie follows Anne's example when she evokes frightening fantasies, learns lessons during re-enactments of biblical episodes, and climbs a roof in response to a provocation.[48] Rémi's perspective allows her to focus specifically on scenes connected to imagination and play, which are pertinent to my discussion here, in that they highlight Lindgren's depiction of yet another free-spirited child. A good example of this is the episode when Mia challenges Mardie to walk across the school roof in *Mardie to the Rescue*, which has a strong resemblance to the scene when Josie Pye dares Anne to walk the ridgepole of the Barry family's kitchen roof. In Rémi's analysis of the two episodes, she considers them liminal spaces for both girls, scenes of transition into new phases in their lives – in Anne's case the passage "from her fictional refuge to the actual world," but for Mardie "the savouring of childhood and of playing at its essence and centre."[49]

Apart from emphasizing playing, the *Mardie* books also contain several episodes that highlight Lindgren's response to Montgomery on the question of disciplining children. There are, for example, several comparable situations, when Montgomery's protagonists are reprimanded for their actions while Mardie is not. In the second chapter of *Mardie*, Mardie invents a mischievous classmate, Rickard, whom she can blame for her own wrongdoing. When she returns home from school one day with a broken slate, she claims that Rickard has thrown it at the wall, although the reader realizes that Mardie has most likely broken the slate herself. This episode is reminiscent of the previously mentioned scene in *Anne of Green Gables*, in which Gilbert teases Anne about her red hair, and she is punished for breaking her slate over his head. Unlike Anne, Mardie is not reprimanded, since she has someone else to blame. The chapter also includes a possible reference to a mischievous act in *Emily of New Moon*. Just like Emily, Mardie cuts her bangs, both girls defying their parent's or guardian's wishes. Both demonstrate a strong and independent will by cutting their hair; however, Mardie avoids any consequences by blaming Rickard, while Emily is punished by her authoritarian aunt.[50] While Emily is subdued, Mardie is established as an imaginative child, who lies to her parents about the circumstances surrounding these events and avoids consequences. Mardie contemplates the possibility of corporal punishment when her mother discovers there is no Rickard, but no such punishment is administered within the narrative framework. The reader later learns that Mardie's parents are against corporal punishment, which renders such a punishment unlikely. Like her literary sisters Pippi and Ann, Mardie is depicted as a child who challenges the norms of obedience and lets her imagination run wild – without any disciplinary actions being taken by adults. Both Mardie and her sister Lisabet exhibit a rebellious and inquisitive nature on several occasions. For example, a feud with their antagonists, the impoverished Mattis and Mia, culminates in a fist fight in the street. In this sense, Mardie becomes yet another example of a norm-breaking female character in Lindgren's canon being set against Montgomery's protagonists.

The best example of Lindgren speaking out against the disciplining of children is the aftermath of Mardie and Mia's roof challenge. On her way down from the roof, Mia steals her teacher's wallet through a window and uses the money to buy sweets. In the dramatic scene following this, Mia is beaten by the teacher in the classroom, in front of her classmates. Although the punishment is administered to her antagonist, Mardie reacts strongly to the abuse, putting an end to it by screaming "No, no, no, no, *no.*"[51] According to Lundqvist, this is the only scene throughout Lindgren's works in which a child is beaten,[52] and Mardie's repeated "no" is perhaps the strongest manifestation of Lindgren's attitudes about the disciplining methods of her time. Lindgren was an advocate against violence and child abuse during her entire career, culminating in her acceptance speech "Aldrig våld!" ["Never Violence!"] when receiving the German book trade's peace prize (Friedenspreis des Deutschen Buchhandels) in 1978.[53] In her speech, she addressed child abuse, corporal punishment, and oppressive child-rearing methods. The year after this speech, and three years after the publication of *Mardie to the Rescue*, corporal punishment was outlawed in Sweden – after a debate that had been ongoing for decades.[54] The ban made Sweden the first country in the world to completely forbid corporal punishment.

Supposedly due to a more hierarchical view on children versus adults than that in Sweden, punishment with disciplinary intent has not received much criticism in Canada until recent decades. Despite extensive research on the effects of corrective assaults on children, corporal punishment was not banned in Canada until 2004. However, within certain limits, caregivers and teachers are still to this day allowed to discipline children between the ages of two to twelve through spanking, as long as the force is minor.[55] In Montgomery's Canada, "moderate and reasonable" corporal punishment was allowed by law and even encouraged as a means for correcting bad behaviour.[56] Despite this general attitude, Montgomery addresses corporal punishment as a topic in much the same way as Lindgren, most notably in an episode when Anne as a teacher feels the pressure to beat a child against her own conviction that this is morally wrong.[57] The pressure on Anne to beat the child comes not from Anne herself, but from the legislated disciplining methods. The two episodes illustrate a similarity in Montgomery's and Lindgren's views on disciplining methods and children's rights. Both Anne and Mardie's parents oppose corporal punishment, and, in this sense, they are all portrayed as progressive, but considering the general views for their respective time and place, Anne's attitude can be regarded as even more forward looking.

As a final example of a critique against adult authority, I would like to conclude with another example of roof climbing in Lindgren's work that carries traces of her reading of *Anne of Green Gables*. In the short story "Hoppa högst" ["The Biggest Leap"] in *Kajsa Kavat och andra barn*, two boys, just like Anne, jump from a roof and hurt themselves.[58] In the short story, the mothers of Albin and Stig have cultivated a rivalry between the two boys that leads them to compete in jumping from the roofs of the outhouse, the woodshed, and finally the barn. Jumping from the barn's roof, they both break a leg. As they lie in their hospital beds, they begin to laugh, asking themselves about the point of their competition. Here, Lindgren links jumping from high places to the mothers' cultivation of rivalry and essentially to bad child rearing. Moreover, she does so in a collection of short stories in which echoes of *Anne of Green Gables* are already noticeably present. Concluding the story with the boys laughing in their hospital beds may appear strange unless the mothers' significance is taken into account. The mothers' foolishness is the cause of the boys' behaviour, and the boys' realization relieves the situation. Consequently, this short story is yet another example of how Lindgren conveys her attitudes toward children and child-rearing methods throughout her texts, from Pippi to Mardie, in a discussion where Montgomery is ever present as a conversation partner.

Because roof climbing and jumping from roofs occur in many of Lindgren's works, the conquering of roofs can be seen in a broader perspective that, in turn, can be linked to the independence of children. In Lindgren's stories, several children, often girls, climb facades and spend time on rooftops. For instance, Pippi effortlessly navigates the rooftop of Villekulla Cottage, making a game of being chased by two policemen. The very positions of the characters in these scenes, where children are placed high up physically, indicate a reversed power structure. Söderberg sees the motif as an influence from Lindgren's childhood reading of girls' fiction, where this is a recurring theme, and she particularly associates it with Lindgren's reading of *Anne of Green Gables*.[59]

In this chapter, I have argued that Montgomery was an important conversation partner for Lindgren as she developed her progressive ideas on child rearing and child autonomy in line with new pedagogical concepts. Lindgren pays tribute to Montgomery's depiction of the dynamics between imaginative children and authoritative adults, but also rewrites them, emphasizing the subversive power of free children. By doing so, Lindgren questions the prevalent process of socialization whereby adults dictate the rules and limit the freedom of children. Lindgren's responsive reading of Montgomery's loving portrayals of unruly children affirms but also subverts them through Lindgren's unconditional belief in the child's right to imagination and play. The result is a critique of contemporary disciplining methods and positive depictions of children breaking social norms and conduct – such as lying and making mischief – in their quest for freedom and sovereignty. Lindgren responds to Montgomery by positioning herself *against* the idea that children ought to be raised according to certain adult rules and *for* a perspective whereby free, playing children are allowed to be exactly that. By portraying children in their own right and allowing them to rebel against the rules of the adult world, Lindgren completes what Montgomery begins.

NOTES

1 Lindgren, *Samuel August från Sevedstorp och Hanna i Hult* [*Samuel August from Sevedstorp and Hanna in Hult*], 61. Unless otherwise indicated, translations of Swedish passages have been made by Hanna Liljeqvist, research assistant at the Swedish Institute for Children's Books. Parts of the argument in this chapter have previously been published in Swedish in Warnqvist, "'Under körsbärsträdet sitter Ann'" ["'Ann Is Sitting under the Cherry Tree'"].

2 See the introduction to this volume, 5–7.

3 See, for example, Edström, *Astrid Lindgren*; Edström, *Astrid Lindgren och sagans makt* [*Astrid Lindgren and the Power of the Fairy Tale*]; Söderberg, "Sprakfålar och musor" ["Wild Girls and Muses"]; and Strömstedt, *Astrid Lindgren*.

4 See, for example, Lindgren, "Anne på Grönkulla och Mannen med stålnävarna" ["Anne of Green Gables and the Man with the Iron Fists"]; Lindgren, *Samuel August*; and Åhmansson's "'Mayflowers Grow in Sweden Too.'" See also the introduction to this volume, 9–11.

5 See Edström, *Astrid Lindgren*, 82, 88–90; Åhmansson, "'Mayflowers Grow in Sweden Too,'" 19–22; Death, "Pippi Långstrump and Anne of Green Gables"; Söderberg, "Sprakfålar och musor"; Warnqvist, "Villa Villekulla ett omstörtat Grönkulla" ["Villekulla Cottage a Subverted Green Gables"]; Warnqvist, "Så hittade Astrid Lindgren sin illbatting" ["How Astrid Lindgren Found Her Unruly Child"]; Warnqvist, "'Under körsbärsträdet sitter Ann'"; and Rémi, "Interactions with Poetry."

6 In an ongoing research project, I study the influence of Montgomery's work on Swedish readers and writers. See, for example, Warnqvist, "'I Experienced a Light that Became a Part of Me,'" and Warnqvist, "Flickan som läsare" ["The Girl as Reader"]. This chapter is a part of this research project. Montgomery's influence on, for instance, Finnish and American readers has also previously been studied by Kannas, "'Emily Equals Childhood and Youth and First Love'"; Ross, "Readers Reading L.M. Montgomery"; and Ross and Warnqvist, "Reading L.M. Montgomery."

7 Espmark, *Dialoger* [*Dialogues*], 25–30.

8 Death, "Pippi Långstrump and Anne of Green Gables," 212–21.

9 Rubio, *Lucy Maud Montgomery*, 75.

10 Waterston, "Marigold and the Magic of Memory," 156; Waterston, *Magic Island*, 22, 154.

11 Lundqvist, *Århundradets barn* [*The Child of the Century*], 15–64.

12 Söderberg, "Sprakfålar och musor," 120–2.

13 Ibid., 15–17, 18.

14 Ibid., 15–64.

15 Quoted in Lundqvist, *Århundradets barn*, 16.

16 Ibid., 16.

17 Lindgren, *Ur-Pippi* [*The Proto-Pippi*].

18 Lindgren, *Pippi Longstocking*, 5; LMM, *AGG*, 13.

19 LMM, *CJ* 2:290 (emphasis in original).

20 LMM, *Alpine Path*, 78.

21 For a discussion on the connotations of red-haired girls, see, for example, J. McMaster, "Taking Control," 58–71.

22 Åhmansson, "'Mayflowers Grow in Sweden Too,'" 20. See also, Söderberg, "Sprakfålar och musor," 117.

23 Death, "Pippi Långstrump and Anne of Green Gables," 213–14. See also, Edström, *Astrid Lindgren*, 88–90.

24 Lindgren, *Pippi Goes Aboard*, 8 (emphasis in original).

25 McMaster, "Taking Control," 59.

26 Death, "Pippi Långstrump and Anne of Green Gables," 213.

27 LMM, *AGG*, 132–3, 158, 163.

28 Edström, *Astrid Lindgren*, 90.

29 Reimer, "Introduction," xiii.

30 Lindgren, *Kajsa Kavat och andra barn* [Brenda Brave and Other Children], 104.

31 LMM, AGG, 121–2.

32 Lindgren, *Kajsa Kavat och andra barn*, 118 (emphasis in original), 120.

33 LMM, AGG, 115.

34 *Chronicles of Avonlea* was not translated into Swedish until 1968, by Birger Bjerre, although Lindgren may have read it in English before this. Like Montgomery's other works, it would have been available in American bookshops in 1948 when Lindgren travelled to the United States as a reporter for the magazine *Damernas värld* [*Ladies' World*]. She may also have come across it in her role as an editor at the publishing house Rabén & Sjögren; Montgomery's American publishing house, L.C. Page and Co., would likely have tried to sell those of her works not yet translated into Swedish to Swedish publishing houses.

35 LMM, AGG, 209. See also, Warnqvist, "Så hittade Astrid Lindgren sin illbatting."

36 Davy has "fuzzy little yellow ringlets," a dimple in one cheek, and an engaging smile (LMM, AA, 68). Lionel is "angelic," with rosy apple-cheeks, "beautiful golden curls," and "his round face was usually a lurking-place for dimples and smiles and sunshine" (LMM, CA, 164, 160). Similarly, Emil has "round blue eyes, a round, apple-cheeked face and a mop of fair hair. In fact he often looked so nice that people might have thought he was a perfect little angel" (Lindgren, *Emil in the Soup Tureen*, 9).

37 See Warnqvist, "Så hittade Astrid Lindgren sin illbatting."

38 Also worth mentioning is that the strict guardians are both careful, even ungenerous, when it comes to financial matters, and primarily worry about the cost of the boys' antics. For Anton, the cost of surgery and the price of the broken soup tureen are his main concerns when Emil's head is stuck in the tureen. When Lionel throws eggs at the henhouse, Judith exclaims, "And eggs at twenty-eight cents a dozen!" (LMM, CA, 161). See Warnqvist, "Så hittade Astrid Lindgren sin illbatting."

39 Montgomery's Anne accidentally serves her friend Diana currant wine instead of raspberry cordial, with the result that she is forbidden to see her friend. Emil's mother makes cherry wine for Mrs Petrell and asks Emil to throw away the fermented cherries. Considering it a waste of good fruit, Emil shares them with his friends, the pig and rooster, intoxicating all of them. Söderberg has also drawn attention to how these scenes create parallels between the novels, arguing that portrayals of drunk children in girls' fiction may have inspired

Lindgren to include the motif (Söderberg, "Sprakfålar och musor," 122). In both novels, members of the community find the housewives' winemaking questionable. See Warnqvist, "Villa Villekulla ett omstörtat Grönkulla."

40 Although Anne is forbidden to see her friend, she does not hesitate when Diana shows up at Green Gables, begging her to help save her younger sister, Minnie May, who has suffered a severe attack of croup. Similarly, Emil saves Alfred from dying from blood poisoning. Emil's parents tell him it is impossible to take Alfred to the doctor in the nearby town of Mariannelund, because of a snowstorm, but Emil refuses to listen and secretly takes Alfred there by horse and sleigh all by himself.

41 See Warnqvist, "Villa Villekulla ett omstörtat Grönkulla."

42 LMM, *AA*, 94.

43 Lindgren, *Emil in the Soup Tureen*, 40.

44 Söderberg, "Sprakfålar och musor," 119.

45 Lundqvist, "Always on the Child's Side," 11. See also Olsson, "Var finns säkerhetsbältena" ["Where Are the Safety Belts"].

46 LMM, *ENM*, 141–2 (emphasis in original).

47 This is primarily because he, in his anger, has said "i hundan," which "almost" is cursing, rather than because he has rebelled against his father (Lindgren, *Stora boken om Emil i Lönneberga* [*The Big Book about Emil in Lönneberga*], 256). Similarly, Davy feels regret after having said "darn" (LMM, *AIs*, 113–16).

48 Rémi, "Interactions with Poetry," 165–90.

49 Ibid., 166.

50 Emily feels such remorse that she cuts the bangs off entirely. As a result, she has to eat her supper in the pantry for a week and is not allowed to go on a much-anticipated trip to Uncle Oliver's. Nor does Emily's punishment end here: she rejoices when her bangs have finally grown back in time for a photograph scheduled to be taken, but Aunt Elizabeth pins her hair back for the picture.

51 Lindgren, *Mardie to the Rescue*, 83 (emphasis in original).

52 Lundqvist, "Always on the Child's Side," 11.

53 Lindgren's speech is now available as an illustrated book, *Never Violence!*

54 See Eva Bergenlöv, *Drabbade barn: Aga och barnmisshandel i Sverige från reformationen till nutid* [*Afflicted Children: Discipline and Child Abuse in Sweden from the Reformation to the Present*]. 2nd ed. (Lund: Nordic Academic Press, 2017), 129–56; Lundqvist, *Århundradets barn*, 38–47, 54–8.

55 See McGillivray and Durrant, "Child Corporal Punishment," 177–200; Durrant, "Corporal Punishment," 99–125.

56 McGillivray and Durrant, "Child Corporal Punishment," 181.

57 LMM, *AA*, 108–16.

58 Both Söderberg and Rémi mention this short story in their analyses but without exploring it in more detail. Söderberg, "Sprakfålar och musor," 121–2; Rémi, "Interactions with Poetry," 189.

59 Söderberg, "Sprakfålar och musor," 121.

8

Absent Fathers: Conversations between L.M. Montgomery and Madeleine L'Engle

HEIDI A. LAWRENCE

Father absence has been explored as a theme in literature and film for at least forty-five years, with scholars examining absentee fathers in modern retellings of William Shakespeare's plays; Jane Austen's works; Sylvia Plath's poetry; the memoirs of contemporary political, literary, and popular figures; and films by directors such as Alfred Hitchcock and Jane Campion.[1] Muriel Whitaker touches on the theme of absent fathers in L.M. Montgomery's work in a 1975 article, following up thirteen years later, in 1998, with an article on missing fathers in Atlantic fiction, including Montgomery's novels.[2] This is significant, because Montgomery's own father, Hugh John Montgomery (1841–1900), was continuously absent from his daughter's life from the time she was twenty-one months old: he abandoned her first when he placed his motherless young daughter with her maternal grandparents; then when he left Maud, now six, to begin his new career, and eventually to start a new family, in Saskatchewan; later, when he failed to support his teen-aged daughter emotionally during the year she spent with his new family; and finally when he died suddenly of pneumonia, leaving his twenty-five-year-old daughter to mourn this final abandonment. In her biography *Lucy Maud Montgomery: The Gift of Wings*, Mary Rubio writes that, after Hugh Montgomery died on 16 January 1900, Maud "was paralyzed" and "did not write about her father's death in her diary until May 1, 1900, when sunshine had started to coax life back into the landscape."[3] Similarly, Madeleine L'Engle's father, Charles Wadsworth Camp

(1879–1936), was absent frequently from her life, starting with her birth during the First World War, when he was serving in France. L'Engle had a nanny, because her parents were rarely at home, and she was away at boarding school for much of her adolescence. Finally, like Maud's, Madeleine's father died far from her, leaving her to spend much of the rest of her life trying to reconcile herself to his absence. Yet the situations of these two women were not unique: the absent father has been a social phenomenon common in North America for over two hundred years, according to historian Robert L. Griswold. In "The History and Politics of Fatherlessness," he explains that, from the late-eighteenth/early-nineteenth century, men began spending more and more time away from their homes "to succeed in a highly competitive business world" and to be actively engaged socially or politically. Griswold warns against disparaging modern fathers as being frequently absent and mythologizing and idealizing fathers of the past as having been always present for their wives and children. Fathers in all walks of life were then, and are now, he points out, often gone from home for both work and leisure.[4]

It was not unusual for circumstances such as those Montgomery and L'Engle faced to arise. A significant body of recent research argues that children need an emotionally and physically present father to develop a sense of stability and emotional, social, and physical well-being. Studies repeatedly show that daughters with absent fathers have poorer relationship skills, may have higher instances of depression, and struggle to trust male authority figures. Leah East, Debra Jackson, and Louise O'Brien demonstrate this in articles published in 2006 and 2007, while Linda Nielsen's 2014 work provides more recent evidence to support these claims.[5] On the other hand, if a father invests significant time and resources in his children, despite prolonged absence, research intimates that his children develop better and more meaningful relationships with him as well as others, as demonstrated by William S. Aquilino in his 2006 study on the relationships of non-custodial fathers with their children.[6] Interestingly, studies also show that children frequently idealize their fathers or invent fantasy fathers to fill the need for a consistent father presence in their lives, much as both Montgomery and L'Engle seem to have done in their fiction and non-fiction. As early as the 1940s, George R. Bach investigated children's imaginative idealizations of absent fathers. In his 1982 study, "On Father Hunger," James M. Herzog also explored the way children reimagine absent fathers.[7]

The main difference between many such childhood fantasies and Montgomery's and L'Engle's idealized fathers is that Montgomery and L'Engle had the skills to rewrite – quite literally – the script of an absent father in ways that shaped fictitious rather than accurate scenarios and explanations for their fathers' behaviour. The intersections between their recrafted scripts demonstrate the conversations between these two authors and their works. The conversations begin with Montgomery's life as shaped in her journals. At age fifteen, in August 1890, Maud moved to Prince Albert to live with her father and stepmother, a situation that lasted only a year. Six months prior to her departure, after mentioning in passing her father's move and remarriage, she records that she feels "very lonesome" in her grandparents' home. This entry hints that being part of a traditional family, with a father, stepmother, and younger sister, would assuage this loneliness. Two months later, she notes her excitement at the possibility of seeing her "darling father again!" lavishing affection on a father who has shown little attention or affection toward her and suggesting an overcompensation for this lack. She then expresses fear that she will be disappointed and that the planned trip to this idealized family and home, about which she has obviously been fantasizing, will not happen. Her journal entries for that year in Saskatchewan begin with excitement at meeting her "dear father again" for the first time in five years and claiming that "he hasn't changed at all,"[8] indicating an idealized and static perception of him, a fantasy father who promises not to disappoint.

Within a week of arriving in Prince Albert, young Maud has admitted that she does not like her new stepmother, claiming that her father has confided in her "that he finds it hard to get along with his wife" and has appealed to her "to put up with some things for his sake." She realizes that this stepmother will never be a mother, referring to her as Mrs Montgomery, and then she assumes the role of a dutiful, Cinderella-like daughter protecting her long-suffering father from a wicked stepmother. Over the next year, Maud periodically records how much she loves her father, but intersperses these entries with notes about how her stepmother is treating her as a servant, requiring her to do the household chores "while Mrs. Montgomery parades the streets or visits with her relatives." One excerpt from Maud's journal sums up the gap between the ideal and the real particularly well: "I *love* it when father and I are alone together for a meal. We can be just as jolly and chummy as we like then, with no one to cast black looks and sneers at us."[9] This is the father-daughter relationship Montgomery had imagined she would recover while in Prince Albert.

After a year in Prince Albert, sixteen-year-old Maud returned to her grandparents' home in Prince Edward Island. Although she would now have been aware that her father was not the caring, supportive parent she had imagined, her journals never articulate such an awareness, but instead fault, in very strong terms, "the atmosphere of suspicion and petty malice and persecution which Mrs. Montgomery seem[ed] to exhale," in which Maud felt herself to be "literally smothering" and from which it was "wonderful to escape."[10] The infrequent references to her father in her journal after she left Prince Albert continue the childhood and adolescent idealization well into adulthood. For instance, she writes about her feelings of grief and loss at learning that her father has died, emphasizing that she always "think[s] of him as [she] used to know him." The phrase "used to know him" subtly suggests that she understands at some level the difference between how she remembered and idealized him before her trip to Prince Albert and her memories of how he actually treated her while she was there. Moreover, this acknowledgment is preceded by a passage fraught with tensions between the ideal and the unacknowledged reality, exposed not only through what she senses to be untrue but also through the dramatic scripting, complete with dialogue, of the exceptional father-daughter relationship: "Father and I have always been so much to each other. He was so good and kind and tender. Long, long ago, before he went west, when I was a tiny girl, we were much together, and how we loved each other! Yet when he went so far away and for so many years we never grew apart, as some might have done. We always remained near and dear in spirit. Oh father, can it really be true that you are dead? Have you left your 'little Maudie' all alone? That was not like you."[11] This nostalgia for her childhood image of her father appears elsewhere in her journals after his death, especially when she thinks about how proud her father was of her writing and how excited he would have been about her publications and the honours she received.[12] She laments that he did not get to see grandchildren, whom he would have loved, naming her second son, stillborn in August 1914, Hugh after her father.[13] She holds onto even the smallest reminders of life as it might have been if her father had been the parent – and grandparent – about whom she dreamed. The nostalgia, however, remains sentimental and dramatic, which clouds a convincing response to a real relationship.

Maud, the daughter of an absent father, attempted to work out in her fiction the unacknowledged and unresolved tensions between idealized and real father. As Rubio states, "The year [in Prince Albert] had been a great disillusionment. But it provided fodder for fiction. Her sense of exploitation would be used in her later writing," adding, "Maud's father's weakness had inflicted the pain on her that most of her future literary heroines were to suffer from – a father's absence or death." Perhaps Rubio's most poignant assessment is that, after her return from Prince Albert, Maud "knew in her heart that she could never count on her father, *ever*, although she always spoke of their undying affection for each other."[14] Instead, she wrote parents into her fiction, whether biological or adoptive, who can be relied on both to train their children and to love them wholeheartedly: the beloved and iconic Matthew and Marilla Cuthbert in *Anne of Green Gables* (1908); Anne and Gilbert Blythe in *Rainbow Valley* (1919), *Rilla of Ingleside* (1921), and *Anne of Ingleside* (1939); Lorraine Lesley in *Magic for Marigold* (1929); Long Alec Gardiner in *Pat of Silver Bush* (1933) and *Mistress Pat* (1935); and Robin and Andrew Stuart in *Jane of Lantern Hill* (1937). In contrast, she also created parents and grandparents who cannot be trusted and do not know how to love, including Mrs Stirling in *The Blue Castle* (1926) and Grandmother Kennedy in *Jane of Lantern Hill*. Then there are those parents who fade in and out of the story and whose absence fosters idealization, such as the fathers of Sara Stanley and of Felix and Beverley King in *The Story Girl* (1911) and *The Golden Road* (1913). Among all these fathers, Douglas Starr, from *Emily of New Moon*, emerges as the father figure most unconditionally idealized by his daughter. However, the tensions between the ideal and real, as have been observed in Montgomery's relationship with her father, are more apparent in the differing perceptions that outsiders hold of him as a parent, husband, and writer than those to which Emily clings for years.

Emily perceives Douglas Starr as a perfect father: loving, spiritually and intellectually nourishing, and trustworthy. Her thoughts reflect Montgomery's own of her father, in defining their relationship as unique and in denying any alternative: "They had always been such chums – they had loved each other so much – it couldn't be that they were to be separated." His behaviour throughout the first part of Emily's life is consistent with this perception, and reflects poorly on Hugh Montgomery's by contrast: unlike Maud's father, he has refused to let maternal relatives bring up his "little beloved Emilykin."

Already, however, questions are being raised about this decision, albeit from the unlikeable Ellen Greene, who thinks she is comforting Emily when telling her that she will find a "good home – better'n you've ever had here" – with the Murrays. Emily's loving father may not abandon her in life, but cannot avoid abandoning her to the unfeeling Murray relatives after his death. Moreover, her "mother's people" present another perspective on this father-daughter relationship when Aunt Ruth deems Emily "spoiled" and without manners, Douglas Starr a "miserable failure," and his leaving Emily "without a cent" as "perfectly disgraceful."[15] Unlike Emily, young Maud never suffered such pecuniary hardships. "*Materially*, I was cared for," Montgomery acknowledges in her journal. However, she did feel that she was "starved and restricted," both "*emotionally* and *socially*," and she rewrote this perceived emotional trauma as the familial life to which Emily's father, through death, abandoned her.[16]

In an attempt to sustain her relationship with her father, Emily "emptie[s] out her soul" in letters to her father "on the road to heaven." The letters become a space in which Emily can express emotions – "of her rapture and her pain"[17] – and explore her determination to write and become a renowned author. The underlying sense throughout all these letters is that Emily's father inspired her to become the author he never had a chance to be, and that she finds strength and support in the idea that he continues to be proud of her efforts from beyond the grave. She incorporates poems that she has written in these letters and points out her improvements in spelling and vocabulary. While Montgomery was able to share the joy of her first publications with her father – he "was *so* pleased" when his daughter published her first poem in a Charlottetown newspaper[18] – and thereafter fantasizes about his pride in her accomplishments, Emily, aged eleven to twelve, can share her aspirations only in an imagined space. When these aspirations begin to be realized in later adolescence and early adulthood, she has long since ceased to write to him, because Aunt Elizabeth found and read the letters, with all Emily's passionate outpourings of perceived injustices. Emily cleanses her conscience with "explanatory notes" and then discovers that she can no longer write a letter to her father as "it no longer mean[s] anything to her. The sense of reality – nearness – of close communion ha[s] gone." In the same way that Montgomery's references and addresses to her father slowly fade throughout the journals, Emily's connection with her father is diminished and then abruptly curtailed:

"perhaps the bitter scene with Aunt Elizabeth had only shaken into dust something out of which the spirit had already departed."[19]

Nevertheless, Emily naturally continues to yearn for confirmation of her abilities. After the events that end her letter writing to her father, she seeks guidance and approval from a variety of other potential father figures. Kate Lawson argues, in her extensive evaluation of father figures and their impact on Emily, that these "various male father-figures in the novel … are shown to be ineffectual, systematically weak or powerless, living marginal lives, and unable to assert traditional male prerogatives of power and rule."[20] However, regardless of their personal failings, Father Cassidy and Mr Carpenter in *Emily of New Moon*, and eventually the family matriarch/patriarch Aunt Elizabeth in *Emily's Quest*, are or become active, responsive readers of Emily's writings. Unlike the letters to her idealized father, the conversations between Emily as writer and Father Cassidy, Mr Carpenter, and Aunt Elizabeth as readers are two-sided: these characters respond directly to Emily's efforts with praise and/or criticism, encouraging her in further efforts. From them, she receives the real help and praise that she could only imagine through the letters to her dead father.

In the last quarter of *Emily of New Moon* and throughout the two sequels, *Emily Climbs* and *Emily's Quest*, thirty-six-year-old Dean Priest, who was Douglas Starr's friend, assumes the mentorship and approval roles that Emily seeks in father figures. However, this father-daughter relationship is haunted by Dean's jealousy of Emily's writing, which Emily herself notices as early as her Shrewsbury High School years. His cruellest rejection occurs when he lies to her and declares her first novel to be "pretty and flimsy and ephemeral."[21] As a result, she burns it and is unable to write again for a long time. Through Dean, Montgomery vents the resentment, which occasionally emerges in her journals, that her father has teased or belittled her about her writing. For instance, Montgomery records in her journal that her father comments about one of her published poems, "Autumn," saying that it "didn't sound much like poetry," because it did not rhyme.[22] While neither Montgomery nor Emily is ultimately obstructed in her progress along the Alpine Path by these dismissive responses to her work, the ideal of a wholly supportive mentor-father cannot be sustained when the reality insists on disrupting the conversation.

The echo of conversations between a daughter and her idealized father reverberates through Montgomery's journals into her *Emily* novels and then into the works of Madeleine L'Engle. In L'Engle's own words, "I adored *Emily of New Moon* and some of the other L.M. Montgomery books and they impelled me because I loved them."[23] The question arises, "Impelled her to do what?" Perhaps reading the *Emily* books inspired L'Engle to persist in climbing her own path toward publication and even fame. Certainly, her childhood journal shows that she drew directly from *Emily of New Moon* for motivation. An entry recorded while she was at boarding school reads, "And now I do swear a vow. I, Madeleine L'Engle Camp, do solemnly vow this day that I will climb the alpine path and write my name on the scroll of fame."[24] This is an unacknowledged but direct reference to the "vow" that Emily makes to "climb the Alpine Path and write [her] name on the scroll of fame."[25] L'Engle repeats her great admiration for Emily as a character in several places in her life-writings, such as in *Walking on Water*: "I read and reread and reread *Emily of New Moon*, by L.M. Montgomery ... especially I loved Emily, because she, too, wanted to be a writer, a real writer; she, too, walked to the beat of a different drum; she had a touch of second sight, that gift which allows us to peek for a moment at the world beyond ordinary space and time."[26] As this tribute establishes, L'Engle was particularly drawn to some of Emily's characteristics, inherited from Montgomery herself: a persistence despite setbacks; an ability to negotiate the expectations and demands of others and to be conciliatory but maintain integrity; and visionary potential and experiences. Reiterating her sense of kinship with Emily, L'Engle writes in *Trailing Clouds of Glory* that "Emily Byrd Starr was my friend and companion, closer to me than any of my classmates at school."[27] In *The Genesis Trilogy*, she expresses the desire to meet Emily someday, insinuating that characters are so "real" that readers can actually interact with them in some sphere, whether in this life or the next.[28] L'Engle's confidence that, as a reader, and especially as a child reader of a much-loved and much-read text, she can "meet" a fictional character enhances her relationship with Montgomery. L'Engle feels that she understands the emotional connection Montgomery had with Emily – the character, of all those she wrote, most like herself. Moreover, this perceived connection between L'Engle as reader and Montgomery as author perhaps underlies L'Engle's creation of a fictionalized narrative for her frequently absent father in her non-fiction writings – similar to what Montgomery creates for the idealized father in her *Emily* novels. Because she sees herself as being so like Emily, L'Engle, too, adapts her father's story to fit her idealization of his heroism, but in much more radical ways than Montgomery's shaping of Hugh Montgomery in her journals or through Douglas Starr.

L'Engle's radical adaptation of her father's story is not an isolated reinvention of a family member's life. Josephine Jones, L'Engle's oldest daughter, comments that, after having read the "Crosswicks Journals," "People would come up to me and say, 'I read all about you. I feel I know you so well,'" but she would constantly remind them, "You have to remember that my mother is a fiction writer." Her mother would often deviate from facts in the volumes she published as non-fiction "journals," especially pertaining to her family. Jones says, "A typical exchange would go like this: 'I loved it when you did such and such.' 'I never did that.' 'Yes, you did! Your mother wrote it in her book!'" Jones made these comments in an interview with historian of children's literature Leonard Marcus in *Listening for Madeleine: A Portrait of Madeleine L'Engle in Many Voices*.[29] By blurring the boundaries between her fiction and non-fiction, L'Engle exerted some agency over her family's narrative. Throughout her biography of Montgomery, Rubio makes a similar observation, although in the context solely of life-writing, when she reminds readers that, as Montgomery recopied her journals between 1919 and 1922, she "hoped to have some control over how her story would eventually be told. There were grievances she wanted to air, and other things she wanted to conceal (or reshape)."[30]

Although L'Engle claims in one of her many reflective books, *The Rock That Is Higher: Story as Truth* (1993), that she was able to examine her emotional state at her father's death through Julie Forrester in her first novel, *The Small Rain*, her additional statement that Julie's death is "far from the facts of" her father's death is questionable based on both her father's own writing and evidence that has emerged since 2004.[31] Rather, L'Engle reveals more about her father's life and death through Julie than she seems to be aware of or able to admit, appearing to transfer much of the anxiety she felt about her father's death onto the mother character in *The Small Rain*. Julie follows the same pattern of behaviour now known about Charles Wadsworth Camp: she is a heavy-smoking alcoholic, who dies of pneumonia after catching a cold. L'Engle seems better able to manage and explore the complexities of her father's experience and her own response to them through defamiliarizing him in the character of Julie. Nevertheless, L'Engle devotes much of her writing about her childhood history, beginning with references in *The Summer of the Great-Grandmother* (1974), to rejecting the close connection between her father's real circumstances and the failures of parental figures in her earlier fiction. Throughout her "Crosswicks Journals," for example, rather than addressing the complexity of her father's character and situation, L'Engle repeatedly insists that her father was gassed during the First World War and suffered related health problems until his death. Marcus, in *Listening for Madeleine*, and Cynthia Zarin, in "The Storyteller," have attempted to resolve the questions of why she continued to tell this story about her father and why she fictionalized narratives to explain his behaviour by candidly debunking L'Engle's story about her father's lungs. Other scholarly work on L'Engle borders on blindly laudatory acceptance of her "non-fiction" rather than careful analytical explorations. Also problematic is that L'Engle's heirs have, to date, refused to grant access to her handwritten journals. Even the recent biography by L'Engle's granddaughters, Charlotte Jones Voiklis and Léna Roy, *Becoming Madeleine*, merely summarizes L'Engle's published accounts of her father's illness and death.[32]

As a result, Marcus's compelling compilation of interviews provides important information that exposes the tensions between the real and the ideal father in L'Engle's fiction and her later non-fiction. First, Marcus notes in the introduction to this collection that "obituaries and Princeton alumni records, among other sources, do not bear out L'Engle's account of her father's illness and death."[33] Second, he includes the interview with Josephine Jones, including her comments on her mother's tendency to heavily fictionalize actual events. In this same interview, Marcus pointedly said to Jones, "There is some question as to whether or not [your grandfather] really was gassed during World War I." Jones replies that, in conversations with her grandmother, she learned that her "grandfather was an alcoholic and my mother could not face that in him. She did not want it to be true that her beloved father was an alcoholic. So here was a plausible explanation for his frequent headaches and need to lie down. It was not that he was hung over but rather that he was suffering the effects of having been gassed in the war."[34] Camp's own work, *History of the 305th Field Artillery* (1919), reveals that he was never gassed. The "Roll of Honor," included in Camp's history, lists all the men who were killed, wounded, or gassed while serving with the 305th field artillery. Camp's name is absent.[35]

The first time L'Engle writes a published version of her father's story, included in *The Summer of the Great-Grandmother*, she says, "I still had not come to terms with my father's death, which occurred during my last year of boarding school. It was a premature death, caused by mustard gas during the First World War; Father would not take his men anywhere he would not go himself, and his action saved most of his men from gassing."[36] The heroism of this contrived story gives L'Engle a mechanism to narrate and explain her father's death as a result of his actions during the great war against evil. While neither Hugh Montgomery nor Douglas Starr engaged in such world-altering events,[37] L'Engle's scripting her father's death to avoid confronting characteristics and behaviour that would blemish her idealized memory of him reflects the pattern already observed with Montgomery and Emily. L'Engle's responsive reading of Montgomery's *Emily* novels in such a personalized manner increasingly blurs the lines between the reality of the circumstances of her father's situation – not only in the false "reality" of her non-fiction, but also in its adaptation to a parental figure in *The Small Rain* and the fantasy father figure in *A Wrinkle in Time.*

L'Engle would have recognized professional connections between her own father and Emily's father, too – both were journalists who attempted to write for a living. L'Engle's first novel, *The Small Rain* (dedicated to her father), hints at the similarities between her father and Emily's father, although she moves the connections in an unexpected direction, choosing to focus on an artistic mother rather than a father. Josephine Jones, when questioned by Marcus, explained that she "would identify her [mother] much more as a daddy's girl," even though L'Engle was much better acquainted with her mother.[38] Like Montgomery in *Emily of New Moon*, L'Engle focuses much more on the absent father than the present adult mentor. She says she could confront memories of her father's life and death by channelling her grief through "the death of Katherine's mother," Julie Forrester, and in so doing, come "close to the truth of what it meant to [her]" and help her "redeem pain through story."[39] It is evident from this reflective comment that Julie can be read as a stand-in for Charles Wadsworth Camp, much as Douglas Starr can be read as a surrogate Hugh Montgomery.

In addition to connections between L'Engle's and Montgomery's non-fiction and fictional father figures, L'Engle compares herself to her main character, Katherine Forrester, saying, "I am not Katherine, though we share much in common," including the dedication with which they approach their art. L'Engle asserts, "No fictional character can ever come only from the author's imagination … The deeper I got into the novel, the more Katherine became Katherine and less Madeleine. But we are sisters, there's no doubt about that."[40] The echoes between L'Engle and Montgomery resound more strongly here, as Katherine resembles Emily. Katherine is ten years old when *The Small Rain* opens. She is described as very small for her age, with "heavy, dark hair" and "deep blue" eyes.[41] In comparison, Emily is eleven and has "glossy, jet-black hair" and "large, purplish-grey eyes."[42] Also like Emily, Katherine is an artist, although a budding concert pianist rather than an author. Just as Emily follows in her father's authorial footsteps, Katherine too follows the career path of a parent, her mother, who was a concert pianist until a car accident incapacitated her. L'Engle's central character aligns with Montgomery's, reflecting L'Engle's conversations with the *Emily* books.

Like Douglas Starr in Emily's life, Julie, despite her failures, remains a constant driving force behind Katherine's aspirations as a pianist. Their relationship is positive – nurturing and secure – unshadowed by her mother's past disappointments. Julie praises Katherine as a "wonderful student," and Katherine feels empowered by her mother's method of instruction, just as Emily feels strengthened and encouraged by her father's approval from beyond the grave. These memories of learning with her mother keep Katherine engaged with her work, even after Julie's death. She embraces the knowledge that her mother would have remained proud of her progress. This is illustrated when, after Katherine plays privately for renowned concert pianist Julien Quimper, he insists that, were Julie still alive, she would be proud of Katherine.[43] Katherine, like Emily, sustains hope that her now-absent parent-artist is both aware of her success and ability and is supportive, even from a place of inaccessibility.

Bolstered by Quimper's insistence that Julie is still supporting her, Katherine frames this hope around the approval of other father figures, just as Emily seeks approval from Cousin Jimmy, Mr Carpenter, and Dean Priest. Specifically, Justin Vigneras becomes Katherine's piano teacher while she is at boarding school in Switzerland. While similar to Dean in that he is significantly older than Katherine, Justin responds to Katherine's gifts without jealousy, seeking to draw them out and help her develop her emotive expression in her playing. In contrast, Dean's attitude toward Emily's writing is that of a father indulging a small child's whim.[44] Justin demonstrates confidence in Katherine's ability to make the most of her situation, and she finds in this the support and approval she needs: "She was suddenly terribly happy, with that sudden winging up of something inside her breast that seemed like the flight of a bird."[45] This imagery reflects some of the imagery Montgomery references during the time when she was considering Emily as a character during 1919 and 1920. In a journal entry dated 31 January 1920, she writes, "One cannot have imagination and the gift of wings, along with the placidity and contentment of those who creep on the earth's solid surface and never open their eyes on aught but material things. But the gift of wings is better than placidity and contentment after all."[46]

Montgomery gives Emily this "gift of wings," the ability to write and through writing to transcend mediocrity, as demonstrated when Emily records in her diary, "I have copied my favourite verse from *The Fringed Gentian* on the inside of the cover. I will read it over every day and remember my vow to 'climb the Alpine Path.' I begin to see that I will have to do a good bit of scrambling, though I once expected, I think, to soar right up to 'that far-off goal' on shining wings."[47] L'Engle gives Katherine that same gift, the "something" that resembles the "flight of a bird," in her music. Albert Peytz, a recalcitrant older gentleman with whom Katherine studies after she leaves the boarding school and Justin's tuition, is reminiscent of Emily's teacher, Mr Carpenter. Like Mr Carpenter, Mr Peytz drives Katherine in ways that bring out her gift and help her to resist "placidity and contentment," as Montgomery calls it. Peytz does not need to pretend that her skill is passable.[48] Instead, he pushes her to the limits of her ability so that she can improve, just as Mr Carpenter does for Emily. Peytz's pride in and approval of Katherine lead her to the confidence in herself that she seeks from those who take the place of her absent parent.

Following this hope of parental/paternal approval and pride in the child, which connects L'Engle to Montgomery through the worlds created in their fiction, a second important shared theme emerges. Like Montgomery's fading memories of her father in her journals and Douglas Starr's inability to be a permanent presence in Emily's life, L'Engle's *A Wrinkle in Time* addresses the effect of an idealized absent father who fails to deliver over the long term. Chantel Lavoie compares fathers in Suzanne Collins's *Gregor the Overlander* and L'Engle's *A Wrinkle in Time*. Lavoie argues that Mr Murry, who "represents God the father working through science … makes a choice for the sake of both scientific advancement and his country, despite his great love for his wife and their four children, understanding that he might not return."[49] L'Engle's fictional father thus correlates with the father she will begin to transform in her published journals over a decade after publishing *A Wrinkle in Time*. Yet, while Mr Murry is initially viewed as almost godlike in his supremacy, fame, and intellect, he, like L'Engle's own father, remains underdeveloped. Largely absent in the novel, he has no central role or influence on the characters' development. It is as if L'Engle was not sure how to write a loving, present father. Even for the Mrs W's, who give Meg, Charles Wallace, and Calvin a picture of Mr Murry, he is not a father, but a hero on the alien planet Camazotz, fighting the "dark Thing." The three women centre him as a warrior against evil, whom the three children then categorize as being of the same stature as artists, musicians, religious leaders, and scientists. The resulting list of important warriors against evil includes Christ, da Vinci, Michelangelo, Shakespeare, Bach, Pasteur, Madame Curie, Einstein, Schweitzer, Gandhi, Buddha, Beethoven, Rembrandt, St Francis, Euclid, and Copernicus.[50] However, L'Engle proceeds to dismantle the heroisms that have been written into Mr Murry's character, and it is unclear whether she is consciously or unconsciously undermining any godlike version of paternal authority she initially gave Mr Murry.

While the Mrs W's present him as a heroic warrior of good, who is fighting evil, during an extended conversation between Calvin O'Keefe and Mr Murry, Mr Murry admits, "Going to Camazotz was a complete accident. I never intended even to leave our own solar system. I was heading for Mars."[51] This reveals that he has simply performed a scientific experiment that went badly wrong and throws into question Meg's celestialized view of him. Rather, Mr Murry is a one-dimensional, mostly ineffectual, largely unheroic character, despite Meg's expectations to the contrary, and this shift is so sudden as to be jarring, as if L'Engle herself did not expect it. Meg's expectations are demonstrated when she finally reunites with her father on Camazotz: "This was the moment that meant that now and forever everything would be all right." Yet for the remainder of the novel, while Mr Murry talks often about returning to Camazotz to save his son, he cannot act. Instead, it is Meg, the character L'Engle has developed most fully, and perhaps to whom she relates best, who returns to save Charles. L'Engle's godlike hero-father is an ordinary, faulty human, who fades into the background, virtually unknown to Meg or to readers,[52] as L'Engle's own father was in many ways unknown to her. Just as Douglas Starr never realizes his potential,[53] so too is Meg's father toppled from his pedestal. For Meg, this unexpected discovery of her father as faulty and unheroic begins almost as soon as she is reunited with him. Her despair and disillusionment become so strong that, for a little while, she verges on hating her father and cannot seem to stop herself from trying to hurt her father emotionally.[54]

In contrast, Montgomery did not need her father or her fictional father figures to be superhuman heroes, and so Emily never feels that she lacks in the same way that Meg does, even though most of Emily's father figures also fade over time. Instead, she finds heroism in little, everyday things. As Emily prepares to leave New Moon to attend high school, Mr Carpenter tells her that it will be good for her to "confine [her writing] to ordinary life." Emily retorts, "There isn't any such thing as ordinary life."[55] She recognizes that everyday life can be marvellous, and she is able to write this into her first published novel, *The Moral of the Rose*. As she develops the story, it becomes "a witty, sparkling rill of human comedy," in which the characters "laughed and scowled and wept and danced – and even made a little love."[56] This suggests that Montgomery's "gift of wings" includes the ability to see ordinary human drama as extraordinary, both in its sorrow and in its humour. But while Emily has her gift of writing letters to her father, as if he has become an extraordinary, supernatural being on the way to heaven, to assuage the pain of his absence, Meg has conversely discovered that even her father's presence is a form of absence, because he cannot meet her expectations of fatherhood. She has to learn to accept him as a failed hero with no supernatural powers. Instead, Mr Murry is successful in familial love, just as Emily's father has been.

In both novels, then, failure and success – and heroism – are measured in emotional rather than social or material terms. When Emily's Aunt Ruth declares that Douglas Starr "was a miserable failure," Emily cries out, "Father wasn't a failure! ... Nobody who was loved as much as he was could be a failure."[57] This love, for Emily, constitutes success. The tension between the real and the ideal absent father in *A Wrinkle in Time* intersects with Emily's persistent love and adoration of her father, again demonstrating the interaction between L'Engle and the *Emily* novels. At the beginning of the novel, Meg wants to save her father because she loves him and misses him. Her love is demonstrated in her joy at sharing information about him; in Calvin's perceptive comment, "You're just crazy about your father, aren't you?"; and in Meg's continued impatience to get to wherever Mr Murry is located.[58] Yet, in the final scenes of the novel, while Mr Murry wants to save Charles Wallace and spare Meg another tesseract, because he loves his children, it is not he who combats evil with good. He becomes impotent to save his son. Instead, it is Meg whose love brings about the denouement. She is able to feel "love and pride" and to ask forgiveness of her father for her unrealistic expectations. As a result of her ability to forgive and love her father despite his flaws, she comes to understand what love can do to save Charles Wallace, too. When "IT made ITS fatal mistake," trying to convince Meg that Mrs Whatsit hates her, Meg suddenly realizes that love is the weapon she possesses to combat IT. She pours her love into Charles Wallace, and when she verbalizes, "I love you! ... I love you, Charles! I love you!" ITS power breaks and she, her family, and Calvin are immediately returned home.[59] Meg's assessment of her father's success or failure, like Emily's, is ultimately couched in her love for him, and she, like Emily, succeeds where her father has failed.

In tracing the conversations between Montgomery's journals and fiction, between Montgomery's fiction and L'Engle's reading, and between L'Engle's fiction and non-fiction, this chapter has argued that each woman, out of adoration, conceived and reconceived her father's life to better fit an emotionally satisfying relationship between her largely absent father and herself. However, these reconceptions were not as easy or as straightforward as Montgomery or L'Engle might have wanted them to be. Each author struggled to create her own "real" world and to rewrite events involving her father, so that they would align more closely with her idealizations of how life ought to be. This struggle evolved because, for both women, the idealization focused on the absent father, the father she did not really know. The lack of substance in the relationships left each author with idealized, yet hollow-sounding, father figures in her novels. Montgomery crafted her journals so that future readers would see only a father who cared and supported her in her work, rather than the father who left her to go West and rarely returned. Her journals then provided material to write a supportive, involved, and inspirational – but dead – father for Emily Starr as an aspiring writer. In comparison, L'Engle "read and reread and reread Emily,"[60] and her fictional and non-fictional reinvention of her own father's life, illness, and death intersects with Montgomery's creation of Douglas Starr. L'Engle, too, hoped to alleviate her father's emotional and physical absence from her life through her fiction and through shaping her journals. Both women needed an acceptable explanation for a father's constant absence, an explanation that would prove her love for her father was well placed. In the quest to supply this explanation, however, the most intriguing junction between Montgomery and L'Engle emerges: neither woman resolved the tensions between the ideal and the real in realizing her own or the fictional absent father. Ultimately, these unresolved tensions became a creative influence for each of them as artists, driving them to multiple attempts at rewriting the perfect father who is always an absent moving force.

ACKNOWLEDGMENT

Many thanks to Lesley Clement for help and suggestions in shaping this chapter.

NOTES

1 See Graham Saunders, "'Missing Mothers and Absent Fathers': Howard Barker's Seven Lears and Elaine Feinstein's Lear's Daughters," *Modern Drama* 42 (1999): 401–10; Christine Gibbs, "Absent Fathers: An Examination of Father-Daughter Relationships in Jane Austen's Novels," *Persuasions: The Jane Austen Journal* 8 (1986): 45–50; Susan E. Schwartz, "The Dead Father Effect on the Psyche of a Daughter – Sylvia Plath," *Journal of Poetry Therapy* 30, no. 4 (2017): 218–27; G. Thomas Couser, "Presenting Absent Fathers in Contemporary Memoir," *Southwest Review* 90, no. 4 (2005): 634–48; Mike Chopra-Gant, "Absent Fathers and 'Moms,' Delinquent Daughters and Mummy's Boys: Envisioning the Postwar American Family in Hitchcock's *Notorious*," *Comparative American Studies* 3, no. 3 (2005): 361–75; "Mothers, Daughters, and (Absent) Fathers in Jane Campion's *The Piano*," *Literature Film Quarterly* 30, no. 1 (2002): 46–58.

2 Whitaker, "'Queer Children': L.M. Montgomery's Heroines"; Whitaker, "Missing Fathers."

3 Rubio, *Lucy Maud Montgomery*, 108.

4 Griswold, "History and Politics of Fatherlessness," 18–20.

5 East, Jackson, and O'Brien, "Father Absence and Adolescent Development"; East, Jackson, and O'Brien, "Disrupted Relationships"; Nielsen, "Young Adult Daughters' Relationships."

6 Aquilino, "Noncustodial Father-Child Relationship."

7 Bach, "Father-Fantasies"; Herzog, "On Father Hunger." See also Adrienne Harris, "'Fathers' and 'Daughters,'" *Psychoanalytic Inquiry* 28 (2008): 39–59.

8 LMM, *CJ* 1:23, 26, 40.
9 Ibid., 42–3, 49, 82–3, 67 (emphasis in original).
10 Ibid., 67.
11 Ibid., 451.
12 Ibid., 451; *CJ* 2:13, 192; *SJ* 5:15, 35.
13 LMM, *CJ* 3:87, 164.
14 Rubio, *Lucy Maud Montgomery*, 66, 68 (emphasis in original).
15 LMM, *ENM*, 3, 14, 15, 19, 10–11, 22; 44, 48.
16 LMM, *CJ* 2:262 (emphasis in original). See this volume's introduction, 9–11, for fuller development of Montgomery's childhood.
17 LMM, *ENM*, 113.
18 LMM, *CJ* 1:53 (emphasis in original).
19 LMM, *ENM*, 379–80.
20 Lawson, "Adolescence and the Trauma," 24. Others who mention father figures as mentors for Emily include Muriel Whitaker, "Queer Children" and "Missing Fathers"; Thomas E. Tausky, "L.M. Montgomery"; and E. Holly Pike, "(Re)Producing" and "The Heroine Who Writes."
21 LMM, *EQ*, 61.
22 LMM, *CJ* 1:459.
23 L'Engle, "GoFish," 291.
24 Voiklis and Roy, *Becoming Madeleine*, 46.
25 LMM, *ENM*, 351.
26 L'Engle, *Walking on Water*, 58.
27 L'Engle, *Trailing Clouds of Glory*, 12.
28 L'Engle, *Genesis Trilogy*, 45.
29 Marcus, *Listening for Madeleine*, 172.
30 Rubio, *Lucy Maud Montgomery*, 273.
31 L'Engle, *Rock That Is Higher*, 222. For contradictory evidence, see Camp, *History of the 305th Field Artillery*; Marcus, *Listening for Madeleine*; Zarin, "The Storyteller."
32 Voiklis and Roy, *Becoming Madeleine*, 26–7.
33 Marcus, *Listening for Madeleine*, 8.
34 Ibid., 171.
35 Camp, *History of the 305th Field Artillery*, 293–96. Other contrasting claims about Camp's health are evidenced in Zarin's *New Yorker* article, "The Storyteller."

36 L'Engle, *Summer of the Great-Grandmother*, 70.

37 Although the 1885 North-West Resistance, organized by the Métis people against the Canadian government, was a localized conflict in Canada and therefore might not be considered "world-altering," Hugh Montgomery did participate, on the side of the Canadian government. See McKenzie and Ledwell, Introduction, 3.

38 Marcus, *Listening for Madeleine*, 170.

39 L'Engle, *Small Rain*, ix; *Rock That Is Higher*, 222.

40 L'Engle, *Small Rain*, ix–x.

41 Ibid., 100, 4, 71.

42 LMM, *ENM*, 5.

43 L'Engle, *Small Rain*, 51–4, 160.

44 LMM, *EQ*, 35–7.

45 L'Engle, *Small Rain*, 92, 109–10. In L'Engle's sequel to *The Small Rain*, titled *A Severed Wasp* (1982), we learn that Katherine does eventually marry Justin, who has remained supportive of her career as a concert pianist.

46 LMM, *CJ* 4:240.

47 LMM, *EC*, 31–2.

48 L'Engle, *Small Rain*, 259, 363.

49 Lavoie, "*Gregor the Overlander* and *A Wrinkle in Time*," 66, 70.

50 L'Engle, *Wrinkle in Time*, 67–8, 82–3; Lavoie, "*Gregor the Overlander* and *A Wrinkle in Time*," 77.

51 L'Engle, *Wrinkle in Time*, 154–5.

52 Ibid., 139–40, 183.

53 LMM, *ENM*, 15.

54 L'Engle, *Wrinkle in Time*, 139–40, 145–6, 159, 161.

55 LMM, *EC*, 104–6.

56 LMM, *EQ*, 171.

57 LMM, *ENM*, 48.

58 L'Engle, *Wrinkle in Time*, 36, 47, 56.

59 Ibid., 183, 187, 194–6.

60 L'Engle, *Walking on Water*, 58.

9

Transformative Girlhood and Twenty-First-Century Girldom in L.M. Montgomery's *Anne of Green Gables*

WILLIAM V. THOMPSON

In her introduction to *All about the Girl: Power, Culture, and Identity,* Anita Harris states that the "category of 'girl' is constantly being constructed and deconstructed." She uses her introduction to outline the range and development of girlhood studies in response to a "diverse and dynamic population." She further comments on the multiplicity of problems facing twenty-first-century girls, identifying the popular idea "that girls lose their resistant and authentic voices when they engage with cultural requirements to shape their identities in line with dominant femininities."[1] Girlhood studies offers a way of understanding multiple girlhoods in relation to media culture, but also raises questions about literary girls and their place within a diverse definition of girlhood across children's and young-adult literature. L.M. Montgomery's *Anne of Green Gables,* a persistently popular girl's text, positions Anne Shirley in relation to a dominant patriarchal community that seeks to define both her femininity and sexuality. In this chapter, I argue for the transformative power of girlhood in *Anne of Green Gables,* which emerges out of Anne's ability to occupy a range of spheres, from the imaginative and the natural to the domestic and the scholastic. While conspicuously nineteenth century in its representations of the feminine and the domestic, Montgomery's text speaks to girls and developing girldom in a similar way to twenty-first-century texts, even if these fictional girls exercise their agency differently than Montgomery's Anne Shirley. Such characters as Suzanne Collins's Katniss (*The Hunger Games* trilogy), J.K. Rowling's Hermione (the *Harry Potter* series), and Disney's Elsa (*Frozen*) have a greater capacity to act; however, they, like Anne, have to negotiate their voices in relation to the constraints of a dominant culture. Girlhood in Avonlea may be more circumscribed than the diverse girlhoods of the twenty-first century, but the fluid, ebullient, sensually charged, transformative nature of Anne's girlhood enables her to develop and retain her voice in the face of dominant constructions of both girlhood and femininity. In this way, girlhood in *Anne of Green Gables* becomes a transformative space, one that holds implications for twenty-first-century diverse girldom, operating across multiple spheres, redefining conventional femininity, and breaking down barriers between girls and women.

Montgomery scholars variously recognize the poignancy and power of Anne's girlhood, examining it within a range of contexts, but not all specifically locating her in the arena of girlhood studies or girls' development. In "*Anne of Green Gables*: A Girl's Reading," Temma Berg argues that Anne's desperate desire for belonging distinguishes the book from a boy's adventure and frames the novel as a feminist text. The feminism of the novel, she asserts, locates itself in Anne's character, her imaginative power, and the ways that imagination empowers women: "Anne wants to be accepted and she makes wanting to be accepted not only acceptable, but courageous and as worthwhile as it is difficult."[2] Irene Gammel, in "Safe Pleasures for Girls: L.M. Montgomery's Erotic Landscapes," frames an examination of Anne's girlhood in terms of the erotic nature of the Prince Edward Island landscape. Gammel states that Montgomery "empowers her girls to be agents in their erotic universe, to indulge in sensualized pleasure without feelings of guilt; indeed, to cultivate and map their erotic imaginary."[3] Gammel's erotic imaginary grounds Montgomery's girl characters firmly in the PEI landscape, with Anne's connection to that landscape finding an immediate expression at the opening of the book in her naming of the White Way of Delight. Such a discussion of girl characters extends to the larger community of women within the *Anne* series. Marah Gubar, in " Where Is the Boy'? The Pleasures of Postponement in the *Anne of Green Gables* Series," argues that female relationships in the *Anne* books have the effect of delaying heterosexual, romantic relationships. She cites a range of examples in which such relationships between women serve to postpone traditional marriage: "By postponing romantic engagements until the last few pages of her narratives or deferring their depiction to a subsequent instalment, Montgomery presents an immense number of confirmed spinsters for whom marriage itself serves as an unconvincing sequel to a long, happy life lived alone or in the company of other women."[4] Finally, Kelly Blewett, in "An Unfortunate Lily Maid: Transgressive Reading in *Anne of Green Gables,*" frames Anne's girlhood in the context of reading and sentimental romance, which in turn becomes the basis of Anne's resistance to conventional constructions of love and marriage. This sampling shows Montgomery scholars positioning Anne's girlhood within contexts that define her variously in relation to her peers, the wider community, and the Prince Edward Island landscape. Whether it is belonging, erotic landscapes, or reading, these contexts frame Anne's desire and adolescent development, but not entirely within the parameters of girldom and the fostering of an authentic voice.

In this volume, "Vulnerable Situations: Boys and Boyhood in the *Emily* Books" by Rita Bode (chapter 3) and "The Performance of the Beautiful Dream Boy in Novels by L.M. Montgomery and Frances Hodgson Burnett" by Margaret Steffler (chapter 4) form a counterpoint to the examination of girls and girldom in *Anne of Green Gables.* Both Bode and Steffler examine Montgomery's representation of boys and boyhood in an historical and literary context, Bode framing her discussion in the context of boys' development and early-twentieth-century boyology, and Steffler examining the idealized figure of the dream boy or the beautiful boy within Montgomery's *Anne* series. These chapters construct boys and boys' development along social and psychological lines, and even in terms of Montgomery's own understanding of boyhood as a parent, but the question of a developing voice recurs specifically in an examination of girls and girls' experience. Girlhood studies provides a lens through which to interrogate Anne's development as an adolescent in Avonlea; it offers a wider arena for locating Anne's development as a girl and young woman, further providing a means of measuring Anne's experience against that of twenty-first-century fictional girls. In "Women, Girls, and the Unfinished Work of Connection: A Critical Review of American Girls' Studies," Janie Victoria Ward and Beth Cooper Benjamin stress the commonalities that exist among girls' lived experience. They explain that, since its inception, the girls' movement has shifted from "a focus on strengthening alliances between girls and women toward a tendency to address girls' needs as a separate entity." In order to avoid reducing girls' experience to a focus on the individual, Ward and Benjamin emphasize the importance of the communal experience for girls: "While the contexts of girls' lives vary by geography, economics, and sexual orientation, among other distinctions, what's lost in this argument is the recognition that all American girls are influenced by, and must negotiate, persistent gender bias in institutions (for examples, schools, health care systems, organized religion) and the ubiquity of American popular culture."[5] Institutionalized gender bias is not simply a challenge to contemporary girls and girls' voices; it is a cornerstone of girls' experience.

By the same token, recognizing the communal nature of girls' experience in no way diminishes the diversity of that experience. In their introduction to *Girls, Texts, Cultures*, Clare Bradford and Mavis Reimer identify this diversity of girls' experience and subject positions within a wide range of scholarly approaches. They state that "as girls have become more publicly visible, they have often become a locus of moral panics, many of which centre upon their bodies and behaviours, and which are exemplified by debates over topics such as the sexualization of young girls, obesity, eating disorders, and consumerism. These flurries of concern are often characterized by generalized and homogenizing depictions of girls, and they tend to state or to imply comparisons with masculine adolescence."[6] Hence comes the need for recognizing the diverse nature of girls' experience in terms of ethnicity, sexuality, and economic status, while noting those places where girls share their experience as girls. Such a communal experience also forms the basis for that of characters from different centuries and genres. Anne shares a struggle in becoming a girl with twenty-first-century characters, such as Katniss, Hermione, and Elsa, particularly in defining her femininity and finding an authentic voice.

Katniss, Hermione, and Elsa are not entirely themselves without a voice, but they, too, face institutionalized and familial gender bias. In *The Hunger Games*, Katniss identifies as both provider and hunter in relation to her family, going so far as to wear her father's old jacket and to use her father's old bow when leaving the confines of District 12 to hunt. Not until she volunteers at the reaping and is subject to a physical makeover in preparation for the Hunger Games does Katniss realize the extent to which she must reconstruct herself as a girl. She must adapt those qualities that will both gain her popularity in the Capitol and keep her alive in the arena. Hermione, in *Harry Potter*, is another type of twenty-first-century girl. She is a know-it-all, a smart girl, one who is rewarded as often as she is told to hold her tongue. As the female third in the group that will eventually hunt for Voldemort's horcruxes all over Britain, Hermione is more knowledgeable about the wizarding world, more emotionally intelligent, and generally more skilled at magic than either Harry or Ron. Nonetheless, Hermione and Harry and their respective skills form a complementary pair: her rationality and his intuition. In *Frozen*, on the other hand, Elsa is a Disney princess, and she is subject to the limitations of such princesses within the Disney canon. Elsa does not, however, remain a princess for long; she is crowned Queen of Arendelle and just as quickly abandons her sister and kingdom to find both her voice and power. For each of these girls, girldom is about finding an authentic and acceptable mode of expression, a way of speaking and acting within a public arena and in the face of hegemonic censure.

For Anne, as well as her twenty-first-century counterparts, girldom is the process of becoming, that period of adolescence lasting longer for girls than for boys. Catherine Driscoll, in *Girls: Feminine Adolescence in Popular Culture and Cultural Theory*, describes the period of adolescence, both historically and in popular culture, as a "disjunction" between physical maturity and social majority. This phase of childhood carries with it a number of descriptors: teenager, adolescent, and pubescent. According to Driscoll, adolescence means more than teenagehood, as the term teenager has become feminized and disempowered, and has a chronological endpoint: "In the twentieth century, adolescence means something other than the teenage stage and implies both pubescence and experience."[7] While Anne is not a teenager in the same way as her twenty-first-century counterparts, she undergoes a protracted adolescence, during which she is subject to the scrutiny of everyone around her, including her peers, as well as the matriarchs and patriarchs of Avonlea.

As the editors point out in the introduction to this volume, many of Montgomery's characters are "tweens" or "teenagers," while Montgomery preferred the terms "boyhood" and "girlhood" to make the distinction between childhood and adulthood.[8] Anne's girlhood, or adolescence, further fits within a larger tradition of girls and adolescence from the late-nineteenth century. Sarah Bilston's *The Awkward Age in Women's Popular Fiction, 1850–1900: Girls and the Transition to Womanhood* examines the adolescent heroine as a transitional figure in late-Victorian fiction. According to Bilston, the fictional girl at the end of the nineteenth century served to both challenge gender norms and reinforce traditional ideas of the feminine: "her restlessness and rebellion could be used to articulate desires for self-determination and independence, secure in the knowledge that wifehood and the third volume could bring the text to a securely traditional conclusion." Despite such a conservative representation of the girl in popular fiction of the *fin de siècle*, Bilston maintains that the girl remains a destabilizing figure: "The figure at the heart of such texts was active, self-confident, articulate, and culturally visible – a figure clearly descended from the transitional girl heroine of the woman's romance novel."[9] Anne is the descendant of such girl characters. She has her roots in these active female characters, but reaches back further to earlier heroines, while simultaneously looking forward to the fictional girls of the twenty-first century.

The gender bias to which Anne is subject as an adolescent is both institutionalized and culturally sanctioned. Anne, of course, is not the only girl in Avonlea to undergo scrutiny of this kind. However, Anne openly seeks to express her voice everywhere in Avonlea, which results in some degree of censure from all quarters. Anne's problem from the opening of the novel is her girlness. The Cuthberts wanted a boy from the asylum, and Matthew returns from Bright River with a girl. Anne is immediately met with Marilla's disapproval. Thus, Anne's experience of being at fault for her own gender comes more from the women of Avonlea than it does the men. According to Rachel Lynde, Anne is "terrible skinny and homely."[10] Anne's passionate response to this criticism of her physical appearance marks her first trial at Green Gables: she must offer an apology for her behaviour toward Rachel Lynde. This trial is consistent with the chief message she receives from the community: she must conform. Anne is subject to the heteronormative, patriarchal values of Avonlea, a system in which both men and women actively participate.

The scrutiny to which Anne is subject finds a resonance with her twenty-first-century counterparts, both in the public and political arenas. In *Harry Potter and the Goblet of Fire*, Hermione endures the scrutiny of her classmates, including Ron, all of whom insist on knowing the identity of Hermione's date to the Yule Ball. Hermione makes herself up for the occasion, so much so that Harry fails to immediately recognize her as he arrives at the Great Hall: "But she didn't look like Hermione at all. She had done something with her hair; it was no longer bushy but sleek and shiny, and twisted up into an elegant knot at the back of her head." Hermione's physical transformation, which is similar to Katniss's and Elsa's transformations, places her in the public eye in such a way as to draw both the envy of other girls and jealousy from Ron. More ominously, Hermione falls foul of Rita Skeeter, after the *Daily Prophet* reporter writes an article about Hagrid's giantess mother. In a *Witch Weekly* article, Skeeter describes Hermione as a duplicitous girl who is playing on the affections of two famous wizards: "Miss Granger, a plain but ambitious girl, seems to have a taste for famous wizards that Harry alone cannot satisfy. Since the arrival at Hogwarts of Viktor Krum, Bulgarian Seeker and hero of the last World Quidditch Cup, Miss Granger has been toying with both boys' affections."[11]

Much like the public scrutiny Anne undergoes from such characters as Mr Phillips and Josie Pye, Hermione constructs her identity and asserts her voice, despite the scrutiny and criticism of those both within and outside of Hogwarts. Anne and Hermione further share a love of learning and a competitive edge. According to Ruthann Mayes-Elma, in *Females and Harry Potter: Not All That Empowering*, Hermione enacts her agency by being a model student, studying hard, and demonstrating her knowledge in the classroom. This is the arena in which Hermione, like Anne, becomes, according to Remus Lupin, "the cleverest witch of your age I've ever met."[12] Mayes-Elma points to the significance of Hermione's initial appearance in the series, in which she wears her school robes on the Hogwarts Express: "Her conscious decision to put her robes on shows a way in which Hermione enacts her agency and thus conveys her attitude about Hogwarts and school in general."[13] Education, for Hermione, is nonetheless more than simply the acquisition of knowledge. Tara Foster, in "'Books! And Cleverness!': Hermione's Wits," identifies Hermione as a warrior and points out that, as early as the first book in the series, she places the defeat of Voldemort above her desire for knowledge: "If faced with expulsion, her greatest weapon will again be her scholarship."[14] Anne Shirley is not a warrior, and she lacks a school uniform; nonetheless, she must negotiate the public sphere of the school and community and is no less intent on performing well against her peers, all the while maintaining a scholastic rivalry with Gilbert Blythe.

Scrutiny for Katniss and Elsa occurs within a wider arena and has dangerously political consequences. Katniss lives under the eyes of the authorities in District 12, but this surveillance takes an altogether more sinister form in the Capitol and the arena. The reaping is broadcast across Panem, but Katniss's every move is filmed and analyzed once she enters the arena for the Seventy-fourth Hunger Games. This scrutiny forces her to act a part, even when she is injured, such as after the fireball attack early in the games: "I almost faint at the sight of my calf. The flesh is a brilliant red covered with blisters. I force myself to take deep, slow breaths, feeling quite certain the cameras are on my face. I can't show weakness at this injury. Not if I want help. Pity does not get you aid."[15] Katniss performs – quite literally – the role of the Girl on Fire, which eventually becomes that of the stylized, highly sexualized Mockingjay, after which she is always accompanied by a camera crew, even on the final mission to assassinate President Snow in the third book of the series. Such political ramifications go far beyond anything Anne experiences in quiet Avonlea; however, Katniss is a twenty-first-century dystopian girl hero, whose roots and determination in the face of difficult situations extend back to adolescent girls such as Anne Shirley. But unlike Anne, Katniss is a political figurehead and a political pawn, earning the direct enmity of President Snow following her trick with the berries that saves her life and Peeta's at the end of the games. Dystopian setting aside, Katniss equally reflects Bilston's transitional, Victorian, fictional girl, who brings the text to a traditional, heteronormative conclusion at the close of the third volume of the series.

Elsa, too, faces the scrutiny of a populace, but she is the heir to the throne of Arendelle, which means her actions are necessarily political at the outset. Elsa defies many of the stereotypes attached to the figure of the Disney princess: she isolates herself, lives with a supernatural power over ice and snow, and does not make choices based on a courtship narrative. During her coronation, Elsa must remove her protective gloves as part of a public ceremony to take up the orb and sceptre of Arendelle. The power she has long kept secret is suddenly on display to the entire kingdom. She struggles to contain herself, then retrieves her gloves and once again masks her power from public sight.[16] The film has been popularly identified as Disney's first feminist fairy tale. According to Amanda Rodriguez and the *Bitch Flicks* website, the "most important relationship in *Frozen*, the one that drives all the action, all the pathos, is that of Anna and her sister Elsa. The two of them love each other very deeply, but they struggle to connect."[17] This struggle to connect further suggests the degree to which heteronormative masculinity can often interfere with female relationships, the very relationship so valued by both Anne and Katniss. Anne has Diana, her bosom friend, while Katniss has her sister Prim, then in the arena Rue, the little girl from District 11 who is killed by one of the career tributes. Hermione lacks the sisterly closeness of such relationships, but both her romantic connection with Viktor Krum and her connection to Harry interfere variously with other relationships, including that with Mrs Weasley, following the publication of the article by Rita Skeeter, and that with Ron, during the hunt for the horcruxes in the final book of the series.

Anne Shirley, however, is not solely subject to the scrutiny and control of the residents of Avonlea; Montgomery's narrator also takes an active part in controlling Anne's presence in the book. Elizabeth Epperly, in *The Fragrance of Sweet-Grass: L.M. Montgomery's Heroines and the Pursuit of Romance*, describes Montgomery's narrator as a "careful stage director,"[18] one for whom Anne is the chief actor in the community of Avonlea. For Epperly, the narrator positions herself sympathetically in relation to Anne. An early example of such a point of sympathy, according to Epperly, occurs as the narrator differentiates between the ordinary and extraordinary observer of the small girl waiting at the Bright River station: "an extraordinary observer might have seen that the chin was very pointed and pronounced; that the big eyes were full of spirit and vivacity … in short, our discerning extraordinary observer might have concluded that no commonplace soul inhabited the body of this stray woman-child of whom shy Matthew Cuthbert was so ludicrously afraid."[19] Epperly explains that "Anne creates herself as the romantic heroine of her own adventures, and the narrator provides the setting and reinforcement for her self-drama."[20]

Sympathy aside, the narrator is careful to control the introduction of Anne's perspective, which, narratively speaking, provides a measure of control over Anne's voice. The narrator delays Anne's position as the focalizing character of the text as she begins to earn her place both at Green Gables and in Avonlea. Anne's soulful response to the White Way of Delight, her collapse into the depths of despair upon learning the Cuthberts had sent for a boy, and her broken-hearted exclamations after getting Diana drunk come in the form of dialogue with Matthew and Marilla, rather than internal reflection. With the exception of chapters 4 and 5, Anne does not fully become the focalizing character of the book until chapter 15, "A Tempest in the School Teapot." Matthew has a chapter – "Matthew Cuthbert Is Surprised" – and Mrs Rachel Lynde has two – "Mrs. Rachel Lynde Is Surprised" and "Mrs. Rachel Lynde Is Properly Horrified." However, the focus of the narrative lies primarily with Marilla for the first fourteen chapters of the book. Marilla is, in relation to Anne, the older, female authority in the domestic sphere. This focus is most evident from chapters 12 to 14. Each of these chapters begins with Marilla wondering about Anne, where she is or what she has done: "It was not until the next Friday that Marilla heard the story of the flower-wreathed hat. She came home from Mrs. Lynde's and called Anne to account."[21] In this way, Marilla becomes the filter through which Anne's voice is heard early in the novel, while simultaneously serving as the domestic purveyor of the hegemonic expectations of the wider Avonlea community.

According to Lesley Clement, in "Mobilizing the Power of the Unseen: Imagining Self / Imagining Others in L.M. Montgomery's *Anne of Green Gables*," Marilla has a discerning eye, with the ability "to see beneath the surface to the inner character or hidden story." Marilla is always aware of Anne's social improprieties, but her deep-seated sense of irony allows her to see beyond Anne's behaviour and recognize the humour in the situations she creates. Clement states that this is Marilla's ability to see both the visible and invisible with respect to the members of the Avonlea community: "Most significantly, Marilla is suggesting the need to read people and events very carefully to penetrate to what lies beneath: the unseen qualities and hidden stories. Among the many, predominantly moral, lessons that Marilla provides Anne, this lesson in learning to look and to see, a lesson in perspective and proportion, is perhaps the most valuable one she has to offer."[22] Such a comment reaffirms Marilla's role with respect to Anne, as caregiver, as teacher, as mentor. Using Marilla as a narrative focus, the narrator carefully positions the older woman in relation to Anne: Anne's is the emerging voice, while Marilla's is the authoritative. Anne always forms the subject of the narration, but in these early chapters, the narrative perspective lies with someone else, whether Matthew, Mrs Lynde, or Marilla.

Despite using Marilla as a focalizing character for much of the first fourteen chapters of the novel, Montgomery's narrator maintains a certain distance from Marilla's character, enough to comment on Marilla's often mixed responses to Anne. Anne's realization that the Cuthberts had requested a boy from the asylum sends her into a paroxysm of grief, which has the effect of tempering Marilla's no-nonsense response: "Something like a reluctant smile, rather rusty from long disuse, mellowed Marilla's grim expression." The "rusty" smile reappears as Anne insists that Marilla call her Anne with an E and becomes a full-fledged smile upon hearing Anne describe Mrs Blewett as a gimlet: "Marilla smothered a smile under the conviction that Anne must be reproved for such a speech." These repressed smiles become a repressed laugh after Anne apologizes to Mrs Lynde, and, as Anne and Marilla walk home to Green Gables in the twilight, Marilla experiences a wash of feeling as Anne slips her hand into the older woman's: "Something warm and pleasant welled up in Marilla's heart at the touch of that thin little hand in her own – a throb of the maternity she had missed, perhaps. Its very unaccustomedness and sweetness disturbed her." As Marilla softens toward Anne, becoming more forgiving of her oddities, the gap between them begins to collapse, and Anne assumes the narrative focus of the novel. Chapter 15, "A Tempest in the School Teapot," begins with Anne commenting on her walk to school with Diana: "'What a splendid day!' said Anne, drawing a long breath. 'Isn't it good just to be alive on a day like this? I pity the people who aren't born yet for missing it.'"[23] Becoming the focalizing character provides Anne and her voice with a greater sense of authority. The narrator never entirely relinquishes control of the narrative, but more and more she assumes Anne's language, particularly the names of places, such as the White Way of Delight, Lover's Lane, or the Dryad's Bubble, all of which reinforce Anne's position within the text. The narrator continues to interject herself, whether on Anne's behalf or as a means of interpreting other characters' responses, but the primary filter from this point forward is Anne.

As Harris suggests, discovering their authentic voices in the face of hegemonic and patriarchal control is a struggle for adolescent girls.[24] While Anne has little trouble vocalizing, it takes time for her to arrive at such an authentic voice. Trinna Frever describes Anne's voice as that of the oral storyteller, suggesting Montgomery's skill as a narrator lies in her ability to evoke oral storytelling as part of her narrative. Frever explains that this skill centres largely on the character of Anne herself: "In addition to the social functions of Anne's speech, her talking serves a narrative function as well, by aligning the text with oral storytelling traditions and the narrative importance of the voice." Frever argues that Montgomery's use of such storytelling elements creates a "polyvocal narrative style," which in turn collapses the traditional narrative hierarchy: "Montgomery provides the reader with page after page of Anne's voice, speaking. Her choice recuperates the reader into the audience of Anne's narration, as if in the room with Anne and Marilla, rather than outside it reading a book. Montgomery uses orality to erode the distancing inherent in the print narrative act, and recasts her audience as listeners to the voice of Anne-as-storyteller."[25] Nonetheless, the narrator interacts with Anne's voice over the course of the book, drawing attention to her manner of expression by borrowing Anne's language and using gentle irony as a means of revealing Anne's foibles.

Unlike the narrator, Marilla as the domestic authority is often repressive with respect to Anne's chattiness. This points to the clear power relationship between the woman and girl within the domestic sphere. Marilla allows Anne her own voice, although more often she is simply unable to quell Anne's natural effusiveness. Marilla allows Anne to impart a narrative as she is taking Anne to see Mrs Hammond to discuss the mistake in having received a girl rather than a boy from the asylum. Marilla sets limits on Anne's narrative, insisting she stick to "bald facts" in the retelling of her history. But Anne cannot stick to bald facts. She has a compulsion to describe and extemporize, as she does in the description of her parents' house in Bolingbroke, Nova Scotia: "I think it must have had honeysuckle over the parlour window and lilacs in the front yard and lilies of the valley just inside the gate. Yes, and muslin curtains in all the windows. Muslin curtains give a house such an air."[26] Anne's description of her parents' house speaks to her need to provide a commentary on everything she sees and thinks, as well as her current desire to have a home at Green Gables.[27]

If finding an authentic voice is part of the challenge facing twenty-first-century girls, such a challenge is equally difficult for Anne. What Anne lacks in her utterances is discernment. She vocalizes her thoughts and feelings, but with little regard for her listener. Storytelling, at its heart, presumes a relationship between teller and listener. Frever insists such a relationship exists within the book, explaining that Anne's narrative function within the text is to bring the reader into a more active participation with her story: "Her speech forms a pattern across the text, a structural thread that binds isolated incidents together, lending coherence to the novel as a whole, drawing the reader into Anne's world through her storytelling, and establishing the relationship between text and reader as one of speaker and listener within an oral storytelling tradition."[28] Anne may find herself in the position of storyteller within the text, but she has to modify and temper her language to gain the appreciation of her audience.

The incident of the Haunted Wood comes closer to storytelling for Anne than many of her earlier utterances, and further demonstrates the power of her imagination to affect her perception of the world. For Anne, the Haunted Wood is set apart from the commonplace; it is rendered romantic and gothic by virtue of the stories it contains. Even here, the stories from the Haunted Wood are fragments; the murdered child, the White Lady, and the headless man all carry their own stories, but they nonetheless have a particular power as a result of their shadowy incompleteness. The gothic nature of Anne's Haunted Wood speaks to more than simply stories. According to Kathleen Ann Miller, in "Haunted Heroines: The Gothic Imagination and the Female Bildungsroman of Jane Austen, Charlotte Brontë, and L.M. Montgomery," the gothic imagination is linked to both romance and the female imagination. She compares Austen's use of the gothic in *Northanger Abbey* to Anne and the Haunted Wood, suggesting the gothic has both an educational and social function for the young woman, furthering the education of both the heroine and the reader: "Austen and Montgomery posit that once the false teachings of Gothic romances – their improper reading and imaginative practices – are swept away, then the heroines will be prepared for their own real-life romantic courtship narratives."[29] For Anne, the Haunted Wood incident is less about gothic romance than it is a lesson in the excesses of the imagination, which, for Miller, is gendered female within the larger tradition of gothic romance. Anne herself recognizes the educational function of the Haunted Wood incident. In her litany of mistakes at the end of the "Lily Maid" chapter, Anne states: "The Haunted Wood mistake cured me of letting my imagination run away with me."[30] The Haunted Wood incident therefore is reduced to an object lesson for Anne, a simple learning opportunity, with all its gothic romance and mystery stripped away. The incident is fraught with emotion, but carries a similar weight to that of putting liniment in the cake or dying her hair green.

Despite Anne's determination to see major incidents in her life at Green Gables as mistakes and object lessons, the courtship narrative Miller describes lies at the heart of Anne's imaginings and developing voice. The earliest evidence of Anne's courtship narrative comes with her insistence that Marilla call her Cordelia, which constitutes Anne's first self-conscious use of language upon arriving at Green Gables. For Anne, the name carries romantic associations. The name itself hints at a story with a romantic heroine at its heart, which Anne later imagines into her room at Green Gables: "I am tall and regal, clad in a gown of trailing white lace, with a pearl cross on my breast and pearls in my hair. My hair is of midnight darkness and my skin is a clear ivory pallor. My name is the Lady Cordelia Fitzgerald. No, it isn't – I can't make *that* seem real."[31] Anne's inability to maintain the fantasy speaks to the limitations of her childish imagination and the inherent eroticism of the image. The figure of Cordelia is pale and languorous; she gazes at herself in a mirror, and despite the cross of pearl, Cordelia seems more than ready for a suitor. The sexual overtones in this picture are too much for Anne at this point in the text, again reinforcing her age and childish imagination.

The courtship narrative is another point at which Anne's experience intersects with her twenty-first-century counterparts. Hermione evokes such a narrative by attending the ball with Viktor Krum, while Katniss throws herself into the fiction of the star-crossed lovers in the arena. Confronted with the possibility of going dateless to the Yule Ball, Ron turns to Hermione, blurting, "Hermione, Neville's right – you *are* a girl."[32] For Ron, the prospect of heterosexual romance turns Hermione into a girl, while Hermione unwillingly finds herself part of a romantic triangle. Katniss and her performance place her in a similar triangle, caught between Peeta in the arena and Gale back home in District 12. Nevertheless, the televised romance becomes a strategy for staying alive. Katniss convinces herself that both she and Peeta are performing the fiction of the star-crossed lovers to the Capitol. But unlike Katniss, Peeta is not acting. Katniss finds herself persisting in a romantic narrative until the final scene in the arena, when she uses the threat of the poison berries to force the Gamemakers to declare both Katniss and Peeta winners of the Seventy-fourth Hunger Games. Katherine Broad, in "The Dandelion in the Spring: Utopia as Romance in Suzanne Collins's *The Hunger Games Trilogy*," explains how the love triangle is bound up with the politics of revolution: "The love triangle plays a significant role in fueling the narrative progression toward a better world. Each boy represents a different path out of dystopia, making the outcome of the romantic choice nothing less than what the future society will be. The courtship narrative therefore says a great deal about Katniss's revolutionary potential and in turn raises significant questions about her revered status as a feminist icon for readers of all ages."[33] Anne has her courtship narrative, as do both Hermione and Katniss. Only Elsa remains ostensibly free. She nonetheless becomes entangled because of Hans's attempt to deceive Anna into marriage; this in turn brings Hans and Anna to ask for

Elsa's blessing, which precipitates the unleashing of Elsa's power. In each case, the courtship narrative is incompatible with a stable feminist position.

These fictional girls also undergo a conspicuous transformation with the introduction of the courtship narrative. Hermione makes herself over for the Yule Ball, becoming unrecognizable to Harry. Katniss, on the other hand, is transformed by Cinna and her prep team into the Girl on Fire: "The creature standing before me in the full-length mirror has come from another world. Where skin shimmers and eyes flash and apparently they make their clothes from jewels. Because my dress, oh, my dress is entirely covered in reflective precious gems, red and yellow and white with bits of blue that accent the tips of the flame design. The slightest movement gives the impression I am engulfed in tongues of fire."[34] Elsa's transformation is at once more complete and potentially more devastating. She becomes the queen of snow and ice as she flees the castle, inadvertently locking Arendelle into an endless winter, and literally shedding her former identity and appearance, beginning with her gloves, as she sings her signature song: "It's time to see what I can do, / To test the limits and break through. / No right, no wrong, no rules for me. / I'm free."[35] Elsa as the queen of snow and ice embodies a female sensuality that stands apart from the courtship narrative; the same is true initially for Katniss as the Girl on Fire.

Becoming subject to heterosexual romance and the courtship narrative, in part, may diminish these characters as strictly feminist heroes; they share, however, a similar predicament with Anne Shirley, an early-twentieth-century feminist pioneer, whose sense of the sensual and the romantic is tied to nature and friendships with other girls. The bond these characters share as girls works to mitigate their attachment to the courtship narrative, but the presence of such a narrative at all undercuts their position in relation to a feminist ideology. *Frozen* is perhaps the clearest example of an attempt at a feminist narrative running at cross purposes to itself. According to Maja Rudloff, in "(Post)Feminist Paradoxes: The Sensibilities of Gender Representation in Disney's *Frozen*," the film remains limited in terms of its depiction of masculine and feminine characters: "When the range of gender images popular culture makes available are increasingly non-diverse and one-dimensional depictions of what femininity and masculinity can mean, it limits the range of possibilities of identification for girls and boys drastically. On the surface, *Frozen* might feature two active, agentic princesses, but they stand as the only female models of identification in a land almost devoid of women."[36] Disney's *Frozen* may limit such means of identification, but the relationship between Elsa and Anna constitutes that sisterly bond characteristic of Anne and Diana's bosom friendship. In *Frozen II*, Elsa and Anna's bond is challenged once again, as Elsa undergoes a further transformation into the fifth spirit, an elemental force of nature, which explains both the source of Elsa's power and her connection to the kingdom of Northuldra, representing the completion of Elsa's story begun in the first film.

Montgomery's text has no lack of female models of identification, nor does Anne. Two incidents later in the book reincorporate Anne's courtship narrative into a new means of expression for Anne: the story of Cordelia and Geraldine, and her account to Mrs Allan of her near-disastrous role as the character of Elaine. Both incidents are equally tied to Anne's courtship narrative. Anne forms the Story Club in direct response to her experience of the incident of the Haunted Wood, turning from storyteller to writer. She convinces herself that getting together with friends to write stories is a more productive use of her time than the imaginings that caused her so much grief in the Haunted Wood. Moreover, the Story Club and the tale of Cordelia and Geraldine are Anne's attempt to find a voice on the page; however, she remains hostage to the tropes of gothic fiction. "The Jealous Rival; or in Death Not Divided" is the account of the friends Cordelia Montmorency and Geraldine Seymour. The text of Anne's story never appears, but Anne explains the plot to Diana, in all its melodramatic glory: "Cordelia was secretly in love with Bertram herself and when Geraldine told her about the engagement she was simply furious, especially when she saw the necklace and the diamond ring. All her affection for Geraldine turned to bitter hate and she vowed that she should never marry Bertram."[37] The excessive melodrama of the story is lost on Anne. The narrator refrains from intervening or commenting on Anne's text, allowing the scene to become a rare case in which Anne becomes the object of humour.[38] This is what Epperly calls the narrator providing the "setting and reinforcement for [Anne's] self-drama."[39] Anne remains convinced of the "tragical" nature of Cordelia and Geraldine's tale: "It's a sad, sweet story. I just cried like a child while I was writing it."[40] Anne as storyteller finds a further expression in the Lily Maid incident, in which Anne learns to save herself while enacting the story of Elaine. In writing the story of Cordelia and Geraldine, Anne's voice is influenced by gothic tropes and novels of romance. Conversely, Anne's account to Mrs Allan following the sinking of the flat on Barry's Pond demonstrates the narrator's willingness to give over control of the narrative to Anne more fully.

The Lily Maid incident carries an inherent contradiction: it reinforces Anne's courtship narrative, while undercutting that same narrative through Anne's response to Gilbert's rescue. Blewett, in "An Unfortunate Lily Maid," and Ann Howey, in "Reading Elaine: Marjorie Richardson's and L.M. Montgomery's Red-Haired Lily Maids," both comment in detail on the Lily Maid incident and Anne's response. According to Blewett, Anne's sentimental, romantic tendencies enable her to read the Tennyson poem subversively, which leads to a revelation about heteronormative romance: "By imaginatively engaging with the Tennyson chivalric poem, Anne explores the idea that the requirements of conventional, heteronormative romance apply to her. This is the cultural expectation, for both the fictitious Anne living in Canada in the late nineteenth century and for the readers who have loved her since; a woman must marry a man and bear children." Blewett reads the Lily Maid scene as a place wherein heteronormative romance takes precedence over Anne's sense of independence: "As Anne plays a maiden trying a final appeal to win the heart of her knight, she attracts a very real male to whom she will have romantic – and sexual – obligation. Thus, far from being a place that does not appreciate romance, as Anne suggests to Marilla, Avonlea is instead a place where romance is unavoidable."[41] Anne comes to terms with her "real male" by the end of the book, but even after her rescue by Gilbert from the bridge piling, Anne's resistance to her own courtship narrative remains fixed.

The scene clearly contributes to Anne's understanding of her courtship narrative and heteronormative romance, but Anne's account of the incident to Mrs Allan provides her with a measure of control over the narrative that she has hitherto not demonstrated. In the description of the sinking of the flat, the narrator creates a temporal shift, allowing Anne herself to take control of the event: " I was horribly frightened,' she told Mrs Allan the next day, 'and it seemed like years while the flat was drifting down to the bridge and the water rising in it every moment. I prayed, Mrs. Allan, most earnestly, but I didn't shut my eyes to pray, for I knew the only way God could save me was to let the flat float close enough to one of the bridge piles for me to climb up on it."[42] According to Howey, the scene offers a poignant contrast between romance and reality on a number of levels. She suggests Montgomery's language in describing the scene – "cloth of gold" and "scrambled to her feet" – reinforces the disparity between Anne and the figure of Elaine: "The contrast between romantic Camelot and prosaic Avonlea becomes more significant in the contrast between Elaine (romantic but passive, dead) and Anne (desiring romance, but active and very much alive). Her agency, her practical determination to act, irrevocably separates her from the romantic heroines she admires."[43]

In telling Mrs Allan about the sinking of the flat, Anne is finding a new voice. She is relating her own experience. This is not the falsehood Anne tells Marilla about the amethyst brooch, nor is it the stories about the white lady or the dead child, and neither is it the tragic tale of Cordelia and Geraldine. Anne has shed her misapprehensions about Marilla's expectations, and she has foregone tales of the haunted wood and gothic tales about dying heroines. Anne describes her own experience forthrightly and clearly; she neither embellishes nor exaggerates. Anne has lived a thrilling, romantic adventure, and she has no compulsion to elaborate it.

The Lily Maid incident provides a peculiar conclusion to Anne's development, which occurs three-quarters of the way through the book. Anne's life and education continue, but she has found her voice. Anne learns some reticence following the Lily Maid chapter: "I have come to the conclusion that it is no use trying to be romantic in Avonlea. It was probably easy enough in towered Camelot hundreds of years ago, but romance is not appreciated now. I feel quite sure that you will soon see a great improvement in me in this respect, Marilla."[44] Anne recognizes that something is lacking in Avonlea, and she determines to become more contained as a result. However, Anne fails, at first, to recognize the significance of her experience. She may have still needed Gilbert to save her from the bridge pile, but Anne rescued herself from the sinking boat. Like her twenty-first-century counterparts, Anne is able to find a voice, recounting her own experience as part of her own narrative. Hermione is able to speak on her own behalf, but she learns to speak on behalf of others, including Hagrid and the house-elves. Katniss is able, with difficulty, to set aside her personal trauma and assume the role of the Mockingjay and speak for the rebels against the Capitol. Elsa finds vulnerability in her grief when confronted with Anna's sacrifice, which in turn allows her to gain control of her powers and enter into a new relationship with Anna and the people of Arendelle, as well as with the kingdom of Northuldra, as the fifth spirit. New and deeper relationships result from each of these girl characters finding a voice, the effects of which extend into the public and political realms. Girlhood is the space wherein such transformation is possible. Anne, Hermione, Katniss, and Elsa are characters who transform both themselves and their fictional worlds, who extend the boundaries of girlhood and invariably broaden what it means to be female.

NOTES

1 Harris, Introduction, *All About the Girl*, xxiv, xxiv, xviii.
2 Berg, "*Anne of Green Gables*: A Girl's Reading," 125.
3 Gammel, "Safe Pleasures for Girls," 118.
4 Gubar, "'Where Is the Boy?'" 48.
5 Ward and Benjamin, "Women, Girls, and the Unfinished Work," 23, 21.
6 Bradford and Reimer, "Introduction: Girls, Texts, Cultures," 12.
7 Driscoll, *Girls*, 48, 52.
8 See introduction to this volume, 3.
9 Bilston, *The Awkward Age in Women's Popular Fiction*, 175, 176.
10 LMM, *AGG*, 76.
11 Rowling, *Harry Potter and the Goblet of Fire*, 349, 432.
12 Rowling, *Harry Potter and the Prisoner of Azkaban*, 368.
13 Mayes-Elma, *Females and Harry Potter*, 79.
14 Foster, "'Books! And Cleverness!'" 108.
15 S. Collins, *Hunger Games*, 179.
16 *Frozen*, 19.00–19:50 min.
17 Rodriguez, "*Frozen*: Disney's First Foray into Feminism."
18 Epperly, *Fragrance of Sweet-Grass*, 21.
19 LMM, *AGG*, 14.
20 Epperly, *Fragrance of Sweet-Grass*, 23.
21 LMM, *AGG*, 98.
22 Clement, "Mobilizing the Power of the Unseen," 57, 58.
23 LMM, *AGG*, 29, 55, 90, 124.
24 Carol Gilligan's *In A Different Voice* is a pioneer work that helps lay the groundwork for such a discussion of girls' voices. Gilligan's text addresses the

development and silencing of women's voices, particularly in the context of "conceptions of self and morality ... experiences of conflict and choice" (2).

25 Frever, "Anne Shirley, Storyteller," 116, 117, 119. The text certainly overflows with Anne's voice, but in important ways, she is less the storyteller than two of Montgomery's other adolescent girls: Emily Byrd Starr and Sara Stanley.

26 LMM, *AGG*, 46.

27 See Lesley Clement's "L.M. Montgomery's Precocious Children: Resisting Adult Narratives of Death, Dying, and the Afterlife" in this volume for further discussion of how Anne exerts control over her life's narrative through her description of her parents' home in Bolingbroke, NS, and her life before her parents died (50–1).

28 Frever, "Anne Shirley, Storyteller," 117.

29 Miller, "Haunted Heroines," 126.

30 LMM, *AGG*, 269 (emphasis in original).

31 Ibid., 72 (emphasis in original).

32 Rowling, *Harry Potter and the Goblet of Fire*, 337 (emphasis in original).

33 Broad, "The Dandelion in the Spring," 18.

34 S. Collins, *Hunger Games*, 120.

35 *Frozen*, 31.15–32.00 min.

36 Rudloff, "(Post)Feminist Paradoxes," 20.

37 LMM, *AGG*, 247.

38 See Clement, "L.M. Montgomery's Precocious Children" in this volume for an alternative interpretation of these incidents (51–2).

39 Epperly, *Fragrance of Sweet-Grass*, 23.

40 LMM, *AGG*, 245.

41 Blewett, "An Unfortunate Lily Maid," 277.

42 LMM, *AGG*, 264.

43 Howey, "Reading Elaine," 97.

44 LMM, *AGG*, 269.

PART FOUR

Continuing Transmediated Conversations: *Anime*, Fanfiction, and Television Adaptations

10

The Problems and Possibilities Inherent in Adaptation: *Emily of New Moon* and *Emily, Girl of the Wind*

YOSHIKO AKAMATSU

The world of *anime* (animation) is booming in Japan and is now recognized as a legitimate art form. It is also a part of the technological industry that the Japanese government is working actively to export under a policy called "Cool Japan." Japanese scholars of children's literature are keenly aware of the enormous popularity of the animated television programs and films that have been adapted from literary texts, and the various problems that arise from them were discussed in nine articles featured in "*Anime* vs Children's Literature" in 2016.[1] As scholar Kei Suyama notes, *anime* and the written texts of children's literature are distinctly different art forms, even when they tell the same story.[2] In 1979, Japanese animators, in association with the Nippon Animation Company, adapted *Anne of Green Gables*, L.M. Montgomery's most famous novel, under the title of *Akage no An* [*Red-haired Anne*] and made it into a tremendously popular *anime*.[3] In 2007, Montgomery's *Emily of New Moon* trilogy[4] was also adapted into *anime* form and was first broadcast on Japanese television under the title of *Kaze no Shoujo Emiri* [*Emily, Girl of the Wind*]. As the literary consultant for this series, I was directly involved with the transformation of Montgomery's trilogy and worked to resolve specific problems that arose during the process. My work with the creators required a certain revisioning of the stories, as the animators and writers strove to represent "cultural markers"[5] that would make the *anime* relevant to a Japanese audience and appealing to people of all ages. This chapter considers how the Japanese animated version of the *Emily* trilogy responds to Montgomery's original literary text, focusing on differences between the two genres. After examining distinctions in scope and structure, I turn to narration, considering the central role that the *anime* creators gave to the "wind," as is demonstrated by the title, including giving a narrative voice and physical manifestation to Emily's Wind Woman and visualizing the natural wind in certain scenes – to great effect. The central role and the attention accorded to the wind, effectively intensifying and developing what the novel suggests and offers, contrasts with the scant attention paid to Emily's own power, her psychic vision, in the *anime*. The absence of that psychic vision results in some simplification of characters and relationships, while the cinematic and animation techniques of the *anime* contribute to the story's emotional intensity. It is the wind, however, that breathes energy and life into the *anime*, marking its difference and originality.

The word "animation" comes from the Greek word for "wind." *Anime* (or "animation") differs from a literary work in that it offers the audience visual action and motion. Professor and media analyst Thomas Lamarre writes, "If we recall that the term animation derives from the Greek *animus* or wind, we come full circle. Animation is an art of wind, an art of opening spaces to channel the flow of the wind. Animation is an art of spacing, of producing intervals through which the wind may blow and turn the wheels, limbs, eyes, and ears of the animator's drawings. The wind of animation arises in gaps that appear between layers of image when you avoid closing the image world. The wind blows through the characters, in their tendency to become weightless and unmoored and in the dynamics of angling their weight through different planes." Although Lamarre was specifically referring to the works of world-renowned Academy Award–winning animator Hayao Miyazaki when he wrote that "the medium (of animation) truly becomes the message (wind power)," I would argue that all animated works have the same characteristic: "In sum, wind-powered animation is the paradigm for a new rootedness."[6] It roots the story (and the audience) in a new medium.

Susan Napier argues, "This very Otherness of the animation form, combined with the extraordinary creative properties of the medium itself ... may be one of its major artistic strengths in the new transnational culture."[7] The transformation of a literary text into its visual manifestation helps a general audience (both those who have not and those who have read the novels) to envision or re-envision a writer's original work. Therefore, many different cinematic and animation techniques are used to render the subtle inner feelings in *anime* productions. For instance, in *Kaze no Shoujo Emiri*, Emily's solitary walk to visit Father Cassidy and to ask him to talk Lofty John out of cutting her beloved bush becomes a much longer walk than usual in episode 7. Likewise, Emily's falling off the cliff near Great-Aunt Nancy's house (episode 16) is a truly horrifying incident in the audience's eyes, because of the animation techniques which make it vivid and enable viewers to viscerally experience Emily's terror. The characters' suppressed feelings are also rendered visually in the *anime*. Emily's love for Teddy manifests itself in her blushing cheeks, without a word spoken, and their exchanged glances suggest their mutual attraction. Each aspect of the production allows readers to deepen their understanding of mystifying or subtle elements within the original texts through a comprehensive art form that includes narration, background music, opening and ending lyric theme songs, and visual images, all of them based on a script that may be modified by the literary consultant's perspectives. Modern technology is used to adapt the book into another way of experiencing children's literature. Keenly conscious of the popularity of the 1979 *anime* based on *Anne of Green Gables*, the creators of the *Emily anime* in 2007 strove to incorporate new animation techniques to impress their audience.

My advice as literary consultant was that the scriptwriters should remain faithful to Montgomery's original texts, but this was not always followed for various reasons: writers had to condense the story from three books to one *anime*; the team wanted to appeal to a twenty-first-century audience of all ages, as well as recreate the era of a century before; and animators wanted to highlight a wide range of animation techniques that the original *Anne anime* team did not have to help them achieve their aims. In a talk recorded on the website of the *Emily anime* and dated 25 August 2007, while the program was being aired, two of the animators and one of the producers discussed how they had tried to keep the *Emily* animation as close as possible to the authorial text.[8] According to the website *Emiri no Sekai* [*The World of Emily*], the director of animation, Harume Kosaka (the only woman taking part in directing and scriptwriting, as well as animation-drawing), indicated that she wanted to develop aspects of the trilogy that would appeal to present-day girls and women, such as a simple lifestyle and a sense of nostalgia for what might be perceived as "the good old days." The NHK program producer, Kenji

Saito, was keen to show the protagonist's struggles to become a writer. Animation producer Hideaki Miyamoto felt it important to highlight Emily's feelings about the beauty of Prince Edward Island. They spoke passionately of their visit to the island in June 2006 and how much it helped them understand the setting of the place that Emily (and Montgomery) loved. Their commentary demonstrates that the creators truly hoped to make the first *anime* of the *Emily* trilogy a unique work that would have a universal appeal for different generations.

Given the limited number of episodes, I suggested that the creators concentrate only on the first book, *Emily of New Moon*, which, like *Anne of Green Gables*, consists of a series of enjoyable vignettes. However, they insisted on covering the entire trilogy, which culminates with the fulfillment of Emily's dream of becoming a writer. They wanted to show the process by which Emily fulfills her ambition, which is very different from the *Anne anime* that ends with the sixteen-year-old girl daydreaming about the future. The producers believed that Emily's struggle to make a living as a writer would arouse more sympathy among twenty-first-century girls, who are more career-oriented than their predecessors.[9] In the final episode, Emily marries Teddy, but the *anime* creators went further: Emily's success as a writer is revealed in a conversation between Emily and her daughter, Lucy. Lucy asks, "And mother's books were published all over the world, weren't they? Was Aunt Elizabeth happy about it?" And Emily answers, "Oh, yes. And so were Cousin Jimmy and Aunt Laura." Emily's published books are shown on the bookshelves of the parlour, where a portrait of a young girl, who resembles Lucy, stands. This house is situated in Prince Edward Island, and looks like the house that was once called the "Disappointed House." Emily and Teddy seem to be living and working there. Lucy continues, saying, "I love Aunt Elizabeth. She always makes me a cup of her special tea," but her chatter is interrupted by a gust of wind, and she catches a vision of the Wind Woman. The *Emily anime* emphasizes the fulfillment of the protagonist's ambition to be a writer and the happiness she has with a family of her own.

The *Emily anime* consists of twenty-six episodes, compared to eighty-three chapters in the trilogy: *Emily of New Moon* (thirty-one), *Emily Climbs* (twenty-five), and *Emily's Quest* (twenty-seven). Compared to this is the *Anne anime*, which consisted of fifty episodes drawn from the thirty-eight chapters of the book. In the process of animating a story, changes are made that will upset some purists who love the original work. Changes that arose in the process of adapting the *Anne anime* were minimal, satisfying fans of the original text.[10] That said, with only twenty-six episodes, the *Emily anime* creators still opted to add certain scenes and perspectives not found in the original books (such as detailing the backgrounds of Emily's friends, giving her a child, having Emily realize her ambition, and more), and some fans took issue with these. As literary consultant, I had no involvement in the visualization process, except for a few scenes in episodes 1 and 26. For instance, I saved Emily's uncle, who had been destined for the cutting-room floor, when the animators thought there were too many relatives in episode 1. I also succeeded in reducing the number of Emily and Teddy's children from four to one in episode 26, insisting that faithful Montgomery readers would be unhappy to see children added that were not in the original Montgomery book. As a compromise, the *anime* team settled on creating just one daughter, Lucy, for Emily and Teddy.[11]

The *Emily anime* can be divided into three parts: episodes 1 to 4, episodes 5 to 23, and episodes 24 to 26. Twenty episodes are based on *Emily of New Moon*, and the balance are from *Emily Climbs* and *Emily's Quest*. In the *anime*, the exposition is over by the end of episode 4, which is called "The Sketch of Four [Children]." The *Emily anime* was promoted as "Another Story of Youth." In this case, "another" is a nod to the *Anne anime* of 1997. Additionally, it suggests the significance of the four main youthful characters: Emily Byrd Starr, Ilse Burnley, Teddy Kent, and Perry Miller. Episode 5 through the early part of episode 23 covers events comprising the structural complications, which deal with the various struggles of Emily and her three friends. The *anime*'s crisis occurs in the later part of episode 23, "Departing Heart." Teddy leaves for Paris after winning first prize for a drawing of his four chums, whereas Emily's hopes are dashed after her novels are rejected by several publishers. Emily feels left behind in Blair Water after her friends graduate from Shrewsbury High School and leave home. Episodes 24 to 26 make up the resolution, ending with Emily's recovery from her creative slump, marriage to Teddy, and success as a novelist. The long stretch of time after high school in the original texts is compressed into a few years in the *Emily anime*.

The producers and writers establish a thread that runs throughout the series with the images of "spring." The concept of spring is taken from what Emily's father, Douglas Starr, says to her near the end of his life: "I want you to be brave … The universe is full of love – and spring comes everywhere."[12] In the adaptation, scriptwriter Mitsuru Shimada adds the lines, "You mustn't be afraid of losing me. You will open many doors into tomorrow."[13] The added dialogue emphasizes her father's wish. It is also effectively echoed throughout the series, both in voice-overs and by Emily herself. Because spring suggests youth, this element suits the story of Emily in her childhood and girlhood. Although the word "spring" does not necessarily connote "youth" in the original text, it does this in the adaptation, as well as connoting "renewal" and "rebirth." The title of the last episode, number 26, is "The Advent of Spring," suggesting that Emily has finally reached her "tomorrow," her goal of becoming a published writer.

Montgomery inserts Emily's letters and diaries to tell her life story. This strategy seems to be a means of entering more intimately into Emily's mind as she writes out her problems, as Montgomery herself did in her own journals. However, there is a consistent third-person narration throughout. In *Emily of New Moon*, the narrator seems to be omniscient, but then manifests herself in the role of Emily's biographer at the beginning of the second chapter of *Emily Climbs*: "This book is not going to be wholly, or even mainly, made up of extracts from Emily's diary; but, by way of linking up matters unimportant enough for a chapter in themselves, and yet necessary for a proper understanding of her personality and environment, I am going to include some more of them. Besides, when one has material ready to hand, why not use it?"[14] The introduction of Emily's "diary" by her biographer is an unusual technique in Montgomery's novel. Elizabeth Waterston calls this technique "an odd and awkward intrusion," but observes that it does "serve to remind the reader of the fact of creation" and to keep the overall focus on Emily as a writer: "The object of the book, after all, is to explore a creative talent in its chrysalis stage."[15] Thus, Montgomery's narrator is human and shows her interest in Emily as the focus of a biography. Mike Cadden rightly suggests that "children's and adolescent literature are genres defined by their audiences, so the voice of the narrator speaking to the implied reader through the narratee is an important consideration in defining them."[16] In the *Emily* books, the biographer's voice as narrator is a literary device that makes the trilogy enjoyable to both children and adults, as is true of so many of Montgomery's novels.

It is through the "Wind," however, that the narration of the *anime* is given substance and brought to life. Since the *anime* genre is comparable to the functioning of wind, as discussed above, the importance of wind in the Emily books emerged as a welcome vehicle for the transition from novel to *anime*. Like the depiction of spring, although more powerful and pervasive, the wind is a natural element of symbolic significance in this animation and is manifested in different ways throughout the episodes, both in conjunction with Emily's special gifts and in the mysterious character, the "Wind Woman," who guides, comforts, and supports her. The *anime* creators introduce Emily as the "Girl of the Wind," possessing what the narrator calls "the flash."[17] This special power or gift is "a sudden heightening of the senses in the presence of nature," as Waterston observes.[18] This heightened state of emotions and creativity results in a "glorious, supreme moment," in which Emily catches "a glimpse of the enchanting realm beyond" and feels that life is "a wonderful, mysterious thing of persistent beauty."[19] Waterston notes, "The flash is sometimes but not always connected with the urge to write. It can come with the recognition of a felicitous word. Many times, of course, Emily writes without experiencing the flash. Conversely, it may come when she is not writing, though there is still a connection with creation."[20] In the *anime*, however, the flash is always closely connected with the urge to write. This clear link strengthens the image of Emily as a writer for a younger audience.

As the title of the *anime* suggests, Emily is described as a person sensitive to the wind. Using both sound and imagery, the "*anime*-tors" were able to create various types of wind throughout the series to highlight the atmosphere: the soft wind blowing around Emily and her father in episode 1; the stormy wind in episode 11, when Perry is mending the farm wall; the cold, death wind on Mr Carpenter's last day in episode 23; and the spring wind blowing around Emily and her daughter in episode 26. The wind functions in many ways in Emily's story: it symbolizes inspiration and creativity; it creates feeling and mood; and it embodies a supportive maternal element in the life of "Emily, Girl of the Wind." In addition, because of the wind, the animated sea surface glitters, reflecting sunlight or moonshine. Natural life on Prince Edward Island is vividly brought into motion through the depiction of the wind.

The opening and closing theme songs created for the *anime* include the word "wind." In the opening song, entitled "*Kaze no Shoujo*" ["Girl of the Wind"], female vocalist Mitoko Horie first asks, "Have you ever seen the colour of the wind, its glimmer over the fields?" In the final song, entitled "*Kaze no Soramimi*" ["The Whisper of the Wind"], another female vocalist, Epo, sings, "Though each person has a glittering star, it sometimes seems lost, hidden by clouds," and then asks, "Is it the whispering wind or someone's voice?" This implies that the wind, as a part of Nature, can offer advice on how to live a meaningful life. Each week, at the beginning and end of the twenty-five-minute program, the audience of the *Emily anime* heard these two songs framing the story and was reminded anew of the significance of the wind.[21]

In the *anime*, ordinary wind sometimes materializes into the "Wind Woman," depicted as a transparent goddess crowned with flowers. When Emily is unable to write after repeated rejections from publishers, she cannot see the Wind Woman, but at the end, when she regains confidence in her writing, she is able to see her once again. Her first novel, self-bound by Emily and circulated among her family, friends, and villagers, is entitled *The Stories of Windy Hill* (created for the *anime*, and not found in Montgomery's novels). In the final episode, Lucy, the daughter of Emily and Teddy Kent (created for this *anime*), inherits her mother's vision, claiming that she too senses the Wind Woman. Although Montgomery's Wind Woman has no voice, in the *anime* she takes on the role of an omniscient narrator. This helps those in the audience with little imagination to follow Emily's artistic development: the Wind Woman appears whenever Emily feels the inspiration to create, linking the flash and creativity, since in the *anime*, Emily is never shown to be gifted with second sight, nor does she have "the Murray look" that intimidates her Aunt Elizabeth.[22]Emily's unusual power is focused solely in her imagination, which allows her to see elements unseen by ordinary people. Although the Wind Woman narrates Emily's story objectively, her words explain what Emily sees and hears, highlighting Emily's response to beauty and nature and her imaginative powers and creativity.

In the *Emily* trilogy, the Wind Woman also acts as a mother figure. In Montgomery's novel, Emily loses her mother when she is young, and she is raised by her father, who educates her at home. This motherless child is isolated, without human friends, yet, in chapter 1, Emily is described as the opposite of lonely: "Emily didn't know she was being pitied and didn't know what lonesomeness meant. She had plenty of company. There was Father – and Mike – and Saucy Sal. The Wind Woman was always around; and there were the trees – Adam-and-Eve, and the Rooster Pine, and all the friendly lady-birches."

The Wind Woman functions partially as a surrogate mother, and, along with Emily's father and other "friends" (nature, trees, and cats), she helps Emily to feel loved, happy, and complete. In the same chapter, there is also a scene of Emily talking to herself, Emily-in-the-glass, as if talking to a friend, explaining how she met the Wind Woman for the first time: "I'm going for a walk with the Wind Woman, dear ... I wish I could take you too. Do you *ever* get out of that room, I wonder. The Wind Woman is going to be out in the fields tonight. She is tall and misty, with thin, grey, silky clothes blowing all about her – and wings like a bat's – only you can see through them – and shining eyes like stars looking through her long, loose hair. She can fly – but to-night she will walk with me all over the fields. She's a *great* friend of mine – the Wind Woman is. I've known her ever since I was six. We're *old, old* friends – but not quite so old as you and I, little Emily-in-the-glass. We've been friends *always*, haven't we?" She had long since treated the reflection of herself as a child-friend, but at six years of age, she also needed a kind mother figure, and the Wind Woman fulfilled that role. The Wind Woman becomes both a surrogate mother and friend. When Emily first arrives at New Moon, she is forced to share a bed with her Aunt Elizabeth, whose stern and repressive manner intimidates little Emily. Unable to sleep, she imagines the Wind Woman's presence at the window and feels safely guarded by her old friend: "'Oh, you're out there, are you, dearest one?' she whispered, stretching out her arms. 'Oh, I'm so glad to hear you. You're such company, Wind Woman. I'm not lonesome any more.'" She joins her friend for an evening flight, "until she coast[s] the shore of dreams and f[alls] soundly asleep" to the sound of the wind singing softly, comforting her as a mother would with a lullaby.[23]

The Wind Woman also plays an influential role when Emily makes major life decisions throughout the trilogy. In *Emily Climbs*, seventeen-year-old Emily has a chance to go to New York, by invitation of the successful writer, Miss Royal, who has admired one of Emily's stories after reading it in a well-established New York magazine. If Emily were to accept the offer, joining the staff of this magazine, she would have the benefit of Miss Royal's advice on her writing. Emily, however, hesitates, wondering, "Would the Wind Woman come to her in the crowded city streets?" Consequently, she decides she would be better off staying "among [her] own people."[24] A symbol of nature, beauty, and creative inspiration, the Wind Woman also personifies the nurturing, maternal spirit that young Emily needs. The Wind Woman continues to play a role in Emily's life as she matures, although not so much as a muse as a supporter. The twenty-three-year-old Emily writes in her diary of a recent day in which she "slip[s] away" to spend time in the beauty of the wilds, and as she "lurk[s]" and "loiter[s]" in her dreamlike surroundings, she has "a tryst with [her] friend of old days, the Wind Woman."[25] For Emily, the Wind Woman's existence is as natural as her own, requiring no deeper explanation. In the *Emily anime*, however, the Wind Woman does not symbolize a surrogate mother but is more a sacred figure, like a goddess of nature and creativity.[26] By visualizing the Wind Woman's transparent appearance, which only Emily can see, the *anime* creators emphasize Emily's special ability, without the need for spoken words.

While Emily's vision of the Wind Woman was carefully crafted by the *anime* creators, Emily's other mysterious power, her psychic vision, was not included. Elizabeth Epperly identifies "a central psychic experience" in each of the *Emily* books: "In *Emily of New Moon*, Emily rescues Beatrice Burnley's reputation; in *Emily Climbs*, she saves a little boy; in *Emily's Quest*, she saves Teddy. Like the literary dimension of Emily's conscious (and unconscious) mind, the psychic experiences, too, belong to Emily the artist. They suggest that Emily is indeed attuned to another, deeper, richer dimension than most people can touch, and they give her legitimacy as an artist. The psychic experiences are to her intuition what the flash is to her visions of beauty: Emily touches the artistic realm within and beyond the world of appearances. Each of the psychic experiences calls out from the deepest places in Emily's spirit."[27] Although Montgomery implies that Emily's psychic experiences are linked to her hidden gifts as an artist, the *anime* creators did not develop these psychic powers. Instead, they concentrated on depicting the vivid world of Emily's imagination, showing how she attains inner growth from the common life she lives with her aunts and cousin at New Moon Farm.

As the *anime* was billed as "Another Story of Youth," Emily's friends, Ilse, Teddy, and Perry, are indispensable to the story, but their characters were simplified from Montgomery's books. In the *anime*, Ilse is not neglected by her father, Dr Burnley, but rather she assists him in his work. Ilse is described as an easy-going girl in contrast to Emily. Her wish to be an elocutionist is not mentioned, but is revealed when she recites some of Emily's poems and entertains those listening. Teddy's gift of drawing is described effectively in the *anime*, but the reason his mother is so unusually attached to him is never mentioned. Perry first appears as the hired boy at New Moon when Emily is brought there, and his illiteracy is emphasized. In the *anime*, he has never learned to read or write because of his impoverished background, but it is his love for Emily that motivates him to learn. The *anime* creators wanted to emphasize that it is Emily's influence that drives Perry's strong desire for learning and success. The creators wanted to stress the importance of education, partly because this television program was being broadcast by the education channel and being viewed by all ages.

In the *anime*, among the adult characters, Dean Priest is a handsome, bespectacled man, who saves Emily from falling off a cliff and encourages her to write her first novel. In the original Montgomery trilogy, he strikes most readers as a somewhat disturbing character: he becomes jealous of Emily's absorption in her writing and develops a secret romantic attraction for her, even at the age of twelve. His sinister nature is highlighted in a physical way, as his nickname "Jarback Priest" shows.[28] However, the *anime* creators cautiously avoided any innuendos about his potentially inappropriate feelings for Emily. Few young readers of the *Emily* series would be aware of Dean's unsavoury aspects in the way that adult readers are. He does not appear again until episode 26, when he attends Emily and Teddy's wedding in the garden of New Moon. His engagement with Emily and her breaking it off are not touched upon in the *anime*, nor are any of the other darker complications of love recounted in the original *Emily* novels. In the *anime*, there is no love triangle among Emily, Ilse, and Teddy. Likewise, Emily's agony over Teddy is portrayed simply as disappointment when she hears the rumour that he is engaged to a painter's daughter in Paris. The strategy of the *Emily anime* was to avoid the complications of extra romantic entanglements found in the original Montgomery novels. Instead, the *anime* audience members are witnesses to the development of love arising from friendship among the two couples of Emily and Teddy, and Ilse and Perry.

This does not, however, mean the *Emily anime* was made solely for children, as noted earlier in this chapter. Viewers of all ages will respond to Emily's loss of both her father and her mentor, Mr Carpenter. Especially memorable is the scene in which Mr Carpenter scolds Emily, who is in a slump because "the flash" has not been coming to her, sternly telling her that "the flash" does not come from somewhere, but is within her. His deathbed scene is heart-wrenching, as well as realistic. Although the agony of his heart attack is emphasized in the *anime*, he manages to say, "Emily, promise me – that you'll never write – to please anybody – but yourself," and "Live under your own hat," as in the original text. He foretells, "You'll get there [to your goal] – sometime – you have the root – of the matter – in you," and declares, "Think how much I'm going to know – in just a few more minutes, Emily. Wiser than anybody else living ... I'll know the truth, Emily." Finally, his last humorous words are "Beware – of – italics," which Emily has always overused.[29] Her mentor's final words are full of love and advice. The *anime* creators strove to include loss as a harsh feature of life, but they were true to the mixture of sadness and humour in Montgomery's text, and portray the lighthearted advice he gives Emily as her mentor until his last breath.

The many clashes between Emily and Aunt Elizabeth and the development of their mutual understanding form a coherent thread throughout the *anime*, as they do in the novels, making the story relevant to both young and older generations. This thread is developed in the *anime* through the association of Emily's mother, Juliet Murray, with a rainbow. In episode 8, titled "Mother's Room," Cousin Jimmy tells Emily the story of Juliet in her younger days. When Juliet was recovering from an illness, she saw a rainbow and wished she would one day be the mother of a girl. A few minutes after hearing Cousin Jimmy's story, Emily herself sees a rainbow after a rainfall and tells Aunt Elizabeth about it. Then her aunt remembers her younger sister Juliet, and begins to soften and let her guard down around Emily. The *anime* creators simplified the complicated story around Emily's mother, Juliet, and her family's disapproval of her marriage to Douglas Starr. Later, when Aunt Elizabeth breaks her leg, Emily reads one of her stories to her bedridden aunt, and those that amuse Aunt Elizabeth become a novel, *The Stories of Windy Hill*.[30] Aunt Elizabeth, who has always regarded novels as sinful, finally admits her enjoyment of them and recognizes Emily's gift as an artist. Their reconciliation is also visualized in the wedding scene in episode 26. Emily, in her wedding gown, embraces Aunt Elizabeth, thanking her aunt for taking her in and raising her at New Moon. As the motif of the rainbow connects Elizabeth, Juliet, and Emily, this *anime* proves itself to be not only a *Bildungsroman* but also the family story of two generations. (In the final episode, 26, it becomes a story of three generations, as Emily's daughter, Lucy, is introduced.) In Japanese culture, children are expected to take care of their aging parents, so the audience, both old and young, would deeply relate to this moment. As chapter 2 of *Emily's Quest* refers to Emily as "a chaser of rainbows,"[31] the rainbow motif is used as a symbol of beauty and art in the novel, but the *anime* creators use it to highlight family union.

The popularity of an *anime* often results in a surge in tourism by Japanese audiences to the place where the work is set, turning the background setting into a sacred place to visit.[32] One good example is the *anime* of *A Dog of Flanders* (1975): Japanese enthusiasts of the *anime* continue to flock to Flanders, as a literary pilgrimage.[33] However, the *Emily anime* did not lead to a tourism boom in Prince Edward Island. Rather, PEI is more recognized as the home and sacred place of Anne Shirley, influenced in no small part by the original *Anne anime* in Japan. The breathtaking PEI landscape is caught and presented more effectively in the *Emily anime* of 2007, but the story of how the outsider Anne changes the Islanders and comes to belong there herself has been more of a draw for the Japanese than the story of the born-and-bred Islander, Emily. Although Emily does change those around her, the focus is more subtle, being mostly on her own personal development.

The *Emily anime* is a would-be writer's *Künstlerroman*, transnationally adapted for a Japanese audience, and the *anime* creators succeed in conveying both the general appeal of its aspiring artist protagonist and the specificity of its time and setting to resonate with a modern-day, non-Canadian viewer. Being an art form between live action and fantasy, *anime* requires a certain amount of imagination to be supplied by the audience.[34] Anna Katorina Gutierrez writes that Japanese *anime* and *manga* tend to be "stripped of the original national and cultural markers," which opens up windows of possibility. "Anime and manga ... are narrative mediums that represent shifts in the perception of childhood, subjectivity and culture from monolithic and stereotypical to global and boundless."[35] The spectacular success of the *Anne anime* led a fresh team of Japanese *anime* creators to breathe new life into Montgomery's *Emily* trilogy.[36] The creative and editorial decisions made to alter, delete, and add to the Japanese *Emily anime* show how cultural markers can be removed or adapted to give an *anime* appeal to other cultures and other generations. Children's literature is brimming with treasures to be adapted by new media industries. If the audience is inspired to seek out and read the original books, they will double their pleasure, finding even more profound meanings and scope for imagination. For people living in this technological twenty-first century, the various ways of enjoying children's literature continue to expand.

APPENDIX

Filmography

Kaze no Shoujo Emily [*Emily, Girl of the Wind*] (2007)

Produced by NHK [Nippon Hoso Kyokai] and TMS Entertainment.

Running Time: 26 episodes x 25 minutes.

NHK airdates: 7 April 2007–29 September 2007.

The Official Website: www.nhk.or.jp/anime/emily/

Cast [Voice Actors]: Tomoko Kawakami (Emily Byrd Starr), Sachiko Kojima (Ilse Burnley), Kouji Miyata (Teddy Kent), Akemi Okamura (Perry Miller), Toshiko Fujita (Elizabeth Murray), Masako Ikeda (Laura Murray), and Rokurou Naya (Jimmy Murray).

Credits: NHK and TMS Entertainment. Based upon the novels, *Emily of New Moon*, *Emily Climbs*, and *Emily's Quest*, written by L.M. Montgomery.

Director: Harume Kosaka. Sound Director: Satoru Koyama. Episode Director: Hiro Kaburagi. Episode Director, Storyboard: Atsushi Nigorikawa. Storyboard: Seiji Okuda. Storyboard, Character Design, Chief Animation Director, Animation Director: Keizou Shimizu. Opening Theme Song Performance, Lyrics, Composition: Epo. Closing Theme Song Performance: Mitsuko Horie. Closing Theme Song Composition, Music: Akira Miyagawa. Key Animation: Jiro Kanai and Kanako Maru. Screenplay, Series Composition: Michiru Shimada. Producer: Hideaki Miyamoto. Literary Consultant: Yoshiko Akamatsu.

DVD: *Kaze no Shoujo Emiri* [*Emily, Girl of the Wind*]. Tokyo: Vap 2007. 7 discs.

Episode List (including scriptwriters and air dates), based on http://emilyofnewmoon.wikia.com/wiki/Kaze_no_Shoujo_Emily/Episodes:

1. "The Girl of the Wind" (Mitsuru Shimada) (7 April 2007)
2. "Pride of the Murrays" (Mitsuru Shimada) (14 April 2007)
3. "Eccentric Ilse" (Mitsuru Shimada) (21 April 2007)
4. "A Sketch of Four" (Makoto Nakamura) (28 April 2007)
5. "First Time on Stage" (Miho Maruo) (5 May 2007)
6. "The Poisoned Apple Incident" (Ritsuko Hayasaka) (12 May 2007)
7. "My Favourite Woods" (Ritsuko Hayasaka) (19 May 2007)

8. "Mother's Room" (Mitsuru Shimada) (26 May 2007)
9. "The Missing Diamond" (Miho Maruo) (2 June 2007)
10. "The Dreamweavers" (Makoto Nakamura) (9 June 2007)
11. "A Contest of Honour" (Mitsuru Shimada) (16 June 2007)
12. "The Only Song in the World" (Ritsuko Hayasaka) (23 June 2007)
13. "Christmas at the Murrays" (Makoto Nakamura) (30 June 2007)
14. "A Picnic by the Sea" (Miho Maruo) (7 July 2007)
15. "The Haunted House" (Ritsuko Hayasaka) (14 July 2007)
16. "Summer Memories" (Miho Maruo) (21 July 2007)
17. "Ilse's Secret" (Mitsuru Shimada) (28 July 2007)
18. "Rhoda's Trap" (Makoto Nakamura) (4 August 2007)
19. "Emily's Failure" (Makoto Nakamura) (11 August 2007)
20. "Growing Up" (Harume Kosaka) (18 August 2007)
21. "Our Dreams" (Ritsuko Hayasaka) (25 August 2007)
22. "Confession under the Snow" (Miho Maruo) (1 September 2007)
23. "Departing Heart" (Harume Kosaka) (8 September 2007)
24. "Those Who Are Left Behind" (Makoto Nakamura) (15 September 2007)
25. "The Snow Is Now Melting" (Mitsuru Shimada) (22 September 2007)
26. "The Advent of Spring" (Harume Kosaka) (29 September 2007)

ACKNOWLEDGMENTS

This paper is based on the essay entitled "Examining the Japanese Animation, *Emily, Girl of the Wind*: *Emily of New Moon*," presented at the international conference, "Lucy Maud Montgomery at Home in Leaskdale: A Centennial Celebration," on 14 October 2011. I thank Dr Lesley Clement, who gave me the chance to develop this theme more deeply and write a paper for this collection. I would also like to thank the three other editors, Dr Holly Pike, Dr Rita Bode, and Dr Margaret Steffler, who gave me useful suggestions, and my two dear friends, Dr Mary H. Rubio and Prof. Lyn Swierski, who always encouraged me during the revision of the paper.

NOTES

1 The periodical *Nippon Jido Bungaku* [*Children's Literature in Japan*] focused on "*Anime* vs Children's Literature" in its September–October 2016 (volume 62, number 5) issue. In it, scholar Akiko Kawabata talks of her students' praise for Disney's adaptations of fairy tales and how she encouraged them to read

the original stories, which then led them to see how American ideology has influenced the alterations made in the Disney adaptations ("Dizuni-anime kara manabu Jidobungaku kenkyuhou" ["How to Study Children's Literature with a View of Disney Animations"], 52–5).

2 Suyama explains how, in 1971, three prominent animators, Isao Takahata, Hayao Miyazaki, and Yoichi Kotabe, hoped to animate Astrid Lindgren's *Pippi Longstocking* for television and visited Sweden to scout locations. Although the animators failed to get Lindgren's permission, Suyama was impressed with their deep respect for the original text and their passionate wish to animate significant literary works. She mentioned the three animators' memorial book, published in 2014, showing their plans to visualize the work as an *anime*. See Suyama, "*Maboroshi no Nagakutsushita no Pippi* kara kangaetakoto" ["What I Learned from *The Pippi Longstocking Anime That Never Came to Be*"], 60–1, and Isao Takahata, Hayao Miyazaki, and Yoichi Kotabe, *Maboroshi no Nagakutsushita no Pippi* [*The Pippi Longstocking Anime That Never Came to Be*] (Tokyo: Iwanami-shoten 2014). Interestingly, after Lindgren's death, her grandchildren asked Miyazaki, who was by then world-famous, to animate *Pippi*, but he was no longer interested in the project. Instead, encouraged by Lindgren's grandchildren, he published a book detailing the background of their plans to animate *Pippi* (Takahata, Miyazaki, and Kotabe, *Maboroshi no Nagakutsushita*, 148–9).

3 Benjamin Lefebvre comments on the *Anne anime* (1997): "Though very little information about this series is available in English, it is still broadcast in Japan on a regular basis." Lefebvre, "L.M. Montgomery," 53.

4 Translations of the *Emily* books into Japanese include those by Hanako Muraoka (1959, 1964, 1967, 1969), Nobuo Kandori (2002), and Naoko Ikematsu (2006).

5 Gutierrez, "Globalization and Glocalization," 13–14. I refer to this article more fully later.

6 Lamarre, *Anime Machine*, 84–5.

7 Napier, *Anime from* Akira *to* Howl's Moving Castle, 292.

8 See Saito, Miyamoto, and Kosaka, three-person talk on website *Emiri no Sekai* [*The World of Emily*].

9 I was told that, if the program had been more popular, the creators might have gone back and added more episodes to fill the gaps in the stories, but that was never realized.

10 One of the changes in the *Anne anime* is the inclusion of the episode of the poisoned apples, which was taken from *Emily of New Moon*. This story is retold as Anne's experience in episode 33 of the *Anne anime*, "An Invitation to Queen's Class." See "*Anne of Green Gables* (1979 TV Series)." https://en.wikipedia.org/wiki/Anne_of_Green_Gables_(1979_TV_series). For other additions, see Akamatsu, "The Continuous Popularity of Red-haired Anne in Japan," 221.

11 The name Lucy is evidently taken from the author's first name. Keen fans may make the connection.

12 LMM, *ENM*, 20.

13 In the original text, Douglas Starr says: "You mustn't be afraid of *anything*, Emily. Death isn't terrible. The universe is full of love – and spring comes everywhere – and in death you open and shut a door" (ibid., 20; emphasis in original). However, in the *anime*, he does not use the word "death," probably because of the compressed form of the *anime* rather than an avoidance of the topic of death.

14 LMM, *EC*, 17.

15 Waterston, *Magic Island*, 130.

16 Cadden, "Voice," 228.

17 LMM, *ENM*, 1.

18 Waterston, *Magic Island*, 119.

19 LMM, *ENM*, 8–9.

20 Waterston, *Magic Island*, 119–20.

21 Lesley Clement noted, when she first read this article, "The opening song directly addresses the audience with a question ('have you ever seen the colour of the wind?'). The closing song generalizes to 'each person' and again addresses the audience with a question. Whereas in Montgomery's text, the wind and the flash pertain to Emily's own particular experiences as an aspiring writer, leaving each individual reader to bridge the gap between Emily's world and her own through imaginative engagement, the *anime* version is less subtle, more direct … it provides a bridge by generalizing beyond Emily's situation and by asking questions."

22 LMM, *ENM*, 130.

23 Ibid., 1, 6 (emphasis in original), 68, 73.

24 LMM, *EC*, 362.

25 LMM, *EQ*, 184.

26 In Lesley Clement's "The Empathic Poetic Sensibility," she looks at the figure of the Wind Woman closely, arguing that, by *Emily's Quest*, the Wind Woman "has become less humanized, less anthropomorphic, more abstract, more metaphoric … but Emily still has reunions with her old friend when her soul needs renewal" (193).

27 Epperly, *Fragrance of Sweet-Grass*, 166–7.

28 LMM, *ENM*, 285. Because by twenty-first-century mores, Dean's physical difference should not be emphasized, the *Emily anime* creators rightly chose not to depict it. In twenty-first-century culture, he also might appear to be a sexual predator, given the difference in their ages. For fuller discussion of Dean Priest, see Rita Bode's chapter in this volume, "Vulnerable Situations," 76–9.

29 LMM, *EQ*, 28–30.

30 Although the stories that amuse Aunt Elizabeth become a book entitled *The Moral of the Rose* in *Emily's Quest*, they are combined as a novel, *The Stories of Windy Hill*, in the *anime*.

31 LMM, *EQ*, 6.

32 Tsugata, *Nippon no Anime wa Naniga Sugoi no ka* [*What Is Cool in Japanese Animation?*], 248.

33 van Dienderen and Volckaert, *Dare ga Nero to Patorassyu o Korosunoka* [*Who Kills Nero and Patrasche?*], 140–3, 148–73.

34 Tsugata, *Animeshon-gaku Nyumon* [*An Introduction to Animation Study*], 40.

35 Gutierrez, "Globalization and Glocalization," 13–14. *Manga* are the Japanese equivalent of comic books or graphic novels.

36 *Emily, Girl of the Wind* (2007) was broadcast as a part of "The *Anime* World Hour" for children, but since it was given an unfavourable time slot, at 7:25 to 7:50 on Saturday mornings, unlike the top time slot given to the *Anne anime* (19:30 to 20:00 on Sunday evening), it had a much smaller audience. Although it was rebroadcast in 2010, it has never been as popular as the *Anne* series. In 2019, anyone interested in the *Emily* series can watch it only on DVD. According to Hideaki Miyamoto, the TMS Entertainment producer of the *Emily* broadcast, the company sold the rights to broadcast *Emily* to twenty-nine countries (nineteen Arabic-speaking countries, seven Italian-speaking countries, Taiwan, Turkey, and Azerbaijan), but not one English-speaking country. The reason for this lapse remains a mystery. Vestiges of their sales promotions and the TMS Entertainment trailer, as well as short clips with Italian subtitles, can still be found on YouTube. On the website *Soyokaze no Oka* [*Breeze Hill*]

(http://breezehill.web.fc2.com/Emily/index.html), enthusiastic fans of the *Emily anime* have posted their passionate requests for the program to be rebroadcast, praising its excellence as a literary adaptation. According to NHK producer Kenji Saito, *anime* programs more than six years old are rarely rebroadcast without powerful public demand. Because the Japanese audience supporting the *Emily anime* was not large enough to warrant its being rebroadcast a third time within six years, it was not revised (Saito, email to Akamatsu, 25 October 2017).

11

Continuing Stories: L.M. Montgomery and Fanfiction in the Digital Era

BALAKA BASU

Fanfiction – the recreational (re)writing of texts – is a literary genre of rapidly growing significance. Abigail Derecho in her brief history of fanfiction identifies it as "a genre that has a long history of appealing to women and minorities, individuals on the cultural margins who used archontic writing as a means to express not only their narrative creativity, but their criticisms of social and political inequities as well."[1] Insightfully defined by Francesca Coppa and Mary Ellen Curtin as "speculative fiction about character,"[2] fanfiction can be even more precisely understood as fantasies about the diegetic positioning of characters in the context of various settings, communities, relationships both textual and paratextual, and eventually all manner of cultural mythologies. Kristina Busse and Karen Hellekson describe the production of fanfiction as "part collaboration and part response to not only the source text, but also the cultural context within and outside the fannish community in which it is produced."[3] They point out that the shift in the method of dissemination of fanfiction from newsletters and zines to internet archives means that "ever-younger fans who previously would not have had access to the fannish culture except through their parents can now enter the fan space effortlessly; financial resources have become less of a concern because access to a computer is the only prerequisite; and national boundaries and time zones have ceased to limit fannish interaction."[4] The nature of fanfiction allows participants to cross generational and socio-economic boundaries in an ongoing exchange of responses to a source text with which they share a fascination, developing new texts that in turn elicit their own responses.

While the creation of fanfiction is evidence of an affective, loving, communal relationship with the source text, this genre of writing is still dismissed in many quarters as overly emotional, purely erotic, and even perverse, a type of amateur and immature engagement with popular texts that produces writing necessarily divorced from literary significance. Produced in staggeringly vast quantities by subcultures with complex vocabularies and traditions that can intimidate the casual reader, fanfiction is perceived by many to be more of a cultural practice than a literary genre, variously denigrated for its pornographic potential and its lack of originality.[5] However, close examination reveals that fan writers are able to create critical dialogue with the originating author in acts of communal storytelling that incorporate allusions and reference points to which other dedicated fan readers and writers may respond. In this chapter, after examining how L.M. Montgomery and her writer heroine Emily themselves engage in practices now associated with fanfiction, I survey four forms of fanfiction that remove Montgomery's novels from her seemingly idyllic and timeless island settings, contextualizing her characters and plots within history and other genres: the sequel set during the Second World War, the modern AU (alternate universe), the gap-filler, and the slash fic, all of which allow the young readers who grow up with her novels to engage in dialogue with the stories they love, a type of literary conversation that Montgomery herself models within her texts.

Emily's reading, which is active rather than passive, resembles twenty-first-century fans' ownership of the texts they love, provoking creative responses. For instance, after reading works by Lord Tennyson, Elizabeth Barrett Browning, and Matthew Arnold, Emily writes, "Teddy lent me 3 books of poetry. One of them was Tennyson and I have learned The Bugle Song off by heart so I will always have it. One was Mrs. Browning. She is lovely. I would like to meet her. I suppose I will when I die but that may be a long time away. The other was just one poem called Sohrab and Rustum. After I went to bed I cried over it. Aunt Elizabeth said 'what are you sniffling about?' I wasn't sniffling – I was weeping sore … I couldn't go to sleep until I had thought out a different end for it – a happy one."[6] The reactions Emily catalogues are those of the fan; they are viscerally felt in the body and attempt to dissolve the boundary between author and reader, producer and consumer. She inscribes Tennyson within her heart in order to possess the poem she loves; she creates a relationship between Barrett Browning and herself; and, most significantly, she interjects her own desired happy ending into Arnold's tragic narrative, a corrective desire that is at the core of many works of fanfiction.

Emily's diaries and her story reflect Montgomery's own experiences from childhood to adulthood as reader, writer, and reader-turned-writer discussed in the introduction to this volume. Depicting Emily as a voracious reader and a life-writer like herself, Montgomery places the child Emily's voice in conversation with that of the narrator through Emily's letters to her dead father in *Emily of New Moon* and through her diary entries in *Emily Climbs* and *Emily's Quest*, creating a form of joint authorship that is referenced explicitly in "Salad Days," the second chapter of *Emily Climbs*: "This book is not going to be wholly, or even mainly, made up of extracts from Emily's diary; but, by way of linking up matters unimportant enough for a chapter in themselves, and yet necessary for a proper understanding of her personality and environment, I am going to include some more of them. Besides, when one has material ready to hand, why not use it?"[7] The narrator's willingness to use the "material" that is "ready to hand" reflects Montgomery's and Emily's practices, and also validates other writers' use of the material Montgomery places at their disposal. As with many fans, Emily's reading frequently makes itself felt within her writing.[8] Like Montgomery, Emily learns her trade through mimicry, from her first poem in blank verse inspired by James Thomson's *Seasons*[9] to her unwitting imitation of Kipling that is pointed out by her teacher, Mr Carpenter, in his review of her work.[10] Like Sara Stanley of *The Story Girl*, whose compelling and fascinating stories are rarely if ever original, Emily is a fan of the oral traditions of her community, incorporating and building upon them in her own writing, transforming and recreating, for instance, the story of "The Woman Who Spanked the King" in *Emily Climbs*.[11] The retelling and versioning that Emily practises signal her immense admiration for the source texts she adapts, just as the creation of fanfiction does for Montgomery's readership and fans.

The possibilities inherent in versioning and adaptation are illustrated in *Emily's Quest*. When Montgomery depicts Emily undertaking the reworking of someone else's narrative, she is adapting an episode from her own experience while working for *The Echo* in Halifax, which she records in her journal. Montgomery, like Emily, was asked to create an ending for a serialized story,

"A Royal Betrothal," after compositors had misplaced the original text. Like Emily, she claims that her "knowledge of royal love affairs [was] limited," and that she was unaccustomed "to write with flippant levity of kings and queens." Nevertheless, Montgomery manages to create a conclusion that passes muster, since "as yet nobody has guessed where the 'seam' comes in."[12] She is, however, curious about the original author's reaction to her unauthorized adaptation, and while she never discovers this in real life, she does imagine it in her fiction when she introduces Mark Greaves, who is horrified by Emily's new ending for the story but enchanted by its author. Neither Montgomery nor Emily engages in this sort of writing from a place of fandom; they have no previous attachment to "A Royal Betrothal," and both are writing professionally. Nevertheless, the ability to solve the puzzle of the story and the weaving of their work into an already extant text are the very project of fanfiction: ludic narrative composition that recalls the way children play make-believe with the narratives they love, reworking and extending them. It is telling that Montgomery uses the metaphor of the "seam" to describe this particular craft. Jane Dawkins, writing about her fanfiction, which is inspired by Jane Austen, describes her fan novel *Letters from Pemberley* as "an old-fashioned patchwork quilt, where in place of the scraps of fabric reminding one of the favorite frocks or shirts whence they came, there is a line or a phrase or a sentence from one of [the original] books or letters stitched alongside the lesser scraps of my own manufacture."[13]

Montgomery's final book, framed by the two world wars, is just such a patchwork sequel, albeit providing only brief glimpses of the characters that readers met as children and who have now grown older. When a version of the book was published in 1974 as *The Road to Yesterday*, these glimpses, lacking the interstitial materials, became even briefer, mirroring the more forced insertion of beloved characters that the two earlier collections, *Chronicles of Avonlea* and *Further Chronicles of Avonlea*, display. Only two of Anne's grandchildren – Gilbert Ford and Walter Blythe – are obliquely referred to, in the story "A Commonplace Woman," where an unpleasant young doctor reflects on both of them as potential rivals for the affection of a beautiful girl he himself hopes to pursue.[14] However, the full novel, *The Blythes Are Quoted*, published in 2009 and comprised of short stories about the people in Glen St Mary and over the harbour, is interspersed with poetry by both a young Walter and an adult Anne. The poems are cut with tiny slices of dialogue that suggest the continuing lives of fans' favourite characters and how they might have developed. In "'Dragged at Anne's Chariot Wheels': L.M. Montgomery and the Sequels to *Anne of Green Gables*," Carole Gerson notes the mixture of feelings from pleasure to frustration that Montgomery records in her journals as she prepares to write her first sequel.[15] While Montgomery wrote the first installments of her various series out of inspiration, she was certainly aware of what her market desired from subsequent instalments. She often regretted the necessity of marrying off her characters,[17] but was aware that her fans demanded this conventional outcome for the characters they had come to love; these traditionally romantic endings, when not offered by Montgomery herself at the instigation of her publishers, are regularly deployed by contemporary fanfiction authors building on the source texts.

Indeed, long before the original structure of *The Blythes Are Quoted* was revealed to readers in Benjamin Lefebvre's afterword,[17] fanfiction writers were spinning off lengthy narratives that included a third generation of young Blythes, Fords, and Merediths dealing with the onslaught of the Second World War. While earlier instalments in the *Anne* series – such as *Anne of Green Gables* and *Anne's House of Dreams* – depict the deaths of Matthew, Anne and Gilbert's first daughter (Joyce), and Captain Jim, Walter's death in *Rilla of Ingleside* is somehow more striking. Unlike Matthew and Captain Jim, he has not yet had time to grow old; unlike Joyce, readers have had opportunities to get to know him as a child in *Rainbow Valley* and as he grows into young adulthood in *Rilla of Ingleside.* His death is *unnatural* and, therefore, all the more horrifying. These two aspects of *Rilla of Ingleside* – the evocation of history by a nostalgic fictional world that is still tied to real time and the use of high drama, tragedy, and romance – provide fanfiction authors with a model they can use to appeal to the emotions of those readers who are immersed in the next generation of Montgomery characters.[18]

The Second World War, then, provides an entry point into the series for fanfiction authors, who can deploy real history coupled with beloved characters to create a tale that feels absolutely authentic. One example of this is a short story, "The Pen and the Sword," written in 2007 by MarnaNightingale. Here, mimicking the style of Dorothy L. Sayers's *The Wimsey Papers* (a series of *Spectator* articles published between 1939 and 1940, which interestingly also continue the story of First World War–era characters during the Second World War), MarnaNightingale employs epistolary excerpts and newspaper articles to tell the story of a family going through the horrors of war for a second time. Grounding her fragmented story – like *The Blythes Are Quoted*, a mixture of genres – in the accounts of novelist Mollie Panter-Downes (1939) and war correspondents Ernie Pyle (1940) and Ross Munro of the *Canadian Press* (1941), whose articles are attributed to Kenneth Ford, she offers a story that, like *Rilla of Ingleside*, is anchored to the historical moment, while also nostalgically focusing on the character development that comes from Gilbert Ford's death, Rilla's and Faith's reactions to the war, and the lives of their children. Here war also serves as an opportunity for new experiences, particularly for women and children: Rilla takes a factory job as a machinist, liking it better than working in Carter Flagg's store; one of Anne's grandchildren, Susan, plans to be a doctor; and Faith, who worked as a Voluntary Aid Detachment nurse in the First World War, mentions how she can sympathize. As well, the daily tidbits that flavour the pages of *Rilla of Ingleside* are there: one article, attributed to Anne, includes the recipe for Susan Baker's war bread, reminding readers of the problems of wartime rationing, even in the Americas. Real life events – like the Canadian forces trying (and failing) to make a beachhead at Dieppe – arouse the passions of the reader.[19] Unlike Austen – who also famously wrote of three or four families in a country town, but kept the Napoleonic wars firmly in the shadows – Montgomery brings the passions and high drama of the world stage into the sleepy villages of Prince Edward Island, which inspire fanfiction spinoffs.

The long novel *Cecilia of Red Apple Farm*, by a fan author who posts under the pseudonym ruby gillis, also directly reworks passages and scenes from the whole range of *Anne* books, set in the late-nineteenth century, to *The Blythes Are Quoted*, set in the early years of the Second World War, to highlight the similarity between her new generation of characters and their ancestors. Cecilia is the daughter of Una Meredith and Shirley Blythe (characters often married off in fanfiction on the strength of one moonlight walk to a dance in the early pages of *Rilla*). Like MarnaNightingale, ruby gillis provides period flavouring in the styles of dresses and behaviour and in references to 1940s popular films and songs. Simultaneously, this setting offers new opportunities to her female character: Cecilia wants to be a doctor, and rather than staying in Canada, she joins up to be a nurse in England. She has a series of romances – one with Sid Gardiner (before he marries May Binnie), and one with her cousin Blythe Meredith, who is this generation's poet – before finally ending up with Marshall Douglas (the son of Mary Vance). Just as Anne initially refuses Gilbert Blythe in favour of Roy Gardner's resemblance to her ideal man in *Anne of the Island,* ruby gillis's Cecilia is fooled by the allure of Sid and Blythe as Roy Gardner–like romantic heroes into believing that she does not truly love her fun, practical, "Gilbert-esque" friend. Published in 2004, *Cecilia of Red Apple Farm* further illustrates the opportunities presented by reusing and reworking a body of texts through its incorporation of Montgomery's poem "I Wish You" as the work of Blythe Meredith. Montgomery includes this poem and attributes it to Anne in *The Blythes Are Quoted*, although ruby gillis could not have known this when writing.[20]

The repetition of names and circumstances might seem derivative, but for readers who have read and reread the original books so many times, the extension of the story world is prized, even if – perhaps even because of – its callbacks to the original text. Due to the tendency of fans to fixate on "the good bits" in a reread, these parts can be taken for the whole. Austen fanfiction demonstrates this aptly. Indeed, Helen Fielding's second *Bridget Jones* novel, *Bridget Jones and the Edge of Reason* (1999), illustrates just such a reading of *Pride and Prejudice*: she shows Bridget, a fan, watching the scene from the 1995 mini-series in which Darcy, dripping in a wet see-through shirt, exits the lake, and then rewinding and rewatching the scene multiple times. How many times might a similar fan reread Walter's letter from Courcelette? This repeated reviewing of selected portions can replace the amplitude of the original novel. With this delimited focus, narrative is no longer seen as a progression, but as a single moment of pleasure, sustained as long as possible. Reading the Second World War as a repetitive sequel to the First World War further highlights this possibility. Even Montgomery seems to do so, as demonstrated in *The Blythes Are Quoted*, with its new generation of characters confusingly named after the old: Walter, Jem, Rilla, Di, Anne, and Gilbert. A variation on Marah Gubar's kinship model,[21] this kind of continuation highlights the blurred boundaries between child and adult characters who are literally related to one another and whose adventures mimic one another.

In a third example of fanfiction set during the Second World War, *Weeping May Tarry*, a long novel by ElouiseBates, Meggie, the heroine, is Shirley's daughter (and also, surprisingly, Paul Irving's granddaughter). In this story, which like *Cecilia of Red Apple Farm* is an instalment of a longer series, Meggie is sent off to a conservatory of music to study singing, aptly combining the traditions of the nostalgic boarding-school novel with "Girl's Own" wartime fiction. Following the tradition of *Magic for Marigold*, which explicitly suggests in its second chapter that the Murrays of Blair Water and the Lesleys of Cloud of Spruce exist in the same universe,[22] ElouiseBates (like many other fanfiction authors, including ruby gillis) suggests that *all* of Montgomery's characters exist in a single universe: Meggie partners briefly with the grandson of Sara Stanley (*The Story Girl* and *The Golden Road*) and is close friends with Jane Stuart (*Jane of Lantern Hill*). Going even further, ElouiseBates introduces the grandchildren of the *What Katy Did* series as friends for Meggie and includes Betsy from Dorothy Canfield Fisher's *Understood Betsy* as Bruce Meredith's wife, creating a world where all the characters of early-twentieth-century girls' fiction seem to have truly lived, where their descendants must cope with victory gardens and dances with soldiers at the Exhibition Grounds, and where kisses are much more commonplace than they once were.[23]

These particular continuers of Montgomery are also desirous of membership in the community of her fans, seeing their literary endeavours as productive of approval from a fellow readership.[24] Likewise, the novels are notable for their sociality – they seem to offer the reader not only a fantasy friendship with the characters themselves but also the very real society of fellow readers of the works. Thus, these fan authors attempt to diversify their stories so that they represent contemporary beliefs regarding multiculturalism; ruby gillis, for instance, introduces into the family by way of marriage a French girl who has had to flee the Nazis due to being Jewish,[25] a situation Montgomery and her contemporaries might have had some difficulty accepting, considering early-twentieth-century attitudes toward interreligious marriage and Montgomery's othering of the German-Jewish peddler who sells Anne green hair dye.

The Second World War thus offers writers of Montgomery fanfiction the loom on which to weave new, more diverse stories, even as *The Blythes Are Quoted*, which also traces the characters' reactions to this new war, demonstrates how these readers-turned-writers followed Montgomery's own trajectory, not knowing that they were doing so. On the subject of fanfiction, young-adult author Patricia C. Wrede writes: "The thing that fascinates me about fanfiction, though, is the way that it models the decision tree that writers go through (whether consciously or unconsciously) to get to their final product. For those of us who do this part mostly unconsciously, it can be interesting and instructing to see the multitude of alternate paths that a story *could* have taken, all laid out more-or-less neatly in different authors' fanfics [... taking a slightly different fork in the road] resulting in the plot veering in a completely new direction. Friends become enemies; enemies become friends; goals and objectives and results shift and change."[26] Within these pieces of fanfiction, then, fan writers are able to follow these decision trees with subsequent generations of characters as well.

Another avenue of access occurs when fan authors transpose historical narratives into the contemporary moment. Perhaps the best-known example of this modern alternate universe [AU] conversion is the television program *Sherlock*, which takes Arthur Conan Doyle's Victorian detective into the twenty-first century. While new cultural contexts appear, the essence of character is meant to be retained. Just as *Sherlock* uses text messages and blogs to substitute for telegraphs and handwritten journals, fans of Montgomery reimagine the relationships between her characters as if they were taking place online. For instance, "Work in Progress" (2012) by verity postulates a friendship between Montgomery's most famous heroines, Anne and Emily. In this piece of fanfiction, Emily circumvents Aunt Elizabeth's injunction against fiction during her time at Shrewsbury High by becoming a blogger who is restricted to the "truth." The story's online summary, a part of which reads "Anne rolls her eyes. 'Is your aunt really going to know if you cheat on your nonfiction with some hot prose on the side?'"[27] shows how the story preserves the character qualities that Montgomery laid out, complete with references to the Murray pride and Anne's orphanhood (figure 11.1). Mr Carpenter's admonitions are spelled out at the beginning of the story:

> "Emily Byrd Starr has a sticky note on her desktop. It reads:
> ITALICS
> CAPITALS
> !!!!!
> "just"
> "really"
> CTRL+F!
> It is almost like having Mr Carpenter in the room with her."[28]

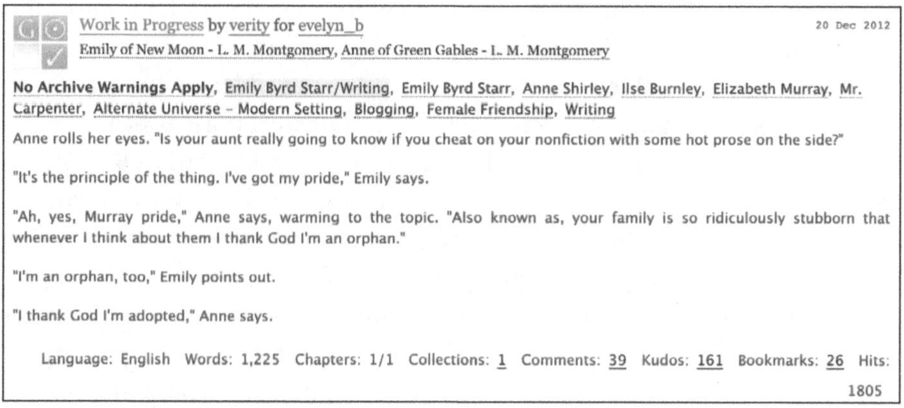

Work in Progress by verity for evelyn_b 20 Dec 2012
Emily of New Moon - L. M. Montgomery, Anne of Green Gables - L. M. Montgomery

No Archive Warnings Apply, Emily Byrd Starr/Writing, Emily Byrd Starr, Anne Shirley, Ilse Burnley, Elizabeth Murray, Mr. Carpenter, Alternate Universe - Modern Setting, Blogging, Female Friendship, Writing

Anne rolls her eyes. "Is your aunt really going to know if you cheat on your nonfiction with some hot prose on the side?"

"It's the principle of the thing. I've got my pride," Emily says.

"Ah, yes, Murray pride," Anne says, warming to the topic. "Also known as, your family is so ridiculously stubborn that whenever I think about them I thank God I'm an orphan."

"I'm an orphan, too," Emily points out.

"I thank God I'm adopted," Anne says.

Language: English Words: 1,225 Chapters: 1/1 Collections: 1 Comments: 39 Kudos: 161 Bookmarks: 26 Hits: 1805

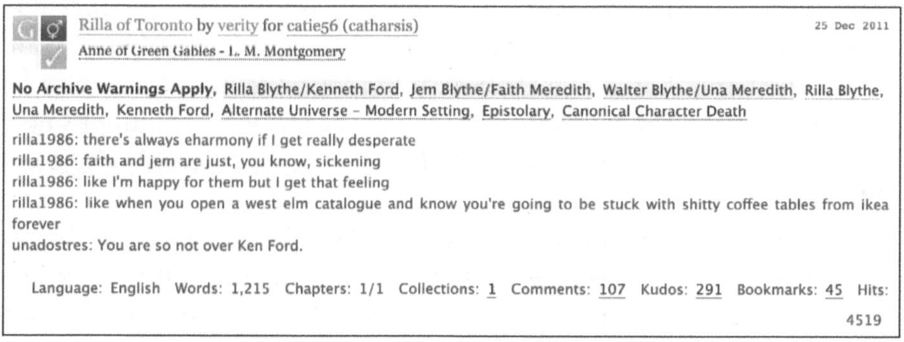

Rilla of Toronto by verity for catie56 (catharsis) 25 Dec 2011
Anne of Green Gables - L. M. Montgomery

No Archive Warnings Apply, Rilla Blythe/Kenneth Ford, Jem Blythe/Faith Meredith, Walter Blythe/Una Meredith, Rilla Blythe, Una Meredith, Kenneth Ford, Alternate Universe - Modern Setting, Epistolary, Canonical Character Death

rilla1986: there's always eharmony if I get really desperate
rilla1986: faith and jem are just, you know, sickening
rilla1986: like I'm happy for them but I get that feeling
rilla1986: like when you open a west elm catalogue and know you're going to be stuck with shitty coffee tables from ikea forever
unadostres: You are so not over Ken Ford.

Language: English Words: 1,215 Chapters: 1/1 Collections: 1 Comments: 107 Kudos: 291 Bookmarks: 45 Hits: 4519

11.1 *Top* Summary of "Work in Progress" by verity, hosted on AO3

11.2 *Bottom* Summary of "Rilla of Toronto" by verity, hosted on AO3

Verity creates humour through the juxtaposition of contemporary social media and allusions to Montgomery's source text. Another story by verity detailing Rilla's romance with Ken Ford and her friendship with Una Meredith, "Rilla of Toronto," takes place mainly through instant messages. In this story, Rilla reflects on her life from eighteen to twenty-five, tracing a continuum from her child self to her new adulthood, underscored by verity's translation of Montgomery's work into contemporary millennial language[29] (figure 11.2).

A third type of fanfiction narrative, the gap-filler, focuses on and expands the implications of the source texts. Moira Walley-Beckett's Netflix/CBC series *Anne with an "E,"* as Laura Robinson shows in chapter 12 of this volume, is somewhat fanfictional in and of itself: as Robinson points out, the show fills gaps by bringing to the fore the darker currents that have always been beneath the seemingly untroubled waters of *Anne of Green Gables*, including Anne's potential post-traumatic stress disorder from the disturbing life she led before coming to Green Gables. This kind of versioning and adaptation tacitly permits fan authors to feel that their versions are just as valid as those produced by professionals. Gap-fillers frequently expand on romantic pairings and in fandom are often referred to by portmanteaux of characters' names that perpetuate some inside joke or work as puns. "Shirbert" – the preferred moniker for Anne and Gilbert – is the latter, and demonstrates how fans posting on sites like Archive of Our Own (AO3), Fanfiction.net, and Wattpad (this last generally populated by younger fans) develop their own language to identify their stories within the community for which they write. One such story, "You caught me staring, but I caught you staring back," by Anuka, clearly inspired more by the television series than the novels, begins with an author's note that reads, "I decided to write some fluff for these two, because I need more Shirbert moments, and season 2 is so far away. I added gifs to make it more vivid."[30] Here, the romance between Anne and Gilbert as depicted by Montgomery and Walley-Beckett is not sufficient for the reader-turned-writer. Anuka wants the gaps in the narrative to be more fully explored than they are on either page or screen and to be made more "vivid" by the inclusion of images that help make the story come alive.

Similarly, "Rilla Blythe's Wedding: A Not Entirely Comprehensive Account" by Scylla also fills a gap: Rilla and Ken's wedding day, a scene that Montgomery leaves to the reader's imagination at the end of *Rilla of Ingleside*. Modelled upon other accounts of weddings within Montgomery's fiction, the story also suggests that accounts of Walter's death have been gravely exaggerated, as he makes a stunning appearance at his sister's wedding. In order to align her work with Montgomery's novel, Scylla ensures that Little Dog Monday's awareness of Walter's death remains, but makes it only a technicality, writing, "His heart had stopped for a full ten seconds – long enough for his Captain to feel for his empty pulse and for Dog Monday to be jolted with the fullness of his death. Little dogs, after all, can only have tender dogs' hearts. Grief to Dog Monday was an all-consuming thing, and when Walter's heart began to beat once more, he was deaf to its spark of joy."[31] After meeting with his eldest sister, Joyce, in heaven – which is, as he had always hoped, Rainbow Valley,

Walter is returned to life so that he may write of peace as well as war (as he did when he was a boy), marry Una, and repair the broken hearts of readers who did not want to lose him.

While heterosexual pairings are the most prevalent in Montgomery fandom, there is room for queer imaginings as well. This very popular genre of fanfiction, known as "slash," is generally defined as stories that centre on same-sex romances between characters, particularly between men. Montgomery slash fiction usually stars Walter Blythe, who may be read as queer: in *Rainbow Valley*, he is considered a "sissy" by his schoolmate, never experiences a romance, dies young, and during the First World War writes a poem which becomes famous, linking him to gay war poets like Siegfried Sassoon and Wilfred Owen. One slash story, "but i don't know who you are" by freyafrida, imagines a bisexual Walter. Told in an enduringly popular sub-genre of fanfiction often referred to as Five Things Plus One (which involves a series of thematically linked but not necessarily chronological scenes), the story is summarized by freyafrida as "Five people Walter thought he wanted, and one person he didn't notice until it was too late."[32] This last person is original to Montgomery's text: Una, whose apparently unreturned attraction to Walter is woven through *Rilla of Ingleside*. The other five potential partners are all alluded to as Walter's close friends, beginning in childhood with Alice Parker from *Anne of Ingleside* and Pat Brewster from *The Blythes Are Quoted* and then carrying on through adolescence and young adulthood with Faith Meredith, Ken Ford, and finally Paul Irving from *Anne of Avonlea*. While his feelings for Faith and Ken are clearly unrequited, Alice, Pat, and Paul all express their own desire for Walter. The inclusion of the famous poet and Walter's "model" uncle, Paul Irving,[33] in particular, illustrates how traits of sensitivity and aesthetic appreciation that challenge traditional ideas about masculinity are frequently interpreted as queer by fan readers and writers.

In another slash fiction, cero_ate's "The Moving Finger Writes, and Having Writ Moves On," Walter discovers his homosexuality while fighting in Europe:

> He wrote half truths and lies once more, when he wrote his Rilla that he could not form poems of the depths of the war. For who could write his sister of the phallic love he had found? He had found his reason in a tow-headed American boy. He meant so much more to Walter than mere

> friendship could explain. He wanted to write, as sweethearts write, of the tempest of joy in the darkest night. But how would they understand? How would they even try to understand he sought not the Dark Lady of Shakespeare but the youth, fair and Wilde? When he was presented with Una's faithful heart, he spurned it. When his tow-headed darling presented his own, Walter took it, greedy for him. His grecian style love, the boy who's [sic] eyes danced, even in the darkest of days. He would do anything to keep him safe. But he could not present him to his family, for their scorn or pity. War had broken him, but made him as well.[34]

Reading this passage, I wonder if cero_ate is also imagining a potentially queer subtext in Walter's own sonnet sequence about Faith Meredith (referenced in *Rilla of Ingleside*)[35] as she brings to life the homosocial experiences of war.

While male/male pairings are generally the most popular stories in fandoms, Montgomery's novels, peopled as they are by communities of girls and women, require that readers who want to queer the text must explore what is called femslash (that is, slash fiction featuring two female characters). Such relationships have been explored within the academic setting. For instance, Laura Robinson remarks in "Bosom Friends: Lesbian Desire and the Anne Books," that the relationship between Anne and Diana uses "the language that readers associate with adult romantic love rather than girlhood affections,"[36] even as it is expressed through the heterosexual paradigm of marriage. One fanfiction author, ArcticLava21, makes it clear that such stories are not merely speculation but instead address key issues of representation. The author's note to ArcticLava21's short Anne/Diana story, "Nature," reads, "Hello everybody! Hope your [sic] having a wonderful day. Before anyone yells at me for 'sexualizing platonic friendships' please note that this is for all those queer kids who grew up pretending. Pretending that he ended up with him instead of her, or desperately wanted representation. Are we good? <3 Enjoy yourselves lovely people."[37] The intended audience of the story, "queer kids who grew up," again establishes the transgenerational kinship between Montgomery's child and adult fans.

All these stories, shared on the Internet, exist in dialogue not just with Montgomery's fiction but with the author herself, and between the fans who read the novels as children and adolescents and the adults that these readers become. Whether fan writers extend the narrative or fill gaps, transpose chronology or queer the text, these pieces of fanfiction allow fans not only to insert themselves into the narrative, but also simultaneously to revivify the original novels, published a century ago. In performing interventions to the text, Montgomery's young fans grow up to reply to the discussions that she began long ago in the pages of her journals and stories, ensuring that all three – author, reader, and text – are continually reborn into a conversation that will never end.

ACKNOWLEDGMENT

This chapter was revised, with the author's permission, by the editorial team. Thank you in particular to Holly Pike.

NOTES

1 Derecho, "Archontic Literature," 76.

2 Coppa, *The Fanfiction Reader*, 12.

3 Busse and Hellekson, "Introduction," 7.

4 Ibid., 13.

5 Tosenberger, "Mature Poets Steal," 4–5.

6 LMM, *ENM*, 221.

7 Ibid., 17.

8 B. Thomas, "What Is Fanfiction,"16.

9 This is an example of Montgomery's including biographical details in *Emily of New Moon*: Montgomery's father "remarked unenthusiastically" that a poem she has "proudly" read to him "didn't sound much like poetry." Montgomery funnels this critique into a comment by Aunt Elizabeth that one of Emily's unrhymed poems, "Autumn" – the same poem that Montgomery's father criticizes – is "*very* blank." LMM, *CJ* 1:459; *ENM*, 119–20 (emphasis in original).

10 LMM, *EC*, 105.

11 LMM, *EC*, chapters 14 and 20.

12 LMM, *CJ* 2:38; *EQ*, chapter 17, part 2.

13 Dawkins, *Letters from Pemberley*, iii.

14 LMM, *Road to Yesterday*, 375.

15 Gerson, "'Dragged at Anne's Chariot Wheels,'" 151. Gerson cites journal entries from 9 October 1907 and 30 June 1908 (LMM, *CJ* 2:174, 193); emphasis in original.

16 See for instance LMM, *CJ* 3:130 on the need to "at least engage Anne [in *Anne of the Island*] for I'll never be given any rest until I do."

17 Lefebvre, "Afterword" to *The Blythes Are Quoted*, 511–20.

18 The misguided third *Anne* movie, *The Continuing Story* by Kevin Sullivan, also attempts to use this technique, while unmooring Anne and Gilbert in time so that they, instead of their children, can experience the First World War first-hand, rather than from the distance of the home front as they do in the novels.

19 MarnaNightingale, "The Pen and the Sword."

20 ruby gillis, "Cecilia of Red Apple Farm."

21 Gubar, "The Hermeneutics of Recuperation," 299–300.

22 LMM, *MM*, 22.

23 ElouiseBates, *Weeping May Tarry*.

24 Busse and Hellekson note that reader commentary is an important aspect of participation in online fanfiction archives ("Introduction," 12).

25 ruby gillis, "Cecilia of Red Apple Farm."

26 Wrede, "Some Uses for Fanfiction" (emphasis in original).

27 verity, "Work in Progress."

28 Ibid.

29 verity, "Rilla of Toronto."

30 Anuka. "You caught me staring."

31 Scylla, "Rilla Blythe's Wedding."

32 Freyafrida. "but i don't know who you are."

33 LMM, *RV*, 22.

34 cero_ate, "The Moving Finger Writes."

35 LMM, *RI*, 16–17.

36 L. Robinson, "'Bosom Friends,'" 21.

37 ArcticLava21, "Nature."

12

Anne with an Edge: CBC-Netflix's Rereading of Montgomery's *Anne of Green Gables*

LAURA M. ROBINSON

Since the centenary of the publication of L.M. Montgomery's *Anne of Green Gables* in 2008 and Montgomery's works entering the public domain in Canada in 2012, there has been a veritable explosion of adaptations and remakes.[1] The most recent reboot is the CBC-Netflix series *Anne* or *Anne with an "E"* that came out in 2017.[2] This is an adaptation with an edge. If we understand adaptations to be rereadings of the precursor text or texts, then this latest version, a "betrayal" according to Sarah Larson in the *New Yorker*,[3] seems to flip Montgomery's novel on its head. However, Moira Walley-Beckett's television series is arguably reading backwards, returning to the novel to foreground the narrative of trauma that was already there.

This chapter examines CBC-Netflix's rather edgy and dark *Anne* by comparing it to Montgomery's novel to consider why Anne and Montgomery have reappeared with such force in this historical moment, and why Netflix renamed and promoted the series in a more feminized and pretty manner than CBC had done originally. Importantly, the figure of Anne represents a version of childhood, and particularly girlhood, which is chronically being rewritten and challenged. Moreover, that construction of girlhood is tied to discourses of both vulnerability and empowerment. Ultimately, this chapter argues that both the pastoral promise of *Anne* the series and the discomfiting darkness that necessarily underwrites that idyllic vision speak to the complicated era in which North Americans presently live. While this darkness lurks in Montgomery's pastoral novel, Walley-Beckett highlights it to make a statement about the impossibility of idealized childhood and the difficulty of locating an ideal at all. Even though Walley-Beckett's rereading of the past is more overtly dark and complicated, she is rereading the past in this way not only to find hope for the future, a message which is very Montgomery, but also to propel individuals to take action to change the future. That hope and call to action are embodied in the figure of the traumatized girl who finds healing and empowerment.

In *Fight Club*, a novel by Chuck Palahniuk adapted into a film, the unnamed narrator aptly states, "everything's a copy of a copy of a copy." In adaptation studies, scholars know this to be very true, as Linda Hutcheon clearly suggests by addressing the chronic impulse for humans to rewrite and reinterpret texts. "Every age," she points out, "can justly claim to be an age of adaptation."[4] Indeed, Montgomery's *Anne of Green Gables* is no different, as it emerges clearly from a tradition or pattern of girls' stories and orphan tales, even if it is not directly reprising a specific story. Constance Classen addresses this quite dramatically in her article "Is 'Anne of Green Gables' an American Import?" citing the numerous similarities between Montgomery's novel and Kate Douglas Wiggin's *Rebecca of Sunnybrook Farm* (1903). While Classen is not claiming that Montgomery's tale is retelling Wiggin's, she certainly provides evidence that Montgomery appears to have borrowed heavily from the earlier novel. She qualifies her position, however: "Montgomery's work had virtues of its own and is not simply a paraphrase of Wiggin's. *Anne*, with its sympathetic, idealized portrayal of rural life with all its drawbacks, is a much lighter and sweeter work than *Rebecca* which is shot throughout with accounts of poverty, theft and dreary small-mindedness. On the other hand, *Rebecca*, with its hard edges, rings truer than *Anne*, in which everything works out rather too well."[5]

Humphrey Carpenter's study, *Secret Gardens*, and my own article on Anne's literary forebears make similar arguments that Montgomery drew upon a growing tradition of girls' stories as a basis for hers.[6] It is worth noting that Carpenter bemoans the appearance of Louisa May Alcott's *Little Women* on the literary scene only because it spawned a generation of what he views as similar but inferior girls' stories, such as *Anne of Green Gables*. While *Anne of Green Gables* may not be an adaptation, the emergence of that character relies upon a tradition that had been developing. Because Montgomery picks up and reinterprets previous stories, Anne herself is a reboot to a degree. Referring to *Anne* as an "original" may overlook an entire literary genealogy and tradition that provides insight into the figure of the girl in different historical and cultural moments. If we can regard Montgomery's *Anne* as a key moment in this tradition of girls' stories, both preceded and followed by other notable texts, then it may change how we view the various adaptations. They, too, become representations of a socio-historical moment that offer up an understanding of the world that produced and received them.

But why do we retell stories that already exist? While critics of the many adaptations of *Anne* have often decried the reinterpretations,[7] the whole notion of an adaptation's merit being determined by its fidelity to the precursor text has been both challenged and recuperated in recent years. As Christa Albrecht-Crane and Dennis Cutchins argue in their introduction to *Adaptation Studies: New Approaches*, "'adaptations' may be understood as 'readings,' paths the filmmakers take through source text(s) that themselves are paths through other texts."[8] Hutcheon points out that "adaptation is repetition, but repetition without replication," meaning that the new version can never be identical to the precursor.[9] Theorizing the compulsion to repeat that appears in texts for children, whether in adaptations or sequels, Mavis Reimer and her co-authors suggest that repetition is consolatory. They point out the limitations of fidelity criticism: "If we think of repetition as sameness, any difference from a standard … is perceived as a negative, as lack," which would explain people's sometimes outraged reactions to adaptations.[10] Rather than a lack, however, the differences might reveal much about the context in which the new version is produced. Albrecht-Crane and Cutchins stress the focus on difference: "Discovering difference then becomes not a quest to uncover the inevitable lack of fidelity, but rather an affirmative focus on how texts form and *in-form* each other."[11] Why retell a story in a different way? Why alter it? What do we need consolation for? How does the newer text cause us to look back at the precursor with a difference?

While it may seem that adaptation theory has accounted for fidelity criticism, Casie Hermansson and Janet Zepernick, in their volume *Where Is Adaptation? Mapping Cultures, Texts, and Contexts*, show that the issue of fidelity still underwrites adaptation studies. They indicate three waves of adaptation studies: one which focused on adaptations from literature to screen, often with an eye to the adaptation's fidelity; one which turned to intertextuality as a way to step away from the original-adaptation binary; and now one that opens up to more genres and approaches, including recuperating "fidelity from the much-maligned rubbish heap of adaptation studies."[12] As they point out, fidelity might matter very much to the viewer, and this is very evident in some responses to *Anne with an "E."* If those familiar with the "original" are distressed by the adaptation, what is the difference that is so affecting and why?

In his review of Walley-Beckett's *Anne* for the *Globe and Mail*, television critic John Doyle demonstrates a keen understanding of the potential work of an adaptation: "'I like imagining better than remembering,' Anne Shirley says at one point, obviously to camouflage pain, but there is emphatic truth in it. And that statement is great context for this adaptation. It imagines rather than remembers or reveres previous versions, no matter how beloved they were. This *Anne* should be approached and appreciated in the same spirit – it's a sublimely reinvigorated *Anne of Green Gables*."[13] For some viewers/readers, the adaptation is the original. I have a colleague who recently discovered the CBC-Netflix version of *Anne*, watching the whole first season three times. Because she had never read it, I loaned her the novel, as well as the Sullivan production. However, for her, the CBC-Netflix version will remain the favoured original text. She told me that she loved the show's return to the past and the comfort it gave. Hers is a fascinating perspective, as the reviews and commentary from those familiar with Montgomery's works are fairly unified in their take that this is a dark, grim version of Montgomery's so-called sunny tale, as I will discuss shortly.

Connected to the consolatory repetition inherent in adaptation is also the repetition without replication, to borrow Hutcheon's phrase, of certain identities. Rhonda Brock-Servais and Matthew Prickett rightly point out that "adaptations of children's literature are haunted by an additional construct – the idea of childhood presented in the original text."[14] In this case, Anne, a girl child, is reproduced and reimagined, which raises several important points. First, as Marnina Gonick suggests, the figure of the girl is not "a universal, biological[ly] grounded condition of female experiences but rather ... produced with[in] shifting sociohistorical, material and discursive contexts."[15] Moreover, that representation can be contradictory. Adaptations of a story with a girl subject and the often-negative responses to the reinterpretation show what Yasmin Jimani, Candis Steenbergen, and Claudia Mitchell have identified as part of understanding and discussing girlhood. "The space of girlhood," they write, "is one of contestation; marked by conflict, resistance, and change."[16] The adaptations can expose the conflict already inherent in the construction of the girl subject in a specific time and place, because audience responses might reveal the gap between expectations and actuality.

Furthermore, adapting Anne is particularly revealing precisely because of Anne's specific identity as a female child, an identity typically associated with vulnerability. As M.C. Kearney states, girls are "a demographic group that has been consistently marginalized, trivialized, and exploited throughout the ages."[17] Similarly, Linda Duits and Liesbet van Zoonen find that, in the discourses of girlhood studies, "implicitly girls are constructed as vulnerable, gullible and in danger, and their possible autonomy, strength and resilience is denied, as are questions of power and identity."[18] Also addressing the "vulnerability discourse" that surrounds girls, both in girlhood studies and also in society in general, Gonick recounts a history of the emergence of the girl subject. She points out that "the changing world brought on by modernity was met with a profound ambivalence. Both women and youth became the symbol for expressing this concern."[19] Based as this novel is on other novels featuring vulnerable fictional girls, Montgomery's Anne and all her adaptations are predicated on her initial marginalized status.

I do not think it is a coincidence that 2017 was the time for a re-emergence and reinterpretation of Canada's most famous girl, as this was and is a time of divisive and explosive politics. Walley-Beckett's reboot is a reaction to North American and world politics of the early twenty-first century, particularly with the 2016 campaign and election of Donald Trump and other such regressively conservative political leaders, populist politicians who are attempting to return American and Canadian politics and social life to an earlier time with fewer rights for women, the LGBTQ2S community, and racialized peoples. Walley-Beckett frequently, if obliquely, makes reference to those regressive politics in her interviews.[20] If the figure of the girl represents vulnerability and disempowerment, and Walley-Beckett's version of Anne certainly highlights those conditions, then this contemporary reboot also uncategorically emphasizes Anne's agency and empowerment at the same time. Peter Stoneley's discussion of the figure of the girl in late-nineteenth- and early-twentieth-century American literature can stand for representations of girlhood from the same time period in Canada. He effectively shows that "the girl ... is instrumental to articulating and assuaging the fear of social change."[21] Stoneley is primarily examining the fear of progressive social change, such as newfound rights for women, around the turn of twentieth-century America. In 2017, the fear could well be regressive social politics, which threaten to erode those same rights. Walley-Beckett's version of Anne highlights her vulnerability and the concomitant trauma in order to expose those regressive ideas.

Let's step back for a minute for a background on the production of this show. The writer of the entire first season, Walley-Beckett, is a Canadian actor and award-winning screenwriter who wrote many episodes of the dark television show *Breaking Bad*, about a high-school teacher turned crystal-meth producer, winning an Emmy for one. She contracted with the Canadian Broadcasting Corporation (CBC) to produce a new version of *Anne* as a television show. Much of the early media attention focused on the unlikely pairing of the crime story *Breaking Bad* with wholesome *Anne of Green Gables*.[22] Netflix got on board afterward, but it is largely seen as a co-production. Until the second season, CBC and Netflix Canada and Netflix international had different titles for the show (*Anne* and *Anne with an "E,"* respectively) and marketed it slightly differently. In Canada, the second season launched on CBC in September 2018 with the title *Anne with an "E"* – without any apparent acknowledgment that the title in season one was different. General consensus in the media (and with the public) is that this television show is very different from the precursor text. Whether reviewers find it "terribly wrong," as *Vanity Fair* declares, or not, they all speak to the "reboot" or "refresh" or "updating" or "reinvigorat[ion]" of the novel by the new series.[23] Walley-Beckett admits that she went "almost completely off book" in writing the series and focused on "drawing out the darkness."[24]

While Joanna Robinson's scathing review in *Vanity Fair* exclaims that Netflix's heroine is "an Anne with PTSD,"[25] many Montgomery scholars have understood the deep trauma that underwrites the supposedly sunshiny novel. Katherine Slater's article on trauma in *Anne of Green Gables* argues that readers' fascination with the novel "is fundamentally connected to the pleasures of witnessing Anne's active healing from early childhood trauma, her movement from isolated fantasy ... to productive social relationships within an embracing community."[26] Montgomery sets the stage for identifying Anne's distress early on, particularly when Anne recounts her pre–Green Gables background to Marilla. Orphaned at three months, passed off to the poor cleaning woman, Mrs Thomas, who had a drunk husband and four children, Anne's earliest years embody suffering and neglect. After Mr Thomas dies when she is eight, Anne is taken in by Mrs Hammond, who has eight children. When Anne is ten, Mr Hammond dies, and Anne is sent to the orphanage. This history is simply recounted by Anne rather than being something that the reader witnesses. It occurs offstage. When Marilla asks if the women were good to Anne, Anne responds: "'O-o-o-h,' faltered Anne. Her sensitive little face suddenly flushed scarlet and embarrassment sat on her brow. 'Oh, they meant to be – I know they meant to be just as good and kind as possible.'" The knowing reader, and Marilla, understand that they were not. Similarly, not only was Anne's sole friend her own reflection, Katie Maurice, a detail that highlights her neglect, but the fact that the bookcase, with no books, had only one pane of glass because "Mr. Thomas smashed [the other] one night when he was slightly intoxicated"[27] reveals the alcoholism and violence that were simply the norm for her, a domestic situation that Budge Wilson dramatized in her prequel *Before Green Gables*.

Even rigid and cold Marilla understands Anne's neglect. She looks at Anne when Mrs Blewett suggests she take her to mind her children and "softened at the sight of the child's pale face with its look of mute misery – the misery of a helpless little creature who finds itself once more caught in the trap from which it had escaped." Certainly, the Cuthberts keep Anne out of a sympathy borne from understanding the trauma she had endured. "We might be some good to her," Matthew responds when Marilla exclaims that Anne is of no use to them and that they should not keep her. Montgomery underscores that identifying that trauma is not necessarily straightforward by showing Marilla finally grasping Anne's reality: "What a starved, unloved life she had had – a life of drudgery and poverty and neglect; for Marilla was shrewd enough to read between the lines of Anne's history and divine the truth."[28] By aligning the reader with Marilla hearing Anne's tale, Montgomery thus encourages her readers to imagine more than Anne reveals and to understand themselves that trauma, or the emotional effect of a devastating event, is often not readily apparent. Her treatment of trauma is gentle and nuanced as she gestures toward the trauma of Anne's past, but skirts around directly confronting the reader with it.

With the transition from print to small screen, Anne's history takes a different bent. The generic conventions of the visual require a dramatization of

Anne's earlier life, which Kevin Sullivan's 1985 television miniseries also did by beginning the story with Anne's child labour in the two impoverished and twin-beset families. However, Walley-Beckett creates a particular focus on the pain and suffering. She explains in an interview with Willa Paskin that she is fascinated by trauma. "I am drawn to the psychology of wounded people," she admits. Thus, she focused on drawing out the darkness of the Anne books.[29] In an interview with Amy Wilkinson, she says, "All the darker aspects of the story are inherently in the book, so I'm not actually reinventing the wheel; I'm just taking us there."[30] Shifting the focus slightly, Walley-Beckett explains in an interview with Joanna Schneller that "I read between the lines, to mine what isn't there but has been there all along,"[31] which places her in a parallel position with Montgomery's Marilla and a reader "read[ing] between the lines of Anne's history."

Walley-Beckett rereads the past to highlight the trauma by imbuing not just Anne but each character with distinct and unhealed trauma, one that seems to have been there all along. Through many flashbacks, usually triggered by something in the present, the viewer sees Anne beaten, bullied, verbally abused, and living in violent and impoverished conditions. Anne is clearly haunted by her past. Walley-Beckett improvises on the backstories of many characters to similarly amplify their underlying trauma. Marilla and Matthew had an older brother, Michael, whose untimely death had a negative, if largely unspoken, impact on both their lives. The actor who portrays Marilla, Geraldine James, carries a worried and sensitive countenance, even if she shows a brusque exterior. This Marilla has had a disappointment in love, as poignant flashbacks make clear. Again, this is hinted at in Montgomery's text when Marilla confesses to Anne that Gilbert's father had been her beau,[32] a confession embellished in the Sullivan miniseries. Walley-Beckett invents another thwarted love when Matthew has flashbacks about his youthful love for Jeannie, the maker of the famous puffed-sleeved dress. Moreover, Matthew's inevitable economic failure is due to some bad decisions on his part and the sinking of a ship carrying Green Gables produce rather than the bankruptcy of the bank he had invested in, a change that places more responsibility for the failure onto Matthew. The effects still wear on his health, as he has a heart attack. Perhaps most "off script" and dark, even more than grifters invading Green Gables at the end of the first season, is Matthew's interrupted attempt at suicide.

Walley-Beckett magnifies the trauma of other characters as well. Gilbert's father is bedridden and dies, leaving Gilbert an orphan just like Anne. Here Walley-Beckett is foregrounding and elaborating a small detail from the novel. Diana explains to Anne that Gilbert will soon be joining the class: "Four years ago his father was sick and had to go out to Alberta for his health and Gilbert went with him" is the only information Montgomery imparts about Gilbert's familial situation.[33] In the television series as well, the French boy Jerry must work instead of attending school, his deepest desire, because his family is so poor. Notably, Jerry has hardly any role in the novel, much less a speaking part. Walley-Beckett's Miss Josephine Barry has recently lost her female life partner. This new Avonlea teems with grieving and wounded people.

Anne's appearance in Avonlea and her trauma enable these characters to begin to heal themselves. Marilla pulls out old love letters after Gilbert's father dies and offers a teary smile, perhaps an indication that she is able to remember him with affection. Matthew reconnects with his old flame, Jeannie, when he enlists her to create a dress for Anne. Jeannie then saves him from suicide. Miss Barry finds some solace in becoming Anne's role model, and Gilbert finds a sympathetic friend in his fellow orphan, Anne, after his father's death. The series shows a chronic woundedness, but also distinct possibilities for healing, notably centred on the orphaned Anne. Writing about the novel, Slater discusses the healing impulse: "In this returning motif of trauma successfully surmounted, Montgomery affirms her commitment to reiterating the power of the Symbolic order. Its repetition suggests that she understands the hunger of many of her readers for witnessing, over and over, the same model that [Catherine Sheldrick] Ross identifies as pleasurable: the outsiders' absorption into an [sic] safe and insular community."[34] In many ways, Walley-Beckett heightens this impulse that Slater identifies in Montgomery's novel by increasing the emphasis on the trauma. The very fact that Anne is so frequently adapted shows a larger and ongoing societal desire for the comfort and pleasure of this story of healing from trauma.

Montgomery's novel is a pastoral, often described as a regional idyll. With its origins in ancient poetry about shepherds and sheep, the pastoral has transmogrified over centuries. M.H. Abrams explains, for instance, that according to William Empson's *Some Versions of Pastoral*, the pastoral is "any work which opposes simple to complicated life, to the advantage of the former: the simple life may be that of the shepherd, the child, or the working man ... Other critics apply the term 'pastoral' to any work which represents a withdrawal to a place apart that is close to the elemental rhythms of nature, where the protagonist gains a new perspective on the complexities, frustrations, and conflicts of the social world."[35] Anne seeks solace in the natural world, a symbol of pastoral peace, and the idyllic Green Gables and Avonlea are far removed from the desperate world of Anne's early childhood. The Sullivan miniseries, at least the first one, with its expansive scenes of the bucolic Prince Edward Island countryside and the beautiful soundtrack by Hagood Hardy, plays up the pastoral mode. What is at the heart of the pastoral is a nostalgic longing for the past, for a golden world – but importantly, an idealized world that never was. The figure of the child and childhood, as Abrams points out, is often connected to the pastoral. Northrop Frye makes a similar connection in the conclusion to his *Literary History of Canada*, referring explicitly to *Anne of Green Gables*: "The pastoral myth in its most common form is associated with childhood or with some earlier social condition – pioneer life, the small town, the habitant rooted to his land – that can be identified with childhood. The nostalgia for a world of peace and protection … is particularly strong in Canada."[36]

Writing about the CBC-Disney co-production of the Montgomery-inspired series *Road to Avonlea*, Aspasia Kotsopoulos explains that "the series suppresses differences and history in its effort to create a utopian vision of the past."[37] While CBC's *Anne* does not present a strictly pastoral vision in the same way that the golden-hued *Road to Avonlea* and the 1985 *Anne of Green Gables* did, the differences in the initial marketing between the Canadian and American broadcasts suggest that the promoters understand the audience's interest in the pastoral mode. First, that the title in Canada was originally simply *Anne* speaks to the iconic status that Montgomery's character holds in this country. Her name is enough to evoke the entire nostalgic apparatus around her. The assumption is that the viewership knows the reference. In the rest of the world, Anne is specified as *Anne with an "E,"* a girl who stands out, is special. What caused a small uproar in Canada was the difference between the American and Canadian promotional ads.[38] Canadian Anne is in a dismal environment with greyish skies. She has bags under her eyes, many visible freckles, imperfect teeth, and looks close to tears. The American version is glowing yellow with a much Photoshopped Anne. That Netflix chose to market this golden world to its audience suggests that it is highlighting the promise of pastoral escape. They even invite the viewer to "visit Green Gables" as those words run across the ad. Entering into the series, it is suggested, is a pastoral escape from a troubled and complicated world. Even though the series Anne is grittier than Montgomery's novel, the pastoral beauty still transports the viewer into a simpler time. Because the marketers could not rely upon the audience in the rest of the world already knowing the pastoral content of *Anne of Green Gables* in the same way a Canadian audience might, they chose to highlight it in the ad. Despite the occasional darkness of the series, Walley-Beckett keeps showing close-ups of Anne revelling in natural beauty, thus keeping the pastoral escape as a focus. Kotsopoulos refers to arguments about this style of television show: "Such discussions of the costume drama seem to demand a recognition of this genre as a kind of fantasy, one in which contemporary desires, anxieties, and fears find displacement into a period setting."[39] In this way, Kotsopoulos suggests, the costume drama trades on nostalgia to highlight the continuity between the past and the present and as a way, then, to mitigate or cope with present anxieties.

The audience turning to a new version of *Anne of Green Gables* might initially expect an idyllic tale of a disenfranchised orphan finally finding a respectable home. This is a story of social mobility, as Anne moves from impoverished labourer to educated middle-class girl. In this case, however, Walley-Beckett shocks the viewer familiar with Montgomery's, or Sullivan's, story by presenting a much more overtly dystopian world, and she locates that world not only in the flashbacks of Anne's younger and socially disadvantaged years but also firmly in the world of largely middle-class Avonlea. The members of the women's group, sounding so progressive as they discuss feminism and welcoming as they invite new adoptive mother Marilla, turn out to be rigid and judgmental women. The bullying and name-calling that Anne endures in Avonlea is far worse than any girlhood rivalry between Anne and Josie Pye that Montgomery constructs.

Stoneley finds that the figure of the girl – "and above all, the middle-class girl – could serve as the vehicle for both nostalgia and optimism."[40] Walley-Beckett's adaptation highlights Anne's identity as being bound up in both emotional states. Always embedded or implied in the pastoral is the dark, complicated, gritty world from which the pastoral offers escape. The theme of darkness overturned by the light is precisely why we keep turning to Anne to reboot. *Anne* comes with the trappings of the nostalgic longing for the healing pastoral past. Reimagining her story allows artists to place the possibility for healing and light into a new complicated or dark context. The many critics weighing in on Sullivan's miniseries, such as Hersey and Howey, rather consistently comment on the show's reflecting "the concerns of many late-twentieth-century viewers."[41] Walley-Beckett's reboot similarly reflects concerns of early twenty-first-century North America. Abrams's definition of the pastoral indicates that "this literary mode serves as an oblique way to criticize the values and hierarchical class structure of the society of its time."[42] Thus, Walley-Beckett's version of *Anne* highlights the darkness that always existed in the past but remained un- or under-represented or that was sublimated by the golden hues of the pastoral. Moreover, she does so in order to create a sense of urgency for optimism and action.

The music that opens the series is also a gloss on Walley-Beckett's message. The Tragically Hip is a band iconic in Canada, especially for middle-class white men of a certain age. The front person, Gord Downie, was diagnosed with brain cancer in 2016 and died in October 2017 at age fifty-three. He spent the last seven months of his life doing charitable works for Indigenous peoples, for cancer, and for children. The outpouring of grief upon news of his death spanned the country, from statements from Prime Minister Justin Trudeau and many artists and musicians on social media, to grieving fans hitting the streets in the Ontario towns of Bobcaygeon and Kingston, to a Toronto Maple Leaf tribute to him before a game. Even a year later, the public expressions of grief continued.[43] Choosing a song by this band inevitably carries with it this entire emotional baggage, at least in Canada. The song "Ahead by a Century" is also a pastoral overturned, which echoes precisely Walley-Beckett's message. The song creates a pastoral sense of a young couple climbing a tree and chatting or staying silent, "with illusions of someday casting a golden light." The golden pastoral represented by the youthful image of climbing a tree and dreaming together is crushed by the rest of the song. The narrator gets stung by a hornet, falls into a nightmare, and takes revenge on the hornets by smoking them out. While being "ahead by a century" refers to Anne's progressiveness, this song also speaks to the inevitable disappointment in the pastoral dream, particularly in the face of hoping for "illusions of someday" with their "golden light."

Walley-Beckett's *Anne* does not descend into nightmares and revenge, but her version does depict her characters actively bringing about change. Marilla's conflict with the Progressive Mothers Sewing Circle is one example. This group ostensibly espouses feminist ideals and progressive beliefs. However, once they hear that Anne has spread stories about the schoolteacher and Prissy, they uninvite Marilla to their meetings and cast judgment upon Anne, as does the rest of Avonlea. Showing much agency, Marilla marches over to berate the women for rejecting, rather than expressing compassion for, an orphan who has experienced and witnessed unspeakable things that no child should. In one of the many dramatic departures from the novel, Anne runs into Ruby's family home, which is rapidly burning to the ground, to shut the windows and doors. She thus saves the house from complete ruin. Walley-Beckett's message is certainly not one of quiet endurance; rather, she shows her characters making powerful and very active choices.

An instructive example of the subtle difference between the active agency of Walley-Beckett's characters and Montgomery's is the scene in which Anne saves Minnie May from the croup. On the surface, both the novel and the television show are largely similar. Anne rises to the moment, with her knowledge gleaned from looking after multiple sets of twins, and acts swiftly to provide medicine and procedures to save Minnie May in the absence of a doctor. However, the scenes differ in the amount of agency Anne exerts. In the novel, Matthew goes for the doctor without being asked, and Anne explains to Diana that she understands where he has gone.[44] In the show, Anne orders Matthew to go for the doctor. Montgomery's Anne is exasperated with the overwhelmed and passive Barry family servant, Mary Joe, and barks orders at her. Wally-Beckett removes Mary Joe and inserts wealthy Miss Josephine Barry in her stead, meaning that Anne is bossing an upper-class woman. With these subtle differences, Walley-Beckett's Anne behaves in an even more empowered manner than Montgomery's does.

Perhaps the most frustrating scene to some, but also a telling alteration, is the bankruptcy story. In Walley-Beckett's version, Matthew tries to take his life in the face of extreme financial woes so that the insurance will provide for Marilla and Anne. Suicide thwarted, Marilla and Anne work out a way to provide for their family. Season one ends with the Cuthberts taking in boarders that the viewer knows to be the criminals who already stole from them and beat Jerry. While this turn of events is desperately bleak and unrelated to anything in Montgomery's novel, Walley-Beckett is highlighting the need for action through this drama. Matthew, Marilla, and Anne must work together to solve their financial difficulties. Walley-Beckett's Avonlea is not a place removed from hardship and crime, and thus it requires an agency that perhaps Montgomery's novel did not necessarily express. As Classen writes, in Montgomery's novel, "everything works out rather too well."[45] This is certainly not the case in Walley-Beckett's series.

Joanna Robinson states in her review that the darkness of the CBC show "feels particularly unwelcome in an already grim 2017."[46] While I agree that, in her Avonlea, Walley-Beckett explores issues that resonate with the downside of contemporary life – such as bullying, bankruptcy, family violence, crime, sexual predators, women's subservient and limited roles, and poverty – rather than presenting a fantasy about an ideal past, I suggest that she does so in the safe genre of the pastoral costume drama to provoke a desire for change. Just before the interview with Schneller, Walley-Beckett was listening to American feminist Gloria Steinem, and she explains that Steinem "was saying that when people have a competent, capable leader in the seat of power, we can sit back and say, 'That's handled' ... But when we don't, that's the moment to activate, to rise, to speak up and fight for change. This is one of those moments." While the pastoral mode allows for a nostalgic escape from the troubles of contemporary life, Walley-Beckett flips the pastoral to motivate her audience to take action against what is dark and troublesome, to strive toward creating an ideal world. "I want to be part of something that raises a voice to move forward," she states. "*Anne* does that for me."[47]

In *Anatomy of Criticism*, Northrop Frye refers to the pastoral as preserving "the theme of escape from society to the extent of idealizing a simplified life in the country or on the frontier" and points out that "such imagery is often used, as it is in the Bible, for the theme of salvation."[48] The pastoral may have the effect of ameliorating a difficult life through presenting the hope that paradise awaits. However, because she flips the pastoral on its head, leading the viewer to crave a pastoral ideal in the frustrating absence of the one the viewer expected, Wally-Beckett's Anne is perhaps more of a catalyst for change than similar girl figures, including other versions of Anne, have been in the past. This pastoral does not just console the audience; it provides a model for fighting against chronic injustice and for working toward a future where exploitation, bullying, violence, crime, and the concomitant trauma can be overcome and healed.

NOTES

1 Montgomery's 1908 *Anne of Green Gables* has inspired a multitude of retellings. Several scholars, such as Benjamin Lefebvre ("Stand by Your Man"), Eleanor Hersey ("'It's All Mine'"), K.L. Poe ("Who's Got the Power?"), Ann F. Howey ("'She Look'd Down to Camelot'"), and Theodore F. Sheckels ("Anne in Hollywood") have explored the earlier cinematic and stage retellings of Anne, the reigning version of which has to date been Kevin Sullivan's production of four miniseries (*Anne of Green Gables*, 1985; *The Sequel*, 1987; *The Continuing Story*, 1998; and *New Beginnings*, 2009). Since the centenary, many more retellings have emerged. In 2016, Breakthrough Entertainment debuted a ninety-minute made-for-television movie, *L.M. Montgomery's Anne of Green Gables*, followed by two sequels in 2017. Add in the abundance of Anne films, musicals, animations, and print reinterpretations, including Montgomery's own sequels, and a whole lot of different Annes are competing for audiences and for cultural primacy.

2 When the series first launched on CBC in 2017, the title was merely *Anne*. The Netflix first season launched as *Anne with an "E"* and was followed not long after by the second season with the same name. There was a blackout of Netflix's second season in Canada, until CBC released the second season. Beginning 23 September 2018, CBC aired the second season with the title *Anne with an "E"* as well.

3 Larson, "How Not to Adapt."

4 Hutcheon, "On the Art of Adaptation," 108.

5 Classen, "Is 'Anne of Green Gables' an American Import?" 48.

6 L. Robinson, "Anne and Her Ancestors." See Carpenter's statement, in which he laments all the "second-rate girls' novels in the Alcott mode that followed the appearance of *Little Women*," many of which featured "girls of unbearable cheerfulness." In a footnote, he refers to *Anne of Green Gables* as one of the lesser novels following the model of Alcott. Carpenter, *Secret Gardens*, 98.

7 For examples, see Poe, "Who's Got the Power?"; Lefebvre, "Stand by Your Man"; Drain, "'Too Much Love-Making.'"

8 Albrecht-Crane and Cutchins, "Introduction," 18.

9 Hutcheon, *Theory of Adaptation*, 7.

10 Reimer et al., "Introduction: The Compulsion to Repeat," 11, 22.

11 Albrecht-Crane and Cutchins, "Introduction," 15 (emphasis in original).

12 Hermansson and Zepernick, "Introduction: Where Is Adaptation?" 6.
13 Doyle, "*Anne of Green Gables* Adaptation."
14 Brock-Servais and Prickett, "From *Bildungsroman* to Romance," 215.
15 Gonick, "'Girl Power,'" 3.
16 Jiwani, Steenbergen, and Mitchell, "Introduction: Surveying the Terrain," xiv.
17 Kearney, "Coalescing: The Development of Girls' Studies," 21.
18 Duits and van Zoonen, "Against Amnesia," 112.
19 Gonick, "'Girl Power' and 'Reviving Ophelia,'" 4.
20 Most explicitly, she seems to make direct reference to Trump as president when she says in an interview with Schneller, "when people have a competent, capable leader in the seat of power, we can sit back and say, 'That's handled.' But when we don't, that's the moment to activate, to rise, to speak up and fight for change. This is one of those moments." See Page, "'Anne with an E,'" and Wilkinson, "*Anne with an E*," for two examples when she discusses bullying, prejudice, and gender parity, among other contemporary issues. In the interview with Page, for instance, she says: "We realized in talking about it that all the conversations in the world right now are inherent and built into the existing L.M. Montgomery stories, the conversations in the world that pertain to Anne, I should say. Conversations like feminism, bullying, and gender parity and equality and prejudice against those who come from away, and it felt incredibly timely." In a conversation with Tony Wong in the *Toronto Star*, Walley-Beckett refers to the #MeToo Movement as well: "I think what we need are more women at the top, we need gender parity. We need men to respect women in the workplace as equals. The rampant predatory, [*sic*] behaviour inflicted on innocent young women has been out of control."
21 Stoneley, *Consumerism and American Girls' Literature, 1860–1940*, 2.
22 See Schneller, "*Breaking Bad* Writer Brings 'Dark Sensibility,'" for example.
23 See Joanna Robinson, "*Anne of Green Gables*: Netflix's Bleak Adaptation Gets It All So Terribly Wrong"; Wilkinson, "*Anne with an E*"; Page, "'Anne with an E'"; and Doyle, "*Anne of Green Gables* Adaptation Is Sublimely Reinvigorated."
24 Paskin, "*Anne of Green Gables* Gets the *Breaking Bad* Treatment."
25 Joanna Robinson, "*Anne of Green Gables*: Netflix's Bleak Adaptation Gets It All So Terribly Wrong."
26 Slater, "The Other Was Whole," 167.
27 LMM, *AGG*, 49 (emphasis in original), 69.
28 Ibid., 54, 35, 49.

29 Paskin, "*Anne of Green Gables* Gets the *Breaking Bad* Treatment."
30 Wilkinson, "*Anne with an E.*"
31 Schneller, "*Breaking Bad* Writer Brings 'Dark Sensibility.'"
32 LMM, *AGG*, 354.
33 Ibid., 130.
34 Slater, "The Other Was Whole," 78. She is citing Ross's "Readers Reading L.M. Montgomery."
35 Abrams, *Glossary of Literary Terms*, 203
36 Frye, "Conclusion to a *Literary History of Canada*," 238–9.
37 Kotsopoulos, "Our Avonlea," 100.
38 See Emma McIntosh, "Canadians Unhappy," for an example.
39 Kotsopoulos, "Our Avonlea," 101.
40 Stoneley, *Consumerism and American Girls' Literature, 1860–1940*, 1.
41 Hersey, "'It's All Mine,'" 131. See also Howey, "'She Look'd Down to Camelot.'"
42 Abrams, *Glossary of Literary Terms*, 204.
43 See for examples Friend, "Gord Downie's Family Hoping to Organize Public Memorial"; Sportsnet Staff, "Watch Maple Leafs Honour Gord Downie Pre-Game Tribute"; and Frisk, "Gord Downie: Anniversary of His Death."
44 LMM, *AGG*, 168–9.
45 Classen, "Is 'Anne of Green Gables' an American Import?" 48.
46 Joanna Robinson, "*Anne of Green Gables*: Netflix's Bleak Adaptation Gets It All So Terribly Wrong."
47 Schneller, "*Breaking Bad* Writer Brings 'Dark Sensibility.'"
48 Frye, *Anatomy of Criticism*, 43.

AFTERWORDS

Preface to the Afterwords

LESLEY D. CLEMENT AND MARGARET STEFFLER

Readers often remember the exact location and circumstances of their initial reading of *Anne of Green Gables*. Adrienne Clarkson, Canada's twenty-sixth governor general, for example, first read *Anne* when she was nine and remembers that the book "was given to me by the next-door neighbours in our apartment building in Ottawa." Clarkson, a journalist, broadcaster, and author, went on to "devour" the entire Montgomery canon and notes that for her, as an "immigrant child" in a refugee family from Hong Kong, Montgomery's books provided "a profound understanding of what Canada is." Through Montgomery's fictional girls, she continues, "I became a Canadian."[1] Creative writers, artists, and performers also report enjoying lively conversations with Montgomery generated by their childhood encounters with her novels. We conclude this volume with a sampling of new conversations from contemporary performers and writers, building on the transmedial focus of the chapters in Part Four of this volume.

The long line of well-known conversations between Montgomery and writers inspired by their childhood reading of her work include those of Margaret Laurence, Margaret Atwood, Jean Little, Rosemary Sutcliff, and Alice Munro.[2] Jane Urquhart's biography of Montgomery in the Extraordinary Canadians series (2009) is, in itself, from beginning to end, a long conversation with Montgomery, as is an earlier biography, Janet Lunn's *Maud's House of*

Dreams (2002). In his review of Lunn's biography for *Quill & Quire*, Canadian children's author Kenneth Oppel writes, "What particularly entranced me about the Emily books as a child was Emily's inextinguishable fire to succeed as a writer – it was Montgomery's fire, too, and reading about it here is one of the pleasures of Lunn's biography."[3] In Oppel's recently published *Inkling* (2018), illustrated by Sydney Smith, it is the protagonist's reading of *Anne of Green Gables* that inspires a verbal and textual representation of Anne "in the depths of despair."[4]

Among the ever-growing number of voices expressing admiration for and affinity with Montgomery's characters are such contemporary Canadian writers as Heather O'Neill, Louise Penny, and C.E. Gatchalian. In March 2018, in response to the "Heritage Minute" on Montgomery, O'Neill, winner of the 2007 Canada Reads competition for her debut novel *Lullabies for Little Criminals*, tweeted that "Lucy Maud Montgomery got me through all my saddest hours when I was ten. (Anne Shirley remains the love of my life)," and she praises Montgomery for "battl[ing] societal norms to create her everlasting ode to the young girl."[5] Award-winning Canadian mystery novelist Penny, in her May 2018 newsletter, relays a conversation she had with her editor Hope Dellon, a "fierce New York intellectual," about their mutual love of Anne of Green Gables, Penny's "first fictional [human] friend," and assumes the voice of Anne when she closes her newsletter with the line "but really, Marilla, one can't stay sad very long in such an interesting world, can one?"[6] Gatchalian, author of the memoir *Double Melancholy: Art, Beauty, and the Making of a Brown Queer Man* (Arsenal Press, 2019), explains how as a "little brown Filipinx boy who had just started feeling the first vague stirrings of queer desire," with no representation in art or literature for role models, he found in Anne an outsider who succeeds through her "transgressive" resistance and her "striv[ing], Herculean, towards unadulterated poetry, beauty, transcendence."[7]

Conversations with Montgomery, especially about difference and belonging, as Clarkson's and Gatchalian's comments suggest, cross ethnic, racial, gender, and socio-economic lines, an appeal witnessed recently in interviews given by twenty-three-year-old Amanda Gorman, the first Youth Poet Laureate of the United States (2017), who presented her poem "The Hill We Climb" at the 2021 presidential inauguration. A *Vogue* magazine article (May 2021) reports that Gorman was a "writer, compulsively, from about age five, stealing time from her sleep to draft short fiction, inspired by *Anne of Green Gables.*"[8] In this and an earlier interview in the *Observer* (New York), Gorman recalls that these first efforts tended to feature "white girls with red hair and blue eyes, very Anne of Green Gables,"[9] until she discovered other "spiritual grandmother[s]" – Toni Morrison, Audre Lorde, Phillis Wheatley, Maya Angelou, and Elizabeth Alexander[10] – who inspired her poems, which comment "on social justice issues such as intersectional feminism and race."[11] But, as she makes clear in an interview for *Interfaith Youth Core* (21 January 2021), the spirit of Anne of Green Gables is one to which she still aspires: "I am quick to be consumed by a problem's complexities and overwhelmed – in mind and spirit – by its magnitude. It's perhaps no surprise, then, that the state of our nation in 2020 – from the pandemic to bigotry laid bare in the murders of George Floyd, Breonna Taylor, and others – left me regularly in the depths of despair. But here's something else you should know about me. I want to be an optimist. I envy Anne's idealism. And so, I make concerted efforts to feed the flame of hope in me whenever possible." The interviewer, Research Fellow Shauna Morin, concludes – about herself and others of her generation who lack confidence in contemporary institutions but "exhibit a knack for recasting challenges as adventures and … set out to conquer them" – that today's young readers will "continue to be uplifted by that plucky orphan, Anne, and her earnest belief that every 'tomorrow is a new day with no mistakes in it yet.'"[12] Montgomery's legacy is captured in the title of Gorman's picture book, *Change Sings: A Children's Anthem* (2021).

This legacy is also captured in conversations that cross genre boundaries through song, television, and dance. A paper presented at the L.M. Montgomery Institute's International Conference in June 2018, entitled "Anne and Aretha: A Harmonious Bond," by Halifax journalist Evelyn White, initiated a social-media flurry when she drew attention to a 2014 *Toronto Star* article in which Richard Ouzounian quotes Aretha Franklin's declaration of her love of Anne of Green Gables, "a can-do kind of girl," and her respect for Marilla, "a lady who knows just how she wants things to go." In a CBC interview months later, White admits that she cannot figure out how a young Black girl in the late 1940s and 1950s came to read *Anne of Green Gables* but hypothesizes that the young Aretha connected to Anne as a motherless girl, who showed independence and a sense of self-confidence.[13] Other connections can be inferred from Ouzounian's article, several with clear links to Franklin's "trademark songs." The singer's definition of a "natural woman" as being "hands-on," doing things in her own way and on her own terms, and comments on "respect" being a "basic human right" bring to mind Anne's feisty defence of her non-conforming behaviour and right to be heard when treated unjustly. And Franklin's closing remarks – "Bad things happen with a lot of people. I'm not immune. I just keep keeping on" – certainly convey Anne's stoicism and optimism.[14]

A second recent conversation occurs in Netflix's popular *Russian Doll.* In a 10 February 2019 CBC article, web journalist Sara Fraser outlines how Emily Byrd Starr made her way into the *Russian Doll* series, explaining that writer and executive producer Allison Silverman framed the idea of Emily when she was looking for something less "sunny" than Anne. In considering Madeleine L'Engle's *A Wrinkle in Time* as a possible intertext for *Russian Doll*, Silverman discovered that L'Engle's favourite book was *Emily of New Moon.*[15] Silverman found Emily to be a much better fit than L'Engle's Meg Murry and thought Montgomery's character "seemed to speak to the concerns that Nadia has and the things she's facing and how she conceives of her place in the world." Emily and Nadia share "childhood abandonment, intense creativity, and a deep love of their cat." Emily's "near-ability to glimpse an other-world of pure beauty and happiness, moments of clarity glimpsed as though behind a thin curtain – something she called 'the flash'" – also worked well with Nadia's predicament and temperament.[16]

Third, and an entirely different medium, is a new full-length ballet by Canada's Ballet Jörgen. Choreographed by Bengt Jörgen, *Anne of Green Gables: The Ballet* premiered with Symphony Nova Scotia to sold-out audiences on 28 and 29 September 2019 in Halifax and began an ambitious two-year tour of nine Canadian provinces and four American states before the program was interrupted by the COVID-19 pandemic in March 2020 and rescheduled until 2021–22. The company's website describes the ballet as "a playful, colourful and evocative production that will transport audiences to early 20th century Atlantic Canada."[17] Lead dancer, Hannah Mae Cruddas, who as a child in Nova Scotia fell in love with Anne, declares that she "always wanted to be joyful and imaginative (like Anne)." In preparation for the role, she reread the books to find references to Anne's body and movement as part of her exploration and testing of "her ballet voice for the character." This careful study of the text resulted in the expression of "Anne's love of talking and her constant flow of words" through "quick, fluid movements" of dance. Cruddas's assessment of Anne as "light and bubbly and expressive" obviously informs the way she understands and plays the role, such as incorporating jumps to convey Anne's excitement.[18]

In the introduction to this volume, we briefly introduced the artists who, in these four afterwords, personally and candidly convey the impact of Montgomery's imagination and vision on their creative work and careers. Like the writers and artists discussed above, these contributors have been profoundly inspired by the otherness, vulnerability, resilience, and spirited energy of Montgomery's characters. We provide more detail and background here.

In "Emily Kent – The Afterlife of Emily of New Moon," Vappu Kannas interviews Vilja-Tuulia Huotarinen and Satu Koskimies, co-authors of the popular novel *Emilia Kent – Runotytön tarina jatkuu* (WSOY, 2018), which continues Emily of New Moon's story beyond the compressed ending of Montgomery's trilogy. The conclusion invites imaginative speculation about the further development not only of Emily and Teddy, but also of engaging characters such as Dean Priest and Ilse. The energetic fun with which the co-authors took up this project accentuates the powerful and haunting presence of Montgomery's narrative in the minds of readers and how her fiction resonates in ways that encourage conversations in the form of fanfiction. The interview demonstrates the continuation of readers' devotion to Montgomery in Finland and worldwide.

Holly Cinnamon, a Canadian actor, director, playwright, songwriter, and teacher currently based in New York City, played the lead role in *Anne and Gilbert – The Musical* (Charlottetown's Guild Theatre, 2016). Cinnamon, who loves "embodying new characters," says "my passion for acting is rooted in my belief in the power of vulnerability, exposing our hearts, fighting for what we believe in and finding empathy and understanding for each other."[19] "Anne's Nature," Cinnamon's contribution of prose and poetry to this volume, recounts her two experiences playing Anne, the first as a high-school student in rural Alberta and the second as a twenty-seven-year-old in PEI following her education and training at the University of Alberta, the National Theatre School of Canada, and the Boston Conservatory. As a red-haired Canadian, Cinnamon felt an early affinity with Anne, and this piece celebrates their many similarities, particularly the bond of "queerness," which she finds empowering.

Rosalee Peppard Lockyer, a women's oral historian from Nova Scotia and "Heritage Ambassador" emerita of the Helen Creighton Folklore Society, conducts extensive research and interviews of elder Canadian women in order to collect their stories, which she then transcribes into "Song Portraits." She believes that "we are strong women because of the strong women before us" and sees women's stories as under-represented. According to Peppard Lockyer, many of those she interviews "often don't believe they have something of value to share." In such cases, Peppard Lockyer poses the question "What is your passion?" and says that "from there it starts to unravel."[20] Her performance of her song portrait of Montgomery, "Rosalee Sings Maud," which was commissioned by the L.M. Montgomery Society of Ontario for Canada 150, debuted in 2017. In her poem for this volume, "My Maud by Katie Maurice," Peppard Lockyer draws on Anne's imaginary friend, Katie Maurice, and the description of Anne as a "stray woman-child."

Kit Pearson, a Canadian children's author, beloved, recognized, and celebrated throughout her career, published her first novel, *The Daring Game*, in 1986 and her most recent, *Be My Love*, in 2019. She often cites the influence of Montgomery, explaining that "as a child I always felt like an outsider, an observer, and then I read *Emily of new moon* by Lucy Maud Montgomery; after that I knew I wanted to be a writer. That book has had an amazing influence – in fact, all three Emily books – on writers in Canada."[21] Well known in mid-career for the popular *Guests of War* trilogy (1998) composed of *The Sky Is Falling* (1989), *Looking at the Moon* (1991), and *The Lights Go on Again* (1993), Pearson was awarded the Governor General's Award for English-language children's literature for *Awake and Dreaming* (1996) and the Vicky Metcalf Award for Literature for Young People in 1998. On 8 May 2019, she was appointed a member of the Order of Canada. Her letter for this volume, "Dear Maud," a form of epistolary fanfiction, speaks to the way in which writers continue to recognize and celebrate the profound influence of Montgomery on their lives and work.

These four afterwords are passionate reminders of ongoing intersections between Montgomery and artists in and beyond Canada.

NOTES

1 Clarkson, "Foreword," ix.

2 See Laurence, "Books that Mattered to Me," 241; Atwood, "Reflection Piece," 225–6, and "Nobody Ever Did Want Me"; for Little and Sutcliff, see Little, "But What About Jane?" 72, 81; Munro, "Afterword," 360–1.

3 Oppel, "Review of *Maud's House of Dreams.*"

4 Oppel, *Inkling*, chapter 5.

5 O'Neill, Tweet.

6 Penny, Newsletter, May 2018.

7 Gatchalian, "Anne Shirley Was the Best Friend a Queer Brown Boy Could Have."

8 St Félix, "The Rise and Rise of Amanda Gorman."

9 Radin, "The First Youth Poet Laureate, Amanda Gorman."

10 St Félix, "The Rise and Rise of Amanda Gorman." Morrison, Lorde, and Wheatley are mentioned in Radin, "The First Youth Poet Laureate, Amanda Gorman."

11 Radin, "The First Youth Poet Laureate, Amanda Gorman."

12 Morin, "The Heroines Who Inspire Me to Keep the Faith."

13 White, "Mainstreet PEI: Anne and Aretha"; Ouzounian, "Aretha Franklin."

14 Ouzounian, "Aretha Franklin."

15 Heidi Lawrence discusses the conversations that L'Engle had with Montgomery and *Emily of New Moon* in chapter 8.

16 Fraser, "Emily of New Moon Gets a Star Turn."

17 Ballet Jörgen, *Anne of Green Gables: The Ballet.*

18 Lawlor, "A Dancing Dartmouth Anne of Green Gables."

19 Cinnamon, "About Holly Cinnamon."

20 Rent, "Peppard Tells Stories of Canadian Women in Song."

21 Flick, "Writing Is the Deepest Pleasure I Know," 16.

Emily Kent – The Afterlife of Emily of New Moon

VAPPU KANNAS

Childhood readings of L.M. Montgomery's *Emily* trilogy have proven inspirational for aspiring authors throughout the world. Alice Munro comes to mind as one of the most famous. She writes in her "Afterword" to *Emily of New Moon* that she first read the book when she was nine or ten years old. She decided that it was "good but different." But what is central to the story of Emily is "the development of a child – and a girl child, at that – into a writer."[1]

Being a writer is so central to Emily's character and the whole trilogy that it is not surprising writers have found in it a guidebook of sorts to what it is like to be an author, how to become one, and how to live a writer's life. However, at the end of the trilogy, Montgomery presents a situation where Emily's career is just beginning, and she is getting married to Teddy Kent. What happens next? Will she be able to balance a career with family life? Will Teddy's artistic career take precedence? Will Emily be able to write, or will she focus on being a wife and mother?

Two Finnish authors, Satu Koskimies and Vilja-Tuulia Huotarinen, have imagined answers to these questions that most readers of the Emily books have wondered about over the years. Although taking over a fictional world created by an admired and iconic author was daunting, Koskimies and Huotarinen thoroughly enjoyed the task. What began as fanfiction became a novel – *Emilia Kent* [*Emily Kent*] (WSOY, 2018). Continuing from the point at which

Emily's Quest ends, *Emilia Kent* explores Emily and Teddy's early married life in the Disappointed House. Teddy's career is soaring, while Emily suffers from writer's block and her responsibilities as a wife. There are also bouts of jealousy, visits from Ilse and Perry, Aunt Elizabeth's health problems, and an uncomfortable surprise appearance by Dean Priest, who asks Emily to read through his travel diaries (in which he pines for Emily) in order to edit them for publication. Reading the novel, one is transported back to Montgomery's familiar world, but what delights the modern reader is the subtle inclusion of a feminist critique of early-twentieth-century gender roles, as well as the realistic depiction of the struggles of a woman writer.

I interviewed Koskimies and Huotarinen on a sunny June afternoon in Helsinki.[2]

VK: When did you first read the *Emily* books?

SK: I was thirteen when a girl I knew recommended the books to me. That's also the first time I mention Emily in my diary. But I knew already when I was eleven that I wanted to be a writer, so Emily and her writing and her connection with nature really spoke to me. I was the same.

VK: Did you grow up in the city or in the countryside?

SK: In the city, in Helsinki, but I spent the summers in the countryside. For me all the places in the *Emily* books are connected to our family's summer house. It's an old nineteenth-century wooden building, and it was clearly "New Moon." This is what often happens to us when we read. We associate the places in the books with our own surroundings.

V-TH: When I first tried to read *Emily of New Moon*, we still lived in the countryside in an old farmhouse with my extended family. I found *Emily of New Moon* among the old books of my aunts and uncles. I was ten years old, and I walked to the garden with the book but couldn't finish it then. The nature descriptions seemed too tedious to me, and the beginning was too slow somehow. Emily's father dies; it's pretty sad. It was too much for a ten-year-old me. So I pushed it aside. Then I read it again when I was a teenager, and suddenly the *Emily* books became very important to me. I read them several times. I remember well, for example, the scene in the church when Emily is hiding from mad Mr Morrison, the charged moment with Teddy afterwards, and all the supernatural experiences in the books. I was writing a poem a day at that moment, and Emily's writing really hit the spot for me.

SK: I didn't read the *Emily* books continually, like some readers that I know. But I always returned to them, for instance when I had love troubles. I read *Emily's Quest* then. Even now it's this feeling that I get that I want to read the *Emily* books, especially the last one in the trilogy, and it always stimulates me in a new way.

V-TH: There's always something new that stirs inside. It's like a treat.

VK: Could you say that Emily has been an important model for wanting to become a writer, a professional writer?

SK: Yes, absolutely. Especially when I was growing up.

V-TH: I had a teacher in high school who was like Mr Carpenter. A very important person and influence, someone who encouraged me to write. He told me to believe in fairies.

SK: I had the total opposite experience. My male teacher was telling me to write more realistically and forget the nature descriptions. I had a long battle with him about my own voice. But maybe it was good that I had to fight for it.

V-TH: I was pretty ambitious from the start, but I remember always thinking that I have to write well enough to be published. This kind of analytical attitude to writing has been reinforced by Emily's example. That you don't get discouraged no matter what.

SK: I wrote poems all the time, even when I was working as a journalist and editor. I always had the dream that I would one day publish a collection of poems. And then I did. But they always went side by side, the writing of poems and fiction and the other work.

VK: How was it to write *Emilia Kent*? To write about a world that was familiar to you?

SK: I couldn't have written the book with anyone except Vilja-Tuulia. We have talked so much about Emily and the books over the years that we have a similar way of looking at them.

V-TH: We're familiar with each other's styles. That's important when you write together, so that you know what the other person sounds like.

SK: It's hard to say now who's written what in the book. I can't tell. And we also edited each other's sentences.

V-TH: The text was always the main thing. And we knew that we could be open about everything, even if we didn't like something. I also didn't want the original *Emily* books to turn into source books or encyclopedias to be mined for information. Some magic about them had to be kept alive. I still believe, even after writing our book, that all the alternative realities exist. All the other what-ifs that come after *Emily's Quest*. But it's nice that we have imagined what the life in the Disappointed House might be like, because Montgomery leaves it up to our imaginations to keep wondering.

VK: In some ways the ending of *Emily's Quest* calls for fanfiction, because it's an open ending. We're not told what their lives will be like, unlike in the *Anne* books.

SK: Everything is so messed up at the end of the book, but then things get settled. The reader can let out a sigh of relief, but there's still this disturbing feeling that an element of danger is hanging about the edges of the ending. That you can't quite relax.

VK: It's interesting that you deal with the aging of Aunt Elizabeth. And Dean Priest is back!

SK: Well, the passing of the years was something we had to deal with. People grow older, and the years bring about all kinds of changes. Many readers have commented on Dean Priest's character. What do you think about him?

VK: I think he's a fascinating character in the original books because he's so contradictory. A bit oppressive, but also encouraging and important to Emily.

SK: It's quite courageous of Montgomery to create this kind of older male character.

V-TH: Dean Priest brings a certain kind of eroticism to the books, even though covertly.

SK: Many readers have told us that Teddy is a mere sidekick in our book. And it's true that our book is about women; it concentrates on the female characters.

VK: You introduce Dean Priest's travel diaries in the book, which I thought was a very interesting change of perspective. We hear about what he's been up to during his travels and get his perspective.

SK: We wanted to explore a little bit how he experienced things, not just how Emily saw him. We tried to depict Dean as a complicated character, not just a fiend.

V-TH: We wanted to show what Emily meant to him while he was travelling. And to show that he's a many-sided character.

VK: In your book, Dean's diaries interestingly reveal that Dean is obsessed with Emily, which I think is a good reading of the original character. Mont-

gomery isn't actually so interested in him once he's off to his travels. She doesn't depict what he does there.
SK: I've always wondered why Montgomery created this older character. It's probably because a younger person couldn't have been so independent, able to travel, etc.
VK: Was it difficult to write about Teddy?
SK: Somebody mentioned that our feminist touch comes out in Teddy's character.
V-TH: But I still see him as a heartthrob. He's surprisingly charismatic for a supporting character. I see Emily and Teddy as a happy couple.
SK: Absolutely. It was meant to be. And we depict them as a happy couple.
VK: You also depict Emily's struggles with writing. She suffers from writer's block.
SK: We wanted her writing to be the centre of our book.
V-TH: Even the original title of the Finnish translation [*Little Poet Girl*] focuses on Emily as a writer, a poet. Her profession is the central thing.
VK: Did you know much about fanfiction before you started your project?
SK: I didn't, at least. I kept asking Vilja-Tuulia if it's okay to do something like this, and she said, yes, there's this thing called fanfiction. And we marched into the publisher's office and asked if we could write something like this, if we can use Montgomery's characters, and they said yes. I wonder what people would say if the book was translated into English. At least we haven't offended anyone.
V-TH: Well, we don't know that. I have a feeling that some readers could be disappointed. But that's how it is with any kind of writing. You have to have a certain sense of freedom in writing, and, after the book is published, it's off your hands. It's important to let it go and let the book live its own life.
VK: This is your interpretation as two Montgomery and Emily fans.
SK: Yes, exactly.
VK: Your book has been categorized as young-adult fiction, even though you deal with adult themes, such as marital problems. But I think this problem of categorization exists already in the original *Emily* books.
V-TH: I think it's problematic in the first place that we categorize books for children or young adults or adults. I read books for all ages. What matters is how the book is written, how it deals with the themes.
VK: Apparently you had fun writing the character of Ilse?

V-TH: Montgomery's original is so good, so excellent.
SK: We did try to come up with all kinds of crazy adjectives that she could use.
V-TH: I still laugh out loud when I read the original lines of Ilse; they feel so fresh, so sharp. Montgomery is superb in writing black humour. And writing fanfiction is imitating. It's easier to imitate something that is well written. The process of writing this book was very different from writing one of my own books. The incompleteness and painstaking work that I connect to my own writing was completely absent. There existed already a ready-made world.

So powerful are the childhood reading experiences and this "ready-made world" of Montgomery's books that they make the readers ask "What happens next?" after the story has ended. It is because of this power that we have books such as *Emilia Kent*.

NOTES

1 Munro, "Afterword," 357–9.

2 This interview has been translated from Finnish to English, edited, and condensed.

Anne's Nature

HOLLY CINNAMON

"You're a queer girl, Anne. I heard before that you were queer. But I believe I'm going to like you real well." – Diana Barry

As an actor, I've played Anne twice.

The first time was in rural Alberta, in a stage adaptation of the first book. I was seventeen, the know-it-all high-school valedictorian who found freedom in drama club, in the realm of imagination. Full of spirit and hormones, I had no idea who I was. But I was headstrong and confident and always right.

The second time was in PEI, in *Anne and Gilbert*, a musical based on the second and third books. I was twenty-seven and had just finished my MFA. I was more complicated, difficult, dark. Like Anne, I had a self-reliance that could come only from being broken and surviving. I had survived an assault. I had come out as a queer woman.

I am a natural redhead, small-town Canadian girl.

Anne has become a guidepost on my journey from girl to woman. I've always felt a deep connection to her – not only because of our red hair, but also because of our strength, our intelligence, our anger, our whimsical worldviews, our divine attraction to beauty, our secret inner lives … our queerness.

There is something different about Anne from the start. It's undeniable. No matter how hard she tries, she does not fit the mould of the ideal little girl. Redheads have always been different – mythologized as devilish, sexual, hot-tempered creatures. But Anne's difference runs deeper than her carrot top.

Anne's primary struggle is with her identity. She is constantly reconciling the labels thrown at her by the culture she lives in:

"Orphan" / "Girl" / "Poor" / "Freckled" / "Carrots!" / "Queer"

These are powerful labels – labels of difference – that she negotiates from childhood. She cannot change how she was born. She cannot change her nature. So, Anne creates a world for herself through her relationship with nature, where the boundaries of identity dissolve.

When I played Anne as a child, I relished her curiosity and her innocent compulsion to question the rules. Anne's lack of conventional upbringing becomes her power. She gets away with expressing herself freely because she doesn't know any better. It is her difference – her queerness – that gives her permission to challenge norms: to ask why right is right and to turn Marilla's world on its head. As Anne grows into a woman, she must negotiate her assimilation into a culture that does not often align with her inner nature.

As a twenty-first-century queer woman, I have found playing Anne to be empowering. I do not have to reduce myself to play her. I do not have to become less complicated or powerful than I am. Anne shows us that there is strength in sensitivity and that a woman with a temper in a contrary culture can still be a heroine.

"Queer" is a label ascribed to Anne to connote her difference and a label I choose for myself today. Granted, the cultural meaning of the term has evolved, been reclaimed. But I recognize my queerness in Anne.

Anne's nature is queer not only because it rebels against cultural norms, but also because it resists definition and limitations in favour of imagination. Her nature is a wild, unclassified territory. It is a world of possibility, play, and magic. She sees through categories to the hearts of all beings. Anne's eye treats everyone equally – from the geranium on the windowsill to the humble mare that pulls the buggy. Old, young, plant, animal, male, female, queer, nonbinary, fluid, free – everything has a soul.

I have fallen in love with Anne's world – a world where all beings are witnessed, dignified, and loved in the beauty of their complicated fullness – a world with less definition and more curiosity than our world today. I wish I could live there for real.

that queer redheaded girl next door
unearths kindred spirits everywhere
her taste does not discriminate
on gender or genus
love is love is love

in flowers she finds friends
in clouds companions
in strangers she searches for similarities

her hair lights a fire she cannot contain
her words once let loose will not withdraw into her mouth
they have changed the air dangerously

conventions collapse confronting her questions
rules recoil from her righteous regard
beliefs buckle
traditions topple
they cannot hold against her
disarming curiosity

Canadians should be polite
aggressions kept passive
just under the surface where they belong
a lesson left unlearned
her nature is resistant
to such stifling false friendliness

that queer redheaded girl next door
does not belong in her time and place
perhaps that is her purpose
and purpose isn't painless

if only a bottle of black dye
could normalize her nature
instead it reveals her roots deep green with envy
for the girl who fits the mould
whom no one will write books about

her difference defines her
her fickle freckles nose foes
carrot-topped

hot-headed
red-faced
rarity

a weed that so longs to be plucked
for the vase with the rest
but hands overlook her
instinctively knowing she could not tolerate
that kitchen table life

it is not her choice to be who she is
it is not her choice to be lonely

her nature cries out against her
steering her from giggling schoolgirls
to bubbling brooks
whose currents
run much deeper
like her own

that queer redheaded girl next door
was sewn from gossamer not gingham

she is not of polished silver
too tarnished for the sideboard drawer
she is of the silver starlight
tickling the pond at secret midnight

her joy is unbridled
her braids all undone
she will not be saddled
untamed
this wild one

only the sunbeam piercing the window understands her
and the soft breeze caressing the cherry blossoms

and the goddess moon lulling alone in an empty sky
these are her bosom friends

their courses unchanged by culture or tradition
their rhythms unwavering
they do not discriminate
her faithful witnesses

My Maud by Katie Maurice

ROSALEE PEPPARD LOCKYER

Like L.M. Montgomery (and Anne), as a child, I had friends of fancy or, using the grown-up term, invisible "imaginary friends." So, as an older child, when I read *Anne of Green Gables*, my initial poignant point of connection was not with Anne, but with Anne's imaginary friend, Katie Maurice. If Anne knew and loved lonely Katie, then Anne and I could be friends. Katie was my door to Anne.

In Montgomery's first description of Anne in chapter 2, I was struck by the phrase "this stray woman-child." Didn't this phrase describe most of Montgomery's heroines? Did it not describe the author as well as her characters? Did it not describe me? And was it not perhaps Katie Maurice, whom I imagine as Anne's best friend, alpha and omega. This phrase and these questions were the seeds of my poem.

MY MAUD

by Katie Maurice

Our world wound 'round her finger
And dripped down from her pen…
But long before,
There was a door
Where it all began.
And there in twisty twilight

Where fairies hide and peek,
She'd tiptoe through her loneliness
With twinkling furtive feet.

The room stood at attention!
Ancient portraits pricked their ears,
And lo, her dim reflection
Unlocked a passage clear.
And all things harsh and hard and dark
Dissolved, unwept, away
And we embraced, face to face;
My friend had come to play!

And from the start
I clutched her heart
Close to my lonely breast,
For we were kindred spirits
From that moment through the rest.
Then from that door we'd run and soar
In flights of fancy, free.
I'd say, "Come on!" and we'd be gone
To Spain or Avonlea.

We rode on steeds.
We did great deeds.
We climbed the Alpine Path
And at the top we had to stop
And shake our heads and laugh.
"You did it, dear!" I proudly cried.
"'Cause you were here, my friend!" she sighed.
And with her there, I could have died
Fulfilled, beloved and satisfied.

* * *

But there was more beyond the door
That beckoned my dear friend
And I, confused, rebuffed the news
Our road had reached its bend.
"I will return!" Her promise burned
In tears all down her face.
But I knew then this was the end,
And rushed for her embrace.

"I promise!" she repeated,
Backing through the twilit door.
We hugged a hundred thousand times
And waved a million more.
And in our heart-torn parting
I blew one final kiss:
A blessèd benediction
On our eternal bliss.

* * *

Down through the years she felt it
Draw her heartstrings now and then,
And echoes of that memory
Would flow out of her pen:
I'd come to her in flashes,
Singing through the Hill of Pines,
Unwind a whiff of mayflowers
In a corner of her mind.

And when she brought her longing heart
Back home to Lover's Lane,
My tears would tumble kisses
Through the mists of summer rain.
And there in fern and silver birch
She felt our olden love.
I'd watch her close her starry eyes

And hurl her heart above!
And I would run to catch it!
And hold it to my breast
Releasing radiant rainbows
From the bonds of loneliness.

* * *

Her flights of fancy faded
As the sands of time ran through,
So patiently, I waited
(As kindred spirits do.)
At last her furtive footsteps
Hastened to my dusky door
And I beheld my bosom friend there
Twinkling, as of yore.

"Come in, my friend! No more pretend,
But live! *here* by my side!
We'll knit the twisty twilight
And purl the eventide.
We'll cast our nets for ages
On the glistening sands of time,
And catch those precious hearts
Who haven't grown up to their minds."

I saw the sorrow leave her;
The cares of life release.
The soul of "this stray woman-child"
Came home to perfect peace.

Where once we walked on pages,
We threw the covers wide
To run with wild abandon now,
Forever, side by side.

Dear Maud

KIT PEARSON

Dear Maud,

When I was twelve years old, I discovered an old trunk full of children's books in my grandparents' basement. My grandmother told me they had belonged to my aunt, and that I was welcome to take them home.

I was very lonely then, having just moved from Vancouver to Edmonton and missing my friends so much that I often cried myself to sleep. My only comfort was reading, so these new books were very welcome.

The first book that I read was the one whose cover appealed to me the most: a pale girl standing by a hill fringed with firs, with a slender moon in the rosy sky. The novel was, of course, your *Emily of New Moon*. The first few pages took me to the cover scene, when Emily at twilight experiences "the flash."

That whole book was like "the flash" to me. I was so transported, so completely immersed in Emily's character and world, that I raced through the novel in one day, tearing off some of the page corners and nibbling on them, as was my wont with the books I literally devoured.

Now I must confess to you, Maud, that I never took much to Anne. She *was* amusing and I cared enough about her to keep reading. But she talked so much I skipped her long conversations, and her constant attempts to please adults irritated me.

Emily, however – probably because, unlike poor, abandoned Anne, she began her life with unconditional love – is never anyone but her own confident, spirited self. I *became* her. When Emily hides under the table and hears her relatives discuss her fate, I was desperate with tension, then so relieved when she goes to New Moon. Your gorgeous evocation of that place – so different from Alberta! – made me long to live there too. I wanted to help skim the cream and bring in the cows, to gaze out the window of the magical room Emily is eventually given.

Although I lacked Emily's courage and fierceness, there were two parts of her character with which I did identify. I, too, sometimes experienced my own version of "the flash," especially when outdoors. And I, too, had yearnings to be a writer – but I didn't recognize that until I met Emily.

So you changed my life, Maud! It was as if a light went on inside me. In that pivotal scene when Mr Carpenter is reading aloud Emily's poems, I lingered over each line, trying to decipher why he thought some were good and some not. When Emily says "I *have* to write," I realized that I did too. I closed up the book, rode my bike to the drugstore, and spent my allowance on a blank notebook, which I began with exactly the same words that Emily uses: "I am going to write a diary, that it may be published when I die."

I poured out my loneliness in that diary and began to feel better. I found the two sequels to *Emily of New Moon* in the library and devoured them just as avidly. There you depicted to me what it was to *be* a writer, such as the agony of negative criticism and the desire to put one's own setting on the literary map.

I'm going to be honest with you, Maud: upon re-reading *Emily* as an adult, I do not find it as faultless as I did at age twelve. The middle is far too long and tedious. Some of your sentences are too yucky to bear: the emphasis on Emily's "fine old ancestors," for example, or how she has a "fairy birthright" because of her pointed elfin ears. In fact, there are far too many comments in the book on how Emily *looks*. Dean Priest's rapture with her is especially creepy.

As in all your fiction, I find your sentimentality and happy endings cloying. I wish you had put some of the darkness of your journals into your novels. But I understand that you were writing most of them to sell, and that your audience then was far different than it is now.

You said in your journals that you took more "intense pleasure" in writing Emily than in any of your other books, and that shows. I find far more positive than negative aspects to the novel, and now I see things I didn't notice as a child: your wonderful humour, for example, especially in Emily's letters to her father and in the ironic portrait of Aunt Elizabeth and the other elders; the continual conflict between duty and pleasure; and how painfully lonely Emily is, even though she doesn't know it. I wonder if you realized how much of *your* childhood loneliness you put in her.

In my own writing, I have been astounded to see how much influence over me you have had. Quite literally, in some cases: in *The Sky Is Falling*, Norah, a rebellious young girl, goes to stay with two women, one strict and one not; in *The Whole Truth*, Polly is healed by going to live on a small, beautiful island, where she starts writing letters to her absent father. Like you, I often depict adults in my books as fully as the child characters. Unfortunately, I am also prone to sentimentality and too-neat endings.

I do none of this on purpose! It's simply that Emily is in my blood. She is so much a part of me that some of her comes out in my own writing. Would I be a different writer if I had discovered *Harriet the Spy* as a child, instead of *Emily*? Would I have written anyway if I had read neither book? Perhaps. All I know is that I am eternally grateful that you set me on your "alpine path." So thank you, Maud! Some of Emily is the best part of me – as she was probably the best part of you.

Your protégé,
Kit Pearson

Bibliography

PRIMARY SOURCES

Fiction

Anne of Avonlea. 1909. Toronto: Tundra, 2014.
Anne of Green Gables. 1908. Toronto: Tundra, 2014.
Anne of Ingleside. 1939. Toronto: Tundra, 2018.
Anne of the Island. 1915. Toronto: Tundra, 2014.
Anne of Windy Poplars. 1936. Toronto: Tundra, 2014.
Anne's House of Dreams. 1917. Toronto: Tundra, 2014.
The Blue Castle. 1926. Toronto: Tundra, 2019.
The Blythes Are Quoted. Edited by Benjamin Lefebvre. Toronto: Viking Canada, 2009.
Chronicles of Avonlea. 1912. Toronto: Seal, 1987.
Emily Climbs. 1925. Toronto: Tundra, 2014.
Emily of New Moon. 1923. Toronto: Tundra, 2014.
Emily's Quest. 1927. Toronto: Tundra, 2014.
The Golden Road. 1913. Toronto: Tundra, 2018.
Jane of Lantern Hill. 1937. Toronto: Tundra, 2018.
Magic for Marigold. 1929. Toronto: Seal, 1988.
Mistress Pat. 1935. Toronto: Tundra, 2018.
Pat of Silver Bush. 1933. Toronto: Tundra, 2019.
Rainbow Valley. 1919. Toronto: Tundra, 2014.
Rilla of Ingleside. 1921. Toronto: Tundra, 2014.
The Road to Yesterday. 1974. New York: Bantam, 1993.

The Story Girl. 1911. Toronto: Tundra, 2018.
A Tangled Web. 1931. Toronto: Seal, 1989.

Life-Writing, Letters, and Essays

After Green Gables: L.M. Montgomery's Letters to Ephraim Weber, 1916–1941. Edited by Hildi Froese Tiessen and Paul Gerard Tiessen. Toronto: University of Toronto Press, 2006.
The Alpine Path: The Story of My Career. 1917. Don Mills, ON: Fitzhenry & Whiteside, 1975.
The Complete Journals of L.M. Montgomery: The PEI Years, 1889–1900. Edited by Mary Rubio and Elizabeth Waterston. Toronto: Oxford University Press, 2012.
The Complete Journals of L.M. Montgomery: The PEI Years, 1901–1911. Edited by Mary Rubio and Elizabeth Waterston. Toronto: Oxford University Press, 2013.
My Dear Mr. M: Letters to G.B. MacMillan. Edited by Francis W.P. Bolger and Elizabeth R. Epperly. Toronto: McGraw-Hill Ryerson, 1980.
"The Gay Days of Old." 1919. In Lefebvre, *The L.M. Montgomery Reader*, 1:163–8.
"How I Began to Write." 1911. In Lefebvre, *The L.M. Montgomery Reader*, 1:67–72.
"Letter 6 – 1 September 1930." In Lefebvre, *The L.M. Montgomery Reader*, 1:268–71.
L.M. Montgomery's Complete Journals: The Ontario Years, 1911–1917. Edited by Jen Rubio. Oakville: Rock's Mills Press, 2016.
L.M. Montgomery's Complete Journals: The Ontario Years, 1918–1921. Edited by Jen Rubio. Oakville: Rock's Mills Press, 2017.
L.M. Montgomery's Complete Journals: The Ontario Years, 1922–1925. Edited by Jen Rubio. Oakville: Rock's Mills Press, 2018.
L.M. Montgomery's Complete Journals: The Ontario Years, 1926–1929. Edited by Jen Rubio. Oakville: Rock's Mills Press, 2017.
L.M. Montgomery's Complete Journals: The Ontario Years, 1930–33. Edited by Jen Rubio. Oakville, ON: Rock's Mills Press, 2019.
The Selected Journals of L.M. Montgomery. Volume 4, 1929–1935. Edited by Mary Rubio and Elizabeth Waterston. Toronto: Oxford University Press, 1998.
The Selected Journals of L.M. Montgomery. Volume 5, 1935–1942. Edited by Mary Rubio and Elizabeth Waterston. Toronto: Oxford University Press, 2004.

SECONDARY SOURCES

Abrams, M.H. *A Glossary of Literary Terms*. 7th ed. Boston: Heinle and Heinle, 1999.
Adams, Gillian. "Secrets and Healing Magic in *The Secret Garden*." In *Triumphs of the Spirit in Children's Literature*, edited by Francelia Butler and Richard Rotert, 42–54. Hamden, CT: Library Professional Publications, 1986.
"Ahead by a Century." Songwriters: Gordon Downie, Johnny Fay, Joseph Paul

Langlois, Robert Baker, and Robert Gordon Sinclair. From *Trouble at the Henhouse* by The Tragically Hip. MCA 1996.

Åhmansson, Gabriella. "'Mayflowers Grow in Sweden Too': L.M. Montgomery, Astrid Lindgren, and the Swedish Literary Consciousness." In Rubio, *Harvesting Thistles*, 14–22.

Akamatsu, Yoshiko. "The Continuous Popularity of *Red-haired Anne* in Japan: An Interview with Yoshiko Akamatsu." In Ledwell and Mitchell, *Anne around the World*, 216–27.

Albrecht-Crane, Christa, and Dennis Cutchins. "Introduction: New Beginnings for Adaptation Studies." In *Adaptation Studies: New Approaches*, edited by Christa Albrecht-Crane and Dennis Cutchins, 11–12. Madison, NJ: Fairleigh Dickinson University Press, 2010.

Alger, Horatio. *Ragged Dick; or, Street Life in New York with Boot Blacks*. 1868. New York: Norton Critical Edition, 2008.

A.M.C. "Letter 5 – 27 August 1930." In Lefebvre, *The L.M. Montgomery Reader*, 1:265–6.

"Another Little Girl." *New York Telegram*, 29 September 1929. In Lefebvre, *The L.M. Montgomery Reader*, 3:298–9.

Anuka. "You caught me staring, but I caught you staring back." *Archive of Our Own*, 2017. https://archiveofourown.org/works/11925471/chapters/26952735.

Aquilino, William S. "The Noncustodial Father-Child Relationship from Adolescence into Young Adulthood." *Journal of Marriage and Family* 68, no. 4 (2006): 929–46.

ArcticLava21. "Nature." *Archive of Our Own*, 2017. https://archiveofourown.org/works/11778819.

Ariès, Philippe. *The Hour of Our Death: The Classic History of Western Attitudes Toward Death over the Last One Thousand Years*. 1977. Translated by Helen Weaver. New York: Knopf, 1981.

Atwood, Margaret. "Nobody Ever Did Want Me." *Guardian*, 29 March 2008. https://www.theguardian.com/books/2008/mar/29/fiction.margaretatwood.

– "Reflection Piece – Revisiting Anne." In Gammel and Epperly, *L.M. Montgomery and Canadian Culture*, 222–6.

Auerbach, Nina. "Jane Austen's Dangerous Charm: Feeling as One Ought about Fanny Price." *Persuasions: The Jane Austen Journal* 2 (1980). http://www.jasna.org/persuasions/printed/number2/auerbach.htm.

Austen, Jane. *Mansfield Park*. London: Penguin, 2012.

Bach, George R. "Father-Fantasies and Father-Typing in Father-Separated Children." *Child Development* 17, nos 1–2 (1946): 63–80.

Bacon, Francis. "Of Death." In *Essays, Civil and Moral*. 1597. *The Harvard Classics*. Vol. 3, part 1. Edited by Charles W. Eliot. New York: P.F. Collier & Son, 1909–14; Bartleby.com, 2001. www.bartleby.com/3/1/.

Ballet Jörgen. *Anne of Green Gables: The Ballet*. https://canadasballetjorgen.ca/anne/.

Barrie, J.M. *Margaret Ogilvy*. 1896. London: Hodder and Stoughton, 1924.

– *Peter Pan*. 1911. New York: Puffin Books, 2013.

Beran, Carol L. "Beautiful Girlhood, a Double Life: Lucy Maud Montgomery, Margaret Laurence, and Alice Munro." *American Review of Canadian Studies* 45, no. 2 (October 2015): 148–60.

Berg, Temma F. "*Anne of Green Gables*: A Girl's Reading." *Children's Literature Association Quarterly* 13, no. 3 (Fall 1988): 124–8.

Bergren, Katherine. *The Global Wordsworth: Romanticism Out of Place*. Lewisburg, PA: Bucknell University Press, 2019.

Bernard, Catherine. "Introduction: Trying to Define Literature's Confluences." *Études britanniques contemporaines* 52 (2017): n.p. journals.openeditions.org/ebc.3511.

Bilston, Sarah. *The Awkward Age in Women's Popular Fiction, 1850–1900: Girls and the Transition to Womanhood*. Oxford: Clarendon, 2004.

Birkin, Andrew. *J.M. Barrie and the Lost Boys: The Real Story behind Peter Pan*. 1979. New Haven: Yale University Press, 2005.

Bjerre, Birger, trans. *Grönkullagrannar: Berättelser från Avonlea* [*Chronicles of Avonlea*]. Lund: Gleerups, 1968.

Blackford, Holly, ed. *100 Years of Anne with an 'e': The Centennial Study of* Anne of Green Gables. Calgary: University of Calgary Press, 2009.

– "Introduction: Anne with an 'e': The Enduring Value of *Anne of Green Gables*." In Blackford, *100 Years of Anne with an 'e*,*'* xi–xxxviii.

Blake, Kathleen. "The Sea-Dream: *Peter Pan* and *Treasure Island*." *Children's Literature* 6 (1977): 165–81.

Blewett, Kelly. "An Unfortunate Lily Maid: Transgressive Reading in *Anne of Green Gables*." *The Lion and the Unicorn* 39, no. 3 (2015): 275–93.

Bloom, Harold. *The Anxiety of Influence: A Theory of Poetry*. New York: Oxford University Press, 1973.

Bode, Rita, and Lesley D. Clement, eds. *L.M. Montgomery's Rainbow Valleys: The Ontario Years, 1911–1942*. Montreal: McGill-Queen's University Press, 2015.

Bode, Rita, and Jean Mitchell, eds. *L.M Montgomery and the Matter of Nature(s)*. Montreal: McGill-Queen's University Press, 2018.

Bradford, Clare, and Mavis Reimer. "Introduction: Girls, Texts, Cultures: Cross-disciplinary Dialogues." *Girls, Texts, Cultures*, edited by Clare Bradford and Mavis Reimer, 1–13. Waterloo, ON: Wilfrid Laurier University Press, 2015.

Broad, Katherine R. "The Dandelion in the Spring: Utopia as Romance in Suzanne Collins's *The Hunger Games* Trilogy." In *Contemporary Dystopian Fiction for Young Adults: Brave New Teenagers*, ed. Balaka Basu, Katherine R. Broad, and Carrie Hintz, 117–30. New York: Routledge, 2014.

Brock-Servais, Rhonda, and Matthew Prickett. "From *Bildungsroman* to Romance to Saturday Morning: *Anne of Green Gables* and Sullivan Entertainment's Adaptations." *The Lion and the Unicorn* 34, no. 2 (April 2010): 214–27.

Bronfen, Elisabeth. *Over Her Dead Body: Death, Femininity, and the Aesthetic.* Manchester: Manchester University Press, 1992.

Burnett, Frances Hodgson. *Little Lord Fauntleroy.* 1886. New York: Charles Scribner's Sons, 2016.

– *The Secret Garden.* 1911. New York: Harper Collins, 1987.

Burnett, Vivian. *The Romantick Lady: The Life Story of an Imagination.* New York: Charles Scribner's Sons, 1927.

Burton, Tara Isabella. "In Defense of Fanny Price." *Paris Review* (10 July 2014). https://www.theparisreview.org/blog/2014/07/10/in-defense-of-fanny-price/.

Busse, Kristina, and Karen Hellekson. "Introduction: Work in Progress." In Hellekson and Busse, *Fan Fiction and Fan Communities*, 5–32.

Butler, Judith. *Gender Trouble: Feminism and the Subversion of Identity.* 1990/1999. New York: Taylor and Francis E-library, 2002.

Cadden, Mike. "Voice." In Nel and Paul, *Keywords for Children's Literature*, 225–28.

Camp, Charles Wadsworth. *History of the 305th Field Artillery.* New York: Country Life Press, 1919.

Careless, Virginia A.S. "L.M. Montgomery and Everybody Else: A Look at the Books." In Hudson and Cooper, *Windows and Words*, 143–74.

Carpenter, Humphrey. *Secret Gardens: A Study of the Golden Age of Children's Literature.* London: George Allen & Unwin, 1985.

Cavert, Mary Beth. "'To the Memory of': Leaskdale and Loss in the Great War." In Bode and Clement, *L.M. Montgomery's Rainbow Valleys*, 35–53.

cero_ate. "The Moving Finger Writes, and Having Writ Moves On." *Archive of Our Own*, 2013. https://archiveofourown.org/works/1093740.

Cinnamon, Holly. "About Holly Cinnamon." https://www.hollycinnamon.com/about/.

Clarkson, Adrienne. "Foreword." Gammel and Epperly, *L.M. Montgomery and Canadian Culture*, ix–xii.

Classen, Constance. "Is 'Anne of Green Gables' an American Import?" *Canadian Children's Literature / Littérature canadienne pour la jeunesse* 55 (1989): 42–50.

Clement, Lesley D. "The Empathic Poetic Sensibility: Discerning and Embodying Nature's Secrets." In Bode and Mitchell, *L.M. Montgomery and the Matter of Nature(s)*, 184–97.

– "From 'Uncanny Beauty' to 'Uncanny Disease': Destabilizing Gender through the Deaths of Ruby Gillis and Walter Blythe and Life of Anne Shirley." In Pike and Robinson, *L.M. Montgomery and Gender*, 44–67.

– "Mobilizing the Power of the Unseen: Imagining Self/Imagining Others in L.M. Montgomery's *Anne of Green Gables.*" *Studies in Canadian Literature / Études en littérature canadienne* 36, no. 1 (2011): 51–68.

– "Toronto's Cultural Scene: Tonic or Toxin for a Sagged Soul?" In Bode and Clement, *L.M. Montgomery's Rainbow Valleys*, 238–60.

– "Visual Culture, Storytelling, and Becoming Emily: An Illustrated Essay." *Journal of L.M. Montgomery Studies* (24 June 2020). https://journaloflmmontgomerystudies.ca/vision-forum/becoming-emily-illustrated-essay.

Collins, Carolyn Strom. *Annotated Bibliography of L.M. Montgomery's Stories and Poems*. Charlottetown: L.M. Montgomery Institute, 2016.

Collins, Suzanne. *The Hunger Games*. New York: Scholastic Press, 2018.

"The Concealment of Art." *Toronto World* (1912). In Lefebvre, *The L.M. Montgomery Reader*, 3:132–3.

Coppa, Francesca. *The Fanfiction Reader: Folk Tales for the Digital Age*. Ann Arbor, MI: University of Michigan Press, 2017.

Cunningham, Hugh. *The Invention of Childhood*. London: BBC Books, 2006.

Davidson, Joyce, and Christine Milligan. "Embodying Emotion, Sensing Space: Introducing Emotional Geographies." *Social and Cultural Geography* 5, no. 4 (2004): 523–32.

Dawkins, Jane. *Letters from Pemberley*. Lincoln, NE: Authors Choice Press, 2003.

Dawson, Janis. "Literary Relations: Anne Shirley and Her American Cousins." *Children's Literature in Education: An International Quarterly* 33, no. 1 (March 2002): 29–51.

Death, Sarah. "Pippi Långstrump and Anne of Green Gables: Tribute and Subversion." In *Proceedings of the Tenth Biennial Conference of the British Association of Scandinavian Studies held at University of Surrey 8–11 April 1995*, edited by Gunilla Anderman and Christine Banér, 212–221. Guildford: University of Surrey, 1996.

Demers, Patricia, ed. *From Instruction to Delight: An Anthology of Children's Literature to 1850*. 3rd ed. Toronto: Oxford University Press, 2008.

Derecho, Abigail. "Archontic Literature: A Definition, a History, and Several Theories of Fan Fiction." In Hellekson and Busse, *Fan Fiction and Fan Communities*, 61–78.

Despotopoulou, Anna. "Fanny's Gaze and the Construction of Feminine Space in *Mansfield Park*." *Modern Language Review* 99, no. 3 (2004): 569–83.

Devereux, Cecily. "Writing with a 'Definite Purpose': L.M. Montgomery, Nellie L. McClung, and the Politics of Imperial Motherhood in Fiction for Children." *Canadian Children's Literature / Littérature canadienne pour la jeunesse* 26:3, no. 99 (Fall 2000): 6–22.

Dickens, Charles. *David Copperfield*. 1850. New York: Norton Critical Edition, 1989.

Dickieson, Brenton. "C.S. Lewis's Theory of Sehnsucht as a Tool for Theorizing L.M. Montgomery's Experience of 'The Flash.'" In *The Faithful Imagination: Papers from the 2018 Francis White Ewbank Colloquium on C.S. Lewis and Friends*, edited by Joe Ricke and Ashley Chu, 144–65. Hamden, CT: Winged Lion Press, 2019.

Dickinson, Emily. "We pray – to Heaven –." *Emily Dickinson Archive*. http://www.edickinson.org/editions/1/image_sets/235748.

Dobson, Joanne. "Reclaiming Sentimental Literature." *American Literature* 69, no. 2 (1997): 263–88.

Douglas, Aileen. "Austen's Enclave: Virtue and Modernity." *Romanticism* 5, no. 2 (2010): 147–60.

Douglas, Ann. *The Feminization of American Culture*. New York: Knopf, 1977.

Douglas, Mary. *Purity and Danger: An Analysis of Concepts of Pollution and Taboo*. New York: Routledge & Kegan Paul, 1966.

Douglas-Fairhurst, Robert. *Victorian Afterlives: The Shaping of Influences in Nineteenth-Century Literature*. Oxford: Oxford University Press, 2004.

Doyle, John. "*Anne of Green Gables* Adaptation Is Sublimely Reinvigorated." *Globe and Mail*, 14 March 2017. https://www.theglobeandmail.com/arts/television/john-doyle-anne-of-green-gables-adaptation-is-sublimely-reinvigorated/article34306598/.

Drain, Susan. "'Too Much Love-Making': *Anne of Green Gables* on Television." *The Lion and the Unicorn* 11, no. 2 (1987): 63–72.

Drew, Lorna. "The Emily Connection: Ann Radcliffe, L.M. Montgomery, and 'the Female Gothic.'" *Canadian Children's Literature / Littérature canadienne pour la jeunesse* 21:1, no. 77 (Spring 1995): 19–32.

Driscoll, Catherine. *Girls: Feminine Adolescence in Popular Culture and Cultural Theory*. New York: Columbia University Press, 2002.

Duits, Linda, and Liesbet van Zoonen. "Against Amnesia: 30+ Years of Girls' Studies." *Feminist Media Studies* 9, no. 1 (2009): 111–15.

Dull, Monique. "Kinship and Nation in *Amelia* (1848) and *Anne of Green Gables* (1908)." In *The Rhetoric of Canadian Writing*, edited by Conny Steenman-Marcusse, 161–78. Amsterdam: Rodopi, 2002. Reprinted in *The L.M. Montgomery Reader*. Vol. 2: *A Critical Heritage*, edited by Benjamin Lefebvre, 277–90. Toronto: University of Toronto Press, 2014.

Durrant, Joan E. "Corporal Punishment: A Violation of the Rights of the Child." In *Children's Rights in Canada: A Question of Commitment*, edited by R. Brian Howe and Katherine Covell, 99–125. Waterloo, ON: Wilfrid Laurier University Press, 2007.

DuVernet, Sylvia. *The Meaning of the Men and the Boys in the Anne Books*. Toronto: University of Toronto Press, 1998.

East, Leah, Debra Jackson, and Louise O'Brien. "Disrupted Relationships: Adult Daughters and Father Absence." *Contemporary Nurse* 23, no. 2 (2007): 252–61. https://doi.org/10.5172/conu.2006.23.2.252.

– "Father Absence and Adolescent Development: A Review of the Literature." *Journal of Child Healthcare* 10, no. 4 (2006): 283–95. DOI: 10.1177/1367493506067869.

"Editorial: On Literary Debts." *Canadian Children's Literature / Littérature canadienne pour la jeunesse* 55 (1989): 2–3.
Edström, Vivi. *Astrid Lindgren: A Critical Study*. Translated by Eivor Cormack. Stockholm: Rabén & Sjögren, 2000.
– *Astrid Lindgren och sagans makt* [*Astrid Lindgren and the Power of the Fairy Tale*]. Stockholm: Rabén & Sjögren, 1997.
ElouiseBates. *Weeping May Tarry*. *FanFiction*, 2008–09. https://www.fanfiction.net/s/4402068/.
Epperly, Elizabeth R. *The Fragrance of Sweet-Grass: L.M. Montgomery's Heroines and the Pursuit of Romance*. Toronto: University of Toronto Press, 1992.
– "L.M. Montgomery and the Changing Times." *Acadiensis: Journal of the History of the Atlantic Region* 17, no. 2 (Spring 1988): 177–85.
– "*Magic for Marigold*: Engendering Questions about What Lasts." In Pike and Robinson, *L.M. Montgomery and Gender*, 331–49.
– Preface to the 2014 Edition. *The Fragrance of Sweet-Grass: L.M. Montgomery's Heroines and the Pursuit of Romance*. Toronto: University of Toronto Press, 2014, ix–xlii.
– "Reading Time: L.M. Montgomery and the 'Alembic of Fiction.'" *Journal of L.M. Montgomery Studies* (5 June 2019). https://journaloflmmontgomerystudies.ca/reading/epperly.
Espmark, Kjell. *Dialoger* [*Dialogues*]. Stockholm: Norstedts, 1985.
Fenwick, Julie. "The Silence of the Mermaid: *Lady Oracle* and *Anne of Green Gables*." *Essays on Canadian Writing* 47 (1992): 51–64.
Fight Club, directed by David Fincher. Twentieth Century Fox, 1999.
Fisher, Mrs Edith Frank. "Letter 1 – 12 August 1930." In Lefebvre, *The L.M. Montgomery Reader*, 1:262–4.
Flick, Jane. "Writing Is the Deepest Pleasure I Know: An Interview with Kit Pearson." *Canadian Children's Literature / Littérature canadienne pour la jeunesse* 202:2, no. 74 (1994): 16–29.
Forbush, William Byron. *The Boy Problem*. 1901. 6th ed. Boston: The Pilgrim Press, 1907. https://archive.org/details/boyproblemooforbuoft/page/n6.
Forest, Natalie. "(Re)Locating Montgomery: Prince Edward Island Romance to Southern Ontario Gothic." In Bode and Clement, *L.M. Montgomery's Rainbow Valleys*, 166–83.
Foster, Tara. "'Books! And Cleverness!': Hermione's Wits." In *Hermione Granger Saves the World: Essays on the Feminist Heroine of Hogwarts*, edited by Christopher E. Bell, 110–24. Jefferson, NC: McFarland & Company, 2012.
Fraser, Sara. "Emily of New Moon Gets a Star Turn in Netflix Hit *Russian Doll*: Move Over, Anne: L.M. Montgomery's Emily Is Ready for Her Close-Up." CBC, 10 February 2019. https://www.cbc.ca/news/canada/prince-edward-island/pei-emily-new-moon-lucy-maud-montgomery-netflix-russian-doll-1.5010353.

Frever, Trinna S. "Anne Shirley, Storyteller: Orality and *Anne of Green Gables*." *Studies in Canadian Literature / Études en canadienne littérature* 30, no. 2 (2005): 115–41.

freyafrida. "but i don't know who you are." *Archive of Our Own*, 2013. https://archiveofourown.org/works/1112515.

Friend, David. "Gord Downie's Family Hoping to Organize Public Memorial." City News, 20 October 2017. https://toronto.citynews.ca/2017/10/20/gord-downies-family-hoping-organize-public-memorial/.

Frisk, Adam. "Gord Downie: Anniversary of His Death." Global News, 17 October 2018. https://globalnews.ca/news/4563214/gord-downie-anniversary-of-his-death/.

Frozen. DVD. Directed by Chris Buck and Jennifer Lee. Burbank, CA: Walt Disney Studios Home Entertainment, 2014.

Frozen II. Directed by Chris Buck and Jennifer Lee. 2019. Burbank, CA: Walt Disney Studios Home Entertainment, 2020.

Frye, Northrop. *Anatomy of Criticism*. Princeton, NJ: Princeton University Press, 1957.

– "Conclusion to a *Literary History of Canada*." 1965. Reprinted in *The Bush Garden: Essays on the Canadian Imagination*, by Northrop Frye, 213–51. Toronto: Anansi, 1971.

Fuller, Miriam Rheingold. "Jane of Green Gables: L.M. Montgomery's Reworking of Austen's Legacy." *Persuasions On-Line* 29, no. 1 (2008). http://www.jasna.org/persuasions/on-line/vol29no1/fuller.html?.

Gallagher, Maureen O. "Across Enemy Lines: Gender and Nationalism in Else Ury's and L.M. Montgomery's Great War Novels." In McKenzie and Ledwell, *L.M. Montgomery and War*, 146–64.

Galletly, Sarah. "L.M. Montgomery and Canadian Mass-Market Magazines." *British Journal of Canadian Studies* 28, no. 2 (2015): 145–65.

Gammel, Irene. "The Eros of Childhood and Early Adolescence in Girl Series: L.M. Montgomery's *Emily* Trilogy." In Hudson and Cooper, *Windows and Words*, 97–118.

– "'I Loved Herman Leard Madly': L.M. Montgomery's Confession of Desire." In *The Intimate Life of L.M. Montgomery*, edited by Irene Gammel, 129–53. Toronto: University of Toronto Press, 2005.

– *Looking for Anne: How Lucy Maud Montgomery Dreamed Up a Literary Classic*. Toronto: Key Porter Books, 2008.

– ed. *Making Avonlea: L.M. Montgomery and Popular Culture*. Toronto: University of Toronto Press, 2002.

– "'My Secret Garden': Dis/Pleasure in L.M. Montgomery and F.P. Grove." *English Studies in Canada* 25, no. 1 (March 1999): 39–65.

– "Safe Pleasures for Girls: L.M. Montgomery's Erotic Landscapes. In Gammel, *Making Avonlea*, 114–27.

Gammel, Irene, and Elizabeth Epperly, eds. *L.M. Montgomery and Canadian Culture*. Toronto: University of Toronto Press, 1999.

Garber, Marjorie. "Over the Influence." *Critical Inquiry* 42 (2016): 731–59.

Gatchalian, C.E. "Anne Shirley Was the Best Friend a Queer Brown Boy Could Have." 13 June 2019. https://electricliterature.com/anne-shirley-was-the-best-friend-a-queer-brown-boy-could-have/.

Gates, Charlene E. "Image, Imagination, and Initiation: Teaching as a Rite of Passage in the Novels of L.M. Montgomery and Laura Ingalls Wilder." *Children's Literature in Education: An International Quarterly* 20, no. 3 (September 1989): 165–73.

Gerson, Carole. "The Canon between the Wars: Field-Notes of a Feminist Literary Archaeologist." In *Canadian Canons: Essays in Literary Value*, edited by Robert Lecker, 45–56, 205–08. Toronto: University of Toronto Press, 1991.

– "'Dragged at Anne's Chariot Wheels': L.M. Montgomery and the Sequels to *Anne of Green Gables*." *Papers of the Bibliographical Society of Canada* 35, no. 2: 143–59.

– "L.M. Montgomery and the Conflictedness of a Woman Writer." In *Storm and Dissonance: L.M. Montgomery and Conflict*, edited by Jean Mitchell, 67–80. Newcastle: Cambridge Scholars Publishing, 2008.

Gerzina, Gretchen Holbrook. *Frances Hodgson Burnett: The Unexpected Life of the Author of* The Secret Garden. New Brunswick, NJ: Rutgers University Press, 2004.

Gibson, H.W. *Boyology; or, Boy Analysis*. 1916. New York: Association Press, 1922. https://archive.org/details/boyologyorboyanaoogibsrich/page/n6.

Gilligan, Carol. *In a Different Voice: Psychological Theory and Women's Development*. Cambridge, MA: Harvard University Press, 1982.

Gonick, Marnina. "'Girl Power' and 'Reviving Ophelia': Constituting the Neoliberal Girl Subject." NWSA *Journal* 18, no. 2 (Summer 2006): 1–23.

Graham, Peter W. "Jane Austen and the Labor of Leisure." *Persuasions: The Jane Austen Journal* 32 (2010): 173–83.

Greer, Germaine. *The Beautiful Boy*. New York: Thames & Hudson, 2003.

Greven, David. "Hawthorne and Influence: Reframing Tradition." *Nathaniel Hawthorne Review* 42, no. 1 (Spring 2016): 1–15.

Griswold, Robert L. "The History and Politics of Fatherlessness." In *Lost Fathers: The Politics of Fatherlessness in America*, edited by Cynthia R. Daniels, 11–32. New York: St Martin's Press, 1998.

Grosz, E.A. *Space, Time, and Perversion: Essays on the Politics of Bodies*. New York: Routledge, 1995.

Gubar, Marah. *Artful Dodgers: Reconceiving the Golden Age of Children's Literature*. New York: Oxford University Press, 2009.

– "The Hermeneutics of Recuperation: What a Kinship-Model Approach to Children's Agency Could Do for Children's Literature and Childhood Studies." *Jeunesse: Young People, Texts, Cultures* 8, no. 1 (2016): 291–310.

– "Risky Business: Talking about Children in Children's Literature Criticism." *Children's Literature Association* 38, no. 4 (2013): 450–7.
– "'Where Is the Boy?': The Pleasures of Postponement in the *Anne of Green Gables* Series." *The Lion and the Unicorn* 25, no. 1 (January 2001): 47–69.
Gutierrez, Anna Katrina. "Globalization and Glocalization." In *The Routledge Companion to International Children's Literature*, edited by John Stephens et al., 11–21. London: Routledge, 2018.
Harris, Anita. "Introduction." In Harris and Fine, *All About the Girl*, xvii–xxv.
Harris, Anita, and Michelle Fine, eds. *All About the Girl: Power, Culture, and Identity*. New York: Routledge, 2004.
Hellekson, Karen, and Kristina Busse, eds. *Fan Fiction and Fan Communities in the Age of the Internet: New Essays*. Jefferson, NC: McFarland, 2006.
Henderson, Desirée. *Grief and Genre in American Literature, 1790–1870*. Burlington, VT: Ashgate, 2011.
Hergin, Stina, trans. *Emily* [*Emily of New Moon*]. Lund: Gleerups, 1955.
Hermansson, Casie, and Janet Zepernick. "Introduction: Where Is Adaptation? Why Ask?" In *Where Is Adaptation? Mapping Cultures, Texts, and Contexts*, edited by Casie Hermansson and Janet Zepernick, 1–10. Philadelphia: John Benjamins, 2018.
Hersey, Eleanor. "'It's All Mine': The Modern Woman as Writer in Sullivan's *Anne of Green Gables* Films." In Gammel, *Making Avonlea*, 131–44.
Herzog, James M. "On Father Hunger: The Father's Role in the Modulation of Aggressive Drive and Fantasy." In *Father and Child: Developmental and Clinical Perspectives*, edited by Stanley H. Cath, Alan R. Gurwitt, and John Munder Ross, 163–74. Boston: Little, Brown, 1982.
Hill, Colin. *Modern Realism in English-Canadian Fiction*. Toronto: University of Toronto Press, 2012.
Himes, Amanda. "Fanny Price and the (Dis)comforts of Home." *Persuasions: The Jane Austen Journal* 27 (2005): 253–60.
Holmes, Nancy. "Romantic Novelist as Naturalist: John Foster and the Bird Woman." In Bode and Mitchell, *L.M. Montgomery and the Matter of Nature(s)*, 58–73.
Honeyman, Susan. *Elusive Childhood: Impossible Representations in Modern Fiction*. Columbus: Ohio State University Press, 2005.
Howey, Ann F. "Reading Elaine: Marjorie Richardson's and L.M. Montgomery's Red-Haired Lily Maids." *Children's Literature Association Quarterly* 32, no.2 (Summer 2007): 86–109.
– "'She Look'd Down to Camelot': Anne Shirley, Sullivan, and the Lady of Shalott." In Gammel, *Making Avonlea*, 160–73.
Hudson, Aïda, and Susan-Ann Cooper, eds. *Windows and Words: A Look at Canadian Children's Literature in English*. Ottawa: University of Ottawa Press, 2003.

Hutcheon, Linda. "On the Art of Adaptation." *Daedalus* 133, no. 2 (Spring 2004): 108–11.

Hutcheon, Linda, with Siobhan O'Flynn. *A Theory of Adaptation*. 2nd edition. London: Routledge, 2013.

Hutchisson, James M., and Stephen R. Pastore. "Sinclair Lewis and Theodore Dreiser: New Letters and a Reexamination of Their Relationship." *American Literary Realism* 32, no. 1 (Fall 1999): 69–81.

Ikematsu, Naoko, trans. *Shingetsu Noen no Emiri* [*Emily of New Moon*]. Tokyo: Shinozaki-shorin, 2006.

"In a Small World." *Nottingham Journal*, 4 October 1929. In Lefebvre, *The L.M. Montgomery Reader*, 3:299–300.

Islander, "Letter 2 – 19 August 1930." In Lefebvre, *The L.M. Montgomery Reader*, 1:264–5.

Jensen, Karin, trans. *Anne på Grönkulla* [*Anne of Green Gables*]. Lund: C.W.K. Gleerups, 1909.

– *Vår vän Anne* [*Anne of Avonlea*]. Lund: C.W.K. Gleerups, 1910.

Jiwani, Yasmin, Candis Steenbergen, and Claudia Mitchell. "Introduction: Surveying the Terrain." In *Girlhood: Redefining the Limits*, edited by Yasmin Jiwani, Candis Steenbergen, and Claudia Mitchell, ix–xvii. Montreal: Black Rose Books, 2006.

Jones, Caroline E. "Idylls of Play: L.M. Montgomery's Child-Worlds." In *Children's Play in Literature: Investigating the Strengths and the Subversions of the Playing Child*, edited by Joyce E. Kelly, 105–23. New York: Routledge, 2018.

Kandori, Nobuo, trans. *Emiri* [*Emily*]. 3 vols. Tokyo: Kaisei-sha, 2002.

Kannas, Vappu. "'Emily Equals Childhood and Youth and First Love': Finnish Readers and L.M. Montgomery's *Anne* and *Emily* Books." In *Reading Today*, edited by Heta Pyrhönen and Janna Kantola, 118–31. London: UCL Press, 2018.

Karr, Clarence. "Addicted to Reading: L.M. Montgomery and the Value of Reading." *Canadian Children's Literature / Littérature canadienne pour la jeunesse* 113–14 (Spring-Summer 2004): 17–33.

Kasmer, Lisa. "'That Was Now the Home': Nationalism and Imperialism in *Mansfield Park*." In *Approaches to Teaching Austen's* Mansfield Park, edited by Marcia McClintock Folsom and John Wiltshire, 216–22. New York: Modern Language Association of America, 2014.

Kaze no Shoujo Emiri [*Emily, Girl of Wind*]. NHK and TMS Entertainment, 2007. http://www6.nhk.or.jp/anime/program/detail.html?i=emily.

Kearney, M.C. "Coalescing: The Development of Girls' Studies." NWSA *Journal* 21, no. 1 (2009): 1–28.

Keen, Paul. "'So – So – *Commonplace*': Romancing the Local in *Anne of Green Gables* and *Aurora Leigh*." In Ledwell and Mitchell, *Anne around the World*, 92–105.

Kelly, George A. *A Theory of Personality: The Psychology of Personal Constructs*. 1955. New York: W.W. Norton & Co., 1963.

Keyser, Elizabeth Lennox. "'Quite Contrary': Frances Hodgson Burnett's *The Secret Garden*." *Children's Literature* 11 (1983): 1–13.

Kidd, Kenneth B. *Making American Boys: Boyology and the Feral Tale*. Minneapolis: University of Minnesota Press, 2004.

Kincaid, James R. *Child-Loving: The Erotic Child and Victorian Culture*. New York: Routledge, 1991.

– *Erotic Innocence: The Culture of Child Molesting*. Durham, NC: Duke University Press, 1998.

Kotsopoulos, Aspasia. "Our Avonlea: Imagining Community in an Imaginary Past." In *Pop Can: Popular Culture in Canada*, edited by Lynne Van Luven and Priscilla L. Walton, 98–106. Toronto: Prentice Hall / Allyn and Bacon Canada, 1999.

Kristeva, Julia. *Desire in Language: A Semiotic Approach to Literature and Art*. 1969. Edited by Leon S. Roudiez. Translated by Thomas Gora, Alice Jardine, and Leon S. Roudiez. New York: Columbia University Press, 1980.

Lamarre, Thomas. *The Anime Machine: A Media Theory of Animation*. Minneapolis: University of Minnesota Press, 2009.

"lapse." *Merriam-Webster*. https://www.merriam-webster.com/dictionary/lapse.

Larson, Sarah. "How Not to Adapt 'Anne of Green Gables.'" *The New Yorker*, 11 May 2017. https://www.newyorker.com/culture/sarah-larson/how-not-to-adapt-anne-of-green-gables.

Laurence, Margaret. "Books That Mattered to Me." In *Margaret Laurence: An Appreciation*, edited by Christl Verduyn, 239–49. Peterborough: Broadview Press, 1988.

Lavoie, Chantel. "*Gregor the Overlander* and *A Wrinkle in Time*: Father Lost, Father Found." *Jeunesse: Young People, Texts, Cultures* 7, no. 2 (2015): 65–85.

Lawlor, Allison. "A Dancing Dartmouth Anne of Green Gables: Ballet to Premiere in Halifax." *The Guardian* (Charlottetown), 23 September 2019. https://www.theguardian.pe.ca/lifestyles/regional-lifestyles/a-dancing-dartmouth-anne-of-green-gables-ballet-to-premiere-in-halifax-355419/.

Lawson, Kate. "Adolescence and the Trauma of Maternal Inheritance in L.M. Montgomery's *Emily of New Moon*." *Canadian Children's Literature / Littérature canadienne pour la jeunesse* 25, no. 2 (1999): 21–41.

– "The Alien at Home: Hearing Voices in L.M. Montgomery's *Emily Climbs* and F.W.H. Myers." *Gothic Studies* 4, no. 2 (2002): 155–66.

Ledwell, Jane, and Jean Mitchell, eds. *Anne around the World: L.M. Montgomery and Her Classic*. Montreal: McGill-Queen's University Press, 2013.

Lee, Katja. *Limelight: Canadian Women and the Rise of Celebrity Autobiography*. Waterloo, ON: Wilfrid Laurier University Press, 2020.

Lefebvre, Benjamin. "Afterword." In *The Blythes Are Quoted* by L.M. Montgomery, 511–20. Toronto: Viking Canada, 2009.
– "Editorial: Assessments and Reassessments." *Canadian Children's Literature / Littérature canadienne pour la jeunesse* 113–14 (2004): 6–13.
– ed. *L.M. Montgomery: A Name for Herself: Selected Writings, 1891–1917*. Toronto: University of Toronto Press, 2018.
– "L.M. Montgomery: An Annotated Filmography." *Canadian Children's Literature / Littérature canadienne pour la jeunesse* 99 (Fall 2000): 43–73.
– ed. *The L.M. Montgomery Reader*. Vol. 1: *A Life in Print*. Toronto: University of Toronto Press, 2013.
– ed. *The L.M. Montgomery Reader*. Vol. 3: *A Legacy in Review*. Toronto: University of Toronto Press, 2015.
– "Pigsties and Sunsets: L. M. Montgomery, *A Tangled Web*, and a Modernism of Her Own." *English Studies in Canada*, 31, no. 4 (December 2005): 123–46.
– "Stand by Your Man: Adapting L.M. Montgomery's *Anne of Green Gables*." *Essays on Canadian Writing* 76 (Spring 2002): 149–69.
L'Engle, Madeleine. *The Genesis Trilogy*. Colorado Springs: Waterbrook, 1997.
– "GoFish Questions for the Author." In *The Young Unicorns*, by Madeleine L'Engle, 291–4. New York: Farrar Straus and Giroux, 1968.
– *The Rock That Is Higher: Story as Truth*. Wheaton, IL: Harold Shaw Publishers, 1993.
– *A Severed Wasp*. New York: Noonday Press/Farrar, Straus, and Giroux, 1982.
– *The Small Rain*. New York: Vanguard, 1945.
– *The Summer of the Great-Grandmother*. San Francisco: Harper and Row, 1974.
– *Trailing Clouds of Glory: Spiritual Values in Children's Literature*. Philadelphia: Westminster Press, 1985.
– *Walking on Water: Reflections on Faith and Art*. New York: Farrar, Straus, and Giroux, 1980.
– *A Wrinkle in Time*. New York: Farrar, Straus, and Giroux, 1962.
Lindgren, Astrid. "Anne på Grönkulla och Mannen med stålnävarna" ["Anne of Green Gables and the Man with the Iron Fists"]. *Bokvännen*, no 10 (1956): 244–5.
– *Emil in the Soup Tureen* [*Emil i Lönneberga*, 1963]. Translated by Lilian Seaton. Leicester: Brockhampton Press, 1970.
– *Kajsa Kavat och andra barn* [*Brenda Brave and Other Children*]. Stockholm: Rabén & Sjögren, 1950.
– *Mardie* [*Madicken*, 1960]. Translated by Patricia Crampton. London: Methuen Children's Books, 1979.
– *Mardie to the Rescue* [*Madicken och Junibackens Pims*, 1976]. Translated by Patricia Crampton. London: Methuen Children's Books, 1981.
– *Never Violence!* Translated by Laurie Thompson. Lidingö: Astrid Lindgren Text, 2018.

– *Pippi Goes Aboard* [*Pippi Långstrump går ombord*, 1946]. Translated by Marianne Turner. London: Oxford University Press, 1971.
– *Pippi Longstocking*. Translated by Edna Hurup. London: Oxford University Press, 1954.
– *Pippi Långstrump* [*Pippi Longstocking*, 1950]. Stockholm: Rabén & Sjögren, 1945.
– *Samuel August från Sevedstorp och Hanna i Hult* [*Samuel August from Sevedstorp and Hanna in Hult*]. Stockholm: Rabén & Sjögren, 1975.
– *Stora boken om Emil i Lönneberga* [*The Big Book about Emil in Lönneberga*]. Stockholm: Rabén & Sjögren, 1989. [Includes *Emil i Lönneberga*, *Nya hyss av Emil i Lönneberga*, and *Än lever Emil i Lönneberga.*]
– *Ur-Pippi* [*Original Pippi*]. Stockholm: Rabén & Sjögren, 2007.
Litster, Jennifer H. "'The Golden Road of Youth': L.M. Montgomery and British Children's Books." *Canadian Children's Literature / Littérature canadienne pour la jeunesse* 113–14 (2004): 56–72.
– "Time Travels and Tangles." Review of *Maud's House of Dreams: The Life of Lucy Maud Montgomery*, by Janet Lunn. *Canadian Children's Literature / Littérature canadienne pour la jeunesse* 109–10 (2003): 117–22.
Little, Jean. "But What about Jane?" *Canadian Children's Literature / Littérature canadienne pour la jeunesse* 1, no. 3 (1975): 71–81.
Lunden, Rolf. "Theodore Dreiser and the Nobel Prize." *American Literature* 50, no.2 (May 1978): 216–29.
Lundqvist, Ulla. "Always on the Child's Side." *Barnboken: Journal of Children's Literature Research*, no. 1–2 (2007): 6–14.
– *Århundradets barn: Fenomenet Pippi Långstrump och dess förutsättningar* [*The Child of the Century: The Phenomenon of Pippi Longstocking, and Its Premises*]. Stockholm: Rabén & Sjögren, 1979.
Lunn, Janet. *Maud's House of Dreams: The Life of Lucy Maud Montgomery*. Toronto: Doubleday Canada, 2002.
MacLulich, T.D. "L.M. Montgomery and the Literary Heroine: Jo, Rebecca, Anne, and Emily." *Canadian Children's Literature / Littérature canadienne pour la jeunesse* 37 (1985): 5–17.
– "L.M. Montgomery's Portraits of the Artist: Realism, Idealism, and the Domestic Imagination." *English Studies in Canada* 11, no. 4 (December 1985): 459–73. Reprinted in Reimer, *Such a Simple Little Tale*, 83–100.
Maher, Susan Naramore. "Recasting Crusoe: Frederick Marryat, R.M. Ballantyne and the Nineteenth-Century Robinsonade." *Children's Literature Association Quarterly* 13, no. 4 (1988): 169–75.
Marcus, Leonard S. *Listening for Madeleine: A Portrait of Madeleine L'Engle in Many Voices*. New York: Farrar, Straus, and Giroux, 2012.
MarnaNightingale. "The Pen and the Sword." *Archive of Our Own*, 2007. https://archiveofourown.org/works/1632692.

Marquis, Albert Nelson, ed. "Alden, Isabella Macdonald." *Who's Who in America: A Biographical Dictionary of Notable Living Men and Women of the United States, 1908–1909*. Chicago: A.N. Marquis and Co., 1908.

Mayes-Elma, Ruthann. *Females and Harry Potter: Not All That Empowering*. Oxford: Roman and Littlefield Publishing, 2006.

McCutcheon, Mark A. "'To Skip or Not to Skip': Shakespearean Romanticism and Curricular Genderpellation in Canadian Popular Culture." *Borrowers and Lenders: The Journal of Shakespeare and Appropriation* 3, no. 1 (Fall-Winter 2007): n.p.

McGillivray, Anne, and Joan E. Durrant, "Child Corporal Punishment: Violence, Law, and Rights." In *Cruel but Not Unusual: Violence in Canadian Families*, edited by Ramona Alaggia and Cathy Vine, 177–200. Waterloo, ON: Wilfrid Laurier University Press, 2006.

McGrath, Robin. "Alice of New Moon: The Influence of Lewis Carroll on L.M. Montgomery's Emily Bird [*sic*] Starr." *Canadian Children's Literature / Littérature canadienne pour la jeunesse* 65 (1992): 62–7.

McIntosh, Emma "Canadians Unhappy after Netflix Retouches 'Anne' Poster for American Audience." *Toronto Star*, 7 April 2017. https://www.thestar.com/entertainment/2017/04/07/canadians-unhappy-after-netflix-retouches-anne-poster-for-american-audience.html.

McKenzie, Andrea, and Jane Ledwell. "Introduction." In McKenzie and Ledwell, *L.M. Montgomery and War*, 3–37.

– eds. *L.M. Montgomery and War*. Montreal: McGill-Queen's University Press, 2017.

McMaster, Juliet. "Taking Control: Hair Red, Black, Gold, and Nut-Brown." In Gammel, *Making Avonlea*, 58–71.

McMaster, Lindsey. "The 'Murray Look': Trauma as Family Legacy in L.M. Montgomery's *Emily of New Moon* Trilogy." *Canadian Children's Literature / Littérature canadienne pour la jeunesse* 34, no. 2 (2008): 50–74.

Mercier, Cathryn M. "Realism." In Nel and Paul, *Keywords for Children's Literature*, 198–201.

Meyer, Susan. "Writing after Anne: L.M. Montgomery's Influence on Canadian Children's Literature." In Ledwell and Mitchell, *Anne around the World*, 262–80.

Miller, Kathleen Ann. "Haunted Heroines: The Gothic Imagination and the Female *Bildungsroman* of Jane Austen, Charlotte Brontë, and L.M. Montgomery." *The Lion and the Unicorn* 34, no. 2 (2010): 125–47.

– "Jane Eyre's Heir: An Intertextual (Re)reading of Charlotte Brontë and L.M. Montgomery's *Emily* Trilogy." *Hotel* 4 (2005): 88–96.

Mintz, Steven. *Huck's Raft: A History of American Childhood*. Cambridge, MA: Harvard University Press, 2004.

Morin, Shauna. "The Heroines Who Inspire Me to Keep the Faith." *Interfaith Youth Core*. Interfaith America, 21 January 2021. https://ifyc.org/article/heroines-who-inspire-me-keep-faith.

Mott, Frank Luther. *A History of American Magazines*. Vol. 3: *1865–1885*. Cambridge, MA: Harvard University Press, 1957.

Mucignat, Rosa. "Theatrical Revolutions and Domestic Reforms: Space and Ideology in Goethe's *Wilhelm Meisters Lehrjahre* and Austen's *Mansfield Park*." *Comparative Critical Studies* 7, no. 1 (2010): 21–40.

Munro, Alice. "Afterword" to *Emily of New Moon* by L.M. Montgomery, 357–61. New Canadian Library series. Toronto: McClelland and Stewart, 1989.

Muraoka, Hanako, trans. *Emiri no Motomerumono* [*Emily's Quest*]. 1969. Tokyo: Shincho-sha, 2008.

– *Emiri wa Noboru* [*Emily Climbs*]. 1967. Tokyo: Shincho-sha, 2007.

– *Kawaii Emiri* [*Emily of New Moon*]. 1964. Tokyo: Shincho-sha, 2008.

– *Kaze no nakano Emiri* [*Emily in the Wind*] and *Ame ni Utau Emiri* [*Emily Who Reads to the Rain*]. Tokyo: Akimoto-shobo, 1959.

Napier, Susan J. *Anime from* Akira *to* Howl's Moving Castle. New York: Palgrave-Macmillan, 2005.

Narbonne, André. "Carlylean Sentiment and the Platonic Triad in *Anne of Green Gables*." *American Review of Canadian Studies* 44, no. 4 (Dec. 2014): 433–47.

– "Lucy Maud Montgomery and Stephen Leacock's Shared Canadian Figure." *Explicator* 72, no. 2 (April-June 2014): 84–7.

Nel, Philip, and Lissa Paul, eds. *Keywords for Children's Literature*. New York: New York University Press, 2011.

Nielsen, Linda. "Young Adult Daughters' Relationships with Their Fathers: Review of Recent Research." *Marriage and Family Review* 50 (2014): 360–72.

Nodelman, Perry. "The Case of Children's Fiction: or The Impossibility of Jacqueline Rose." *Children's Literature Association Quarterly* 10, no. 3 (Fall 1985): 98–100.

– *The Hidden Adult: Defining Children's Literature*. Baltimore: The Johns Hopkins University Press, 2008.

Olsson, Lotta. "Var finns säkerhetsbältena, vuxennärvaron, allergitesten och kostcirkeln?" ["Where Are the Safety Belts, Adults' Presence, Allergy Tests, and Eating Advice?"]. In *Samfundet de Nio. Litterär kalender 2006*, edited by Gunnar Harding. Stockholm: Norstedts, 2006.

O'Neill, Heather. Tweet. 8 March 2018. https://twitter.com/lethal_heroine/status/971771772747091969?lang=en.

Oppel, Kenneth. *Inkling*. Illustrated by Sydney Smith. Toronto: HarperCollins, 2018.

– Review of *Maud's House of Dreams*, by Janet Lunn. *Quill & Quire*, October 2002. https://quillandquire.com/review/maud-s-house-of-dreams/.

An Outsider. "Letter 3 – 22 August 1930." In Lefebvre, *The L.M. Montgomery Reader*, 1:265–6.

Ouzounian, Richard. "Aretha Franklin Says She Is Feeling Super: The Queen of Soul Loves Canada's Sweetheart." *Toronto Star*, 18 April 2014. https://www.thestar.com/entertainment/stage/2014/04/18/aretha_franklin_says_shes_feeling_super.html.

Pacey, Desmond. *Creative Writing in Canada: A Short History of English-Canadian Literature*. 1952. Revised edition. Toronto: Ryerson, 1961.

Page, Aubrey. "'Anne with an E': How 'Breaking Bad's' Moira Walley-Beckett Is Updating Anne for 2017." Collider.com, 12 May 2017. http://collider.com/anne-with-an-e-moira walley-beckett-interview/.

Parrish, Sonya Lawson. "Shadows and Houses: Politics and Place in *Our Nig* and *Mansfield Park*." *MP Journal* 2, no. 4 (2009): 38–48.

Paskin, Willa. "*Anne of Green Gables* Gets the *Breaking Bad* Treatment." *Sydney Morning Herald*, 12 May 2017. https://www.smh.com.au/lifestyle/why-a-breaking-bad-writerhas-dared-to-darken-childhood-classic-green-gables-20170511-gw2 8sx.html.

Pearce, Sharyn. "Constructing a 'New Girl': Gender and National Identity in *Anne of Green Gables* and *Seven Little Australians*." In Blackford, *100 Years of Anne with an 'e,'* 229–45.

Penny, Louise. Newsletter, May 2018. https://mailchi.mp/louisepenny/2018may?e=792d907659.

Phelps, Elizabeth Stuart. *Beyond the Gates*. Boston: Houghton Mifflin Company, 1883.

– *The Gates Ajar*. 1868. Boston: Houghton Mifflin Company, 1910.

– *The Gates Between*. Boston: Houghton Mifflin Company, 1887.

Pike, E. Holly. "The Heroine Who Writes and Her Creator." In Rubio, *Harvesting Thistles*, 50–7.

– "(Re)Producing Canadian Literature: L.M. Montgomery's Emily Novels." In Gammel and Epperly, *L.M. Montgomery and Canadian Culture*, 64–76.

Pike, E. Holly, and Laura M. Robinson, eds. *L.M. Montgomery and Gender*. Montreal: McGill-Queen's University Press, 2021.

Plotz, Judith. *Romanticism and the Vocation of Childhood*. New York: Palgrave, 2001.

Poe, K.L. "Who's Got the Power? Montgomery, Sullivan, and the Unsuspecting Viewer." In Gammel, *Making Avonlea*, 145–59.

Posey, Catherine. "Ethereal Etchings: Connecting with the Natural World in Lucy Maud Montgomery's *Anne of Green Gables* (1908), *Emily of New Moon* (1923), and *Magic for Marigold* (1929)." In *Knowing Their Place? Identity and Space in Children's Literature*, edited by Terri Doughty and Dawn Thompson, 95–108. Newcastle upon Tyne, UK: Cambridge Scholars Publishing, 2011.

Proehl, Kristen. "'love of kindred spirits': Queer Friendship and the Evangelical Bildungsroman from *The Wide, Wide World* to *Anne of Green Gables*." In *Saving the World: Girlhood and Evangelicalism in Nineteenth-Century Literature*, edited by Allison Giffen and Robin L. Cadwallader, 171–87. New York: Routledge, 2018.

Radin, Sara. "The First Youth Poet Laureate, Amanda Gorman Wants You to Know Her Work Goes Beyond Words." *Observer*, New York, 9 April 2019. https://

observer.com/2019/04/amanda-gorman-youth-poet-laureate-future-projects-women-in-the-world-summit/.

"Realism." *The Cambridge Guide to Literature in English.* 2nd ed. Edited by Ian Ousby. Cambridge: Cambridge University Press, 2000.

Reimer, Mavis. "Introduction: Discourses of Home in Canadian Children's Literature." In *Home Words: Discourses of Children's Literature in Canada*, edited by Mavis Reimer, xi–xx. Waterloo, ON: Wilfrid Laurier University Press, 2008.

– ed. *Such a Simple Little Tale: Critical Responses to L.M. Montgomery's* Anne of Green Gables. Metuchen, NJ: Scarecrow Press, 1992.

Reimer, Mavis, Nyala Ali, Deanna England, and Melanie Dennis Unrau. "Introduction: The Compulsion to Repeat." In *Seriality and Texts for Young People: The Compulsion to Repeat*, edited by Mavis Reimer, Nyala Ali, Deanna England, and Melanie Dennis Unrau, 1–33. London: Palgrave Macmillan, 2014.

Rémi, Cornelia. "Interactions with Poetry: Metapoetic Games with Anne in Astrid Lindgren's *Madicken*." In Blackford, *100 Years of Anne with an 'e,'* 165–90.

Renan, Ernest. *The Apostles.* 1866. Translated and edited by Joseph Henry Allen. Boston: Little, Brown, and Company, 1903. https://www.scribd.com/document/98153883/The-Apostles-Ernest-Renan-Allen-Translation-1903.

Rent, Suzanne. "Peppard Tells Stories of Canadian Women in Song." *Saltwire Network*, 12 November 2018. https://www.saltwire.com/news/local/peppard-tells-stories-of-canadian-women-in-song-258693/?location=nova-scotia.

Richardson, Alan. "Reluctant Lords and Lame Princes: Engendering the Male Child in Nineteenth-Century Juvenile Fiction." *Children's Literature* 21 (1993): 3–19.

Ricou, Laurie. *Everyday Magic: Child Languages in Canadian Literature.* Vancouver: University of British Columbia Press, 1987.

Robinson, Jenny. "How Katy Lied: Pictures of Joy and Pain in *What Katy Did* and Other American Girls' Stories." In *The Radiant Hour: Versions of Youth in American Culture*, edited by Neil Campbell, 88–114. Exeter: University of Exeter Press, 2000.

Robinson, Joanna. "*Anne of Green Gables*: Netflix's Bleak Adaptation Gets It All So Terribly Wrong." *Vanity Fair*, 12 May 2017. https://www.vanityfair.com/hollywood/2017/05/anne-of-green-gables-netflix-review-anne-with-an-e-bleak-sad-wrong.

Robinson, Laura M. "Anne and Her Ancestors: Self-Reflexivity from Yonge to Alcott to Montgomery." In Blackford, *100 Years of Anne with an 'e,'* 125–42.

– "'Bosom Friends': Lesbian Desire and the Anne Books," *Canadian Literature* 180 (Spring 2004): 12–28.

– "Remodeling *An Old-Fashioned Girl*: Troubling Girlhood in Ann-Marie MacDonald's *Fall on Your Knees*." *Canadian Literature* 186 (Autumn 2005): 30–45.

Rodriguez, Amanda. "*Frozen*: Disney's First Foray into Feminism." *The Bitch Flicks Website*. 2 December 2013. http://www.btchflcks.com/2013/12/frozen-disneys-first-foray-into-feminism.html#.XU7lhDHsZfx.

Rose, Jacqueline. *The Case of Peter Pan; or, The Impossibility of Children's Fiction*. London: Macmillan, 1984.

Ross, Catherine Sheldrick. "Calling Back the Ghost of the Old-Time Heroine: Duncan, Montgomery, Atwood, Laurence, and Munro." *Studies in Canadian Literature* 4, no. 1 (1979): 43–58.

– "Readers Reading L.M. Montgomery." In Rubio, *Harvesting Thistles*, 23–35.

Ross, Catherine Sheldrick, and Åsa Warnqvist. "Reading L.M. Montgomery: What Adult Swedish and Canadian Readers Told Us." *Journal of L.M. Montgomery Studies* (13 May 2020). https://journaloflmmontgomerystudies.ca/reading/ross-warnqvist.

Ross, Rita. "Cultural Heroines and Canadian Imaginaries: Evangeline and Anne." In *Contemporary Canadian Fiction*, edited by Carol L. Beran, 51–70. Toronto: Salem-Grey House, 2014.

Rowling, J.K. *Harry Potter and the Goblet of Fire*. London: Pottermore Publishing, 2015.

– *Harry Potter and the Prisoner of Azkaban*. London: Pottermore Publishing, 2015.

Roy, Wendy. "Home as Middle Ground in Adaptations of *Anne of Green Gables* and *Jalna*." *International Journal of Canadian Studies / Revue internationale d'etudes canadiennes* 48 (2014): 9–31.

– *The Next Instalment: Serials, Sequels, and Adaptations of Nellie L. McClung, L.M. Montgomery, and Mazo de la Roche*. Waterloo, ON: Wilfrid Laurier University Press, 2019.

Rubio, Mary. "*Anne of Green Gables*: The Architect of Adolescence." In Reimer, *Such a Simple Little Tale*, 65–82.

– ed. *Harvesting Thistles: The Textual Garden of L.M. Montgomery*. Guelph: Canadian Children's Press, 1994.

– *Lucy Maud Montgomery: The Gift of Wings*. Toronto: Doubleday, 2008.

– "Satire, Realism, and Imagination in *Anne of Green Gables*." *Canadian Children's Literature / Littérature canadienne pour la jeunesse* 1, no. 3 (1975): 27–36.

Rubio, Mary, and Elizabeth Waterston. "Introduction." In *The Selected Journals of L.M. Montgomery*.Vol. 1: *1889–1910*. Toronto: Oxford University Press, 1985.

– "Introduction." In *The Complete Journals of L.M Montgomery*. Vol. 1: *The PEI Years, 1889–1900*, edited by Mary Rubio and Elizabeth Waterston, ix–xi. Toronto: Oxford University Press, 2012.

ruby gillis. *Cecilia of Red Apple Farm*. *FanFiction*, 2004–09. https://www.fanfiction.net/s/2026830/.

Rudd, David. *Reading the Child in Children's Literature*. Basingstoke: Palgrave Macmillan, 2013.

Rudloff, Maja. "(Post)Feminist Paradoxes: The Sensibilities of Gender Representation in Disney's *Frozen*." *Outskirts: Feminisms along the Edge* 35 (November 2016): 1–20.

Russell, Ruth Weber, D.W. Russell, and Rea Wilmshurst. "Introduction." In *Lucy Maud Montgomery: A Preliminary Bibliography*, xi–xix. Waterloo, ON: University of Waterloo Library, 1986.

Rutherford, Mildred Lewis, ed. "Isabella McDonald Alden." In *American Authors: A Hand-book of American Literature from Early Colonial to Living Writers*. Atlanta, GA: Franklin Printing and Publishing Company, 1894.

Sabatini, Sandra. *Making Babies: Infants in Canadian Fiction*. Waterloo, ON: Wilfrid Laurier University Press, 2003.

Saito, Kenji, Hideaki Miyamoto, and Harume Kosaka. Three-person talk on website *Emiri no Sekai* [*The World of Emily*]. http://www.vap.co.jp/emily/commentary.html.

Sánchez-Eppler, Karen. "Childhood." In Nel and Paul, *Keywords for Children's Literature*, 35–41.

Sandilands, Catriona. "Fire, Fantasy, and Futurity: Queer Ecology Visits Silver Bush." In Bode and Mitchell, *L.M. Montgomery and the Matter of Nature(s)*, 27–41.

Sardella-Ayres, Dawn. "Under the Umbrella: The Author-Heroine's Love Triangle." *Canadian Children's Literature / Littérature canadienne pour la jeunesse* 105–6 (Spring-Summer 2002): 100–13.

Scharnhorst, Gary. "Demythologizing Alger." In *Ragged Dick; or, Street Life in New York with Boot Blacks: Authoritative Text, Contexts, Criticism*, edited by Hildegard Hoeller, 182–98. New York: Norton Critical Edition, 2008.

Schneider, M. Lucy. "The Little White Attic and the East Room: Their Function in *Mansfield Park*." *Modern Philology* 63, no. 3 (1966): 227–35.

Schneller, Johanna. "*Breaking Bad* Writer Brings 'Dark Sensibility' to *Anne of Green Gables*." *Globe and Mail*, 17 March 2017. https://www.theglobeandmail.com/arts/television/breaking-bad-writer-brings-dark-sensibility-to-anne-of-green-gables/article34336503/.

Scylla. "Rilla Blythe's Wedding: A Not Entirely Comprehensive Account." *Archive of Our Own*, 2009. https://archiveofourown.org/works/32919.

Seelye, John D. *Jane Eyre's American Daughters: From* The Wide, Wide World *to* Anne of Green Gables*: A Study of Marginalized Maidens and What They Mean*. Newark: Delaware University Press, 2005.

Sewell, Elizabeth. *The Field of Nonsense*. London: Chatto and Windus, 1952.

Seymour, Jessica. "Writing across Platforms: Adapting Classics through Social Media." In *Minding the Gap: Writing across Thresholds*, edited by Thom Conroy and Gail Pittaway, 105–15. Cambridge: Cambridge Scholars Publishing, 2015.

Sheckels, Theodore F. "Anne in Hollywood: The Americanization of a Canadian Icon." In Gammel and Epperly, *L.M. Montgomery and Canadian Culture*, 183–91.

– *The Island Motif in the Fiction of L.M. Montgomery, Margaret Laurence, Margaret Atwood, and Other Canadian Women Novelists*. New York: Peter Lang, 2003.

"Simple Story, but Fine Character Drawing." *The Pioneer*, 23 March 1930. In Lefebvre, *The L.M. Montgomery Reader*, 3:305.

Slater, Katharine. "'The Other Was Whole': *Anne of Green Gables*, Trauma and Mirroring." *The Lion and the Unicorn* 34, no. 2 (April 2010): 167–87.

Söderberg, Eva. "Sprakfålar och musor. Om Astrid Lindgrens förhållande till några flickboksklassiker" ["Wild Girls and Muses: On Astrid Lindgren's Relationship to Some Girls' Books Classics"]. In *Makt och vanmakt: Texter från ett genusteoretiskt seminarium*, edited by Ingeborg Nordin Hennel, 115–45. Härnösand: Mitthögskolan, Institutionen för kultur och humaniora, 1998.

Soja, Edward W. *Postmodern Geographies: The Reassertion of Space in Critical Social Theory*. London: Verso, 1989.

Sportsnet Staff. "Watch Maple Leafs Honour Gord Downie in Pre-Game Tribute." Sportsnet.ca, 18 October 2017. https://www.sportsnet.ca/hockey/nhl/watch-maple-leafs-honour-gord-downie-pre-game-tribute/.

Steffler, Margaret. "'Being a Christian' and a Presbyterian in Leaskdale." In Bode and Clement, *L.M. Montgomery's Rainbow Valleys*, 54–73.

– "Brian O'Connal and Emily Byrd Starr: The Inheritors of Wordsworth's 'Gentle Breeze.'" In Hudson and Cooper, *Windows and Words*, 87–96.

Stewart, Susan. *Nonsense: Aspects of Intertextuality in Folklore and Literature*, 1980. Baltimore, MD: Johns Hopkins University Press, 1989.

St Félix, Doreen. "The Rise and Rise of Amanda Gorman." *Vogue*, May 2021. https://www.vogue.com/article/amanda-gorman-cover-may-2021.

Stoneley, Peter. *Consumerism and American Girls' Literature, 1860–1940*. Cambridge: Cambridge University Press, 2003.

"Strange to Modern Girls." *Auckland Star*, 25 January 1930. In Lefebvre, *The L.M. Montgomery Reader*, 3:305.

Strömstedt, Margareta. *Astrid Lindgren: En levnadsteckning* [*Astrid Lindgren: A Life*]. 4th ed. Stockholm: Pan, 2003.

"Studies in Canadian Village Life." *The Scotsman* (21 October 1909). In Lefebvre, *The L.M. Montgomery Reader*, 3:77.

"Suffused with Whimsicality." *Montreal Daily Star*, 26 October 1929. In Lefebvre, *The L.M. Montgomery Reader*, 3:302–3.

Sullivan, Kevin, director, producer, writer. *Anne of Green Gables*. Sullivan Entertainment Presents, 2000.

Sutherland, Kate. "Advocating for Authors and Battling Critics in Toronto: Montgomery and the Canadian Authors Association." In Bode and Clement, *L.M. Montgomery's Rainbow Valleys*, 223–37.

Suyama, Kei. "*Maboroshi no Nagakutsushita* no *Pippi* kara kangaetakoto" ["What I Learned from *The Pippi Longstocking Anime that Never Came to Be*"]. *Nippon Jido Bungaku* 62, no. 5 (September-October 2016): 60–3.

Takahata, Isao, Hayao Miyazaki, and Yoichi Kotabe. *Maboroshi no Nagakutsushita no Pippi* [*The Pippi Longstocking Anime That Never Came to Be*]. Tokyo: Iwanami-shoten 2014.

Tausky, Thomas E. "L.M. Montgomery and 'The Alpine Path, So Hard, So Steep.'" *Canadian Children's Literature / Littérature canadienne pour la jeunesse* 30 (1983): 5–20.

Thacker, Andrew. "The Idea of a Critical Literary Geography." *New Formations* 57 (2005–06): 56–73.

Thomas, Bronwen. "What Is Fanfiction and Why Are People Saying Such Nice Things about It?" *Storyworlds: A Journal of Narrative Studies* 3 (2011): 1–24.

Thomas, Clara. "Anne Shirley's American Cousin: *The Girl of the Limberlost.*" In Rubio, *Harvesting Thistles*, 58–63.

Toner, Christopher. "'With What Intense Desire She Wants Her Home': Jane Austen on Home as Telos." *Persuasions: The Jane Austen Journal On-Line* 36, no. 1 (2015). http://www.jasna.org/publications/persuasions-online/vol36no1/toner/.

Tosenberger, Catherine. "Mature Poets Steal: Children's Literature and the Unpublishability of Fanfiction." *Children's Literature Association Quarterly* 39, no. 1 (2014): 4–27.

Trites, Roberta Seelinger. *Disturbing the Universe: Power and Repression in Adolescent Literature*. Iowa City: University of Iowa Press, 2000.

Tsugata, Nobuyuki. *Animeshon-gaku Nyumon* [*An Introduction to Animation Study*]. Tokyo: Heibon-sha, 2005.

– *Nippon no Anime wa Naniga Sugoi no ka* [*What Is Cool in Japanese Animation?*]. Tokyo: Shoden-sha, 2014.

Tunc, Tanfer Emin. "Teaching *Anne* and *Antonia* in Turkey: Feminist Girlhood in L.M. Montgomery's *Anne of Green Gables* and Willa Cather's *My Antonia.*" In Ledwell and Mitchell, *Anne around the World*, 200–15.

Twain, Mark. *The Adventures of Huckleberry Finn*. 1884. New York: Norton Critical Edition, 1977.

"Unlucky in Love." *Murdoch Mysteries* (season 9, episode 12). CBC. CBLT, Toronto. 1 February 2016. https://www.dailymotion.com/video/x6cvh2m.

Urquhart, Jane. Afterword to *Emily Climbs* by L.M. Montgomery, 330–4. New Canadian Library series. Toronto: McClelland and Stewart, 1989.

– *L.M. Montgomery*. Extraordinary Canadians series. Toronto: Penguin Canada, 2009.

van Dienderen, An, and Didier Volckaert. *Dare ga Nero to Patorassyu o Korosunoka?* [*Who Kills Nero and Patrasche?*]. Translated by Kaori Shiozaki. Tokyo: Iwanami-shoten, 2015.

verity. "Rilla of Toronto." *Archive of Our Own*, 2011. https://archiveofourown.org/works/302886.

– "Work in Progress." *Archive of Our Own*, 2012. https://archiveofourown.org/works/601499.

Voiklis, Charlotte Jones, and Lena Roy. *Becoming Madeleine*. New York: Farrar, Straus, and Giroux, 2018.

Walley-Beckett, Moira, screenwriter and producer. *Anne/Anne with an "E."* Season One. CBC Television/Netflix. Pelican Ballet and Northwood Entertainment, 2017.

Ward, Janie Victoria, and Beth Cooper Benjamin. "Women, Girls, and the Unfinished Work of Connection: A Critical Review of American Girls' Studies." In Harris and Fine, *All about the* Girl, 3–14.

Warnqvist, Åsa. "'I Experienced a Light that Became a Part of Me': Reading *Anne of Green Gables* in Sweden." In Ledwell and Mitchell, *Anne around the World*, 228–42.

– Flickan som läsare: Exemplet *Anne på Grönkulla*" ["The Girl as Reader: The Case of *Anne of Green Gables*"]. In *Flicktion: Perspektiv på flickan i fiktionen* [*Flicktion: Perspectives on the Girl in Fiction*], edited by Eva Söderberg, Mia Österlund, and Bodil Fomark, 29–41. Malmö: Universus Academic Press, 2013.

– "Så hittade Astrid Lindgren sin illbatting" ["That's How Astrid Lindgren Found Her Unruly Child"]. Under strecket, *Svenska Dagbladet*, 25 May 2013. n.p.

– "'Under körsbärsträdet sitter Ann': Dialogen med L.M. Montgomery i Astrid Lindgrens verk" ["'Anne Is Sitting under the Cherry Tree.' A Dialogue with L.M. Montgomery in Astrid Lindgren's Work"]. In *Nya läsningar av Astrid Lindgren*, edited by Helene Ehriander and Martin Hellström, 103–21. Stockholm: Liber, 2015.

– "Villa Villekulla ett omstörtat Grönkulla" ["Villekulla Cottage a Subverted Green Gables"]. Under strecket, *Svenska Dagbladet*, 22 December 2008. n.p.

Waterston, Elizabeth. "Leaskdale: L.M. Montgomery's Rainbow Valley." In Bode and Clement, *L.M. Montgomery's Rainbow Valleys*, 21–32.

– "Lucy Maud Montgomery." In *The Clear Spirit: Twenty Canadian Women and Their Times*, edited by Mary Quayle Innis, 189–220. Toronto: University of Toronto Press, 1966.

– *Magic Island: The Fictions of L.M. Montgomery*. Toronto: Oxford University Press, 2008.

– "Marigold and the Magic of Memory." In Rubio, *Harvesting Thistles*, 155–66.

– *Rapt in Plaid: Canadian Literature and Scottish Tradition*. Toronto: University of Toronto Press, 2001.

Wendell, Susan. *The Rejected Body: Feminist Philosophical Reflections on Disability*. New York: Routledge, 1996.

Whitaker, Muriel A. "Missing Fathers: A Development Motif in Some Atlantic Fiction." In *Children's Voices in Atlantic Literature and Culture: Essays on Childhood*, edited by Hillary Thompson, 44–52. Guelph: Canadian Children's Press, 1998.

– "'Queer Children': L.M. Montgomery's Heroines." *Canadian Children's Literature / Littérature canadienne pour la jeunesse* 1, no. 3 (1975): 50–9.

White, Evelyn. "Anne and Aretha: A Harmonious Bond." Paper presented at L.M. Montgomery Institute's 13th Biennial International Conference, University of Prince Edward Island, Charlottetown, 21 June 2018.

– "Mainstreet PEI: Anne and Aretha." Interview with Kerry Campbell, CBC, 17 August 2018. https://www.cbc.ca/player/play/1302582851512.

Wilkinson, Amy. "*Anne with an E*: How Creator Moira Walley-Beckett Reimagined the Classic." *Entertainment Weekly*, 11 May 2017. https://ew.com/tv/2017/05/11/anne interview-moira-walley-beckett/.

Willard, Frances E., and Mary A. Livermore, eds. "Alden, Mrs Isabella Macdonald." In *A Woman of the Century: Fourteen Hundred–seventy Biographical Sketches, Accompanied by Portraits of Leading American Women in All Walks of Life*. Buffalo: Charles Wells Moulton, 1893.

Wilson, Budge. *Before Green Gables*. Toronto: Penguin Canada, 2008.

Wolf, Virginia L. "Paradise Lost? The Displacement of Myth in Children's Novels Set on Islands." *Studies in the Literary Imagination* 18, no. 2 (1985): 47–63.

Wong, Tony. "Anne with an E's Moira Walley-Beckett Is the Most Significant New Canadian Showrunner in a Generation." *Toronto Star*, 27 August 2018. https://www.thestar.com/entertainment/television/2018/08/27/the-surging-talent-running-anne-with-an-e-talks-metoo-annes-damage-and-more.html.

Wordsworth, William. "Lines Composed a Few Miles above Tintern Abbey, On Revisiting the Banks of the Wye during a Tour. July 13, 1798." In *William Wordsworth: The Poems*, 357–62.

– "Ode: Intimations of Immortality from Recollections of Early Childhood." In *William Wordsworth: The Poems*, 523–9.

– *The Prelude, 1799, 1805, 1850*. Edited by Jonathan Wordsworth, M.H. Abrams, and Stephen Gill. New York: Norton, 1979.

– *William Wordsworth: The Poems*. Vol. 1. Edited by John O. Hayden. Harmondsworth: Penguin, 1977.

Woster, Emily S. *Intertextuality and Life Writing: The Reading Autobiography of L.M. Montgomery*. PhD dissertation, Department of English, Illinois State University, 2013.

– "Old Years and Old Books: Montgomery's Ontario Reading and Self-Fashioning." In Bode and Clement, *L.M. Montgomery's Rainbow Valleys*, 151–65.

– "The Readings of a Writer: The Literary Landscape Created by L.M. Montgomery's Love of Literature." *CREArTA* 5 (2005): 209–22.

Woster, Emily S, and Kate Scarth. "Welcome to the *Journal of L.M. Montgomery Studies*." L.M. Montgomery Institute, University of Prince Edward Island, 5 June 2019. https://journaloflmmontgomerystudies.ca/jlmms/1/1/welcome-journal-lm-montgomery-studies#footnoteref19_nydc936.

Wrede, Patricia. "Some Uses for Fanfiction." *Six Impossible Things*, 11 May 2011. https://www.pcwrede.com/some-uses-for-fanfiction/.

Wullschläger, Jackie. *Inventing Wonderland: Victorian Childhood as Seen through the Lives and Fantasies of Lewis Carroll, Edward Lear, J.M. Barrie, Kenneth Grahame, and A.A. Milne*. New York: The Free Press, 1995.

York, Lorraine. "'How a Girl from Canada Break the Bigtime': Esi Edugyan and the Next Generation of Literary Celebrity in Canada." *Canadian Literature* 217 (Summer 2013): 18–33.

– *Literary Celebrity in Canada*. Toronto: University of Toronto Press, 2007.

Young, Craig, and Duncan Light. "Interrogating Spaces of and for the Dead as 'Alternative Space': Cemeteries, Corpses, and Sites of Dark Tourism." *International Review of Social Research* 6, no. 2 (2016): 61–72.

Zarin, Cynthia. "The Storyteller: Fact, Fiction, and the Books of Madeleine L'Engle." *New Yorker*, 12 April 2004. https://www.newyorker.com/magazine/2004/04/12/the-storyteller-cynthia-zarin.

Contributors

YOSHIKO AKAMATSU, PhD, is professor at Notre Dame Seishin University in Okayama, Japan. She translated Montgomery's posthumous collection of short stories, *Akin to Anne: Tales of Other Orphans* (1989). Her articles on Montgomery include "Japanese Readings of *Anne of Green Gables*" (1999), "The Continuous Popularity of *Red-Haired Anne* in Japan" (2013), and "During and after the World Wars: L.M. Montgomery and the Canadian Missionary Connection in Japan" (2015). The paper "The Awakening of Awe-Inspiring Girls: From a Viewpoint of the Japanese Novel *Daiana from the Bookstore*" is under review with the *Journal of L.M. Montgomery Studies*. She is on the editorial board of the *Journal of L.M. Montgomery Studies*.

BALAKA BASU is associate professor of English at UNC Charlotte, where she works on literature for young people, critical theory, popular culture, and the digital humanities. She holds a BA in English from Cornell University and a PhD in English from the Graduate Center, CUNY. She is currently working on her third book and first monograph, *Fanfiction: Poetics and Genre* (contracted by Louisiana State University Press). She presents regularly at the L.M. Montgomery Institute's biennial conference at UPEI and is serving a five-year term as associate editor for the *Children's Literature Association Quarterly*.

RITA BODE is professor of English literature at Trent University. Her work on Montgomery has appeared in *CREArTA* and *Storm and Dissonance: L.M. Montgomery and Conflict*, and she is co-editor of two volumes of essays on Montgomery: with Lesley D. Clement, *L.M. Montgomery's Rainbow Valleys: The Ontario*

Years, 1911–42 (MQUP, 2015), and with Jean Mitchell, *L.M. Montgomery and the Matter of Nature(s)* (MQUP, 2018), which won ACQL's 2018 Gabrielle Roy Prize (English) for the best book-length study in Canadian and Quebec literary criticism. She is also a volume editor in Oxford University Press's "The Complete Works of Edith Wharton," working on the novellas. Other recent publications include the co-edited volume, with Monika Elbert, *American Women's Regionalist Fiction: Mapping the Gothic* (Palgrave 2021) and articles or chapters in the areas of transatlantic studies and American women writers of the long nineteenth century.

LESLEY D. CLEMENT, past visiting scholar at the L.M. Montgomery Institute (UPEI, July 2019–June 2021) and co-editor of the *Journal of L.M. Montgomery Studies*, has held teaching and administrative positions at various Canadian universities, most recently Lakehead-Orillia. She has published on visual literacy, visual culture, empathy, and death in picture books and in Montgomery's writings. Her work on Montgomery appears in *Studies in Canadian Literature*, *L.M. Montgomery's Rainbow Valleys*, *L.M. Montgomery and the Matter of Nature(s)*, the *Journal of L.M. Montgomery Studies*, and *L.M. Montgomery and Gender*. Recent projects include co-editing, with Rita Bode, *L.M. Montgomery's Rainbow Valleys: The Ontario Years, 1911–1942* (MQUP, 2015); and, with Leyli Jamali, *Global Perspectives on Death in Children's Literature* (Routledge, 2016).

VAPPU KANNAS holds a PhD in English from the University of Helsinki, Finland. Her dissertation examines the journals of L.M. Montgomery and the depictions of romance in them. She has published articles on Montgomery in *The Looking Glass*, *Reading Today*, and *L.M. Montgomery and Gender*. She is a novelist, translator, and poet. She has published a collaborative chapbook, *As an Eel through the Body*, co-written with Canadian poet Shannon Maguire (Dancing Girl Press, 2016); a poetry collection, based on Montgomery's life, *Morsian* (Ntamo, 2018); and two novels, *Rosa Clay* (Kustantamo S&S, 2020) and *Kirjeitä Japaniin* (Kustantamo S&S, 2021).

HEIDI A. LAWRENCE received her PhD from the University of Glasgow, UK. She studies the intersections between ecopsychology and its praxis, ecotherapy, in children's and adolescent literature, with special interest in imaginative and fantastic literature She has participated in international literature conferences, including the L.M. Montgomery Institute's biennial conference, MLA, IRSCL, ChLA, and ASLE, presenting on Montgomery, Louisa May Alcott, Madeleine L'Engle, and other children's literature authors. She holds MA degrees in English (Brigham Young University) and Medieval Studies (University of Leeds, UK) and an MPhil in English Literature (University of York, UK). She works as adjunct faculty at Brigham Young University.

E. HOLLY PIKE is an independent scholar, formerly associate professor of English at Grenfell Campus, Memorial University, where she taught literary history, women writers, and children's literature. She has given many conference presentations on L.M. Montgomery and has published on Montgomery's works in a number of collections, including *L.M. Montgomery's Rainbow Valleys* and *100 Years of Anne with an "e."* She and Laura M. Robinson co-edited *L.M. Montgomery and Gender* (MQUP, 2021). She has also published on Elizabeth Gaskell and Jane Austen and is on the editorial board of the *Journal of L.M. Montgomery Studies*.

LAURA M. ROBINSON is professor of English and theatre/women's and gender studies at Acadia University. She specializes in Canadian women's writing, children's literature, and feminist theory. Former visiting scholar at the L.M. Montgomery Institute (UPEI), she has published many articles on Montgomery's work, in addition to articles on Canadian writers Margaret Atwood and Ann-Marie MacDonald and Americans Louisa May Alcott and Eleanor H. Porter. She curated a travelling and virtual exhibit entitled "The Canadian Home Front: L.M. Montgomery's Reflections on the First World War." She also acted as a consultant on Historica Canada's L.M. Montgomery Heritage Minute and the Inspiring Places: L.M. Montgomery Literary Tour in PEI. With E. Holly Pike, she edited the collection *L.M. Montgomery and Gender* (MQUP, 2021).

KATE SCARTH is the chair of L.M. Montgomery Studies and assistant professor in the Applied Communication, Leadership, and Culture (ACLC) program at the University of Prince Edward Island. She has published on L.M. Montgomery, Jane Austen, and Charlotte Smith in publications including the *European Romantic Review* and *Women's Writing*. Major current projects include her book manuscript, *Romantic Suburbs* (under contract with the University of Toronto Press), the *Journal of L.M. Montgomery Studies* (as founding editor), *Halifax Literary Landmarks*, and *Your L.M. Montgomery Story* project (as project co-leader).

MARGARET STEFFLER is professor emerita of English literature at Trent University. Her work on Montgomery has been published in *Making Avonlea: L.M. Montgomery and Popular Culture*; *Windows and Words: A Look at Canadian Children's Literature*; *Storm and Dissonance: L.M. Montgomery and Conflict*; *CREArTA*; *Anne's World: New Perspectives on Anne of Green Gables*; and *L.M. Montgomery's Rainbow Valleys: The Ontario Years, 1911–1942*. She is the editor of two volumes of P.K. Page's work published by Porcupine's Quill: *Mexican Journal* (2015) and *Metamorphosis: Selected Children's Literature* (2020). Recent publications include articles on Sylvia Fraser, Alice Munro, and Miriam Toews.

WILLIAM V. THOMPSON is associate professor at MacEwan University in Edmonton, Alberta, where he teaches a range of courses in children's and young-adult literature and science fiction. He has written on J.K. Rowling and C.S. Lewis, and his essay "The Shadow on the House of Dreams: L.M. Montgomery's Re-Visioning of Anne" appeared in the volume *L.M. Montgomery's Rainbow Valleys: The Ontario Years, 1911–1942*. He also writes personal essays and short fiction, and his essay "My Cowboy Cousin" was nominated for a Pushcart Prize by Zone 3 Press, winning an honorable mention in the 2021 Tom Howard/John H. Reid Fiction and Essay Contest.

BONNIE J. TULLOCH is a PhD candidate and UBC public scholar in the School of Information at the University of British Columbia. Her doctoral work examines the intersections between information, communication, and storytelling as they relate to youth engagement with Internet memes. Her other research interests include children's and young-adult literature, with a focus on nonsense poetry and island fiction. She is the 2018 recipient of the L.M. Montgomery Institute's Elizabeth R. Epperly Award for Outstanding Early Career Paper.

ÅSA WARNQVIST is docent and director of the Swedish Institute for Children's Books in Stockholm, Sweden. She is also affiliated with Linnæus University in Växjö, Sweden. Her research has primarily focused on book market studies, gender studies, and normativity studies. Her current research is on depictions of fat characters in Nordic children's and young adult fiction and Swedish reading responses to L.M. Montgomery's writing. She has co-edited several collections, most recently, *Silence and Silencing in Children's Literature* (2021). Warnqvist was the vice-president of IRSCL from 2017 to 2021 and the primary organizer of the IRSCL Congress 2019 in Stockholm. She is a former visiting scholar (2011–13) at the L.M. Montgomery Institute (UPEI) and a member of the editorial board of the *Journal of L.M. Montgomery Studies*. She also coordinated the 2009 international conference "L.M. Montgomery – Writer of the World" in Uppsala, Sweden, with Dr Gabriella Åhmansson.

Index

www.ingramcontent.com/pod-product-compliance
Lightning Source LLC
LaVergne TN
LVHW041358090826
845264LV00023B/191
* 9 7 8 0 2 2 8 0 1 3 8 9 1 *